THE CONCISE DICTIONARY OF ARCHITECTURAL AND DESIGN HISTORY

Frederic H. Jones, Ph.D

CRISP PUBLICATIONS, INC.
Los Altos, California

THE CONCISE DICTIONARY OF ARCHITECTURAL AND DESIGN HISTORY

Frederic H. Jones, Ph.D

CREDITS
Editor in Chief: **Frederic H. Jones, Ph.D**
Associate Editor: **Regina Sandoval**
Contributing Editors: **Linda Sandoval**
Judith Jones
Eleanor Kuykendall
Book Design: **Frederic H. Jones, Ph.D**
Cover Design: **Barbara Ravizza**

Library of Congress Catalog Card Number 91-70350
Jones, Frederic H., Ph.D
The Concise Dictionary of Architectural and Design History
ISBN 1-56052-069-8

INTRODUCTION

The Concise Dictionary of Architectural and Design History

This project has truly been a labor of love. Words have been a fascination for me all my life. I have collections of dictionaries, glossaries, word lists, etc. in many languages and on many subjects. I suppose it was just a matter of time before I was compelled to undertake a word list project of my own. I hope you find it both interesting and useful.

Many of the words and definitions included here were provided by historic dictionaries of architecture and design including the late 19th century edition by Russell Sturgis. Many of the illustrations have also been derived from these sources. In all cases the language and definitions were updated when necessary. Another primary source of words and their definitions were various associations and trade organizations. They include: The Illumination Engineering Society, Carpet and Rug Institute, Western Institute of Cabinetmakers, and many others. I wish to acknowledge their invaluable assistance and hasten to add that errors, no doubt, derive from my translation rather than from their creation.

My hope is that this and the other dictionaries in the series serve as introductory aids to students of design and architecture. The need to know both the meaning of obscure words and the obscure meanings of familiar words is one that a student of any profession encounters early in their studies. In fact the very "putting on of the mantle" of the language of the profession is the very essence of engaging the profession. We find ourselves sounding and thinking like designers and eventually we become the thing we emulate. This list of words will serve as an incomplete but helpful map on this journey.

I, in the process of editing this dictionary encountered many words and illustrations that would extend beyond the scope of any single dictionary. I have also been very involved in the contemporary process of automating the very word management and drawing management tools essential to design practice. I speak of the computer of course. I therefore have combined the extensive database of words and images and the computer and am making available an electronic "encyclopedia" of architecture and design. If you are interested in this product please contact me at 39315 Zacate Avenue, Fremont, CA 94538.

Frederic H. Jones, Ph.D

A

Aaron's-rod: An ornament consisting of a straight molding of rounded section with leafage or scroll work seeming to emerge from it.

Abacus: The uppermost member of a capital, a plain square slab in the Grecian Doric style, but in other styles often molded or otherwise enriched. Egyptian and Asiatic capitals are often without the abacus.

Acanthus: (A) A plant growing freely in the lands of the Mediterranean, having large leaves, deeply cleft; the sharp pointed leaves of some species strongly resembling those of the familiar field and roadside thistles, *Carduus* (or *Cnicus*, Gray) *Lanceolatus*, *Virginianus*, and others. The two species commonly described and figured, *Acanthus mollis* and *A. spinosus*, are very different in the character of the leaves. (B) In Greek, Greco-Roman, Byzantine, Romanesque, and neoclassic architecture, a kind of decorative leafage, assumed to be studied, or to have been studied originally from the plant.

Accolade: An ornamental treatment of the archivolt or hood molding of an arch or of the moldings of an apparent arch, or of a form resembling an arch, as in late Gothic work; consisting of a reverse curve tangent on either side to the curves of the arch or its moldings, and rising to a finial or other ornament above.

Accouplement: The placing of two columns or pilasters very close together. This device is common in neoclassic church fronts, and the like, and is most effective when several pairs of columns form together a colonnade, as in the celebrated example of the east front of the Louvre. It was almost unknown to Greek or Greco-Roman builders, so far as modern research enables us to say. In the revived classic styles it is considered essential that the capitals should not coalesce; but in medieval work it is common for them to form one block. The placing of a column closely in front of an anta or a pilaster is not considered accouplement.

Acropodium: A pedestal for a statue, especially when large and high and adorned with unusual richness. A terminal pedestal or gaine when resting upon representations of the human foot, or even of the feet of animals, is sometimes specially called acropodium; but the term in this sense is inaccurate and has no classical warrant.

Acropolis: The fortified stronghold or citadel of a Greek city, usually a steep eminence near its center, as at Athens, Corinth, or Tiryns. The shrine of the patron divinity of the city or state was sometimes situated within or upon it, as at Athens. The Athenian Acropolis was, indeed, the artistic as well as the military center of the city and state. Besides the magnificent propylaea by which it was entered, it was adorned with temples and shrines of great beauty, including the Parthenon, Erechtheion, and temple of Nike Apteros. The Acropolis of Corinth was called the Acrocorinthos.

Acroteral, Acroterial: Pertaining to, or having the form of, an acroterium.

Acroteria: Plinths for statues or decoration. They occur at the apex and ends of a pediment.

Acroterium: (A) In Classic architecture, a pedestal for a statue or similar decorative feature at the apex, or at each of the lower corners of a pediment. None of ancient times remains in place; but in Neo-classic work they are frequent. (B) By extension, from the preceding definition, but improperly, a statue or other decorative feature supported on such a pedestal.

Addorsed: Usually two animal figures placed symmetrically back to back. Commonly seen on capitals.

Adytum: The inner sanctuary of a Greek temple. A private sanctuary or chamber.

Aedes: In Roman architecture, any building. A distinction was maintained between *templum*, a regularly consecrated structure, or enclosure, and *aedes sacra*, which was a building set apart for pious purposes but not regularly consecrated. In modern inscriptions the term is applied to any public building and is accepted as the equivalent of the English word.

Aedicula: In Roman architecture, a small building; by extension, a shrine set up within a large edifice. Such a shrine may be a mere box or enclosure of wood, or, perhaps, only a screen with pedestal and statue in front of it.

Aedicule: Framing of a window or door with two columns or piers and supporting a lintel or pediment. In Classical architecture, a shrine framed by two columns and supporting an entablature and pediment.

Aedile: A Roman city officer, having special charge of public buildings and streets, and of municipal affairs generally.

Aedility: The government or the care of a city considered with reference to the public buildings, streets, squares, water supply, and other similar functions and duties.

Aerugo: The composition formed upon ancient bronzes by exposure; usually being carbonate of copper, but differing in composition according to the nature of the metal or the soil in which it may have been buried.

Aesymnium: A building erected by or in honor of a person named Aesymnios; especially a tomb in Megara named by Pausanian.

Affronted: Usually two animal figures placed symmetrically facing each other. Commonly seen on capitals.

Agger: In Roman building, a large mound or rampart, as of earth. It is applied to the great mound which backs the early wall of Rome, the agger of Servius Tullius, and sometimes to that wall itself, because consisting mainly of an embankment merely faced with dressed stone.

Agiasterium: In the early church, a sanctuary; especially, that part of a basilica in which the altar was set up.

Agnus Dei: A representation in painting or sculpture of the lamb as typical of Christ.

Agora: In Greek archaeology, the market place or open square in a town, nearly corresponding to the Italian Forum. Covered porticoes (see stoa) were built along the sides of the square, in some cases. But little that is certain has been ascertained concerning the arrangement of any agora of Classical Greece.

Agrafe: (A) A cramp or hook used in building; a term used in different senses, but rare. (B) The sculpture in relief put upon the keystone of an arch in ancient Roman and in Neoclassic work. Thus, the archivolt of the Arch of Titus is enriched by an elaborate scroll ornament, upon which is placed a figure almost completely detached from the background.

Aileron: A half gable, such as closes the end of a penthouse roof, or of the aisle of a church. The term signifies, of course, one of two wings. In Neoclassic architecture an attempt is frequently made to disguise the actual structure, the sloping roof of the aisle; and the aileron takes a nearly independent place as a wing wall shaped like a scroll, as in S. Maria Novella, at Florence; or commonly, like a quarter circle or similar curve, as in S. Zacharia, Venice.

Aisle: (A) In a building whose interior is divided into parts by rows of columns or piers, one of the side divisions, usually lower and smaller than the middle division. In ancient Roman basilicas, Christian basilicas, and the greater number of churches of all epochs, the aisles are straight and parallel, adjoining the nave, the choir, and the higher and chief part of the transept, or such of these divisions as may exist; where, however, the termination of east end, west end, or transept is finished in a rounded apse, the aisle may be continued around the curve. In round churches the aisle is concentric with the nave, and surrounds it. In a few churches there are two aisles on each side of the nave; in a very few, as in the Cathedral of Antwerp, there are three on each side. In many cruciform churches the aisle stops at the transept; in others it returns along one side only, usually the east side, of the transept; in very large churches it sometimes returns on each side, so that a cross section through the transept resembles a similar section across the nave. In most churches from the fifth century A.D. to the present time, the roofs of the aisles are lower than the nave roof, etc., so as to allow the direct admission of light through windows pierced in the higher walls above; but in Roman-

esque churches of central France and on the Rhine the aisles are but little lower than the vaulted nave, etc., from lack of skill on the part of the builders, who needed the resistance of the aisle roofs to the higher vaults; and there is a small class of later churches in which nave and aisles are nearly of the same height. Churches of this class are called *Hallenkirchen* in Germany, that is, churches resembling halls. Such are the cathedrals (S. Stephen) at Vienna in Austria, that of Carcassonne in southern France, that of Erfurt on the Rhine, and the Church of S. Sebaldus in Nuremberg, Bavaria. The nave vault may be crowned up a little higher than the aisle vault; but there is no clerestory wall with windows. The aisle is usually only one story in height; but in a few Romanesque churches, such as the Cathedral of Tournai in Belgium and in one or two later ones, such as the Cathedral Notre Dame of Paris, there is an upper story, usually called a gallery, and probably used in the Middle Ages as a place of safekeeping for the property of persons going on a pilgrimage or a crusade. (B) By extension, any one of the longitudinal divisions of an oblong basilica or church; thus, the name of the higher part of the choir is called the middle aisle, and a church with two aisles on each side is said to be five-aisled.

4

This use of the term is to be contrasted with the French use of *nef* for any longitudinal division. (C) By extension, and, perhaps, by confusion with alley, a walk or passage in a church, or any hall arranged for an audience, giving access to the seats. In this sense wholly popular and modern.

Aisled: Furnished with aisles; most common in combination, forming a term distinguishing the number of aisles, as the Cathedral of Antwerp is seven-aisled. In these cases, the nave is considered as one of the aisles, and the term expresses the number of separate parallel divisions of the structure.

Alabastrites: In Roman archaeology, a semiprecious stone, probably the Oriental or calcareous alabaster.

Album: In Roman archaeology, a contrivance for displaying publicly legal and other notices. One form of the album seems to have been a panel of whitened wall, as has been found in Pompeii.

Alette: In Roman architecture, and in styles derived from this, those parts of a pier which flank the central pilaster or engaged column, and which form the abutments of the arches.

Alexandrine: (A) Concerning Alexander the Great and his successors, their dominions and their cities and buildings. (B) Concerning the city of Alexandria in Egypt.

Alhambra: A group of buildings on a hill above the city of Granada in southern Spain, forming a fortress palace or *alcazar* of the Moorish kings of Andalusia. The unfinished palace of Charles V adjoins the Moorish buildings. The celebrated decorations of the courts and rooms are partly in ceramic tiles, partly in molded and painted plaster on a wooden framework.

Alien Priory: A small monastery dependent upon a larger one which is in another country.

Alipterion: An adjoining room in a Roman bath; called also eloeothesium and unctuarium.

Almonry: A place, sometimes a separate house, where the alms of a great abbey or of a city or a magnate were distributed.

Alms gate: In an abbey or manor house the gate in the bounding wall or courtyard wall where alms were distributed.

Altar frontal: See antependium.

Altar: A table or structure used in religious places and rites to hold a sacrifice or offering to a deity.

Altar-tomb: A tomb resembling an altar but not used for one.

Ambo: A Bible stand used in a Christian church for the reading of the Gospel and Epistle.

Amphiprostyle: A temple with porticos at each end and no columns at the sides.

Amphitheater: A circular sports, exhibition, or theatrical space enclosed by tiers of seats. In ancient times the site of gladiatorial contests.

Ancones: Projections left on blocks of stone or carvings used to lift them into position. Brackets beside a doorway that support a cornice.

Androsphinx: An Egyptian sphinx of the kind which combines the head of a man with a lion's body.

Angular Capital: An Ionic capital with the volutes turned outward and all four sides alike.

Anta: In Classical architecture a pilaster which does not conform to the primary order of the building.

Antechurch: An addition to the west end of a church. It usually resembles a narthex or porch.

Antefixae: Ornamental blocks used to conceal the ends of tiles on the edge of a roof.

Antependium: A cloth or metal altar covering that hangs over the front edge.

Anthemion: Classical ornament based on honeysuckle flowers and leaves.

Apophyge: A curve that occurs at the top and bottom of a column where the shaft joins the base or capital.

Apse: A polygonal or semicircular vault. Often occurs in a chapel or chancel.

Apteral: A Classical building with the columns at the ends rather than the sides.

Aqueduct: A channel constructed to carry water. It is often elevated.

Arabesque: A piece of decorative scroll work or other ornament not closely studied from nature. Although the term is taken from Arabian, that is Eastern, ornament, it is applied generally to work of European design. The paintings in Roman houses discovered in Pompeii or on the Palatine, at Rome, the sculptured reliefs of the same epoch when they cover broad panels instead of

6

narrow bands, and the imitations of such Roman work in the fifteenth and sixteenth centuries are commonly called arabesques.

Araeostyle: An arrangement of columns spaced four diameters apart.

Arcade, intersecting: In the Romanesque architecture of the north, one whose archivolts cross one another, being curved in imitation of interlacing bands. Many instances of this curious decoration exist in England; it is naturally limited to purely decorative arcades not large in scale nor deeply recessed.

Arcade, surface: An arcade or system of arches built against the surface of a wall, or partially or wholly imbedded in it, generally for decoration, as frequently in Romanesque and Medieval architecture; a blind arcade. Also called wall arcade.

Arcade: (A) Two or more arches with their imposts, piers, columns, or the like taken together and considered as a single architectural feature. It is more common to use the term for a considerable number of arches, and especially where they are small and where the whole feature is as much decorative as useful. Thus, one of the four sides of a vaulted cloister would be more commonly spoken of as an ambulatory, or a gallery, although

the word arcade might be used for the row of arches as they are seen from the garth within. The arcade is a favorite decorative feature in nearly all arcuated styles and especially in those of the Middle Ages. Thus, in the front of a Gothic cathedral there is very commonly a large arcade raised high above the portals and having each of its arches filled with a statue. In the well-known front of Notre Dame in Paris an arcade of 29 arches comes immediately above the great doorways. Each of these arches is filled with a statue of a king or a queen, and the whole is known as the Royal Gallery, a term used in connection with other churches as well. High up in the front, above the great rose-window, is a second arcade of four great double arches to each tower and four similar ones between the towers; these last open and showing the peak of the roof beyond, while minor arches adorn the buttresses. This second arcade is on a great scale, the larger arches having about 8' span and rising 24' above the bases of their columns, while yet the arcade is purely ornamental, except in so far as it covers a narrow gallery for the caretakers or workmen. Similar arcades are used in the interior of Gothic churches and very commonly in English architecture. It is certainly a more dignified and worthy system of design when these arcades can be used to stiffen the walls which they adorn, and to a certain extent this is done in the Romanesque and Gothic work; still, however, the arcade is usually a purely decorative feature. (B) A single arched opening, with its abutment, etc.; rare in this usage, which is borrowed from the French; but occurring in carefully written matter, as when a Roman memorial arch is spoken of as having one, two, or three arcades. (C) In English, and forming part of a proper name, a covered gallery with shops or booths along its side. The Lowther Arcade and Burlington Arcade are well-known buildings of this sort in London. One in Milan is described under Galleria. There is no English name for this kind of structure, which is the nearest European approach to the Oriental bazaar. Enterprises of the sort are not common, and neither in French, Italian, nor English is there a special name for them.

Arch, chancel: The arch at the west end of a chancel.

Arch, diaphragm: A transverse arch across the nave of a church.

Arch, rear: An arch spanning a window opening or doorway inside a wall.

Arch, scoinson: An arch carrying a part only of the thickness of a wall, as behind a window frame; or one of slight reveal forming a flat niche or recessed panel.

Arch: (A) A structural member rounded vertically to span an opening or recess; in this sense the term is used either for a decorative or memorial building, of which an upward curving member forms the principal feature and spans a gate or passage below, or for the member itself, considered as a firm and resistant curved bar capable of bearing weight and pressure. In this, the original sense, a wicker device thrown across a street or passage and covered with foliage and flowers is as much an arch as a more permanent structure. (B) A mechanical means of spanning an opening by heavy wedge-shaped solids which mutually keep one another in place and which transform the vertical pressure of the superincumbent load into two lateral components transmitted to the abutments. The shape is indifferent, although arches are generally curved. The width or thickness, horizontally, is also indifferent, although an arch which acts as a roof and covers much horizontal space is called a vault.

The constructional arch has been known from great antiquity, but it was rarely used by the ancients except for drains or similar underground and hidden conveniences. It appears, however, that the Assyrian builders used it freely as a means of roofing their long and narrow palace walls. Assyrian vaults were built of unbaked brick put together with mortar, so that the anchor vault became a continuous and massive shell. On the other hand, the Etruscans from a very early time understood the principle of the arch so well that they built arches of cut stone in large separate voussoirs put together without mortar. For us, the Etruscans were the originators of the true self-supporting arch. It was adopted from them by the Romans; but both these nations confined themselves almost exclusively to the semicircular arch, both in spanning openings in walls and for purposes of vaulting. The pointed arch seems to have been known as early as the round arch. It is, indeed, an obvious way of making an arch which shall have greater height in proportion to its width, and which shall in this way be stronger, because having less outward thrust. Its use in pre-Gothic, as in early Islamic architecture, and in Romanesque buildings, as in S. Front at Perigueus, is merely occasional and because of some preference on the part of the individual builder.

The three-centered arch and the four-centered arch are both much used in the transitional work of the sixteenth century in Northern Europe. The segmental arch has hardly been used for decorative purposes, except occasionally in the Louis Quatorze style, before the present half century; it is now rather common in French work, and it may be that more could be made of it, architecturally speaking, than in the past. The flat arch is used commonly to produce a similitude of trabeated construction when in reality the stones accessible are too small for the great spans required. Thus, in Roman and Neo-classic buildings, the epistyle or architrave between two columns is often made of separate voussoirs in this way, as in the Pantheon of Paris. Mechanically, an arch may be considered as any piece or assemblage of pieces so arranged over an opening that the vertical pressure of the supported loan is transformed into two lateral inclined pressures on the abutments.

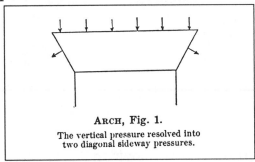

ARCH, Fig. 1.
The vertical pressure resolved into
two diagonal sideway pressures.

Considered in this light, then, the stone window head shown in Fig. 1 is truly an arch. The stone is wedge-shaped; and it will be readily seen that the load on it has a tendency to force this wedge down into the window opening by pushing the adjoining masonry away to the right and left, as shown by the arrows.

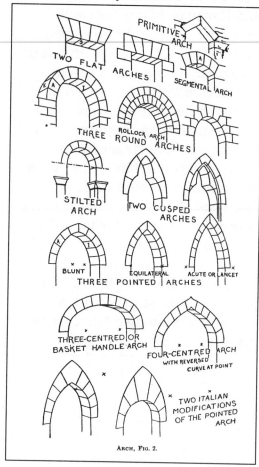

Arch, Fig. 2.

An arch slightly more elaborate is the primitive arch shown in Fig. 2. Here

two wedge-shaped stones lean against each other, and each one transmits pressures similar to those just described, the pressures at the respective upper ends counteracting each other. This form of arch may be compared to a pair of rafters whose tiebeam has been removed and its function fulfilled by a weight at the feet of the rafters.

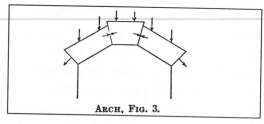

Arch, Fig. 3.

To go a step farther, we have an arch made of three stones, as shown in Fig. 3, each one of which is acting as an independent wedge tending to force its way inward, and so exerting a lateral pressure at each of its oblique ends, while the combination of all these six pressures results in a lateral push on each abutment as shown by the arrows. This lateral push, in Figs. 2 and 3, is similar to that in Fig. 1, from which it differs in direction, owing to the inclination of the end pieces; were these more steeply inclined they would evidently exert a push more nearly vertical. Hence, the higher the arch in proportion to its span, the less lateral push will it exert. The foregoing considerations will be found to apply equally well to all of the arches shown in Fig. 2, or to any other similar construction of wedge-shaped pieces. It will also be observed that, in the case of two or more such wedges, each one is being acted upon by the adjoining pieces, which tend to force it outward; this tendency is overcome only by proper and more or less uniform distribution of the loads to be carried. The lateral pressure on the abutment is known as the thrust, and resistance to this force was the subject of constant experiment in the church building of the Middle Ages, resulting in the elaborate systems of engaged and flying buttresses.

Arches may be divided according to their form into the following classes:

(1) The flat arch; (2) The arch with one center; (a) Semicircular or round arch; (b) Segmental arch; (c) Horseshoe arch. (3) The arch with two centers; (a) Equilateral pointed arch; (b) Lancet arch; (c) Drop arch or blunt pointed arch; (d) Pointed horseshoe arch; (e) Drop arch in the second sense. These five varieties are what is known as pointed arches; the first three being those in use in many styles. (4) With three centers; (a) Basket handle arch; (b) The round arch with reversed curve at crown. (5) Arches with four centers; (a) That form of pointed arch in which two of the centers are on the springing line and two below; (b) That in which a two-centered arch is prolonged at top with a reversed curve. It is evident that a six-centered arch might be composed by giving to the form (6) A reversed curve as in the other instances; but such subdivisions may be continued indefinitely; thus a five-centered arch might be developed out of the basket handle arch; and so on. An arch is divisible into the haunches, or reins, and the crown. An arch is made up of voussoirs, of which there may be one in the middle occupying the center of the crown and called a keystone. The inner side of the arch ring is called the intrados. The outer side of the arch ring is called the extrados, or back. When an arch is laid down on paper the horizontal line which passes through the center in the plane of the arch, if there is but one, or which connects two centers, and which (except in the segmental arches, one- or two-centered) marks the place at which the curve of the arch joins the vertical line of the abutment, is called the springing line. The height from the springing line to the intrados (or to the line which in a drawing represents the intrados) is the height or rise; sometimes called the versed line. The width between

the two points of juncture above mentioned is the span. That part of an arch which forms a part of the face of the wall is called the face of the arch, or very commonly, the archivolt. Parts of the construction immediately dependent upon or connected with an arch are the abutment; impost; skew back; spandrel; springer.

Archaic: Pertaining to or having the character of extremely early and primitive work. As applied to different branches of art, the term refers to different but specific periods; as, for example, in Greek art, to the formative period between the Heroic or Homeric Age, and the middle or end of the sixth century B.C. Archaic is distinguished from primitive art by its evidence of those definite progressive tendencies which give form to the later and more perfect art.

Architrave: A molded frame surrounding a window or door. The lowest part of an entablature.

Archivolt: A continuous architrave molding on the face of an arch.

Arcuated: A building structurally dependent on arches, in contrast to a trabeated building.

Arena: The open space of an amphitheater. A building primarily used for sports and exhibitions.

Astragal: Small circular section molding usually with bead and reel decoration.

Astylar: A facade without pilasters or columns.

Atlantes: Columns or supports carved in the form of male figures. Used extensively by German Baroque architects.

Atrium: The inner open court of a building surrounded on multiple sides by the building or roof, often occurring in residential structures. A colonnaded quadrangle in Medieval church architecture.

Attic Base: Base of a Greek Ionic column. It consists of two large rings of convex molding joined by a spreading concave molding.

Attic Storey: A room or upper story in a building or house often directly under the roof. In Classical architecture, a story above the main entablature of a building.

Aumbry: A storage space or cupboard used to store ritual vessels in a church.

B

Back: (A) The more remote or further side of any member or part of a building, or what may have seemed more remote to the designer. (B) The rear of a building, in any sense. Where both of the longer faces of a large building are treated with nearly equal architectural effect, that face which has not the principal entrance will be the back. Churches, while they often have a front, can hardly be said to have a back, because the chancel end, commonly called the east end, is peculiarly important in the ecclesiological sense, and frequently has exceptionally important architectural features. In the plural, as "the backs," that side of a long row of buildings which is opposite their principal fronts, as in Cambridge University (England), where the term covers the buildings as seen from the river. (C) The top or upper surface or portion of a member, as the back of a hand rail; the back of an arch, meaning the extrados. (D) In composition, the reverse or inner side; a lining or the like.

Baldachin, Baldaquin: (A) A canopy made of a textile fabric (originally of baudekyn; a precious stuff brought from Baldacca or Baghdad), used in processions, placed over an episcopal chair and throne of state, or suspended over an altar where there is no ciborium. (B) A permanent canopy, especially above the high altar of a church; in this sense applied to the most massive and permanent structures, as the bronze baldachin in S. Peter's at Rome which is stated to be 95' high.

Balistraria: Cross-shaped openings in Medieval military battlements. Used to fire bows while affording protection.

Balk: (A) A heavy piece of timber, of any kind not in the log. A squared timber. (B) By extension from the above meaning, in primitive country houses of Great Britain, a loft formed by laying planks or poles on the balks or main timbers of the framing. Commonly in the plural.

Ball flower: A globular ornament frequently occurring in the hollow moldings of English Gothic architecture. It suggests a flower with three, or rarely four, petals nearly closed over an inner ball, and is repeated at short intervals to give points of light in the darkness of the hollow. Isolated four-part flowers are sometimes found in late Norman work.

Balustrade: A short series of pillars or balusters terminated on top with a rail.

Barocco: Irregular; informal; unexpected; not according to the traditions of the schools. The term seems to be the Italian form of an original Spanish or Portuguese word, the French form of which is *baroque*. According to the tastes and opinions of the person who used it, the term is either one of reproach or a mere qualification descriptive of the decorative art of a certain period.

Baroque: (A) Same as Rococo; used in this sense by many French writers and by English writers who follow them. (B) Same as Barocco. In this sense it is rather as a term of reproach that the adjective *baroque* is applied to architecture. It is used in this way without very exact meaning, characterizing rather the late Neo-classic architecture as of the middle of the seventeenth century; but applied also to the Jesuit style, and even to the Italian architecture of Bernini and Carlo Maderno; and in general for anything assumed to be excessive, extravagant, and in bad taste.

Bartizan: A small turret rising from the top angle of a tower or parapet.

Bas-Relief: (A) A form of sculpture in which the figures project but slightly from the general background; low relief; as, for example, in the frieze of the Parthenon. (B) Any sculptured work thus executed in low relief. Bas-relief is especially used as an adjunct to architecture. The contrasting treatment of sculpture is high relief or *alto-rilievo*.

Base Block: A block of any material, generally with little or no ornament, forming the lowest member of a base, or itself fulfilling the functions of a base; specifically, a member sometimes applied to the foot of a door or window trim.

Base: The lowest part or the lowest main division of anything, as of a column, pier, the front of a building or of a pavilion, tower, or the like. The term is used independently in the following senses: (A) The lowest of the three principal parts of a column, when the column is so divided. Many Egyptian columns and the columns of the Grecian Doric order have no bases; moreover, in other styles many pillars, which, from their approximately cylindrical form are called columns, have no base in the strict sense here given to the term. The traditional base of the Ionic columns of one of the porches of the Erechtheum in Athens is made of, first, a group of hollow moldings divided by narrow fillets, below this a larger cove between two fillets, and below this a convex molding almost semicylindrical in section, called generally a torus. The Attic base, so called, consists of the following members, beginning at the top: a convex moulding of nearly semicylindrical section; a scotia between two fillets; another convex molding somewhat larger than the upper one. The base of the Medieval columns, Eastern and Western, Byzantine, Romanesque, and Gothic, are extraordinarily varied, and it is evident that the artist tried many combinations of moldings, retaining for frequent use only those which were the most agreeable to the eye and expressive of the function of the base, which is, of course, to extend somewhat the area of pressure. As the use of the square plinth below the base had been adopted from Roman practice and had become very common, the Medieval builders adopted a spur to fill each of the four corners of this plinth and to extend still more the even pressure of the base upon the plinth. (B) The lowest part of a wall or pier, especially if ornamented by moldings or by a projecting feature decorated by panelling or sculpture. In this sense the term is incapable of accurate and exhaustive definition, as the lowermost course of stone in the exterior of a wall, where it shows above the pavement or the surface of the ground, is capable of an infinite variety of artistic treatments. Hence, (C) A member of any material applied as a finish or protection at the foot of a wall, or the like, especially in interior finish, as a baseboard forming part of the wooden trim of a room.

Basilica (so-called, at Paestum): A building standing among the ruins of the ancient Paestum (Greek, *Poseidonia*; modern Italian, *Pesto)* on the coast of Campania. It resembles a Doric temple, but has the peculiarity of a row of columns through the middle, and in consequence an uneven number on each of the narrower fronts. Also, there are no traces of a wall which might have enclosed the naos. For these reasons it has been called a basilica, according to the ancient or pagan type; that is to say, a portico for public resort.

Basilica: A church with a nave and two or more aisles. The nave is higher and wider than the aisles. In Classical architecture it refers to a large meeting hall.

Bastion: A projection at the angle of a fortification.

Bay leaf garland: Classical decoration used to enrich torus molding.

Beakhead: Roll molding ornamented with a row of bird or animal heads. Common in Norman architecture.

Beehive: Conical with curved sides, having a shape such as that of the tomb known as the Treasury of Atreus.

Bergere: (French) A small upholstered armchair.

Billet: Molding made up of several bands of raised cylinders or square pieces at regular intervals. Common in Romanesque architecture.

Blind tracery: Tracery applied to wall surfaces and wood panels. Common in Gothic architecture.

Block: (A) A piece of stone or terra cotta prepared, or partly prepared, for building. (B) A mass projecting from a larger piece of stone, as in some unfinished masonry of the Greeks. (C) In carpentry or joiner's work, any small, more or less symmetrical, piece of wood, used for whatever purpose, as behind a wainscot, or other work which is to stand out from a wall; under any horizontal member to give it a proper level; in the angle between the sides of a box; the top and front rail of a chest of drawers or cabinet, or the like; a traditional means of giving stiffness or support where there is no room for braced framing. (D) A row or mass of buildings closely connected together, or a single structure which, perhaps divided by party walls contains a number of stores or shops with dwellings above them, or dwellings only, or small apartment houses. (In this sense, peculiarly American.)

Blocking Course: A projecting stone cornice at the base of a building. In Classical architecture, a plain stone course with a cornice at the top of a building.

Boss: (A) A projecting mass of stone, usually not large and commonly intended to be cut away after the completion of the work. (B) A mass projecting, as in *A*, but intended as a permanent feature; thus, in Gothic architecture, the molded sill course of a window, or row of windows, is often terminated by sculptured projections of the sort. The most common use of the term is for the carved keystone of Gothic vaults. Where the different ribs meet at the top of the vault such a piece of stone (called by the French *clef*) is an almost essential feature, and this, if treated in a decorative way, is the boss. Those of the thirteenth century are sometimes of great richness. In later times they often took the form of the pendant.

Brattishing: Ornamental cresting on top of a cornice or screen. Often is carved or molded in the form of leaves and flowers.

16

Bucrane, Bucranium: An ox skull, used as a symbolic decoration in Roman architecture, in which it had a sacrificial significance, and was confined to altars and temples. It appears to have originated in the primitive practice of affixing the skulls of the oxen sacrificed to the frieze, or other parts, of the temple of the god worshipped. As a decoration, it was associated with garlands, festoons, and fillets. In Renaissance decoration in Italy it occurs as an arbitrary ornament destitute of particular significance. Its inappropriateness, however, prevented its general adoption.

Byzantine: Architecture of a style chiefly developed in the domains and during the existence of the Byzantine Empire, generally from 476-1200, from which it spread westward into Italy, whence its influence radiated into France and Germany; and northward into Russia, where it dominated ecclesiastical design. It was developed almost exclusively in ecclesiastical buildings, and was the distinctive style of the Eastern or Greek church. It was in reality a style of transition, leading from the Classic Roman architecture to the Romanesque and Gothic styles of the West on one hand, and to the Islamic styles of the East on the other. Its

chief distinction is the revolution in structural design brought about by the invention of the dome on pendentives, and its greatest monument, Hagia Sophia at Constantinople (Istanbul) is one of the really great buildings of the world; yet the majority of its productions were small in scale and timid in construction, and it never carried to their logical conclusion the great principles exhibited in its early masterpieces. It therefore presents the spectacle of an arrested development, of precocious and brillian promise unfulfilled; the decline of the empire began before its arts had reached their culmination.

INTERIOR OF Sta SOPHIA, CONSTANTINOPLE.

C

Ca': The Venetian abbreviation of the word *casa* (house). In this sense it is used as a part of a common title of many dwelling houses, including some important structures, each of which would be called *palazzo* in other Italian cities.

Campanile (pl. campanili): In Italian, a bell tower; hence, a bell tower of Italian design or general character, especially a church tower more or less completely separated from the rest of the building, and generally having no buttress nor any marked break in its outline, which is square, unbuttressed, plain, and with nearly all its decorative effect near the top in connection with the belfry chamber. Such towers are abundant in Italy during all the Medieval epoch, and their general character was preserved in the Renaissance and post-Renaissance styles. Among the largest existing are those of the Cathedral of Cremona in Lombardy, of S. Mark's Church in Venice, and of the Piazza dei Signori in Verona. The exquisitely graceful campanile of S. Zeno of Verona has a two-story belfry, and it has been noted by recent observers that its sides are not strictly vertical, but have a slight entasis.

Cancello: A latticed screen used in early churches to separate the choir from the main area of the church.

Cancellus (pl. cancelli): In Latin, usually in the plural, any barrier or screen formed with bars; particularly the bar between the court and spectators in a pagan basilica, and between the clergy, or clergy and choir, and the congregation in a Christian basilica, whence chancel. The cancelli of antiquity might be of bronze, iron, stone, or wood.

Candelabrum: (A) In Latin, a lampstand. Some of those known to us are very small and low; but those which are of interest architecturally are high and of considerable pretensions. Some of these are of bronze, and very slender; but others are cut in marble or fine grained stone, and are sometimes 5' or 6' high, and very massive. The forms of these last have entered somewhat into Neo-classic decoration. (B) A candlestick made decorative by wrought work, in metal, enamel, or the like; especially one having several sockets for candles, and of large size. (C) A modified column, small and decorated, and usually engaged. The typical form is that of a rapidly tapering shaft with a florid capital, the whole emerging from a cluster of leafage below.

Canopy: (A) A rooflike structure usually supported on pillars or projecting from a wall, and serving rather a decorative than a protective purpose. It may be movable, as when carried above an important person in a procession, and may consist of an awning of silk or other material supported on poles; or it may be of light material and permanently placed, as above a bedside, whether supported by the posts or hung from the ceiling; or it may be of solid material. In a Gothic niche, the canopy is the most important part. (B) Bed drapery that hangs from posts or the ceiling.

Cap: The crowning or terminal feature of a vertical member of any structure, either fitting closely upon it or extending somewhat beyond it in horizontal dimensions; thus distinguished from a finial. The capital of a column, pilaster, or pier, the subbase or cornicelike finish of a pedestal, the cast-iron head of an iron or timber post, the crowning horizontal timber of a stud partition, a timber bolster on a post to diminish the unsupported span of the superstructure, are alike called caps, and the term is also used of a wall coping, door lintel, or handrail as of a balustrade.

Capella: In Italian, a chapel.

Capital, basket: A hemispherical capital decorated with a wicker basket-like design. Prominent in Byzantine architecture.

Capital, bell: Capital in the form of a reversed bell. The bell is often decorated with carvings.

Capital, block: Capital cut from a cube with the lower parts rounded off to the circular shaft. Prominent in Romanesque and Byzantine architecture.

Capital, crocket: A capital formed with stylized leaves with ending rolled over as small volutes. Prominent in Early Gothic architecture.

Capital, double: One furnished with a dosseret.

Capital, lotus: A capital in the form of a lotus bud. An Egyptian style.

Capital, palm: A capital in the form of the crown of a palm tree. An Egyptian style.

Capital, protomai: A capital, usually with half-figures of animals projecting from the corners.

Capital, scalloped: A block capital in which the single lunette on each face is formed into one or more truncated cones.

Capital: The head or crown of a column.

Caryatid: A column made in the form of a female figure. Columns or pilasters carved all or partially as human figures.

Cashel: In Irish archaeology, an enclosing wall of rough stone, intended either for defence as forming part of a rude fort, or enclosing a church or several sacred buildings. By some writers the term has been adopted for general use as meaning an enclosure of rough stonework.

Castle: A fortified house or living structure.

Castrum: A Roman military camp.

Catacomb: An underground cemetery or series of linked underground passages.

Catacumba: (A) A catacomb, the low Latin form of the word. (B) The courtyard or atrium preceding a Christian basilica.

Cathedra: The bishop's chair in a cathedral church. Usually placed behind the high altar.

Cathedral: (more properly cathedral church). The church in which is set up the Bishop's Throne or Cathedra. This church may be considered as the bishop's throne room; or, if the choir is considered as the throne room, then the cathedral with chapter house and other accessories, and the actual residence of the bishop, together with the cloisters and other enclosed spaces, may be considered as the episcopal palace, resembling a royal or grand ducal palace in having rooms for business and ceremony combined in the same building with the residence of the prince and his officers and attendants. The cathedral itself is not necessarily large nor splendid, nor is there any architectural style or character which can be said to belong to it in a peculiar sense. In Athens, the old cathedral, which was used without interruption until the middle of the nineteenth century, remains one of the smallest churches in the world, and capable of containing a congregation of only a few score.

Caulcole: Stalk rising from the leaves of a Corinthian capital.

Cavalier: A raised earth-platform or military fort used for gun placement.

Cave dwelling: A natural cave occupied by humans as a dwelling place. Caves have been so occupied in all ages. In Europe there are caves that were occupied long ago for an extended period; but in America, while numerous natural caves have been inhabited, the duration of the residence within them was comparatively short. Some caves were walled up in front, leaving only a doorway. Many of those existing in the Southwestern United States were very small, and were nothing more than storage vaults. In the huge cavelike recesses of the sandstone cliffs of the Southwest, houses and villages have been constructed by American Indians of the Pueblo type, and these structures are often described as cave dwellings, though they properly belong to the class cliff dwelling.

Cell: (A) Compartment of a rib vault or groin. (B) A sleeping room in a monastery.

Cella: Main body of a Classical temple. It housed the cult image

Celure: Paneled and decorated part of a wagon roof. Often above an altar.

Central tower: In a special sense, that at the crossing of a church, and therefore resting upon open arches and detached piers. One of the most remarkable is that of the Creisker at Saint-Pol-de-Leon; another (much higher) is at Salisbury; but many exist in all the Medieval styles, and many more have been ruined by the burning of the roofs of the churches. The towers named above are

crowned by stone spires. Other central towers are finished as lanterns, as in S. Ouen at Rouen. The cupola at the crossing of a Byzantine or a Neoclassic church is to be compared with the central tower.

Chain course: A bond course of stone headers fastened together continuously by metal cramps. A noted example is the triple chain course in the choir of Notre Dame, Paris (1195).

Chalet: A wooden dwelling house of the type common in Switzerland. The chalets are of two different types as for the structure: (A) the type derived from the log house, of heavy beams placed upon the other and crossed at the angle; (B) the framework building, a structure of posts and beams, with the wall merely filled in with thick boards, or even bricks, etc.

Chancel, high: The central or principal part of a chancel in a large church where there are aisles or a deambulatory. The need of the term comes from the confusion between the use of choir, chancel, etc., to denote particular sacred enclosures, and the use of the same terms to denote the entire easterly division of the building.

Chancel: That portion of a church set apart for the use of the clergy, and where the holy Eucharist is celebrated, and the divine office is chanted. It is situated at the rear, and therefore properly eastward, of the nave, from which in large churches it is separated by a screen or rail, and, as its floor is higher than the nave, it is approached by one or more steps. The chancel is often divided into two parts, the choir and sanctuary, separated by the altar rail. The division nearest the nave is the choir (the place of the singers), and the division east of the choir is the sanctuary (the place of the high altar), the place referred to by S. Ambrose (A.D. 397) in the following words addressed by him to the Emperor Theodosius, "The priests alone, O Emperor, are permitted to enter within the rail of the altar-retire (to the nave), then, and remain with the rest of the laity." The altar is in the center of the sanctuary; the credence (or the table for the bread and wine, the sacred vessels, and the missal) is on the south side; and near by in a wall recess is the *piscina*-a drain to receive the washing of the priest's hands and that of the sacred vessels. On the same side, but to the west, is a sedilia, divided into three seats, for the officiating clergy at the sacrifice; and on the north side, in the case of a cathedral church, the bishop's throne is now placed; anciently it was placed behind, and higher than, the altar.

The term is, however, frequently used to denote the sanctuary only, as distinguished from the choir.

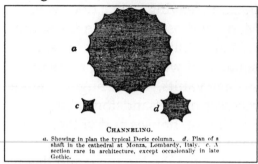

CHANNELING.
a. Showing in plan the typical Doric column. *d.* Plan of a shaft in the cathedral at Monza, Lombardy, Italy. *c.* A section rare in architecture, except occasionally in late Gothic.

Channel: Any furrow or groove, whether for carrying off water or for any other purpose. A street gutter in England is sometimes called a channel. In Greek Doric architecture it is applied to the grooves of the triglyphs and columns; those of the columns being called by this name to distinguish them from the flutes of the Ionic and Corinthian orders; though this distinction is not always maintained.

Chantry chapel: A chapel within a church or attached to a church dedicated to the founder or those designated by the founder. Formerly used to celebrate mass in their honor.

Chaori: A large porch to a Brahman temple in India, used especially for marriage ceremonies. It is sometimes identical with the *mantapa*, and sometimes precedes it, forming in area the largest feature of the temple.

Chaplet: A bead molding carved into the semblance of a string of beads or pearls; a carved astragal or baguette.

Chapter room: (A) Same as chapter house. (B) A room provided for the stated meetings of a chapter in its proper sense of an assembly of canons or members of an honorary order; hence, by extension, the place of meeting of a branch or suborganization of a large association.

Checker: (A) Any decoration which divides a surface into equal squares treated alternately in different ways, as with different colors or with high and low relief. (B) A form of diaper ornament in which the compartments are uniformly square, as in late Romanesque and in Gothic surface carving. (C) With the article, one of the squares in checker work.

Cherub: (A) A symbolic, or allegorical, decoration consisting of an infant's head with wings, common in late Italian seventeenth-century carving, and on English and American tombstones of the seventeenth and eighteenth centuries. (B) In the art of the sixteenth century and later, a naked child in any religious or liturgical representation. These figures are not often winged. (C) In ancient Jewish and in Byzantine art a symbolic figure with six wings, as on the Ark in Solomon's Temple, and on the pendentives of Hagia Sophia, Constantinople (Istanbul).

Chevron: A zigzag molding. Common in Romanesque architecture.

Choir screen: Wood, metal, or masonry partition separating the choir from the nave and trancepts of a church. It is similar to the iconostasis in an Orthodox church.

Choir: (A) Primarily, that part of a church in which the singers were accommodated. In Catholic churches, where there were many persons employed to sing the mass and other services of the church, the space allowed for these singers and the clergy became very large; hence arose the signification *B*, which, however, is to be understood as inaccurate, and a loose term for that which has no accurate one. (B) In a church, that part of the main structure which is in great part occupied by the choir proper, *A*, above. This, in a cruciform church, will be that arm of the cross which is farthest from the main entrance; that is to say, at the east end of the church when oriented in the usual manner. Thus, in a large church, the term choir has two very different meanings: first, the actual enclosure in which the clergy and choristers perform their duty; and second, one great arm or extension of the building including the rounded apse, if there is one, and the deambulatory surrounding that apse, if there is one. The choir, being considered the most sacred part of the church, was often built in advance of the rest of the structure, and on this account many of the large churches of Europe have a choir of different date from the other parts. The floor of the choir is often raised higher than that of the nave. Where there is a crypt, this may occupy the whole space below the choir, the floor of which will then be much elevated; thus, at S. Zeno in Verona, the number of steps up to the choir floor and down to the crypt are about equal; and in S. Miniato al Monte, near Florence, the disposition is about the same, with 16 rather steep steps leading up to the choir floor. In England, a similar arrangement exists in the cathedrals of Rochester and Canterbury.

Chultune: A subterranean chamber of irregular shape as built by the ancient Mayas, often in the cavity left by the extraction of zaccab from the pockets in which it occurs. Usually single and from 10'-15' below the surface, with a well-like opening at the top covered by a slab. The walls, roof, and floor were sometimes of dressed stone finished with a coat of stucco. Supposed to have been reservoirs, but also used as sepulchres.

Churrigueresque: Spanish and Latin Baroque architecture characterized by extreme and fancy detail.

Ciborium: A canopy suspended over a high altar in a church. Typically in the form of a dome resting on columns.

Circus: In city planning, a circular street junction. A long oblong Roman building with rounded ends and tiered seats on three sides used for horse racing.

Clearstory: That part of a building which rises above roofs of other parts, and which has windows in its walls. The term is especially used for Medieval churches, whose division into a central nave and side aisles of less width and height made the opening up of the wider central nave a natural and obvious arrangement. It dates back, therefore, at least as far as the earliest Christian basilicas. A similar arrangement is, however, traceable in some buildings of Roman antiquity. The term, if used for such buildings, is used with a sense of extending the application of it beyond its usual meaning.

Close: The plot of ground occupied by a cathedral and its dependent buildings, and formerly always enclosed by a wall. The closes of some English cathedrals are extensive, and contain fine trees of great age; the buildings also, being grouped in a picturesque fashion, give a parklike character to the whole.

Coliseum: The largest Roman amphitheater known to us. It stands in Rome southeast of the Forum, in a flat which continues the valley in which the Forum is situated. Its exterior is well preserved for about four-fifths of its perimeter, except that the fittings of the uppermost part are uncertain. It was built by Vespasian and his son and successor, Titus, at least as far as the top of the third story of the exterior, the solid wall with pilasters forming the fourth story having been added in the third century. (Also spelled colosseum.)

Colonnade: A number of columns arranged in order, usually in one line, and considered in connection with all the details of the order, and sometimes with the roof, pavement, stylobate, and other adjuncts. The term is usually limited to structures in which the columns carry an architrave, and excludes the arcade. When a colonnade is carried along three or four sides of the exterior of a building, or of a large court or garden, it is called a peristyle. When attached to a building to which it serves as entrance porch, it is called a portico; and this meaning is often extended to roofed colonnades of any description. Colonnades in Grecian architecture are peculiar in the placing of the corner column, as in the exteriors of Doric temples, at a smaller distance from the two neighboring columns than the other columns are from one another, this on account of the supposed need of greater effect of solidity at that point. The columns being all set somewhat out of the true vertical the corner column is put the most out of plumb. The Grecian and Greco-Roman builders did not employ coupled columns; but this modification was introduced soon after the revival of Classical architecture in the fifteenth century, and some of the most important architectural effects of the last four centuries have been produced by this arrangement, such as the great colonnade of the Louvre, built in the reign of Louis XIV.

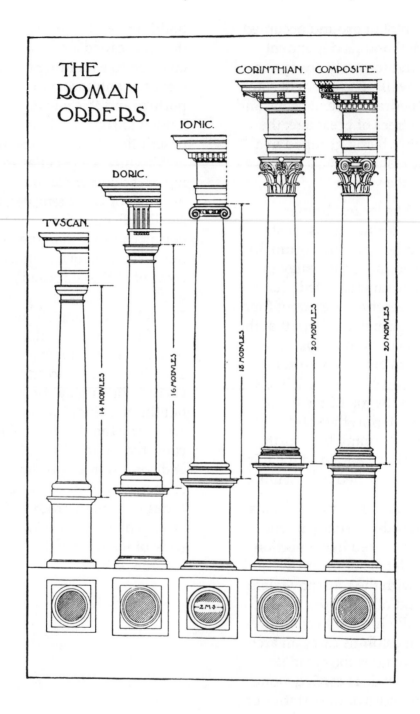

Column, coupled: In plural, coupled columns; those set in a pair or in pairs. These may be in a continuous colonnade, as a peristyle or portico, and the disposition is then called araeostyle.

Column, knotted: A column, the shaft of which is shaped to appear as if tied in a knot, or as if composed of two ropelike parts interlacing.

Column, manubial: Properly, a column decorated with spoils of the enemy; hence a triumphal or memorial column of any kind.

Column, midwall: A column or the like which carries a part of a wall much thicker than its own diameter and which, therefore, stands about halfway between the face and the back of the wall, its axis being about the same as the axis of the wall. In some Medieval styles, slender columns are seen carrying very thick walls which rest upon them, and this disposition affects greatly the general design.

Column, rostral: (A) The columna rostrata or pillar adorned with the beaks of ships, which stood in the Roman Forum, having been originally erected in commemoration of the victory of C. Dullius, 260 B.C. Other memorial and votive pillars of similar character were erected at different times, generally, as it appears, in commemoration of naval victories. (B) In modern usage, a pillar in which sculptured representations or suggestions of beaks of ships are used as decorative additions; sometimes erected either along or in connection with other monuments in recognition of naval prowess.

Column, symbolical: A column used to support a representative figure or emblem, as the columns of S. Mark in Venice and other cities of the ancient Venetian dominion; or to commemorate an event or person, as a rostral column, the column of Trajan, the column in the Place Vendome in Paris, etc.

Column, Trinity: A monument of slender and shaftlike proportions built triangular in plan, for at least a part of its height, as a specially sacred memorial. Several exist in Europe, but all of the seventeenth and eighteenth centuries, from which it appears that the fashion is of late origin.

Column, unbending: A column of which the diameter is of such proportion to its height, that, under vertical pressure, it cannot be fractured transversely by any tendency to lateral bending. This proportion of safety varies according to the material used,

27

a column of iron or steel being much more slender for a given service than one of stone or marble, which finds its idea of stability in the proportions of the Greek orders.

Column, wreathed: A column so shaped as to present a twisted or spiral form.

Column: (A) A pillar or post; a pier rather slender than thick and especially one that carried a weight and acts as an upright supporting member. In this general sense, the word has been applied to the supporting parts of iron frames of all sorts; so that where the uprights of a piece of carpentry work would commonly be called posts, the cast-iron or wrought-iron uprights are called columns. (B) In special architectural sense, a supporting member of stone or some material used in close imitation of stone and composed of three parts, capital, shaft, and base; the shaft, moreover, being either cylindrical or approximately so, that is, a many-sided prism, or a reeded or fluted body whose general shape is cylindrical. In this sense a column need not carry a weight at all large in proportion to its mass; thus the decorative use of columns for memorial purposes involves the placing of a statue, a bust, a globe, a vase, or similar object slight in proportion to the column itself as the only weight superimposed upon the capital. The term is still employed where some one of the above characteristics do not exist; thus, in the earliest columnar architecture, that of the Egyptians, there is no base, and the earliest columnar structures of the Greeks, namely those of the Doric order, were also without bases. Capitals are, however, universal, and are to be considered as mainly decorative in character.

Columna rostrata: An ornamental column decorated with ships' prows. From Roman architecture.

Columnar: (A) Having the characteristics or form of a column. (B) Composed, or partly composed, of a column or columns; having columns as the principal, or as a very important, element of a design or structure.

Common room: In an English college, a room which forms the place of gathering of the fellows and others, who control the affairs of the college, and who generally live in its buildings. It is, however, the hall, and not the common room, which is used for dinner and usually for other meals. The term originating in Oxford is general now except in Cambridge.

Composite order: One of the five orders recognized by the Neo-classic architects and described by the writers of the sixteenth century. In its original form it is a Classical Roman adaption of the Corinthian order; one of very many modifications which that order received to make it still richer and more elaborate, especially in the ornamentation of the capitals. As described by the sixteenth century writers, the capital consists of volutes and ovolo between them, borrowed, with modifications, from the Ionic capital; and of the circle of acanthus leaves applied to the lower part of the bell as used in the Corinthian capital.

Concalli: In Aztec building, a storehouse.

Confessio: A chamber in Medieval churches under the altar housing a relic.

Coping: A cap or covering placed on a wall or horizontal opening to shed water.

Corbeille: In French, a basket. Employed in English in the eighteenth century to designate any basket-like architectural member, especially capitals resembling baskets either in form or decoration; now obsolete. (Written also *corbeil* and sometimes confused with corbel.)

Corbel: A bracket of that form which is best fitted to ordinary conditions of cut stone or of other masonry; in French, the corresponding term *corbeau* is limited to a bracket having, particularly, two opposite vertical sides, as distinguished from the *cul de lampe*, which has a generally pyramidal or conical shape. In this limited sense a modillion is a corbel; but the term corbel is used more commonly for Medieval and outlying styles of architecture. In English books the term has a special application to those wall brackets of many forms which in Gothic architecture serve as starting places for vaulting ribs. Sometimes these are simple *culs de lampe*; but sometimes they are dwarf vaulting shafts, with caps and bases.

Corinthian order: One of the five orders recognized by the Italian architects of the sixteenth century and described by the writers of that time. It is one of the three orders used by the Greeks, but its origin was late in the independent development of Greek architecture, and there are only a very few monuments of pre-Roman time in which it is known to have existed. Of these the most important is the circular building at Epidaurus. The little building in Athens known as the Choragic Monument of Lysicrates is another instance. This order was adopted by the Romans of the empire as their favorite one for elaborate work, and in some of their monuments is treated with great beauty, even the buildings erected far away from the center of the empire retaining great charm of elaboration, as in Palmyra and Baalbek, in the palace at Spalato, the Maison Carree at Nimes, and, especially, at Athens in the temple of Olympian Zeus, which was finished, and probably entirely built, under Hadrian.

Cornice: The crowning member of a wall; or part of a wall; as a coping or water table treated architecturally. It has several special meanings. (A) In the Classical entablature, the uppermost of its three principal members. It may crown a colonnade, a dado or basement wall, a porch, or even a purely ornamental feature, like the casing of a window. In buildings of Classical design having more than one story, a cornice crowns the whole wall, and is proportioned rather to the height of that wall than to the height of the uppermost order if the building is of columnar architecture. In this sense the wall cornice has been said to have been borrowed from the order. (B) In architecture other than Greco-Roman and its imitations, the uppermost feature of a wall of masonry. Thus, the cornice of

many Romanesque churches consists of a slab of stone projecting a few inches from the face of a wall and supported, or apparently supported, where it overhangs, by corbels. Such a cornice may or may not carry a gutter. In some cases a row of small arches (a blind arcade) is formed under the top of the wall, and seems to carry the projecting stone. In the fully developed Gothic style the cornice generally consists of three members: first and lowest, a sculptured band; second, a drip molding of considerable projection, the hollow beneath which is apt to be dwelt upon as forming an effective line of shadow; third, the steeply inclined weathering above, which is continued either to the gutter or is carried up so high as to form the face of the gutter cut in the stone behind it, or which carries a parapet of some sort. In wooden buildings there is confusion between B and C. (C) So much of the roof as projects beyond the face of the wall and affords shelter to the uppermost windows, besides giving shadow. It is the eaves treated in a decorative way. B is often called wall cornice. C is called also roof cornice. It is to be observed that when the uppermost courses of the main wall have no projection, or very little, it is common to say that the building has no cornice. Thus, the Ducal Palace of Venice has on its two principal fronts a course of marble decorated with a cove, a fillet, and a bead, but not more than four courses of brick in total height and having no more than 7" projection, although at least 85' above the pavement of the square; but this slight coping carries a series of battlement-like upright ornaments of marble 7' high. In some high modern buildings with flat roofs, the cornice has been treated in a similar manner, and a parapet replaces its projection so far as architectural effect is concerned. By extension, the term applies to a similar decorative member of whatever material, similarly placed, as at the top of a piece of furniture, of an interior wall or partition, or the like. Thus, cornices in the interiors of houses are usually formed of a series of plaster moldings. (D) A piece of light woodwork, embossed metal, or the like, which is set horizontally at the top of a window casing within, either to conceal the rod and rings which carry the curtains, or to form a lambrequin as part of the upholstery, or to give emphasis to the height of the window. In this sense, the term is allied with the Italian use of the same word for a frame, as of a picture, a bas-relief, or the like, from which usage arises the frequent misunderstanding in descriptions of Italian interiors, the mountings and settings of pictures, or the like.

Couple: To arrange, set, or unite in pairs. The term is used in combination with a great variety of structural terms, and is generally self-explanatory. Coupled columns are those which are united in pairs, the two columns of the pair being very close together, as in the arrangement called araeostyle. The arrangement is not known to have existed in antiquity. It is often thought that the first instance of it is the great colonnade of the Louvre which was built in the seventeenth century. Coupled pilasters occur in the Palazzo Stoppani Caffarelli (Vidoni) and the Palazzo Chigi, in Rome, both of the sixteenth century.

Coussinet: (French; occasionally transferred into English in one or another of its various meanings) (A) The lowest stone or *voussoir* of an arch, resting on the impost and having its upper surface inclined toward the center of the arch. (B) The whole band or cushion of the Ionic capital, including the two volutes and the flat or depressed band connecting them.

Credence: (French) Sideboard. A table or shelf near an altar in a church to hold the elements of the Eucharist.

Crepidoma: The stepped base of a Greek temple.

Cross, archiepiscopal: One which, having the general character of the Latin cross, has two horizontal bars instead of one.

Cross, city: In the Middle Ages, a structure with a raised platform from which public addresses could be made, laws and edicts proclaimed, and the like; usually, a steeplelike ornamental building ending in a cross. In some instances, this structure was high and elaborate enough to supply a pulpit or stand for the speaker, raised above the pavement at the base.

Cross, consecration: One used with others in the ceremony of consecrating a church. Such crosses were frequently made a part of the permanent interior decoration of a building.

Cross, Greek: One which has the two bars of equal length and crossing one another in the middle, so that the four arms are equal. It is customary to speak of churches whose nave, choir, and transept arms are equal, or approximately equal, in length as built on the plan of a Greek cross.

Cross, market: Same as city cross; the term arising from the common

usage of locating such crosses in the principal market place of a town.

Cross, memorial: Any cross erected in memory of a person or event. Many city crosses, preaching crosses, and the like were originally memorial crosses.

Cross, Papal: A modification of the Latin cross, having three horizontal arms.

Cross, poultry: The market cross at Salisbury, Wiltshire, England.

Cross, prayer: One erected in a village or at the crossing of important roads, or the like; generally, with a small altar at which mass could be said on certain occasions, and with a figure of Christ or a group of the Virgin and Child. A very few of these still exist, at least in part; one is mentioned as standing at Royal (Puy de Dome). A few of these were in bronze, and drawings of some have been preserved.

Cross, preaching: A cross erected by the roadside, or in the market place of a town, generally upon a stone platform, approached by a few steps, called a Calvary, where monks or friars could address the people. It was generally a simple structure, the cross forming the finial of a stone shaft. In market places, however, the preaching cross was often a polygonal building richly decorated with an open vaulted story below, and a spire above with pinnacles and statues. Memorial crosses were, on occasion at least, preaching crosses.

Cross, S. Andrew's: A saltire, that is a cross with four equal arms, but set diagonally.

Cross, tau: An object having the form of a capital T, associated with certain early mysteries of faith which were perhaps derived from the Ankh.

Cross, wayside: A cross erected by the side of a road in Roman Catholic countries as a station for prayer, or to commemorate a local event, as a murder or other tragedy.

Cross, Latin: One which has an upright much longer than the crossbar, or, in other words, which has three arms equal or nearly equal in length, and the fourth much longer. The ordinary Romanesque and Gothic church in Western Europe, and all the churches which succeeded the Classical revival, and in which the nave is longer than the choir and much longer than either arm of the transept, is commonly spoken of as being built on the plan of a Latin cross.

Cross: Any object consisting primarily of two straight or nearly straight pieces forming right angles with one another, whether a mere delineation on a flat surface or a solid, freestanding piece, or something partaking of both natures.

Crossbanding: In the construction of flush doors, the veneer which is placed between the core and face veneers with the direction of the grain at right angles to that of the face veneer.

Crown: (A) The head of anything, especially of an arch or vault. Like haunch, the term is applied to a part of an arch which cannot be limited exactly. By extension, used attributively, as crown cornice, crown molding, and the like. (B) A decorative termination, as of a tower or turret, which is assumed to resemble a crown.

Crypt: A vault for relics and burials in a church or cemetery. They may be below or above the ground or floor.

Cryptoporticus: An enclosed gallery with pierced walls rather than columns. Common in Roman architecture.

Crystal palace: An exhibition building composed in large part of iron and glass; a popular term. The original one was that built in Hyde Park, London, for the great exhibition of 1851, the first international exhibition.

Cum (In Latin, *with*, the preposition): In English ecclesiological use, denoting the combination of two parishes into one; in such phrases as Bolton-cum-Stowe.

Cupola: (A) A bowl-shaped vault; and the imitation of such a vault in lighter materials. The significance of the term is in its form, and while it is erroneous to speak of a lath and plaster imitation of a Gothic roof as a vault, it is still correct to call a bowl-shaped roof a cupola even if it is hung from the roof timbers.

Curtain: (A) In fortification, the wall between two towers or bastions, and in this sense accurately descriptive of a part of the defensive works. (B) By extension, in a building having pavilions, projecting masses, and the like, the flat wall between any two such masses.

Cusp: Properly a point; in architecture, a point made by the intersection of two curved lines or members; especially in Gothic windows, tracery, etc., where the arch is diversified on its intrados by foliation the curves of which are tangent to the inner edge

of the larger arch. The simplest are those seen in the ordinary cusped arch. Gothic tracery affords many instances of the more elaborate sorts.

Cyclopean masonry: Masonry in preclassical Greek architecture made of irregular stones.

Cyma reversa: See molding, reverse ogee.

Cymatium: In Classical architecture, the top member of a cornice in an entablature.

D

Dado: (A) In Italian, a tessera or die; hence the flat face of a pedestal between the base and cap. In English it denotes a continuous pedestal or wainscot, including the base and cap molding, or sometimes only the plane surface between the base board and cap molding of such a continuous pedestal. A panelled wooden dado is generally called a wainscot; the words are often used erroneously as if synonymous. Dado is not usually used of an external pedestal course. (B) A groove formed by dadoing.

Dagoba: In Buddhist architecture, a shrine for relics. For those set up within a temple and having a position akin to that of the chasse or reliquary in Christian ecclesiology.

Dalan, Dallan: In Persian and Indian architecture, a veranda, or sometimes a more stately hall of reception, but always more or less open to the weather with a roof carried on columns, or the like.

Dar: In Indian and Persian architecture, a gateway. The term enters into many compounds, as buildings are named from the gateways which they cover or protect, and gateways themselves take names from the roads passing through them, the cities to which these roads lead, and the like.

Decastyle: A portico with 10 fronted columns.

Decoration: (A) The act or art of making beautiful or attractive. (B) The result of a deliberate attempt to beautify or adorn. In this sense, used more especially for sculpture, painting, inlay, or similar added ornamentation.

Della Robia ware: Relief sculpture that originated by the della Robbia family and that has been glazed with tin.

Demicolumn: A column sunken halfway into a wall. Not a pilaster.

Demilune: (French) A crescent-shaped outwork built into a moat or a fort. Semicircular.

Dentil, Venetian: One of a series of square blocks alternating with sloping surfaces, as described below. Also, the ornament so produced in general. A square-edged projecting fillet, or listel, is cut either on one edge or alternately on one and on the other side, so as to produce sloping surfaces which occupy half the width of the fillet. In this way a projection and a depression alternate along each cut side or edge of the fillet; the projections on one side, of the double cut form, corresponding to the depressions on the other. The same form occurs, though rarely, in French Romanesque. There are other forms of square-edged ornament peculiar to Venetian architecture, some of which deserve the name dentil as well as the above-described form, but the term is generally limited as stated.

Dentil: A small rectangular block, forming one of a series closely set in a row, generally between two moldings, and intended for ornamental effect by alternation of light, shade, and shadow. Rows of dentils are found under the corona of an Ionic or Corinthian cornice. One of the earliest examples is in the cornice of the caryatid porch of the Erechtheum, Athens; another is that of the Choragic Monument of Lysicrates, while in Roman Ionic and even Roman Doric buildings it is a very common feature. In the Roman Corinthian, also, there is a row of dentils between two moldings under the modillions. The proportions of Classic dentils are very considerable; in some of the best examples the width and projection are each equal to two thirds the height, and the inter-dentil or space is one-third the height; which approximates to one-sixth the lower diameter of the column. In Byzantine, especially Veneto-Byzantine, architecture a form of double alternating dentil is used.

Device: A pictorial or sculptured design, usually emblematic or symbolical, expressing a sentiment and often accompanied by a motto in which the same or a similar sentiment is put into words. The device (called also *impresa* or *imprezza*) was common in the sixteenth and seventeenth centuries, and a simple one or a single element or part of one is often found in architectural decoration. The device is freely taken by any person at pleasure; and it differs in this from heraldic bearings which are always the direct gift or grant of a superior authority.

Diameter: (A) An imaginary line through the center of a circle or sphere, and terminating in the perimeter or surface; a similar line in a circular cylinder. (B) The length of a diameter in sense *A*. In the system of proportions devised by the Italian architects of the Classic revival (Vignola, Palladio, Scamozzi, etc.) for the Classic orders, the diameter of the lower part of the shaft of a column was taken as a standard of dimension for all parts of the order. It was divided into two modules, and these into parts or minutes, 12 for the Tuscan and Doric, eighteen for the Ionic, Corinthian, and Composite orders.

Other writers have used other subdivisions. This highly artificial analysis of the proportions, establishing a rigid and arbitrary canon, was evidently unknown to the Romans, although with their love of system they developed certain traditional rules, more or less flexible. Vitruvius gives certain of these, employing the term *crassitudo* for the diameter of the shaft as a unit for certain measurements and spacings; but he does not make it the basis of a whole system of detailed proportions as do the Italian classicists.

Dipteral: Composed of, or provided with, two rows of columns; especially when applied to a Greek temple, having two rows of columns on all sides.

Diptych: Panels with religious designs on them and that open in the manner of a screen door.

Divan: (A) A council chamber, court, or state room, especially in the Levant or among Islamic peoples generally. (B) A room, especially in the Levant, having one side entirely open, as toward a garden, and a floor raised by one or two steps. (C) In the West, a broad and long seat, composed of a mattress or long cushion either laid directly on the floor or upon a low bench. Sometimes used for sofa or couch.

Dodecastyle: A portico with 12 frontal columns.

Dome: (A) A building; generally one of importance, and a public building rather than a dwelling: "Here, hard by Vesta's temple, Build we a stately dome."-Macaulay. In this sense used only in poetry or in a loose and general way. The use, Italian, of the word *duomo*, and the corresponding German word *dom*, applied to a cathedral church, seems to have had no influence in England. (B) A cupola; more commonly used for a large one covering a good part of a building. In this sense also it is loose and inaccurate, and it would be far better if the word cupola were used exclusively for a roof of this kind. (C) An evenly curved vault on a circular base.

Dome, Gothic: A structure supposed to be possible or conceivable; at once a true cupola and Gothic in structure and design. A true cupola could not exist in Gothic architecture. When, however, a vaulted compartment is much crowned-up, the rounded forms approach those of a dome in this sense.

Domus: A single-family Roman house.

Doric order: (A) One of the five orders, recognized by the Italian writers of the sixteenth century, to whom, however, Greek architecture was almost wholly unknown. (B) The style of architecture used in the greater number of Greek temples known to us, and of which the Parthenon serves as the type.

Dress circle: Originally, in British theaters, the first balcony containing the boxes, and set apart for the wealthier class of the audience, who were supposed to appear in evening dress. It usually extended around three sides of the auditorium, the pit being either enclosed by it, or extending under it. In modern times, the term is used more or less indiscriminately to mean a similar part of a theater either on the main floor, or on a balcony above the orchestra, and next in importance to the latter, and most often without boxes.

Drum: (A) One of the nearly cylindrical pieces of which a shaft of a column is built up when it is not a monolith. (B) The vertical wall, circular or polygonal in plan, which carries the rounded part of a cupola; called also *tambour*. The drum applies chiefly to the exterior of buildings; thus, in the Pantheon or in the Church of Hagia Sophia there is no drum; the Cathedral of Florence has a very high octagonal drum pierced with an occulus in each face; and S.

Paul's in London has a very lofty drum, which may be considered as having three parts, a plain basement, a lofty peristyle crowned by a parapet and surrounding a sloping circular wall pierced with windows, and an attic, which last carried the cupola itself.

Dugout: A dwelling wholly or partly constructed in the ground, preferably in a bank or slope. The walls are continued upward or outward from the excavation by utilizing the earth thrown out, together with sod or stones, or both. The walls above ground, or the front where the excavation is in a slope, are finished with sod, stone, boards, canvas, or logs, according to the resources of the locality of the individual builder. The roof is usually of earth and sod on poles, with a slight pitch to each side, but it may be of any material available.

E

Easter sepulchre: A shallow arched recess or niche in the north side of the chancel, for the reception of the sacred elements between their consecration on Maundy Thursday and the Easter High Mass.

Eaves: The lower portion of a sloping roof near the walls; especially, such a part projecting beyond the walls, and forming an overhanging drip for water.

Ecclesiology: The study of church services, church building, and the practices which pertain to these.

Echal: The enclosure of the Ark in a synagogue.

Egg and anchor; egg and dart; egg and tongue: An ornament applied to a convex rounded molding, and consisting of a series of approximately oval projecting rounded surfaces of small size, each one surrounded by a groove and a raised rim, between which rims are inserted, one between every pair of the "eggs" with their enclosing ridges, a sharp-pointed member calculated to contrast in the most forcible way with the soft rounded surfaces between which it is set. This pointed member is called a dart, anchor, or tongue, according to its shape, and the name of the ornament is sometimes varied accordingly. Ornaments of this kind are found in Greek buildings of the Ionic style, dating from a time as early as the fourth century B.C. It is there varied from the plainest nearly egg-shaped rounds with mere ridges following their contour, and others as simply taking the place of the "darts" between, to a much more elaborate design in which the eggs are turned into leaves with mid-rib strongly marked, and the darts between modified in a like direction. They are also, even in the placing, from the chief ornament of the cap molding and several inches in height, to one of many horizontal parallel bands, each as small as allows of effective working of the ornament in marble. The ornament was taken as the single decoration of the Roman Doric capital; the ovolo so decorated is the chief characteristic of this order.

Echauguette: A turret, watch tower, or other place, provided for guards or watchment; usually, in Medieval fortifications, corbelled out from a curtain wall or from a salient angle, and dominating the battlements, either open or with a roof. Hence, in modern usage, an angle turret springing from a corbel or *cul de lampe,* as in many late Gothic and early Renaissance houses in France and Germany.

Egyptian style: A style characterized by pyramids, lotus columns, and pylons originated by the ancient Egyptians.

Embankment: A banking or building of a dyke, pier, causeway, or similar solid mass; hence, by extension, the result of such work, especially in the form of a waterside street. The term is used to translate foreign words, such as the Italian and Venetian *riva, fondamenta,* and *molo;* also, for the French *quai,* for which the English quay is not always an adequate translation.

Embrasure: (A) An enlargement of a door or window opening, at the inside face of the wall, by means of splayed sides. Especially, in military construction, such an enlargement designed to afford a more extended range of vision from the inside by means of the sloping sides, while not increasing the outside opening. Hence, (B) In military architecture, any opening through, or depression at the top of, a wall or parapet for discharging missiles; as a loophole, crenelle, or the like, because usually so splayed.

Empire style: A Neo-classic style that originated from the French First Empire and was very elaborate.

En suite: In French, forming a series; in English, especially said of rooms opening into another with doors carefully placed opposite one another.

Engaged column: A round pilaster-like member, generally ornamental in character, without utility and most commonly built with the wall, or as part of the wall, whose courses of stone are continued through the shaft. Even where the engaged column is a piece of costly and beautiful material, and is therefore not continuous with the structure of the wall, it is to be considered as a pilaster with a rounded horizontal section, rather than as a column.

English Regency style: A style similar to the *Directoire* and *Empire* styles. Its decoration involved many styles such as Chinese and Egyptian motifs.

Entablature: In Grecian, Greco-Roman, and Neo-classic architecture, the whole horizontal mass of material carried upon the columns and extending upward as far as, and including, the first decidedly projecting course of material, drip molding, or the like. It is always divided into three parts, succeeding one another vertically, except that a few very exceptional buildings, or parts of buildings, generally small and elaborate in their decorative treatment, may dispense with one of these parts. The architrave or epistyle is the lintel course which rests immediately upon the abaci of the columns; upon this rests the frieze, which in Doric architecture is divided into the alternative members, called triglyphs and metopes, and upon this rests the cornice. This uppermost member is the front or exterior face of the horizontal course of stones which is supposed to take the beams of the roof and also the gutter which received the roof water. Where there is no real structure of the sort, and the order is a mere decoration, the parts succeed one another in exactly the same manner, whether the upright members are columns, engaged columns, pilasters, or a wall. In some varieties of the orders, even as admitted by the recognized authorities, the architrave is greatly diminished in proportion to the other members, and the frieze is proportionally widened. This peculiarity occurs especially in the Roman form of the Doric order. Within the strict regulations laid down by the sixteenth century writers, there are many minor freedoms allowed the designer; thus in the Roman Doric order, the architrave is often divided horizontally into two fascias, though more often left plain. So in the Ionic order there are more usually three fascias, and this division is repeated in the Corinthian order, but with the offset between the fascias molded, or even more richly sculptured; while yet in each of these orders there are sometimes but two fascias. The combination of moldings which makes up the cornice may also vary; and the placing of the triglyphs in the frieze of the Doric order may follow more or less closely the original Greek distribution.

Entasis: An intentional swelling in a column.

Epinaos: In Grecian arhaeology, a back vestibule, as of a temple; opposed to a *pronaos*.

Escutcheon: (A) In heraldry, the surface upon which are charged the devices borne by any one as peculiar and distinctive to him or her. The form of the escutcheon is generally shieldlike, affecting the outline of the knight's shield as employed at any epoch; but, in the Neo-classic art of the seventeenth and eighteenth centuries, it is often an oval and sometimes surrounded by scrollwork, while the escutcheon borne by women is lozenge-shaped. The charges should be applied to the escutcheon in color; but it has been recognized at all epochs that a slight relief may be made to answer the purpose; thus, a fesse or pale charged upon an escutcheon may be represented in sculpture by very slight relief from the surface or field of the escutcheon, a relief only sufficient to cast a slight shadow at its edge. (B) By extension, from the above definition, a small plate or the like, generally of metal and more or less ornamental, used for many specific purposes; as about a keyhole to protect the edges and pierced to admit the key; or inscribed with a name or number as a doorplate. (C) A metal plate used to protect veneering around a keyhole.

Eustyle: An arrangement of columns two and a quarter diameters apart.

Exedra: A semicircular or rectangular recess with seats. A niche at the end of a room and opening onto a larger space.

Extrados: The outer face of an arch or vault.

Eyelet: A small opening for light and air, or for the discharge of missiles, in the wall or parapet of a Medieval castle; usually widening toward the interior, or backed by an embrasure. The opening was usually round or square, or else extremely long and narrow; sometimes with a cross slit, or enlarged at the center or ends by a round aperture for the discharge of firearms.

F

Facade: The architectural front of a building; not necessarily the principal front, but any face or presentation of a structure which is nearly in one plane, and is treated in the main as a single vertical wall with but minor modifications.

FAÇADE: CATHEDRAL, CREMONA; NORTH TRANSEPT.
This, having no intimate connection with the side walls, is essentially a façade.

Thus, if a large building presents toward one street a front consisting of the ends of two projecting wings with a low wall between them enclosing a courtyard, that would be hardly a facade, but rather two fa-cades of the two pavilions. With buildings which present on all sides fronts of similar or equivalent elaborateness of treatment, it is, perhaps, incorrect to speak of a facade; thus, in a great church, although the west front may be described by this term, it is inaccurate because that front would not be what it is were it presented without the flanks or north and south sides. The facade rather comes of street architecture and of buildings which have but one front considered of sufficient importance to receive architectural treatment.

Face: (A) To dress or finish one or more faces of a piece, member, or structure. (B) To provide with a relatively highly finished face by the application of a finer or more elaborately worked material.

Facet: Any one of the several polygonal faces of a crystal or cut jewel; hence, any one of the faces or plane surfaces of a stone cut into like forms, as in rusticated masonry where each is dressed to a pyramidal projection. There are many examples in Italy, among them the exterior east facade of the Doges's Palace at Venice and the Palazzo dei Diamanti at Bologna.

Faience: (French) Terra cotta. Pottery of coarse or dark colored body covered by an opaque coating, such as enamel, which may be elaborately painted. This is the proper significa-tion, and it covers all the beautiful decorative wares of Italy from the fifteenth to the eighteenth centuries, including the richest varieties of ma-jolica, and also the various potteries of France of slightly later epoch, such as those of Rouen, Nevers, Moustiers, and many more. These wares are of-ten very soft, both enamel and body; but when used for external decora-tion such as wall tiles and the like, the same effects of color and brillian-cy are possible with an extremely hard and enduring substance, and the greatest epochs have been marked by the production of cresting tiles, ridge tiles, finials for painted roofs, and the like, which are perfect-ly durable.

Falling mold: In stair building, a full-sized pattern of the side of a wreath. It is cut out of a thin piece of veneer, or the like, following the lines of the developed (*i.e.* unrolled or opened out) curved elevation, and is then bent around the wreath to give the actual lines of the steps, mold-ings, and other parts.

Fan window: Decorative work abounding in fanlike patterns; espe-cially fan vaulting, and the imitation of this and of late lierne vaulting, in

the carved stone canopies of tombs and the like.

Fane: (A) A temple, especially one devoted to worship; hence, a place of worship of any kind, but in a general and somewhat poetical sense. The word *profane* is connected with this as meaning outside of (before) the fane. (B) A weathercock; a vane. The term means originally a flag (German *fahne*), and in the present signification is probably confused with vane.

Fanlight: A semicircular window over a door. Common in Georgian and Regency architecture.

Fasces: The ancient Roman emblem of civil authority, a number of rods bound together with an axe into a cylindrical bundle. It appears fre-quently in Roman and in modern carved decoration.

Fascia: In Latin, a bandage, a strip; hence, (A) Any one of the long nar-row bands or divisions of the Ionic architrave, each projecting slightly beyond the one below. (B) In mod-ern usage, any similar band, as a string course or belt, or the plane face of a cornice or like member, but al-ways a vertical surface, and broader than a mere fillet.

Fastigium: In Latin, the crest or top of a roof; the whole roof or upper part or side of anything; especially, a roof having pediments or gables, as distinguished from one which does not affect in this way the exterior of the building. In no sense common in English usage, but originating the adjectives fatigiate and the French *faite.*

Fauces: (Latin plural noun, the throat, etc.). A passage, inlet, or the like; a passage in a house, and generally, in Roman archaeology, such a passage, especially if from the atrium to the *peristylium,* or garden. Some authorities, however, assume that the only passage properly called *fauces* is that from the *vesitulum* to the atrium. The main reason for this seems to be the general giving of Greek names to all rooms, etc., back and beyond the atrium, while the old Latin names remain to the rooms of the original house.

Favissa: An underground cellar or reservoir under a Roman temple for the storage either of water, or, more generally, of worn-out and useless sacred implements and furnishings of the temple.

Feathering: The cusping of tracery; the elaboration of tracery by means of cusps. The term is not common; introduced in the early years of Me-

dieval archaeological research, it has been generally replaced by foliation.

Fence: A structure, as of bars, posts, and the like, used to enclose fields, gardens, orchards, etc.

Fenestella: (A) Generally, a small glazed opening in an altar, shrine, or reliquary, to afford a view of the relics it contains. (B) A small niche on the south side of an altar above a piscina or credence. (C) Sometimes an opening for a bell at the top of a gable.

Fenestral : A small window, or (in old English usage) a window filled with oiled paper or cloth instead of glass. Of, or pertaining to, a window.

Fenestration: (A) The arrangement in a building of its windows, especially the more important and larger ones. In this sense fenestration is nearly the same thing as the providing of daylight for the interiors of buildings. (B) The art of adorning or designing architecturally the exterior of a building by the proper arrangement and apportioning of windows and doors considered together as openings in the wall, affording spots of darkness contrasting with the lighted surface of the wall, and also convenient spots for concentrating ornamental treatment.

Feretory: A reliquary designed to be carried in a procession.

Ferme ornee: A farm, and especially the buildings and gardens of a farm, treated in a decorative manner, and generally the residence of a person of means who carries on agriculture, stock-raising, or the like, for personal gratification. Such buildings are not to be confused with farm buildings of the continent of Europe, or the small manor houses of England of the seventeenth and earlier centuries, although these may be extremely elaborate in their architectural character. Such a farm, as many of those in Normandy and northern France, was the center of very serious agricultural and money-making occupations, but the conditions of the time required defensible buildings, and the spirit of the time required architectural treatment.

Festoon: Anything hanging in a natural catenary curve; especially in Classical and Neo-classical architecture, the representation of a garland of flowers, fruits, and the like, hanging from two points, heaviest at the middle and lightest at the points of suspension.

Fillet: (A) A relatively small and narrow flat molding, generally as a plain band in a group of moldings; either of rectangular section, projecting, or sunk, from the general surface; or simply a flat surface included between other moldings. (B) A thin strip of material having more or less the form of a fillet in sense *A*.

Finial: (A) A boss, a knob, or a more elaborate ornament at the point of a spire or pinnacle. The finials which crown the pinnacles in Gothic churches are often of great beauty; their position bringing their ornamental treatment against the sky and thus causing them to be less clearly seen, does not prevent them from being among the richest and most effective parts of the associated sculpture of the edifice. (B) A knob in the shape of fruit of foliage used as decoration found on the top of a bedpost of a lamp. (C) The terminating ornament of a gable, canopy, rod, or post.

Fire altar: An altar used for burnt sacrifices. The altars of antiquity were, many of them, of this kind. Where the altar is of stone and small, especially if it is decorated with sculpture, the inference may be that the substances burned would be small in quantity and symbolic or representative of the whole sacrifice; and such altars when within a house or temple may be supposed to have been used for burning incense; or, at least, not for animal sacrifices.

Flamboyant: (A) Having to do with the late French Gothic window traceries, which are so arranged that the openings between the stone piers are no longer circles, either with or without cusps, and triangles between the circles, but take the shapes of flames. The stone piers are cut in S curves and meet at acute angles, and the general aspect of the openings may be thought to resemble flames rising either vertically or at an angle with the vertical. The term is French, but in France the significance is generally applied to that which gives out flame or resembles flame, or to what is very brilliant and shining. It is less used in a strictly architectural sense in France than in England. (B) Having to do with the French Gothic of the late fifteenth and early sixteenth centuries; namely, that which has flamboyant window tracery.

Flan: To splay the side of an opening, as the jambs of a door or window. (Rare or local English.)

Flat: One story of a building, and hence the whole, or a considerable part, of a story used as a residence.

Fleche: In French, a spire, large or small. In English, usually a comparatively small, slender spire surmounting and forming part of the construction of a roof, as is common at the junction of the nave and transept roofs of French Gothic churches; and may include the lower story of the same structure with vertical walls or uprights.

Fleur-De-Lis; -Lys: (More properly *Fleur de Loys*, that is to say, flower of Louis, rather than lily flower.) An ornament long associated with the royal power in France, consisting of three leaflike pointed members above and three, or one, below a horizontal crossbar. Of the three upper ones the middle one stands erect, the two others are strongly curved outward and downward, one on either side. The lower members are treated in a similar though less pronounced fashion, but in very abstract and simple forms are sometimes united into one mass. It is stated that this ornament was first borne as an heraldic charge by Louis VII of France, who died in 1180. The escutcheon of the kings of France was afterward charged with *fleur-de-lis*, two above, side by side, and one below. The first of these arrangements is called, in heraldic language, "France Ancient"; the second, "France Modern."

Fleuron: In French usage, a plastic semblance of a vegetable form used as the crowning feature of a decorative member, as a finial, *e'pi*, or the like.

Floriate, Floriated: Carved with leaves and foliage or made to resemble or suggest flowers; *e.g.*, many Medieval capitals, finials, and moldings, particularly in the fourteenth and fifteenth centuries.

Florid: Highly ornate; extremely rich to the point of over-decoration; a term applied in general to works of any style or period; but more specifically used also to characterize the art of several periods in which a style having reached its culmination has passed into a stage of excessive display ending in extravagance and decline.

Flute: A groove or channel; channels which are parallel or nearly so, and used to a decorative purpose. The most common of this decoration is in the shafts of columns, those of Grecian and Greco-Roman origin being commonly so treated. It is customary to distinguish between the channels which adorn the shaft of the Greek Doric order and which are elliptical in section, and separated one from another by a common arris, from the flutes of the Ionic and Corinthian orders, which are circular in section, deeper in proportion, and are separated one from another by a narrow fillet. This distinction is not always maintained. Flutes are used in other than straight lines in such work as the strigil ornament.

Fluting: Concave groves on the shaft of a column or other surface.

Fly gallery: In a theater, one of the galleries over the stage, from which parts of the scenery are hung and managed. Commonly spoken of as the flies.

Fly: In a theater, the space above the stage, and concealed from the front by the wall above the proscenium arch.

Fodera, fodero: In Italian, a lining, as of a garment; hence, a casing or veneering, as of marble.

Foil: In tracery, any one of several lobes, circular, or nearly so, tangent to the inner side of a larger arc, as of an arch, and meeting each other in points, called cusps, projecting inward from the arch, or circle. Three such lobes make a trefoil; four, a quatrefoil; five, a cinquefoil, or quintefoil; six, a sexfoil; and a large number, a multifoil. Mere cusps on an arch produce foils only when connected by arcs, usually more than semicircles. When the foils are very small and numerous, as in Moorish arches, the arch is called cusped arch rather than a multifoil arch. Foils are encountered occasionally in early

Medieval (Romanesque) work and in late florid work, but they characterize especially the Middle Pointed period in France, England, and Germany.

Foliate: (A) Made, provided, or adorned with foils, as in Medieval tracery. When a foil is adorned with subordinate foils the tracery is said to be double foliate; if these are again adorned with minute foils, it is triple foliate. Tracery with cusps may be foliate even when the cusps are joined, not by true circular arcs, but by other curved outlines. (B) To form into leaves or leaflike shapes. (C) To adorn with foliation.

Foliation: The state of being foliate; foliate decoration.

Fondamenta: In Italian, an embankment or quay constructed along the side of a water channel. In English usage, the term applies especially to those in Venice, which form stone-paved thoroughfares along many of the canals, the term being used in the names of such streets.

Font over: A lid for a baptismal font; usually movable, and suspended above the font either by a counterpoise or by a swinging crane, to all of which apparatus a highly decorative character is generally given. The cover, or lid proper, is usually carried out in the same architectural de-sign, agreeing with that of the font itself. In a few cases the font is enclosed at the top with an immovable structure; a sort of prolongation upward of the bowl itself, but opening on one side, at least, by means of a door.

Font: A baptismal basin in which the water for the administration of baptism is contained, or into which it is poured, or both.

Foot base: A molding above a plinth.

Footing stone: Any stone intended for the construction of a footing; especially, a broad, flat stone for forming the base course of a foundation.

Footstall: (A) The lowermost part of a supporting member, as of a pier or pillar, having generally some distinctive architectural treatment; thus the molded footstall of a Medieval pillar corresponds to the base of a Greco-Roman column. (B) The pedestal which supports a pillar, altar, statue, or the like.

Footstone: Same as a kneeler, when situated at the foot of the slope of a gable wall.

Fore choir: Same as antechoir.

Forecourt: The outer court of a large building, or assemblage of buildings.

The entrance to a palace or a public building of importance is commonly through an outer court, the forecourt, which gives access to many different doorways, and which is reached from without by a gate, or gates, in an iron railing. Where the main buildings consist of a center and two wings which advance on either side, the fourth side being closed by a railing or a wall or lower and subordinate buildings, the court within is commonly the forecourt, as there will be no outer one. Vehicles are commonly excluded from the forecourt, except the carriages of distinguished personages.

Formeret: In French usage, a longitudinal arch of a series of vaults. In a French Gothic church of the usual type the formerets are the arches in the outer side walls and the corresponding ones along the inside of the aisles, forming part of the support of the clearstory.

Fornication: The process, or act, of covering with a vault; vaulted roofing or covering.

Forniciform: In the shape of a vaulted roof or ceiling.

Fornix: An arch or vault, especially under a building; a triumphal arch; a sally port in a wall; the Classical Latin term akin to *fornus* and *furnus* (an

oven), and thus to furnace, and the root word of several terms given above, signifying arched, or vaulted. In the late Latin it is used for a brothel (in Rome, often an underground vaulted chamber), whence the use of the term fornication in the criminal sense.

Fort: A fortified post, usually small, and often one out of many such works which together make up a fortress. By extension, the term is applied to advance posts of a civilized government among savage or barbarous people, even if the fortifications are slight and rather formal than for real defence.

Fortification: (A) The art and practice of making a post defensible, as in protecting a city against attack or in providing a place of shelter which will enable a small number to hold out against the attack of a larger force. (B) A structure, or series of structures, for the purpose described above.

Fortress: A strong place; a town or city furnished with a citadel and surrounded by fortifications, or more rarely a post fortified in an elaborate way though not having within its walls any inhabited district; a strong and extensive fortified place of any epoch.

Forum (pl. fora): In Roman archaeology, a public market place or open square; used in earlier ages as the one principal center of a town. The Roman Forum (Forum Romanum; Forum Magnum) was the narrow valley between the Palatine hill on the southwest, the Capitoline Hill on the northwest and the Viminal Hill on the northeast, the ground rising slowly toward the southeast to the Celian Hill. This small space could hardly be enlarged because of the rising ground on every side of it, and also because of the important buildings with which it was surrounded and which encroached upon it on every side. The temples whose ruins still remain were late edifices; but they stood on the sites of much earlier buildings, which sites were sacred and could not well be abandoned. But the building emperors seem to have been little inclined to enlarge the original forum even where that might have been done, on the northeast, but rather to have added open squares of their own which they surrounded with stately buildings and which vastly surpassed the Forum Magnum in splendor as well as in size. Besides those which are known to have existed, it is altogether probable that the great structures north of the Capitol, and which are associated with the names of the Antonine em-perors, were also grouped around fora. The fora of other Italian cities occupy but little place in archaeological study, but there were many towns in Italy, in Cis-Alpine Gaul, etc., whose names are composed with the term, as Forum Appil in Latium, Forum Cornelium, now Imola, in north Italy, Forum Julii, now Frejus, on the French Riviera.

Fosse: A ditch used in defence.

Foundation stone: (A) One stone of a foundation; or prepared for or fit for a foundation. (B) One such stone prepared to be laid with especial ceremony.

Fountain: Originally, a spring or continuous supply of water, natural or artificial, and hence, architecturally, a structure or artificial setting or mounting of such a water supply; often extensive, costly, and architecturally splendid. Fountains are of two principal kinds; (1) Those of which offer a basin or several basins into which the water falls, and allow the water to be taken either direct from the spout or dipped from the basin; (2) those which are intended chiefly for decorative effect and only casually, and sometimes not at all, for the purposes of persons wishing to draw water.

Foyer: In French, a room for gatherings or meetings; especially, in theatrical language, the room of meeting for the actors, the dancers, or other persons connected with the theater, and to which, under certain conditions, other persons, such as patrons of the theater, are admitted.

Fractable, Fract table: A coping upon the gable wall of a building when carried above the roof to form a parapet; especially, when broken into curves, steps, or the like. Special names have been given to different portions of the fractable, according to the various outlines of the gable; a flat portion at the bottom being copied with a foot table; curved portions with boltels or bottles; a rectangular step with its copings is a square.

Frame house, Framed house: A house built by means of a framework, usually of timber and scantling. This, in modern times, is covered outside by boarding, shingling, sheet metal, and the like, and within by wood sheathing or by plaster. In the Middle Ages and in the fifteenth and following centuries timber houses throughout Europe were elaborately framed, but were not sheathed as above described.

Frater, Frater house: Same as refectory in a monastic establishment. (Sometimes fratery and fratry.)

Fresco: A painting painted on wet lime plaster.

Fresco-Secco: This is a poor substitute for fresco. When the plaster is perfectly dry, the surface is rubbed with pumice stone, and late on the day previous to that on which the painting is to be commenced, the plaster must be carefully washed with water into which a small portion of lime has been infused. The following morning the wall must be again washed. Afterward, the cartoon is fastened up, the outline pounced, the artist commences his work. The colors used in this method are similar to those employed in true fresco. The limewater necessarily yields a very feeble protecting crust of carbonate of lime, too feeble, according to some experiments, to protect the pigments. But there are those who believe this method to be a success.

Fretwork: In general, any decoration of frets or meanders. Hence more particularly, in modern times, interlaced openwork of wood, metal, or stone; reticulated openwork, especially such as is intricate and composed of small units like the Arabic *meshrebeeyeh*.

Friary: A monastery for the occupancy of a class of monks known as friars.

Frigidarium: In a Roman bathing establishment the cold room; usually the large room in which was the bath of unheated water. This, in a great establishment like those in Rome, was frequently a large swimming tank.

Front: One face of a building, or of a large member of a building, as a pavilion or the like, especially the most important face considered from the point of view of its architectural character or its visibility from without. When used in any less specific sense, the term is usually qualified. Thus, if a house stands at the corner of two streets, the side in which the entrance door is placed is commonly spoken of as the front, and the face on the other street as the end or side wall; but this side may again be called the front on such a street.

Frontal: (A) Formerly, a small pediment or like decoration over a door window, or niche. (B) A decorative covering for the front of an altar below the table; commonly of cloth, like a lambrequin or valence, embroidered and covering only part of the front; sometimes of wood carved and painted, sometimes of gold or silver set with gems.

Frontispiece: The principal facade, or part of a facade, of a building, especially when this is much more decorative than the rest, and is in a sense separated from it in design; more especially, a subordinate feature as a porch, a doorway treated more elaborately than the rest of the facade, and more or less as a separate composition applied to the front.

Fronton: In French, a pediment; and by extension, any member occupying nearly the same position, either fronting a roof, or surmounting a window opening, or the like. In English usage, rare and generally confined to a pediment-shaped member crowning the architrave of an opening.

Frustum: (A) In geometry, a truncated cone or pyramid; or, more accurately, that portion of any solid left between its base and a plane which cuts off the apex or upper portion parallel to its base; hence, (B) A drum of a column, or of a pier when the section of the pier comprises one piece.

Full-centered: Semicircular; said of an arch. Obviously a translation (partially erroneous) of the French term *plein cintre*.

Fumoir: In French, a smoking room; especially, one in a public building or place of public resort, or the like.

Fusarole: A molding of convex rounded section, commonly carved into beads or the like; as under an ovolo or echinus, in a Classic capital, or forming part of an architrave.

G

Gable: A more or less triangular-shaped piece of wall closing the end of a double pitched or gable roof. The top of the wall may be bounded by the two slopes of the roof when this overhangs; or it may form a parapet following, more of less, the slopes of the roof behind. Hence, any piece of wall of the same general shape, having a more purely ornamental purpose. The French make a distinction between the *pignon*, which is properly the enclosure of the roof at either end, and the *gable*, which is more commonly ornamental; but in English no separate term has been introduced. It is often impossible to fix the lower boundary of a gable; but also very often a horizontal band, either of projecting moldings or of merely ornamental inlay, is carried across, usually for the artistic purpose of holding the parts firmly together in appearance. The only use of gables in Classical architecture is in the pediments, and even this is rare in other than temple architecture. In the Medieval styles, however, the gable, both constructive and ornamental, large and small, is a very important item in the general decorative system. In the earlier post-Gothic styles, especially in the north of Europe, such as the German Re-naissance and the Elizabethan in England, the gable, whether forming a part of the main structure, or serving as the front of the dormer, is the chief decorative feature.

Gablet: A miniature gable, usually employed as a decoration, especially in Gothic building, where it is used chiefly as a decorative form of coping, as on a buttress, pinnacle, or the like; to decorate and emphasize an arch, as in a decorative arcade, or in a church facade.

Gaine: Anything having the shape of a sheath; hence, the lower part of a terminal or hermes where a shaft of rectangular section tapers toward the base on which it stands. The term is also, in common usage, extended to pilasters of like outline having a capital in place of a human head.

Galbe: In French, the general outline, the exterior proportions and character, especially and primarily, of an architectural or decorative composition. Used in the same sense in English, and expressing an idea covered by no one English word.

Galilee porch: Same as Galilee. The term originated in the old habit of calling many halls, such as sacristies, outside chapels, rooms in the triforium, etc., by the name of galilee, which called for the further discrimination conveyed by the compound term.

Galilee: In English churches, a subordinate and accessory room, usually near the entrance. The original use of the terms and its derivation is uncertain.

Galleria: In Italian, a gallery; in most of the English senses of the word, especially a covered and lighted way for foot passengers, with booths and shops. The Galleria Vittore Emmanuele, in Milan, is an important structure of this sort, spacious and very lofty, opening on two important streets and upon the Piazza del Duomo, and sheltering the entrance and show windows of shops of good character.

Gallery of mirrors, Hall of mirrors: A large room in which the decoration is composed to a large degree of mirrors. In the eighteenth century, when looking-glasses, originally coming from Venice, were esteemed, this kind of decoration was put to use. The most important instance is the Galerie des Glaces at Versailles, a room 240 feet long, with large windows on one side and mirrors in casings, or frames, opposite them, the mirrors being not in large sheets, which at that time were not to be had, but arranged like the panes or lights of a window with sash bars.

Gallery: (A) A room or hall much longer than its breadth. In old English practice the term seems to have conveyed two meanings: (1) that of a place of amusement, the term probably derived from "gala" and (2) that of a passage from room to room, commonly used to store and display family portraits, suits of armor, banners, trophies of the chase, etc. (hence the modern term for a room or store devoted to the display or sale of artworks. (B) A mezzanine supported on columns overlooking the interior space of a building. (C) The upper story above and isle in a church, usually oven onto the nave. (D) A shopping arcade. (E) A railing that protects the exterior of furniture.

Garden, formal: The art and practice of landscape architecture when applied to designs of a regular and symmetrical character; that is, with little reference to natural dispositions, but rather on a geometrical plan with straight walks, clipped hedges, carefully arranged grouping of trees, and a comparatively large amount of architectural adornment in the way of parapets, terraces, pedestals, and the like.

Garden, hanging: (*Horto Pensilis*) (A term taken from Pliny's *Natural History*.) One supported on vaults or arches and carried high above the streets of a town. Those of Babylon were of very great size, but nothing is known of their construction nor of the way in which the soil was maintained in proper condition.

Garden: A tract of ground usually but not always open to the sky, in which plants, flowers, and/or vegetables are grown under special care; distinguished from a field under cultivation by the more constant and minute care which it receives.

Garden house: (A) A house situated in a garden; usually a summer house, a more or less open place of shelter for temporary use. (B) A dwelling house having a garden attached to it, especially such a dwelling in or close to a city.

Garderobe: Originally, a place for the safe keeping of garments, etc. By extension, in French, a latrine; used in English in Medieval archaeology as garderobe tower, that in which the latrines were placed.

Gargoyle: A water spout, especially one projecting from a gutter and intended to throw the water away from the walls and foundations. In Medieval architecture, the gargoyles, which had to be very numerous because of the many gutters which were carried on the tops of flying buttresses, and higher and lower walls, were often very decorative, consisting of stone images of grotesque animals, and the like, or, in smaller buildings, of iron or lead.

Garret: (A) Originally, and expressing its probable derivation from the French *guerite*, a watchtower, a place for a watchman, a corbelled turret, or the like; in this sense obsolete. (B) The open space in any building beneath the roof and above the uppermost story of finished rooms. Thus, in a house with a double pitch roof, the garret is usually high in the middle; but as the beams which form the ceiling of the topmost story are made to serve as tie beams for the roof, the height of the garret diminishes to nothing at the eaves.

Garth: A planted enclosure; a term connected with garden in derivation as in meaning. Especially, in modern usage, the open space of a cloister; that piece of ground which is enclosed by the ambulatories.

Gatch: Plaster as used in Persia for decorative purposes.

Gate chambers: (A) A room of any kind in a gate building, as a gate tower or gate house. (B) A sunken panel, box, or recess into which one fold of a gate may be received when it is opened widely and is not to be allowed to block the passage.

Gate house: (A) A building enclosing or accompanying a gateway of an important building; often in ancient buildings made defensible and always containing rooms in which the gate keeper and others might be lodged. (B) A gate keeper's lodge, if forming a house by itself. (C) In hydraulic engineering, a building within which the water gates of a reservoir are situated, or in which the regulation and management of those gates is carried on.

Gate Tower: A gate house of considerable height and size, and either fortified, or of architectural pretension. The entrances of fortified cities, Medieval strong castles, and the like, have been commonly arranged in gate towers, by means of an archway affording entrance to the ground floor of the tower, and another one leading into the tower from the court. Each of these archways allows of defensible appliances, as strong gates, a portcullis, loopholes or embrasures for archers, musketeers, or military engines; and some gate towers are arranged so that the assailants on forcing one gateway find themselves in a court open to the missiles from

above, and from which they cannot emerge without forcing another gateway or retreating.

Geison: In Greek and Greco-Roman architecture, the projection from the face of a wall of the coping or eaves; especially the broad shelf in front of the tympanum of a pediment and formed by the top of the cornice of the entablature below. The triangular panel may be flush with the face of the architrave of this lower entablature, or may be set farther in, making the recess for the statuary or the like so much deeper and increasing the width of the geison. In the Parthenon at Athens this projection, or the width of the geison, is nearly three feet. The term is often extended so as to imply the mass of cut stone itself which projects and forms the cornice of the horizontal entablature.

Geminate: Coupled, especially in columnar architecture, said of coupled columns in a colonnade.

Georgian architecture: That of the reigns of the four Georges in England, namely from 1714 to 1830. The term is more usually employed for the architecture of the earlier reigns. Thus Buckingham Palace, built under George IV, would not so often be called a building of the

Georgian style as a piece of nineteenth century architecture. On the other hand, the churches of S. Mary Woolworth, S. Martin's-in-the-Fields, and Somerset House are specimens of the earliest and latest buildings which are more usually designated by the term we are considering. Architecture of the same epoch in America has been called, generally, colonial, or old colonial; but some writers have applied the term Georgian to this also, as an expletive more accurate and more descriptive.

Ghat, Ghaut: In India, a landing place with steps and a broad quay, as on the bank of one of the great navigable rivers. There is often on the land side of the quay a piece of architectural walling with a gateway carried through it, much resembling the gates in the outward wall of a fortified city.

Ghetto: In ancient cities of Europe, especially in Italy, the Jewish quarter; a district to which the Jews were confined. The old ghetto is often found to be full of relatively unaltered ancient buildings, and in some cities that quarter is peculiarly interesting to students. The ghetto of Rome, undisturbed until 1887, surrounded the so-called Poticus Octaviae, the building named after Octavia, the sister of Augustus, and partly rebuilt under

Septimus Severus. The ghetto was therefore close to the Tiber and lay between the theater of Marcellus (Palazzo Orsini Savelli) on the southeast, and the Church of S. Maria in Monticelli on the northwest; lying therefore due west from the Campidoglio and hardly more than one quarter of a mile distant.

Giglio: A flower-shaped ornament recognized as the special bearing or badge of the city of Florence. It strongly resembles the *fleur-de-lis*, but has on either side of the central spike a slender flower stalk. Its forms, also, are in a sense fixed and definite, whereas the *fleur-de-lis* has been used for many purposes, and in many ages and countries, and has no one form which can be positively called the correct one. It has been called in some heraldic books "*Fleur-de-lis* Florence."

Girandole: A candlestick with several sockets for candles, usually made into a decorative object and sometimes large and very elaborate. This method of lighting apartments was introduced in the seventeenth century. It is to be noted that there are three chief forms in which candlesticks intended for grouping many candles together are made: lusters, or chandeliers in the usual sense, which hang from above; girandoles, called also candelabra, or candela-brums, which stand on a solid base and branch above; and, finally, wall brackets, called also by an extension of another term, either appliques, or sconces. Of these, girandoles are capable of the most splendid effect, and they sometimes are so permanent and massive as to form part of the architectural decoration of a large apartment.

Girdle: A band, usually horizontal; especially one ringing the shaft of a column.

Glasis: The ground sloping from the top of a military parapet.

Glebe house: A house provided for the occupancy of the incumbent of an ecclesiastical living.

Glebe: The piece of land considered as belonging for the time to the holder of an ecclesiastical benefice in connection with the Church of England. It is sometimes treated as including buildings, the house provided for the incumbent, and its appurtenances.

Glory: In religious art, an appearance as of light emanating from the person, which is indicated in a way often very conventional and abstract, in painting, sculpture, and decoration of different sorts. The use of this attribute seems to be of Eastern origin, and the Buddhist and other parts of Asia, since the tenth century, offer many instances of this method of distinguishing the important and most sacred personage in a composition. This term may be taken as the general one including all the special forms known by the terms aureola, or aureole, which surrounds the whole person; halo, which surrounds the head only; nimbus, which, in its original signification of a cloud, should be as general as glory, but is most commonly used as synonymous with halo; and Vesica Piscis, which is the aureole, only of a special pointed, oval shape. In Medieval architectural sculpture, the glory of any kind was often treated simply as a frame in relief, often carved with leafage, and as completely an architectural molding or group of moldings as the archivolt of a window; its position surrounding a sacred personage explaining its especial significance, while its presence called attention to the figure which it surrounded.

Glyph: Literally, a cutting of any sort; any one of many grooves, channels, flutes, or the like, usually vertical or nearly vertical.

Glyptothek: A building for the exhibition of sculpture; the term being introduced as the name of the building erected by the care of Ludwig I of

Bavaria, 1825-1848, while still crown prince. The immediate purpose was to provide a home for the sculptures brought from the Temple of Aegina. The term *glyptothek* may be taken as a modern German modification of it.

Golden Section: A Classical proportion. It is defined as a line cut in such a way that the smaller section is to the greater as the greater is to the whole. It was considered a fundamental and divinely given design principal in the Renaissance.

Gopura: In Indian architecture, a gateway, as of a town or temple enclosure; especially, in the writing of European students of Eastern art, a gateway tower; *i.e.*, one built above the main entrance to a temple, as if to call attention to its position.

Gorge: In some orders of columnar architecture, a band around the shaft near the top, or forming part of the capital near the bottom; a fillet or narrow member which seems to divide the capital from the shaft. In those orders, such as Roman Doric, in which the capital proper is a small, thin molding, the gorge is used to give to the capital a certain height and mass, and it may then be a band of some inches in width between two groups of moldings, the whole forming a necking which is larger than the capital itself.

Gorgon: In architectural sculpture, the representation of a gorgon's head. In earlier work it was without serpents; in later work, with many and much involved and convoluted serpentine bodies surrounding the face. It is represented as borne upon the aegis carried by Pallas Athene, and occurs in Grecian architectural sculpture, especially of the earlier work.

Gothic architecture: (A) That of the Goths properly so called. This is not now traceable nor to be identified except in Spain, where a very early Romanesque may be ascribed to the Visigothic kingdom, before the Moorish conquest. Even of this, no complete buildings can be named, but separate capitals and some larger members are built into Moorish and other buildings. (B) That of populations already skilled in building, but brought under Gothic rule. Of this, the most important instance remaining is that of Ravenna: the buildings erected under the rule of Theodoric (King of the Ostrogoths from 475 A.D., King of Italy from 493), and which show a peculiar modification of Latin architecture. (C) That which originated in northern central France about the middle of the twelfth century, and which at the close of that century had spread over what is now northern France; while detached buildings in England, in northern Spain, and on the Rhine were beginning to show its influence. In this sense, the term is an invention of the Classical Renaissance, and expressed contempt. The thirteenth century was the time of complete development of the style; but in spite of very serious modifications which are often spoken of as corruptions or signs of decay, the style which may be properly called Gothic continued to prevail in France until 1500, in Germany and in Spain nearly as long, an in England until even later. France was always its chief center, the architecture of no other country equalling it in dignity or beauty, in perfectly rational and logical working out of its principals, or in beauty of sculptured detail. The essence of Gothic architecture is in its vaulting.

Gothic style: A furniture style with designs popular in the Middle Ages.

Gradine: In Italian, a step; hence, in English writing on Italian art, the superalter, a raised shelf set above the altar and at its back, usually as long as the mensa, one-third or one-fourth as wide, and having the front closed in. This front is frequently adorned with paintings, and this narrow row of pictures is called the predella.

Graecostasis: In the Roman Forum, a platform or tribune, so called because the ambassadors from the state of Greece (as later of other foreign powers) were supposed to stand there during certain ceremonies held in the Forum, in which there was speaking from the rostra near at hand. Explorations have uncovered what is thought to be the later rostra, and beneath and within this is a platform with a rounded front which has generally been thought the original *graecostasis*. According to this theory, the platform was not in use under the Empire.

Graffito: In Italian, a scratching or incising upon rough material, as a plastered wall; the term is applied especially to the ancient scratched inscriptions which have been of value to modern archaeologists.

Grange: Originally, a granary; hence, a farmstead; the buildings of a farm taken together. The term was used at first in a special significance of a group of buildings connected with the agricultural department of a monastery, a large manor house, or the like, but it does not appear that the term was long limited to this signification. With Shakespeare and other writers of the reign of Elizabeth I the term is common in the sense of a farming place of any kind.

Grave monument: The structure raised upon or near a grave to mark its place, and usually to record the name, etc., of the deceased. The simplest form is the heaped-up mound of earth covered with sod. This was often, in old English graveyards, held in place by a light net or lattice of osiers which were allowed to decay before being removed. The addition of a gravestone of any sort seems to have been in Christendom the more usual step to take in the way of a more permanent memorial; but in many parts of Europe it has been for centuries customary to erect small crosslike memorials of wood or wrought iron, and upon these is often placed some tablet or frame within which perishable memorials, such as an inscription on paper, can be preserved for a time. On some of these tablets are placed usually very small paintings of souls in purgatory; and a similar memorial acting as a cenotaph is often placed as near as possible to the spot where the person has been drowned, killed by robbers, or by accident; the purpose in each case being to request the prayers of the passer-by. Grave monuments in the open air were seldom more elaborate than this, previous to our own time of elaborate and extensive cemeteries; it is not uncommon to set up a monument of considerable height and elaboration and frequently of many thousand dollars' cost at, or near, the grave in such a cemetery. The obelisk, column, or other shaft, or the still more elaborate tombal structure so put up sometimes serves as a memorial of the graves of a number of persons, as those belonging to the same family.

Gravestone: A stone marking a place of burial; the simplest form of tomb; often called tombstone. It is but seldom that a memorial slab (the simplest form of cenotaph) is called by this name. Among the Greeks, graves in the open air were marked by upright stones carved sometimes into the shape of pillars of circular section, sometimes into flat slabs decorated on one side, or on both, and often adorned by an ornamental crown, and sometimes by a piece of sculpture, a statue, group, figure of a beast, or an imaginary monster, or an imitation of a funeral vase, sometimes of great size.

Grecque: A meander; especially one of the simplest kind, the line of which make right angles with one another and are few, and arranged in one sequence.

Green Room: Same as foyer, in the sense of a place of meeting of the actors in a theater; the original English

63

word for such a room, which, however, was generally a very poor and plain room originally hung and furnished with green, though no particular reason for that custom is alleged.

Griffin: In a decorative art, an imaginary creature compounded of lion and eagle. The more common representations show lion's paws, eagle's wings, and a head furnished with a hooked beak. In Greco-Roman art these creatures occur in sculptured friezes on marble urns, and the like, but they are more effectively used in Italian Romanesque art, where admirably designed creatures of this sort are used for the supports of the columns of church porches.

Grille: In French, a grating of any sort, especially of light ironwork, such as a gridiron, or a grate of a fireplace. Architecturally, in French, and by adoption in English, a defence of metal, usually wrought-iron bars, high enough and close set enough to prevent the passage of a body, and serving in this way to enclose a courtyard or the grounds around a public building; or to fill up the place between two masonry piers, or between two pavilions of a building. The term in English is generally restricted to something rather elaborate and

architectural in character. In this sense the word is used sometimes for a metal window guard, even when the opening is small. It is customary also to use the term as synonymous with gate when a doorway is closed by a swinging or sliding grating instead of a solid door.

Grisaille: Painting in monochrome, especially in rather delicate gray. By extension, any flat ornamentation which is devoid of effects of color; thus, ornamental windows composed of uncolored but rough and not perfectly transparent glass set in lead sash are commonly said to be *en grisaille*. The term is generally used as a French word.

Groin arch: A piece of arched construction forming in some way the angle between two simple vaults. The term has no accurate significance, and is applied erroneously to the diagonal rib of a ribbed vault, and also to the whole of a groined vault taken together. The only sense in which it can be rightly used seems to be in the series of larger and more carefully dressed stones laid as *voussoirs* in the angle between intersecting arches in which stones the groin is worked.

Groin point: A mason's term to designate the actual arris, or groin.

64

Groin rib: The diagonal rib in a ribbed vault occupying the place where a groin might be constructed; an erroneous expression, as a ribbed vault is not groined.

Groin: The arris formed by the salient between two intersecting vaults. In the most common form of vaulting with groins the vaults which intersect one another are simple barrel vaults, and each groin, beginning at the spring in a solid angle usually of 90°, increases in obtuseness of angle as it ascends, and, where the vaults are of equal height, gradually passes into nothing, the surfaces being practically continuous at the crown of the vault. A sharp edge resulting from the intersection of vaulting surfaces.

Groining: Properly, the meeting of simple vaults, such as barrel vaults, at an angle so as to form a more elaborate structure. By extension, the building of groined vaults generally.

Grotesque: A Roman wall ornament made up of sphinxes, foliage, medallions, etc., executed in stucco or paint.

Grotto: An artificial cave with waterfalls or fountains.

Grouped: Standing in close proximity to one another but not in contact; said of columns when more than two are brought near together, especially in the case of the compound piers of Gothic architecture, where a large central column or pier has small shafts set a few inches from it, as especially in Salisbury Cathedral. Such a pier is described as consisting of grouped shafts.

Guard house: (A) A building, as in a fortress, a prison, or the like, in which the guard is stationed. (B) The term retained in certain districts for a jail or place of confinement.

Guglia: In Italian, a building or part of a building, having the shape of a pyramid, obelisk, or pinnacle. Any building having a generally upright and slender form, when not easily classified under some other technical name; thus, a small pagoda or *tope*, or a monument of undescribed architectural character, or an elaborate German stove of enamelled earthenware may be said to be a *guglia* or of guglia form.

Guilloche: An ornament composed of curved lines usually intersecting with one another, differing from a fret or meander which is composed of straight lines. As the French term *guilloche* has no such exact and limited meaning, so the English term is often used for any ornament composed of interlacing lines, bands, ribbons, or the like.

Gula: A molding or group of moldings having a large hollow, as a cave or cavetto. The term is used also as synonymous with ogee.

Gutta: In Grecian Doric Architecture, one of a number of small circular ornaments in low relief which are cut on the under side of the mutules and the regulae.

Gymnasium: (A) A place for physical exercise, as (1) among the ancient Greeks, a public place more or less official and governmental in character in which the young men were duly exercised. (2) In modern times, a large and high room, sometimes forming a building by itself, and treated architecturally, but always arranged for the reception of gymnastic apparatus, such as vertical and horizontal bars, ladders, swinging ropes, trapezes, and the like. (B) In Germany, and elsewhere in imitation of Germany, a high school.

Gynaeceum, Gynaecium: (A) In Greek archaeology, that part of a large dwelling which is devoted to the women, hence, the family rooms as distinguished from the more public rooms where the master and his soldiers or male dependents commonly lived. (B) In modern times a

harem; the living place of the women in a dwelling of any nation or epoch. (C) In ecclesiology, that part of a church occupied by women to the exclusion of men, as in early Christian practice, and still to a certain extent in the East.

H

Hacienda: In Spanish America the chief house on an estate or very large farm, and hence and more often, the estate itself as a whole.

Haematinum: In Latin, red; used absolutely as representing the phrase *haematinum vitrum*, red glass; in this sense, the term has been applied to Roman glass of deep red color, as in the fragments of tile which have been found.

Hagioscope: In ecclesiological usage, an opening through a wall or pier, as in a church, and pierced in such a direction that a person in the aisle or transept can see the altar. Called also squint, and more rarely *loricula*. Openings of this character are not uncommon, but it is not certain that they were originally intended for the purpose mentioned.

Haikal screen: The screen of a sanctuary; in Eastern Christian churches, to other sects than Greek, that which corresponds to the Iconostasis.

Haikal: In Arabic, a sanctuary; a holy place. Used by writers on the archaeology of the Levant for a shrine of a Christian church in the East.

Half-relief: Sculpture in relief, between bas-relief and alto-relief; a term of no accurate or precise value.

Hall church: A church with aisles but without clearstories, the interior of which is a hall of approximately uniform height throughout.

Halo: That form of the glory which is represented around the head alone.

Hance: In Great Britain, the curve of shorter radius which adjoins the impost at either side of a three-centered, or similar arch. By extension, a corbel at either end of a lintel of a door or window opening, and this because the corbel and the lintel taken together approach the form of a many-centered curve. The term seems to have been originally equivalent to a lintel, and then by confusion with the word haunch to have gained its meaning as given above. It is probably obsolete.

Hanging buttress: The semblance of a buttress, usually having the upper part, the weathering, etc., like other buttresses of the same building, and put in to carry out the sequence; supported, however, upon a corbel or in some similar way, and not firmly based upon the ground. Such an addition might be of use as enabling a greater weight of masonry to be applied at the haunches of an arch above; but of course is not a buttress in the proper sense.

Harmonic proportions: An ancient system of architectural proportion built on musical harmony. The system is built on the fact that a plucked string 1/2 the length of an otherwise identical string will sound one octave higher. If 2/3 the length, it will sound 1/5 higher; and if 3/4 the length, it will shound 1/4 higher than the longer string. Architects accordingly defined harmonious rooms or buildings as those which conformed to the same ratios. This system was rediscovered in the Renaissance and lauded, adopted and elaborated on by such theorists as Alberti and Palladio.

Hathoric: Having to do with the Egyptian goddess Hathor. Used especially of capitals in the later architecture of Egypt characterized by masks of the goddess.

Hathplace: Same as estrade or dais in the sense of a raised platform. In this sense, probably derived from corruptions of *haut-pas* and *hault-pace*; by confusion with halfpace, whose origin moreover is doubtful, a landing or platform on a staircase.

Haunch: That portion of indefinite extent which is included between the crown and the abutments of an arch.

Hearse: Originally a grating of any kind, as a portcullis at the gate of a fortress, or a fence around and perhaps above a tomb; in this latter sense either temporary and intended for the display of burning candles, drapery of rich stuffs, and the like on occasions of ceremonies; or of iron as a permanent protection. By extension in the sixteenth century and later, a temporary structure of wood, canvas, and the like, set up as part of the display at a public funeral, as of a prince. It was arranged like a temporary triumphal arch in the streets to receive banners, heraldic devices, and the like. It is by an extension of this meaning that its modern significance of a vehicle to transport the deceased has come in. Also herse.

Hecatonstylon: A building having 100 columns.

Heel: (A) A molding called *cyma reversa*. (B) That part of an upright post or of a rafter in the sloping part of a roof which rests upon the sill or plate.

Heelpost: (A) A post or stanchion at the free end of the partition of a stall. (B) A post to receive the hinges of a gate; either a part of the gate, or the stationary support to which the gate is hung. The term appears to have no certain meaning, unless in the sense of definition *A*.

Helix: A spiral motif, for example the inner spiral of the volute on a Corinthian capital.

Heptastylar; -style: (A) Having seven columns; said of a portico. (B) Having a portico of seven columns at one or at each end; said of a building such as a temple.

Heraldry: The art and science of the herald; the only branch of which at all connected with architecture is the determination and marshalling of arms.

Hermes: In Greek archeology, a figure having the head, or head and bust, of a god resting upon a plain, blocklike shaft. It is supposed that the use of these figures is of very remote antiquity. By extension, and especially at Athens, any four-cornered pillar finished at top with an indication, however slight, of a human head; such figures were considered as inviolable on account of their use in marking boundaries of landed property.

Heroum: Greek (*heroon*). A building or sacred enclosure dedicated to a hero, that is to say, to a person greater than the ordinary, whether considered as a demigod or not. Hence, by

extension, a tomb or cenotaph, as when dedicated to a personage of great dignity. In this latter sense, used both in Latin of the Classical period and in the Greek of the Byzantine empire.

Hexaprostyle: Having a portico of six columns in front; that is, hexastyle at one end and without columns along the sides.

Hexastylos: A hexastyle building.

Hieracosphinx: An Egyptian sphinx of the kind which combines the head of a hawk with a lion's body.

Hieroglyph: A figure usually or frequently representative of some object, as an animal, a weapon, a utensil, or the like; or else a simple zigzag, circle, parallelogram, oval, or similar conventional representation of a well-known object too complex to be readily represented; standing for a sound as a syllable, and in this way forming part of an inscription.

Hieron: In Classical, especially Greek, archaeology, a holy place of any kind, especially a *temenos*; that is to say, the sacred enclosure of a temple or shrine. The hieron of Asklepios at Epidauros, that of Zeus at Olympia, that of Apollo at Delphi, and that of Hera at Argos were celebrated in antiquity for the crowd of interesting buildings, monuments, statues, and other works of art which they contained, and each of these has been more or less thoroughly explored by modern archaeologists.

Hill fort: A rude defensive post occupying the summit of a hill or a strong position among hills, as, in antiquity, those which grew to be the citadels of important towns; and, as in India, the works of native tribes. Especially, an earthwork of North American Indians encircling the summit of a bluff or hill.

Hindpost: Same as heelpost, as in the partitions between stalls in a stable.

Hip knob: A vertically projecting pinnacle, ending in a finial, ball, or similar feature, and situated at the end of the ridgepole in a hipped roof. The hip rafters meet at that point, and sometimes in their framing require a central vertical piece, of which the hip knob is the natural decorative termination. The hip knob is, however, more commonly a mere ornament of the form called for at that place, and sometimes forms part of the metal or pottery covering of the end of the ridge.

Hippodrome: In Grecian archaeology, a place provided for horse racing, chariot racing, and the like. It is

probable that none was ever as large and elaborate as even a Roman third-class circus, and the majority of them were probably very simple and temporary in their construction, natural hillsides being used as far as possible to provide sloping arrangement of seats.

Hollow newel: The newel or central shaft of a winding stair when constructed as a hollow cylinder, as sometimes in circular masonry stairs. Sometimes erroneously applied to the open well in such a stair when constructed without a newel, and which is properly an open newel. The best-known instance of the use of a hollow newel in the former strict sense is in the central staircase of the Chateau of Chambord. Here, the space inside the newel is occupied at its upper end by a secondary circular stair.

Holy sepulchre: The sepulchre in which the body of Christ lay between his burial and resurrection. Its supposed site is marked by a church at Jerusalem.

Honeycomb work: Primarily, any kind of decorative work forming a pattern with a reticulated mesh resembling or suggestive of a honeycomb. Particularly a system of decoration widely used in the Islamic styles of architecture upon pendentives, corbelled-out masonry, and niche heads, and consisting of an intricate combination of minute brackets, inverted pyramids, and tiny squinches successively projecting row over row; the aggregation of niches and hollows, of geometric forms, producing the suggestion of a broken honeycomb. This work, which is more commonly called stalactite work, is sometimes wrought in stone, but more often in plaster; and in interiors is richly painted and gilded. It is a conspicuous element in the architecture of Cairo, North Africa, and of the Spanish Moors; slightly less so of the Persian and Turkish architecture, and is hardly at all found in that of Moslem India.

Horizontal cornice: Same as geison; a term used to distinguish it from the raking cornice of the pediment above.

Horn center: A small disk, originally of transparent horn, with three minute pointed legs, to be placed on a drawing at the center of a required circle or arc, to protect the paper from injury by the point of the compasses.

Horn: (A) Something projecting, usually of small size, and tapering more or less toward a point. One of the four angles of a Corinthian abacus is in this sense a horn; and the term may be applied to one of the strong-stemmed projections terminating in leaf form which were characteristic of thirteenth century Gothic sculpture. (French *crochet*.) (B) A volute like that of an Ionic capital, for which the more extended term ram's horn would seem to be more appropriate.

Horseshoe: (Used attributively.) Having the form and somewhat resembling a horseshoe, as a horseshoe arch; or suggesting the idea of that form; this being very often remote from the actual curved shape.

Hospitium: In Roman archaeology, a guest chamber, or, by extension, a place such as an inn, where strangers were habitually entertained.

Hypaethral: (A) Without a roof; said of a building or part of a building. (B) Having a part unroofed; said of a building as a temple, in which a court of considerable size is left uncovered, as described under *hypaethros*.

Hypaethros (A) In Greek (used by Roman writers), open to the sky; uncovered by a roof. The term is also applied to walks between porticoes and amid vegetation. Hardly in use in English. (B) Used absolutely, an uncovered or unroofed or partially unroofed building. The term is also applied to a temple of one particular class, which is described as decastyle and dipteral with the middle part unroofed, and as having a kind of peristyle two stories high in the middle, this apparently enclosing the open space. Here again the word is hardly in English use; the space may be called hypaethral court. (C) A hypaethral building, or one having a hypaethral opening.

Hypaethrum: In late Latin, an unroofed building or part of a building.

Hyperoon: In Greek architecture, apparently an upper story. It is the word used in the *Acts of the Apostles*, 22:8.

Hyperthyrum: A part of the architrave of a doorway, apparently confined to the top of the door. It is sometimes translated lintel, sometimes frieze.

Hypobasis: A lower base (compare hypopodium).

Hypocaust: A chamber for the reception and generally for the distribution of heat. Apparently, in Greek and Greco-Roman writing, any kind of stove or furnace, large or small, but used by modern archaeologists especially for the continuous flues beneath the floor and within the walls of some Roman buildings by means of which the rooms appear to have been warmed.

Hypogaeum: A building below ground, or that part of a building which is under ground; used by ancient writers apparently for any cellar, but by moderns chiefly for a rock-cut tomb, or the like.

Hypophyge: A hollow curve, especially that at the top of a Classical shaft where it increases a little in thickness below the necking of the capital; a modern term coined to correspond with the Vitruvian term *apophyge*.

Hypopodium: A lower podium; the basement or lowermost story of a podium when this is high and divided architecturally into several parts.

Hyposcenium: In a Greek or Greco-Roman theater, an important part of the structure of the *skene* or part appropriated to the actors. The term is generally used by modern archaeologists for the wall supporting the front of the stage, and which was often decorated.

Hypostyle: Having large and numerous columns; columnar in a special sense, as having the roof supported by columns in several rows; said especially of several great halls of Egyptian and other antiquity.

Hypotrachelium: (A) In Classical architecture, a member between the capital proper and the shaft proper, perhaps a part of one or the other, and perhaps a third member, the exact signification being doubtful. (B) The groove between the shaft and the necking on a Doric column.

I

Icon: An image, especially a portrait or likeness of something. In common usage, a sacred picture such as those which are made in Russia and other countries where the Greek church prevails; but properly, any sacred representation when the term is used in connection with Eastern art. Thus, it is proper to say that the icons of the iconostasis are in modern times usually painted but were in ancient times often inlaid or even carved.

Iconography: The study of that branch of art which consists largely of portraits or of imaginary portraits, and other representations of sacred significance. In architecture, especially, the study of religious pictures, sculptures, inlays, etc., which have representative significance.

Iconostasis: In the Greek church a screen between the sanctuary and the body of the church; usually in one plane only; a wall built from side to side of a sanctuary and having three doorways. The term signifies image bearing, derived evidently from the habit of covering the screen with paintings. It appears to be a general rule in the Greek church to conceal from the laity the altar itself and the celebration of the mass. In a Coptic church a screen conceals the three altars, as in the Greek church it conceals the single altar.

Imbrex: (A) In Latin, a bent or curved tile approaching in form a half cylinder, either for making pipes, gutters, etc., or for covering the joints of roof tiling. (B) One of the scales or subdivisions of imbricated ornament.

Imbricated: Covered with or consisting of a pattern as described in imbrication.

Imbrication: A covering as of a surface with a pattern resembling overlapping scales. The original significance is a tiling in which rounded forms occur, such as are made by the overlapping edges of imbrices. But the term is extended to include all patterns which seem to resemble overlapping scales, and even such scales themselves, as in the pods of plants, or the skins of fish. Considered as an ornamental pattern the character of the lines and surfaces may be almost anything which can be associated with scalework.

Impasto: In Italian, the surface of painting and the combining of pigments which produce that surface; used commonly in English to express the technical quality of the painter's technique.

Impluvium: (A) Same as *compluvium*, i.e., the hypaethral opening so arranged that rain water flows through it into the space below. (B) The cistern or tank in a Roman atrium, courtyard, or garden; the receptacle for the water flowing through the compluvium from the roofs. This tank was often made very decorative, and its borders were a favorite place for the busts, small bronze statues, and the like, with which the residence of a wealthy Roman in later times was commonly adorned. (C) The open or unroofed space below the hypaethral opening, whether filled or partly filled by a cistern or not. The Latin word, meaning simply that which is rained upon, easily lent itself to these different significations; *B* is much the most common in modern usage.

Impost Block: A member which gives direct support to one side of an arch, or to the adjoining parts of two arches; as in many wall openings in Italian Medieval and Neo-classic work where that member is worked into the semblance of a capital; and in the heavy abacus of a Byzantine capital in some early Italian buildings.

Impost: The uppermost part of an abutment; that part from which an arch springs direct. As in the case of the haunch and crown of an arch, so

it is impossible to fix the exact limits of the impost. It often happens that a single stone contains within itself at once the impost and the first or lowest part of a haunch.

Impulvium: Rectangular basins in the center of the atrium of a Roman house.

Incantada: The ruins of a late Roman building in Salonica, Turkey in Europe. It is generally in the Corinthian style, and its purpose is not perfectly understood. Only five columns remain with their entablature, above which rises a low attic with engaged figure sculpture. The work appears to be of the second century A.D.

Inclination: Slope of any kind; especially in building that which has to do with decorative effect as contrasted with batter, which is the slope of walls made thicker at the base for strength, or in a fortification for defense; and slope which is more commonly applied to a roof or ramp of a staircase. Thus, the axes of a Doric column in Greek work are found to have been generally inclined to the vertical, and in Medieval work, walls and pillars are continually set with an incline. The angle of inclination is that which a roof, a ramp, or other essentially sloping member makes, either with the horizontal plane, or with a vertical plane. It is rare that this is estimated by builders in terms of mathematical science, as in so many degrees and minutes. More commonly it is estimated by the horizontal dimensions compared with the vertical dimensions. Thus a carpenter will say that the inclination of a roof is three (horizontal) to two (vertical).

Incrustation: The covering of any thing with an outer shell or crust. (A) The covering of a whole surface with such a material, as when a wall of brick is entirely concealed with marble slabs or with mosaic. (B) The adornment or diversifying of a surface by partial covering which is, however, of considerable proportionate size. Thus, a brick wall may be adorned with incrustations of marble covering a fourth or a sixth of its whole surface, and the term would not be used for the mere inlaying of a few narrow bands. A metal box is said to have incrustations of enamel, or to be adorned with incrusted enamels, when the enamels themselves are somewhat elaborate compositions and are affixed as entire works of art upon the surface.

Insula: In Roman archaeology, a block in a town; thus, in the discoveries at Pompeii each separate space bounded by four streets is called an *insula,* whether it contains one house or many.

Insular: Standing alone; connected with no other structure, so as to be visible on every side; said of a building. The more usual word is detached.

Intaglio: Incised work of any sort, especially engraving in fine stones. In English the term is but rarely used in a more general sense.

Inter: The Latin preposition and adverb signifying between; used in English in many compound words, each of which expresses the relation of the spaces between members in a series to the members themselves. Thus, interjoist is the space between two joints; intercolumn, the space between two columns, meaning thereby their shafts; and intercolumniation the same thing as intercolumn, but with the added meaning of the whole art of spacing columns with relation to the thickness or their shafts.

Interaxial: (A) Coming between the axes; said of a member which is left between the main lines of composition and is in a sense disregarded, it being held that the symmetry or sequence of the greater features which are distributed upon the axes makes it possible to put in minor details as convenience demands. (B) Based upon the axes, especially upon a double series of axes forming right angles with each other; said of a system of planning. Erroneous or forced in this sense.

Intercolumniation: (A) The space between the shafts of two adjacent columns. (B) The ratio of the diameter of a shaft to the space between two shafts. An intercolumniation is usually considered the distance in the clear between the lower parts of the shafts; sometimes, however, it is taken as the distance from center to center of columns. Ordinarily, it is described in terms of the diameter or semidiameter taken at the bottom of the shaft, though its absolute dimension may of course be used. The term, though not necessarily limited to Classic styles, is chiefly employed in describing Classic colonnades. The terminology of the subject is derived from Vitruvius, who describes five kinds of temples, as follows: picnostyle, with columns set 1-1/2 diameters apart; systyle, 2 diameters; eustyle, 2-1/4, with a central intercolumniation of 3 diameters; diastyle, 3 diameters, of which he says the architraves often fail through being too long; and finally, araeostyle, a window spacing with architraves of wood.

Interlace: To cross and recross, as if woven; said of different cords, bands, withes, or the like, or of a single piece of flexible material returning upon itself. By extension, to seem to interlace, as of a sculptured ornament resembling a band crossing and recrossing itself, or of several bands seeming to cross one another, first above, then below.

Intercupola: (A) The space between two cupolas. (B) The space between the two shells of a cupola; especially in the few cases in which this member is built of solid masonry, as in S. Peter's at Rome, or the Cathedral at Florence, the space between the inner and the outer shells often being utilized for staircases and the like.

Interfenestration: (A) The space between two windows. (B) The art or disposing windows and, by extension, doors and other openings.

Interglyph: The space between two of the grooves or cusps, as in a triglyph; usually, a flat surface below which the groove itself has been sunk.

Interlacing arch: More properly, interlacing archivolt; one of several which seem to cross one another and produce a continuous interwoven pattern, as in an intersecting arcade.

Intermodillion: The space between two modillions, as in an architrave.

Intermural: Built between walls; said of something not commonly so placed, as a stairway. Intermural stairways are treated with great effect in Italian palazzi, the largest of them being, perhaps, the Scala Regia of the Vatican. In the Ducal Palace at Venice there are two, the celebrated Scala d'Oro and the Scala dei Censori. The term is extended to apply to stairways of which the enclosing walls are pierced with arches, so as to be very open. Fine examples of these are numerous throughout Italy, those of Genoa being especially showy and attractive.

International Style: A style of architecture that has no particular regional characteristics.

Intertriglyph: The space between two triglyphs in a Doric frieze. Called also metope.

Intinerary pillar: A pillar serving as a guidepost at the meeting of two or more roads, and, more, especially, one having the distances to different cities inscribed upon it. The term is generally limited to such pillars in Classical Roman usage, and this because of the Roman itineraries or official descriptions of the roads through a province or a section of the empire,

upon which chartlike records the pillars were clearly marked.

Intonaco: In preparation for fresco painting, the final smooth coat of plastering upon which, while wet, the color is applied by the artist, (in Italian, also *intonico, scialbo.*)

Intrados: (A) The inner face of an arch or vault generally forming the concave underside, or soffit. (B) The line in which the surface above defined intersects the face of the arch.

Invert: An inverted arched construction, as the bottom of a built drain or sewer; an abbreviation of inverted arch or vault.

Ionic Order: One of the five orders recognized by the Italian writers of the sixteenth century. The order is of Greek origin, although it received a greater development on the shores of Asia Minor, a country inhabited by the Ionian Greeks, than in the mother land itself; yet the earliest existing buildings which are assuredly of this style are of the mainland of Greece, and other great islands which have always been closely connected with it. This remark applies only to the fully or partially developed Ionic order, for what are called proto-Ionic capitals have been found in considerable numbers in the non-Greek lands farther removed from the shores of the Mediterranean as well as in Greece itself. The most important instances of the, as yet, imperfect Ionic capital are still, however, those found at Athens, in some ruins on the Trojan plain, thought to be those of the ancient Neandria, at Naucrates in Egypt, and in the islands of Delos and Lesbos. In all of these the capital is almost devoid of horizontal lines, and consists of two volutes which spring from the shaft, as if the designer had studied a reed or other succulent stem of circular section which had been split for a short distance down the middle and rolled away from the center in two scrolls. In some cases, this appearance of nature study is made stronger by the introduction into the design of a strongly marked and sometimes double band which surrounds the circular shaft just above the separation of the two volutes. In others, as in a well-known example at Athens, covered with brilliant painting, the capital has gone a step farther in its development, and is a solid block adorned merely by the appearance of two scrolls treated from the same common center.

All these proto-Ionic capitals tend to overset the theory advanced by some archaeologists, reasoning backward from the developed capital, that the decoration by volutes came of the adornment of a horizontal block, the ends of which were carved in this easy and obvious way. The perfected capital is, indeed, not wanting in strongly marked horizontal lines, and even those of earlier times than that of the highest development, as perhaps of the sixth century B.C., like one discovered at Delphi, show a very strongly marked flat table, the ends of which only are worked into the volutes. This flat table being supported by an ovolo molding, forming a complete circle and resting upon the shaft, and adorned with very large oves, needs nothing but the refinement of its parts to make it the perfected capital of the Erechtheum. This refinement was more needed in the Ionic capital than in some others, because the form is in itself somewhat irrational, and suggests in a disagreeable way the oozing out of a more plastic material under the superincumbent weight. Thoughts of this kind disappear when the highly wrought design of the fifth century capital is studied.

The fluting of the shaft does not appear in the earliest examples; but, in those which seem to be of the fifth century, like that of Delphi mentioned above, there are channels like those of the Doric columns, but more numerous, and in the fifth century these are succeeded by the well-known flutings, 24 in number, and separated by narrow fillets instead of meeting at the sharp arrises, as in the channels named above. The base underwent fewer important changes during the period of which we can judge, for the practice of fluting horizontally the large torus of the base came in at a very early epoch, and this remained the most important characteristic of the order after the volutes of its capital. When the Ionic shaft is set upon the Attic base, it loses much of its distinction. The bases of the little temple of Nike Apteros at Athens seem to combine the two ideas, the combination of flutes resting upon a part, at least, of the attic base; and a somewhat similar attempt was made in the famous Erechtheum. The flutings and the arrangement of the base are of peculiar importance to students, because the Corinthian order when it began was, in the main, the Ionic order with a newly invented capital. In connection with the Ionic order there are some beautifully imagined ornamental devices in less common use. Thus, the pilasters which are used with the Ionic column are sometimes of singular beauty, having simply fluted shafts with a capital consisting of a band of anthemions, with egg and dart moldings above, and a base with right flutings and sometimes a kind of guilloche adorning the torus. Moreover, it is in connection with this order that the most perfect instance of the caryatid occurs, namely, in the Erechtheum at Athens. The entablature and the other parts of the temple seem to have been the subject of thought and study as careful as that given to buildings of the Grecian Doric order. The frieze, having no triglyphus, is sometimes adorned with a continuous band of figures, those of the Erechtheum having been planted on and made of different material, so as to show some contrast of color, even without the use of painting and gilding. The frieze of the temple of Nike Apteros was also adorned with figures on a very small scale. Ionic temples were numerous on the Grecian shores of Asia Minor and Syria. The most curious instance of the introduction of the order in a place which seems incongruous is the well known portico of the Propylaea of the Acropolis at Athens. There, while the outer colonnades on both sides are pure Doric of a perfect type, the columns which front upon the continuous passage of the roadway through the portico from west to east are Ionic; but of necessity their entablature is very far removed from the full perfection of the order.

Isocephalous: Having the heads nearly on a horizontal line; said especially of human figures in a frieze or band, as a painting or bas-relief. Rarely extended to arches in an arcuated construction when for any reason the crowns and not the springing lines are brought nearly to a horizontal plane.

Isodomum: Same as Greek masonry. The term signifies of equal make, and is applied properly only to such stonework as is laid in courses of equal height.

Italian furniture: Furniture characterized by six different styles. The Pre-renaissance (1100-1400) style modeled Byzantine and Gothic art. The *Quattrocento* (1400-1500) style had very classic and simple details. The *Cinquecento* (1500-1600) style was dominated by rich and elaborate carvings. The *Baroque* (1650-1700) style was characterized by exaggerated and ornate designs. The *Settecento* (1700-1750) style had lavish but elegant designs. The other styles duplicated *Directoire*, Louis XVI, and Hepplewhite styles.

J

Jacobean architecture: That of the reign of James I; or, by extension, that of the period covering the reign of the Stuart family and the brief interval of the Commonwealth. This covers roughly the seventeenth century. Up to the beginning of this century the domestic work of England had developed slowly on natural lines, corresponding to the needs of the people and the desires and ambitions of their artists, who were taught in the school of the ecclesiastical architecture of their time. After this time it began to be affected more and more by foreign ideas, Italian and French. For a century England had been using the orders and so in a way trying to keep in touch with the march of affairs in Italy; but it was not until the educated architect appeared that the orders were sufficiently understood to be used with accuracy. From this time on there was a marked change in planning and in construction. For the first time in England's history the architect appears; and, with his advent, the skilled mechanic, who could interpret and carry out the surveyor's sketch, began to disappear. In this lies the interpretation of the successes and failures of Jacobean and later work. There was more knowledge needed to design, and less knowledge to execute. Classic knowledge, which had hitherto but modified detail, now made itself felt in the plan and the elevations. The square house took the place of the old forms, the oblong auditorium replaced the three-aisled church. Both were in harmony with the times and the general sentiment of the English people; but it was an English people in whom it is difficult to recognize those who made England famous under Elizabeth I. Inigo Jones, working indifferently in the fast failing Gothic or in the new Classic, marked the early phases of Jacobean. In both styles he showed himself a master; but his Gothic is not better than that of his less well-known predecessors, and his Classic would hardly have placed him in the first rank in Italy and France.

Wren, who is by far the most marked figure in the period, was a man of great ability and great reserve. Hampered by limited knowledge, by multiplicity of interests, and by an enormous quantity of work, he yet produced buildings which in dignity, simplicity, and good proportion stand fairly unrivalled. Wren was always distinctly English, and he laid the foundation of all that was best in the Queen Anne and Georgian times.

Jacobean work was founded on the Italian work of Palladio, who represents the closing phases of the great Italian Renaissance. It gave England Classic plans and Classic laws, but in so doing it led the way to a time when the science of architecture killed all the more vital qualities.

Jacquemart: A figure, usually of metal, the arms of which move by clockwork at certain hours, and which, with a mallet or the like, strikes the hours, the quarters, etc., upon a bell. These figures are generally in pairs, one on each side of a bell, but this apparently for mere symmetry, or to make a somewhat more imposing group.

Janus: (A) An ancient Italian god, represented with two faces looking in opposite directions, and supposed to preside over the beginning of everything. His temple, so often alluded to in literature, appears to have been a very small structure, probably of bronze, consisting of little more than the two doors on opposite faces of the structure, which doors were open during time of war. (B) By extension, any temple of Janus, or building dedicated to Janus; especially Janus quadrifrons, a building having four faces. Such buildings, forming almost cubical masses, and pierced with four archways or by two barrel

vaults crossing one another in the middle and continuing from face to face, were not uncommon in the city of Rome. These appear to have been akin to the arched, and probably vaulted, structures which connected the great colonnaded streets of the Syrian cities, Antioch, Gerasa, Palmyra. Some of those in Rome are stated to have been used for shelter only, but their size was not great, and they could have formed only a part, perhaps the central part, of the shelter referred to. Only one remains in condition. It is that which belonged to the Forum Boarium, and near which is the Church of S. Giorgio al Velabro. It is known that this once had another story.

Jesse window: One in which the Tree of Jesse is represented in the design of the colored glass; or, more rarely, in the stone tracery.

Jetty: (A) A pier projecting from the land into a piece of water, to allow vessels to land passengers and freight, or to serve as a breakwater. The term is used in landscape architecture for such a pier when of small scale and on the margin of an ornamental lake, or a river treated as part of a park. (B) An overhanging portion of a building, especially a story overhanging the one below, as is common in Medieval houses.

83

K

Keyhole: A hole for the reception of a key, in any sense; more specifically, the aperture by which a key is inserted into a lock.

Keystone: A key or wedge of stone; in general, the same as voussoir. The term is usually restricted to mean a voussoir at the crown of the arch, coming thus in the middle of the archivolt, although any voussoir may be considered as a key, especially the last one placed, which thus *keys* the whole system together.

Kiosk, Kiosque: (A) In the Levant, a summer palace, a pavilion, or place of temporary resort. (B) A small and usually open building used for subordinate or temporary purposes. In this sense, the term is applied to Oriental summer houses and garden houses, in Paris to the booths in which newspapers and the like are sold, and generally to a roofed pavilion for musicians, a place of shelter in a public park, or the like.

Kirk: A place of Christian worship, especially in Scotland. The term is the Lowland Scotch form of the word church.

Kneeler, Kneestone: A more or less triangular stone at the slope of a gable wall; cut so as to have a horizontal bed while the outer face may conform, wholly or in part, to the slope of the gable. The term footstone is commonly applied to a single such stone forming the lower end of the coping on the slope and serving to resist the push of the more commonly sloping stones above.

Knot work: Ornament in relief, resembling interlaced work.

Knotted columns: A carved stone support formed of two or four columns with their shafts tied into knots. Found in Romanesque architecture.

Knotted pier: A pair or a group of shafts treated as described under knotted columns.

L

Labrum: (In Latin, a contraction of *lavabrum*, a bathtub) In Roman archaeology, one of the stone bathing tubs, of which many exist in the museums of Italy. They are sometimes made of very precious material, hard granite or porphyry, and have a little carefully chosen ornamentation.

Labyrinth: (A) In Greek archaeology, a complicated building, with many corridors and rooms, through which it was difficult to find one's way. The term also is applied to a cave. The Labyrinth of Egypt is described by Herodotus, but the ruins as they exist near the ancient Lake Moeris, in the province of Fayoum, show no trace of the splendor of the buildings as they once may have possessed. The labyrinth of Crete, in which Minotaur was confined, is perhaps wholly mythical. The Labyrinth in the tomb of Porsena at Clusium was apparently merely the tomb itself, but a building so large and of such unusual character for a tomb that the term was applied to it in admiration. (B) A maze of any description. In modern times, generally a fantastic arrangement of lofty and thick hedges in a garden, as at Hampton Court, where it is somewhat difficult to find one's way to the center. (C) A drawing or other representation on a flat surface of a maze, so elaborate that, even with the whole plan before him or her, the student is puzzled as to the right course to follow to reach the center. In architecture such labyrinths are inlaid in the pavements of churches of the Middle Ages, where they are sometimes 30' or more in diameter. They were supposed to be emblematic either of the difficulty and uncertainty of the Christian's progress through this world, or they were, as some think, of purely mystical meaning, connected with some legend now lost and held traditionally by the masons. It has been remarked that they contain no religious emblems whatever. They were very numerous in the Middle Ages, but a great number of these have been destroyed when the pavements were relaid.

Laconicum: In Roman archaeology, the hot room or suarium of a thermal establishment.

Lacunar: (In Latin, an abbreviated form of *lacunarium*, from *lacuna*, a gap, an opening.) (A) A ceiling adorned by sunken panels, but usually a horizontal one; also, any under surface so adorned, as the soffit of a projecting cornice, the underside of an epistyle, or the like. (B) A single panel forming part of such a ceiling.

In this sense, much more common in English. The lacunar, then, is the same as a caisson, but applied to a horizontal surface, and not to a cupola or vault.

Lady chapel: A chapel dedicated to the Virgin Mary.

Lalique: A type of French glass that has low-relief designs. The designs are molded, pressed, and then engraved on the glass.

Lambrequin: A decorative member; a band usually horizontal and more or less fringed, lobed, or notched on the lower edge. (A) In upholstery, the usual meaning is a short broad curtain covering the rings and rod or other fastening at the top of long curtains, such as those for a door or window. (B) In ceramics, the band around the top of the body of a richly decorated vase, as in many Chinese porcelain. These significations mark the two extremes of the common and the more remote meaning of the term; it is applicable to any similar stripe, band, cornice, and the like, but strictly as a piece of ornamentation.

Lancet window: A thin pointed window in the form of an arch.

Lancet style: That style of Gothic architecture which is distinguished by the use of the lancet arch, as the

Early English.

LANCET: TRIFORIUM OF CHOIR, LE MANS CATHEDRAL.

Lancet: (A) Same as lancet window. (B) One light shaped like a lancet window of a large traceried window. In this sense the word is used by artists in stained glass; as a cartoon for one of the lancets of such a window.

Lantern cross: A churchyard cross topped in the shape of a lantern.

Lantern: (A) Any structure rising above the roof of a building and having openings in its sides by which the interior of the building is lighted. (B) A structure for surrounding and protecting a beacon or signal light, as on a lighthouse, having sides of glass held by the slightest framework practicable. (C) An eighteenth century oil lamp with a candle in the lamp or lantern or a modern light fixture suspended from the ceiling or a wall.

Larmier: A drip, especially when forming a somewhat elaborate member, as in a cornice, water table, or the like.

Lateran: Originally in Latin, *Lateranus*, the family name of a branch of a great Roman gens; by extension, belonging to or forming part of the mansion and gardens of this family on the Caelian Hill, near the southeastern extremity of Rome, and in later times, to the buildings erected upon the same site. The Lateran Basilica, or Church of S. Giovanni Laterano, is a very ancient church, which has been repeatedly altered, having especially a late Neo-classic facade turned toward the east. This has been for many years the Cathedral of the Bishop of Rome (the Pope), and, therefore, the central church of the Roman Catholic world; S. Peter's being a parish church, or, from another point of view, the principal chapel of the Vatican Palace.

Lattice: A system of small, light bars crossing each other at regular intervals. In modern country houses this is often made of laths, or light strips of wood forming regular square or lozenge-shaped openings. In Oriental work, as in the houses of Cairo and other Levantine cities, the projecting windows are filled with very elaborate lattices. A similar filling for windows was once common in England, replacing glass, and shutting out much of the snow and rain. A lattice painted red was the sign of the tavern. The term is extended to cover glazed sashes in which the sash bars form square or lozenge-shaped openings filled with pieces of glass of the same shape. Also, in recent times and in composition, a large structure of similar form. Thus, an iron girder having a web composed of diagonal braces is commonly known as a lattice girder. A distinction is sometimes made, in iron construction, between latticing and lacing: the former applying to a double diagonal system or bars crossing each other; the latter restricted to mean a single series arranged in zig-zag.

Leading: The process and the result of executing any work in lead, specifically, a system of lead sash bars to receive glass.

Lean-To: In the United States, a small extension to a building with a roof that has but one slope, and therefore appears to lean against the main house. Also any similar building constructed against some other object, as the shelter sometimes made by Indians by laying poles against a fallen tree trunk.

Lectern: Originally a high sloping desk standing in the middle of the choir, often accompanied by a pair of tall candlesticks, and used as a rest for the service book, from whence the hebdomadrius reads or sings certain portions of the canonical hours, the antiphons, and lessons. It can be either fixed or movable, and sometimes the desk is double; if so, it is made so as to revolve. Lecterns came into use at an early date, and were made very precious with costly materials, gold, silver, marble, and mosaics. Pope Leo III (795-816) gave one to S. Peter's Church at Rome, made of the purest silver.

Lectorium: The place in a Christian church from which parts of the Scripture are read. Hence, by extension, same as lectern.

Ledge: (A) A relatively small projecting member or molding, as a stop bead, a fillet. (B) A member of wood fulfilling the functions of a cleat, but frequently much larger. Thus, the cross pieces at the top and bottom of a batten door are known as ledges, as also the much larger members performing a similar function in a partition or sheet piling.

Ledger: In general, any member intended to occupy an incumbent position. Often in combination. (A) One of the longitudinal horizontal timbers of a scaffold, secured to the uprights and supporting the putlogs. (B) A flat stone used as the top or finish of a structure, as a tomb.

Lenox: American china first manufactured in 1889 and considered competitive with European china.

Lesche: In Greek archaeology, a place of social gathering, perhaps a club-house (literally, "talking place"). There seem to have been many buildings called by this name in Grecian lands. The most celebrated is that of the Knidians (people of Knidos) in the sacred enclosure at Delphi; it is described by Pausanias, and alluded to by Plutarch and other ancient writers. The recent excavations have uncovered what are admitted to be the ruins of this building. Pausanias described at length the paintings by Polygnotus in this building.

Letter: To add letters to, furnish with letters or lettering in the sense of description, titles, legends, etc. By extension, to furnish with numerals, as well as ordinary lettering; as when a drawing is said to be lettered in the sense of having all its terms and measurements given upon it.

Libbey glass: A nineteenth century glass company specializing in cut glass.

Lich stone: A stone at the entrance to a churchyard, intended to receive a bier.

Lich Gate: A covered gate at the main entrance of a churchyard, usually protected by a spreading gable roof.

Light: (A) The volume of daylight received in a room, corridor, or the like. The term is often used in composition, as in the subtitle borrowed light. By extension, a similar volume of light from an artificial source; as a closet may have a borrowed light from a room lighted by electricity. (B) An opening or medium through which daylight may pass, as a pane (called generally by glaziers and carpenters a light) of glass. More especially the opening between two mullions or window bars in a decorative window, the glass of which is commonly in irregular or other small pieces, hardly called lights in this case. (C) An artificial source of light; a means of providing light. (D) Radiant energy that is capable of exciting the retina and producing a visual sensation. The visible portion of the electromagnetic spectrum extends from about 380 to 770 nm.

Limoges: Manufactory of fine china named after the city in France for which it is located.

Linen Pattern: A carved design, common in late Gothic and sixteenth-century woodwork, and supposed to represent a loosely folded cloth. The usual form suggests a square cloth like a napkin folded accurately with deliberate decorative purpose; hence, called often napkin pattern.

Linenfold: A decorative element that looks similar to a scroll or folded cloth. Tudor panelling in the form of vertically folded linen.

Lintel: A beam or the like over an opening, which carried the weight of the wall above it. It may be of wood, or iron, or of stone. The bearings of its ends on the jambs of the opening must be sufficient to prevent injury from pressure to the material, either of the lintel or of the jamb; and if the opening is very wide, it may be necessary to consider also the strength of the foundations under the jambs, upon which the entire weight above the opening must come. A horizontal beam or stone bridging an opening.

Lion motif: An ancient Egyptian decorating style used on furniture.

Lip: A rounded overhanging edge or member, especially when curving outward and downward, as a spout or drip.

List: The rough edge, with or without bark, of a board as sawn from a log. The enclosure or border of anything; hence, in the plural, the temporary barrier separating from the spectators a tilting ground, or place for athletic sports of any sort, as well as the place set apart for a judicial combat. Lists were put up on all occasions of jousts, tournaments, archery practice, and the like, during the Middle Ages and the fifteenth and sixteenth centuries, and the term is often applied to the ground itself so enclosed.

Loculus (pl. loculi): In a catacomb used for a burial, or columbarium, one of the recesses used when large enough to receive a dead body with or without a coffin, and when smaller to receive the cinerary urn. It was customary to close the mouth of the loculus with a slab of stone or with masonry.

Locutorium: A place for conversation; especially the parlour of a monastic establishment.

Lodge: A masons' workshop within a Medieval church or castle during construction.

Loggia (pl. Loggie): In Italian architecture, a roofed structure open on at least one side and affording a protected sitting place out of doors; commonly a prominent part of a building and forming a porch or gallery, but not infrequently an independent structure serving as a public shelter. The loggia is a frequent and important feature of the architecture of the Italian palazzi, and, less frequently, of the public buildings and open squares; but the term is hardly to be used in connection with such colonnades and like structures as are intended to serve certain positive purposes; *e.g.*, an ambulatory, or covered passageway. In its application to private residences, it corresponds very closely to the veranda of the country houses of the United States; but the word, in its adopted English sense, is restricted to mean a subordinate, partially enclosed space forming a room open to the air, but still contained within the body of the building.

Lookout: (A) A seat, platform, or more elaborate structure at a considerable height to afford an unobstructed view, as for a sentry. (B) A short wooden bracket or cantilever, one end of which is secured in a wall so that it projects on the outside to support an overhanging portion of a

roof, cornice, or the like. Generally concealed by the supported structure.

Lookum: A small roof, as a penthouse; used to shelter a hoisting wheel and its tackle.

Loop: (A) The crenel or open part of a battlement; the space between two merlons, usually having a low breast wall. Loop and crest is an old term for the whole battlement. (B) A loophole or loop window.

Loose box: An enclosed portion of a stable, larger than a stall of the usual size, to accommodate one or more horses, which are left free to move about within it.

Lotus: In art, the ornament supposed to be based upon one of several water plants, as a water lily of Egypt, or one of Mesopotamia. The lotus which is thought to have furnished the original theme for Egyptian design is not found now in Egypt, but in India. The Egyptian designs are, however, perfectly adapted to purely decorative purposes.

Louis Quatorze Architecture: In French, that of Louis XIV, the King who succeeded in 1643 and who died in 1715, after the longest reign in French history. The style called *l'architecture Louis Quatorze* hardly developed itself until 20 years after the King's succession, previous to which time the style of the preceding reign continued. Under the influence of great ministers the Church of the Sorbonne was built about 1650, a massive and costly chapel of great architectural interest, and a few years later the Church of the Val-de-Grace, the work of Francois Mansart. Cardinal Mazarin, who died in 1661, left directions for the construction of college buildings which soon after became the Institute of France and still stand on the south bank of the Seine. That wing of the Chateau of Blois which was built for Gaston d'Orleans, younger brother of Louis XIV, was built, as well as the building last named above by Francois Mansart. After 1670, however, the King imposed upon the architects whom he employed the grand style which be especially affected; and this, beginning in Levau's buildings, the Pavillon de Flore on the Seine, forming anciently the angle between the water gallery of the Louvre and the Tuileries, and the eastern front of the Louvre with its famous colonnade by Claud Perrault soon went on to the vast constructions of Marly and Versailles. The Hotel des Invalides, the design of Bruant, was begun in 1670, and the large Church of S. Louis was built with it; but the famous southern part of the church, the

Dome des Invalides, is of the later years of this long reign. Interior decoration had a great share in the outlay of thought and money of this reign, its most triumphant structure being the Gallery of Apollo in the Louvre. Churches of great interest were built, of which the most important is the Church of S. Roch in Paris, all except its front, which is of a much later period.

Louis Quinze Architecture: In French, that of Louis XV, the King who succeeded in 1715 and reigned until 1774. The style known as *l'architecture Louis Quinze* is often cited as trivial and as expending its force in tasteless ornamentation; but this common view can hardly be held by students of the whole body of building of this long reign. The years of the Regency, closing with the death of Philip, Duke of Orleans, in 1723, were indeed years rather of delicate design in private houses and their furniture than of grandiose public buildings; but the noble buildings of the Place de la Concorde in Paris, the work of Gabriel, the completion of the Chapel of Versailles by Robert de Cortte, and the front of the Church of S. Roch by the same artist, the Chateaux of Nancy and Luneville in Lorraine by Boffrand, the Church of S. Sulpice by Oppenord, completed by

Servandoni, and the Pantheon of Paris by Soufflot, are buildings of such singular importance, and expressing so liberal and intelligent a spirit of originality in Neo-classic design, that they may confidently be set against the similar buildings in any previous reign.

Louis Seize Architecture: In French, that of Louis XVI, the King who succeeded in 1774 and was beheaded in 1793. The art known as the style *Louis Seize* is expressed but in few important monuments, for the trouble of the whole reign, and that which brought the great Revolution to its first outbreak, was a threatening national bankruptcy. The delicate taste which marked the curious revival of severity and simplicity, as opposed to the overdone scrollwork and magnificence of the rocaille decoration common in the previous reign, is chiefly known to us by internal decoration, as in the panelling and painting of boudoirs and libraries in private houses and at Versailles and Fontainebleau, and in the exquisite furniture which was made for those rooms. Even in Paris only one complete building represents the taste of the time, the palace in miniature, on the *quai*, south of the Seine, which, built as a private hotel, is now a part of the office and place of reception of the Legion of Honour. The theater of Bordeaux by Louis is often pronounced by French students the noblest monument of this reign; but the mere addition to an otherwise utilitarian building of a dodecastyle portico of Corinthian columns can hardly be accounted as making up a building characteristic of a style.

Louis XIV style: Same as *Louis Quatorze.*

Louis XV style: Same as *Louis Quinze.*

Louis XVI style: Same as *Louis Seize.*

Lozenge: A figure used in decoration, having the shape of an oblique parallelogram; usually one of a series.

Lych Gate: Same as lich gate.

M

Macellum: In Roman archaeology, a market, especially for provisions. The only instance known to us where the plan can easily be made out is that of Pompeii. There, a tholos, really a 12 sided enclosure, and apparently a mere roof supported on stone pillars, occupied the middle point, while all around the place was entirely open to the air, and the very small shops which fronted on the open space were without windows or back rooms. A colonnade forming a cloister faced the open space on either side. Although the building is small and could never have had architectural pretensions, there are remains of painting of great interest.

Machicolation: A projecting series of corbels often surmounting the walls of later Medieval fortifications, and carrying an overhanging portion of the stone floor of the rampart, the floor having openings between the corbels for the delivery of missiles on the enemy below. The parapet or battlement is constructed along the outer ends of the corbels.

Magazine: A place of storage of any kind; especially, in modern use, of explosives and projectiles; an abbreviation of powder magazine.

Majolica: Fourteenth century earthenware produced in Spain and Italy. It is glazed with tin and has painted designs.

Mandoral: A figure of the general form of an almond; especially in Christian symbology a representation in art of the Vesica Piscis.

Mannerist style: Sixteenth and seventeenth century styles having grotesque human figures. This style was a revolt against rational styles.

Manor house: A country house. A medium-sized unfortified Medieval house.

Manse: In north Britain, and in literary use elsewhere, the dwelling of a Protestant clergyman.

Mansion: A large, and usually costly and elegant, dwelling house.

Manueline style: A Portuguese architectural style after King Manuel the Fortunate.

Marquetry: Inlay composed of thin veneers of hard wood, ivory, and other costly materials, usually fixed to a wooden backing.

Marquise: In French, a roof put up out of doors to shelter the approach to a doorway, or the like; and less massive than that which forms part of a porch, cloister, or the like. By extension, the term may signify any out-of-door shelter which is somewhat unusual in character; thus, a carriage porch, which is not very common in France, is sometimes so called.

Martello tower: A round low gun-tower.

Martyrium: A place where are deposited the relics of a martyr. In mediaeval ecclesiology, a shrine, a sepulchre, or a crypt.

Mascaron: A human or partly human face, or, more rarely, the front of a head of a lion or other beast, more or less caricatured; used as an architectural ornament, especially in the later Neo-classic styles, as in the Italian work of the seventeenth century. The faces are apt to be highly grotesque, representing rather satyrs or fauns than men, and exaggerated modification of animal heads. These are purely ornamental, and decorate keystones and the like. They should not be confounded with the lions' heads used as spouts or gargoyles.

Mask: A representation in art of the front part of the head of a human, beast, or fantastic creature. In architecture, usually called mascaron.

Mason's mark: The signature or mark of the mason who executed a

building. Common on Gothic and Romanesque buildings.

Mastaba: In Egyptian archaeology, a tomb of the more architectural sort; built above ground, having usually a very plain exterior, rectangular in form, with a flat roof, from which form has come the name, which signifies a bench. The exterior, therefore, is usually very plain, only the doorway having some slight architectural treatment, but there is sometimes great splendor of sculptured and painted decorations within. In most cases the *mastaba* has a shaft leading to a tomb chamber excavated in the rock at a considerable depth. Usually there is a small, narrow chamber, either entirely concealed in the masonry and without access, or having a very small passage. This chamber, the *serdab*, was intended for a staute of the deceased, and the passage was probably to allow the smoke of incense to pass

Mausoleum: A large and splendid tomb or cenotaph. The name was first applied to the building said by Pliny to have been erected in honor of King Mausoleu of Caria, in Asia Minor in the fourth century B.C.

Medallion: Properly a sculptured tablet, panel, or similar member, treated decoratively or forming part of a decorative composition of which it is the central or a prominent feature. By extension, such a decorative member, whether carved or flat, as in color decoration. The term is usually restricted to mean a member approximately round or oval.

Megalith: A large stone block. Usually undressed or roughly dressed. For example, the stones of Stonehinge.

Megalithic: Literally, consisting of great stones, a term applied to ancient monuments of prehistoric or of unknown date, and distinguished for the size of the rock masses. The most distinguished megalithic monument is Stonehenge in Salisbury Plain, in the south of England. The one which covers the most ground is, if the detached stones arranged in lines and circles be considered all together, that at Karnak, in Brittany. The monuments most generally described as megalithic are Bilithon, which is any monument consisting of two stones only, or any part of a larger group consisting of two stones. One stone is laid flatwise or lengthwise upon top of a larger one, or a larger and approximately cylindrical stone is supported upon a smaller one, the whole bearing a resemblance to a mushroom. Catstone; A form of menhir. Cromlech; A large top stone supported tablewise upon several smaller ones. These latter may be of the nature of walls to an inner chamber of which the great stone forms the roof. Cyclolith; Dolmen; Same as cromlech; the Breton term, commonly used throughout France. Galgal; Same as cairn. Loggan; A rough stone so supported on a small projection of its surface that it can be rocked slightly without moving from its place; called also logan stone from a misconception of the origin of the term, which appears to be in its capacity of having a rocking motion. Menantol; A stone through which a hole has been bored. These are rather numerous in Ireland and Cornwall, and exist in many parts of the world. Such a stone may form part of a larger monument, a cromlech, or the like. Menhir; A single stone set upright. Ortholith; A single row of large stones. Parallelith; Two rows of stones forming an avenue and, therefore, arranged nearly parallel one with another. It is rare to find more rows than two. Peristalith; An arrangement of large stones around the outside of a mound and, therefore, if the mound is nearly circular, forming a kind of ring. The term is suggested by peristyle and conveys the idea of columns around a sekos. Trilithon; A group of three stones of monumental character. The monument of Stonehenge, as it is known to moderns, is composed mainly of trilithons. The Cairn and the Cistvaen or Kistvaen are sometimes included, but are not necessarily megalithic. The study of megalithic monuments passes insensibly into that of other buildings of unknown date; thus the kisvaen and the cromlech were frequently the cores or central chambers of earth mounds.

Megaron: In Greek archaeology, the largest hall of an ancient residence such as the fortress palaces of Tiryns and Mycenae. It is considered as equivalent to the Andron; the women's apartment being naturally smaller and more retired, while the megaron served for the assembly of soldiers and servants as well as the residents.

Meissen: An eighteenth century German porcelain also known as Dresden.

Membretto: In Italian, a subordinate member, as of a building; in English, same as alette.

Memorial window: One which is so treated as to be a monument to a person, a number of persons, or a cause. Especially, a window of which the decorative glass is so treated as to furnish an inscription, a symbolic picture, or a decorative distribution of emblems and attributes.

Menhir: A stone monument of prehistoric or uncertain time, consisting of a single unhewn stone of great size set upright.

Merlon: One of the higher portions of a battlement.

Metope: In a Doric entablature, that part of the front which is interposed between two triglyphs. The term implies, etymologically, the space between the triglyphs, whether open or closed; but in architecture it is applied almost exclusively to the slab or block of stone which fills this space, and this because we have no Grecian monument in which metopes have been left open. That they were so in early times appears from several passages in Greek literature. The metopes, considered as blocks of marble, were made the medium for very elaborate sculpture and painted decoration, and that from an early time. The painted metopes have generally lost their decoration to such an extent that they are no longer easily understood. As the metope was of necessity a nearly square tablet, without constructional utility, it became natural to use an elaborate kind of sculpture for its decoration. Thus, in the Parthenon, the very highest relief is used, relief so high that the heads and limbs are sometimes detached from the background. The theme, or artistic subject, of each metope is generally limited to its own small surface, and a certain monotony of treatment follows the constant repetition of bodies of centaurs and warriors in violent action, or, as on the east front of the Thescion, the labors of Hercules.

Metroon: A shrine or sanctuary of the Great Mother, or Mother of the Gods; called also Basileia, or Queen, a deity of whom little has been ascertained by modern scholars.

Meurtriere: A small loophole in a fort or military structure sized for a musket or gun barrel.

Mihrab: A niche for prayer in a mosque.

Miliary pillar: A Roman milestone; one of those pillars which were set up at intervals of 1,000 paces along the Roman highroads in all parts of the Empire.

Minaret: A tower attached to a mosque, and used only for the announcement by the *mueddin* of the hour of prayer.

Minbar: The high pulpit in a mosque.

Minster: Originally, a conventional church; but, as the large churches of certain monasteries have been famous long after the other buildings have disappeared, therefore, a large and important church; the principal church of a town, whether a cathedral or not. Buildings known by this name especially are those of York and Beverly, in Yorkshire, England, and those of some Protestant cities on the Continent, as of Bonn on the Rhine and Basle in Switzerland.

Minton porcelain: Earthenware decorated in the Chinese, style and first produced in 1793.

Mirador: A bay window, oriel window, loggia, or balcony arranged to command a prospect; hardly in use, except in describing Spanish architecture.

Miserere: A hinged seat in a choir stall, which, when turned up, affords a higher support as a resting place for a singer when standing. The bracket on the underside of the seat of a hinged choir stall which serves as a seat or rest during choir.

Misericord: In monastic architecture, a room, usually a separate building, devoted to meals of which meat formed a part. It was not in all convents and monasteries that this was allowed at any time, and it seems never to have been served in the frater or refectory.

Mitre, Miter: A bevel or oblique cut on each one of two parts which are to be joined end to end at an angle.

Moat hill: A tumulus surrounded by a moat. These remains of prehistoric antiquity, though often called barrows, are more commonly remains of dwellings or fortifications.

Moat: A large trench; especially one drawn around a building for defensive purposes. The moats of Medieval castles were of great importance, the height to the battlements being increased in this way by 30' or 40', and approach to the base of the wall made almost impracticable. The sixteenth century chateau of France had frequently moats which were intended to be filled with water and which enclosed both the house and also a certain surface of ground devoted to gardens, both for pleasure and for domestic purposes. In England the term moat house is not uncommon in local nomenclature as given to a manor house formerly, if not now, moated.

Modelling: The art and practice of making a model, especially the working of a plastic material into a desired shape, as a step in the study of an artist's thought.

Modillion: One of a series of projecting corbels or bracket-like members supporting the corona of a cornice, especially in the Corinthian and the Composite orders. While the distinction cannot always be made between modillion and console, where the latter is used in a series, yet the former term appears not to be applied to such a member used singly, nor to one not of a Classic type.

Module: A standard, usually of length, by which the proportionate measurements of a building are supposed to be determined. According to Vitruvius, the front of a Doric building, if columnar, is, when tetrastyle, to be divided into 28 parts; if hexastyle, into 44 parts; and that each of these parts is a "modulus," called by the Greeks *embates*. He says, further, that the thickness of a column (shaft) should be two moduli, the height with the capital, 14, the height of the capital alone, one module, and its width 1-1/6; and he applies similar rules to the entablature. Starting from these loosely written chapters, which even its author could hardly have thought authoritative, or even exact, the writers of the Italian Renaissance and their imitators have laid down exact proportionate measurements for all parts of the order, dividing the module into parts called minutes, in English, 12, 18, or 30 of them to a module; and taking the module itself, now a semidiameter, now a whole diameter, now the third of a diameter, now a fraction of the height of a column.

Molding, annular: Any molding, of whatever section, which forms a ring about a surface of revolution, as a shaft, base or capital. The fillet, torus, etc., of a Classic base, the astragal of the necking, the echinus and annuli of the capital, are all annular moldings.

Molding, anthemion: One decorated by anthemions.

Molding, balection: In panelled work, a molding next to the stiles and rails and projecting beyond the plane of their face.

Molding, bead : Cylindrical molding with ornament resembling a string of beads. Common in Romanesque architecture.

Molding, bed: The molding or group of moldings immediately beneath the projecting soffit of a cornice or a similar projecting surface. In the Ionic and Corinthian cornices, in particular, the moldings below the dentil band.

Molding, bird's beak: A molding having a profile like a bird's beak;

convex on the upper or outer face and concave on the lower or inner face.

Molding, cable: A form or molding resembling a rope or cable, used occasionally in the Romanesque or round-arched period of Medieval architecture. The slender twisted shafts of late Gothic architecture in Florence and Venice, as applied to the angles of buildings, are sometimes called cable moldings.

Molding, calf's tongue: One formed by a series of pendant, pointed, tongue-like members relieved against a plane or, more usually, a curved surface. This decoration is commonly found in archivolts of early Medieval British architecture, the tongues, in such cases, radiating from a common center.

Molding, chain: A molding in the form of a chain with links; occasionally met with in Norman and Romanesque buildings.

Molding, chevron: A molding adorned with chevrons, or zigzags, as in Norman and some Romanesque portals. The chevrons are usually of cylindrical section, and alternately convex and concave.

Molding, nebuly: An overhanging band whose lower, projecting edge is shaped to a continuous undulating curve. The term is evidently derived from the heraldic adjective nebulee or nebuly, while the member so described is hardly to be considered as a molding. Common in Romanesque architecture and perhaps derived from the so-called wave molding.

Molding, pellet: In Romanesque architecture, a fillet or small fascia ornamented with small hemispherical projections. Pellet ornamentation is the treatment of any surface with similar projections arranged geometrically or in patterns; especially used in pottery. The ornamentation of fasciae with succession of flat disks in Romanesque architecture is sometimes called pellet molding.

Molding, reverse ogee: A double curved molding, it is convex above and concave below.

Molding, star: In Romanesque architecture, a molding whose surface is carved into a succession of projecting starlike shapes.

Molding, wave: A decoration for flat numbers, as a fascia, composed of a succession of similar undulations somewhat resembling curling waves, first used in Greek architecture and common in all derived styles.

Molding: (A) The plane, curved, broken, irregular, or compound surface formed at the face of any piece or member by casting, cutting, or otherwise shaping and modelling the material, so as to produce modulations of light, shade, and shadow. The term is generally understood as meaning such a surface when continued uniformly to a considerable extent, as a continuous band or a series of small parts. (B) By extension, a piece of material worked with a molding or group of moldings, in sense *A*, on one or more sides; the piece being usually just large enough to receive the molding so worked and to afford one or two plane surfaces by which it is secured in place for decorative or other purpose. (C) From the common use of wooden moldings made separate and very cheaply, in the molding mill, any slender strip of material planed and finished, used for covering joints, concealing wires, and the like.

Monastery: A building or group of buildings arranged for the occupancy of members of a religious order, or of persons desiring religious seclusion. The term is commonly understood as meaning such a place for monks, as distinguished from a nunnery; but there appears to be no authority for this restriction, the term including properly the establishments of either sex, and thus being synonymous with convent.

Monochromy: The use of one color in a design, as distinguished from work in many colors; the production of unicoloured instead of multicolored designs. This is generally held to signify not the use of several different blues (as cobalt blue, Prussian blue, and the like), or of several different reds in one composition, but rather the use of color of single character, made darker and lighter either by the mixture of white or black with the original tint, or, when transparent colors are used, the putting on of a color in fewer or more numerous coats. The term is much more commonly employed for decorative work in gray or some other neutral color. When light and shade is considered by itself with out reference to the local colors of the objects viewed in light, in shade, and in shadow, the result is usually a work in monochromy.

Monogram: A combination of two or more letters, which, when so combined, stand for a word or phrase; usually, a single word, as a proper name. Combinations of letters which form the initials of different names, as when a piece of silver is marked with the initials of the

owner, are not monograms, but ciphers.

Monolith: An architectural member, as an obelisk, the shaft of a column, or the like, when consisting of a single stone. Monoliths in unusual conditions are especially described by this term, as the roof of the tomb of Theodoric at Ravenna.

Monopodium: The solid and permanent part of a Roman table, as in a triclinium. This was commonly of masonry or cut stone, and different table tops seem to have been brought in and taken away with the dishes, much as in modern times we use large trays. These supports for tables are found in houses at Pompeii.

Monopteron, Monopteros: In Greek architecture, a circular peripteral building, as a temple, having only a single row of columns.

Monostyle: Having but a single shaft; said of a pier, as in a church, and in distinction to compound; thus, the nave piers of Notre Dame, in Paris, are monostyle; that is to say, are single round columns with capital and base, whereas those of Reims Cathedral are clustered piers.

Monotrigyphic: In the Doric order, having one trigylph over the space between two columns, the space between the centers of two adjoining columns being equal to the width of two triglyphs and two metopes.

Monstrance: In ecclesiology, a receptacle of any kind in which the Host is displayed, as distinguished from a vessel in which wafers are kept for security. In modern practice, the term is used exclusively for small and portable vessels of the sort.

Montant: A slender, vertical member. The term is French, and, in its adapted use, of uncertain significance; perhaps most generally used as the equivalent of mullion, or muntin.

Moresque (properly same as Moorish): Moresque design or composition; decoration by means of more or less geometrical figures and interlacing bands, flat or in slight relief, and commonly in brilliant color, as that of the Alhambra.

Mosaic: surface decoration or design made up of small pieces of glass, marble or stone.

Mosque: The building which for Moslems takes the place of the church among Christians and the synagogue among Jews; that is to say, a specially appointed place for prayer and exhortation. Attendance there is enjoined by the law of Islam.

An Islamic building used for communal prayer.

Motive: In fine art, primarily, the subject of a work of art, as when it is said that the motive of a wall painting in a church is Biblical, or legendary, or drawn from the history of a saint or other personage. By extension, and more commonly, the peculiar character of a work of art, either considered in its entirety or in its details. Thus, it may be said that the motives of Gothic sculpture are rather vigorous action, portraiture, grotesque imaginings of monsters, or the like, than religious representation. So it is often said of a building of one epoch or style that it has some motives drawn from another and earlier style. A person who denies to Italian Gothic the character of true Gothic architecture may yet say that it offers admirable Gothic motives.

Mutule: A flat member slightly projecting from the soffit of the Doric cornice, placed one over each triglyph and one over each metope, and of about the width of the former.

N

Nailhead: A small projecting feature, usually ornamental and common in Romanesque sculpture, thought to resemble the projecting head of an old-fashioned wrought nail; as a rough four-sided pyramid.

Naos: The principal sanctuary or chamber in a Greek temple which contained the statue of the god.

Narthex: In early Christian and Byzantine architecture, the great porch or vestibule at the end farthest from the altar and sanctuary, and therefore just within the main entrance to the church. In the simplest, early buildings it was merely a part of the church screened or railed off, and often an aisle carried across the church as in pre-Christian basilicas, but in the larger buildings it is a separate room. The familiar type of narthex is a room as long as the combined width of the naves and aisles, having a door into each of these divisions, and corresponding doors to the outer air. The term has been extended in use to all church vestibules having this form and character. Thus, the great entrance porch of S. Peter's at Rome is often called the narthex. The term is also used loosely for any enclosed vestibule of entrance to a religious building. As to the original use of the narthex, when persons not fully admitted to Christian fellowship were separated from the members of the church, distinctions were made by which some were admitted to the church proper, others not beyond the narthex, and others again not beyond the atrium and its porticoes. It is also asserted that in some instances the women of the congregation occupied the narthex, but this may be a mistake for the gallery over the narthex, which with the other galleries of a church, was often appropriated to the women.

Nave: (A) Anciently, that part of a church which was nearest to the common entrance, and which was appropriated to the general congregation of the laity, while the choir and transepts were reserved for the clergy and others. In this sense the term includes the central and side portions alike, or the nave in sense *B* with its adjacent aisles. (B) The chief division of a building, especially of such a building as contains but one very large room divided by piers or columns. Thus, in a church, the middle, and usually the highest, part is called the nave when there are aisles on both sides. The term nave, then, denotes the whole space between the two rows of piers or columns and from floor to roof, including the height of the clearstory. As there is no special term, other than nave, for the central and highest part of the choir or chancel, or of the transept, when there are aisles to such part of the church, we may say, the nave and aisles of the choir. This is strictly in accordance with definition *B*, above, but it is rarely used, and a circumlocution replaces it.

Neck molding: A necking which takes the form of a molding of any sort.

Neck: A part of a column considered as interposed between the spreading or ornamental part of the capital and the shaft. This is sometimes enclosed between two neck moldings and may even receive a separate decoration.

Necking: (A) Same as Neck. (B) A molding or group of moldings separating the capital from the shaft. (C) In a general sense, any ornamental member at the lower part of a capital. Also called gorgerin.

Necropolis: A city of the dead; applied generally to collections of ancient graves or tombs, considered as the objects of exploration; rarely used for a modern cemetery.

Neoantique: (A) Same as neoclassic. (B) Characterizing any special move-

ment in modern architecture involving the study of ancient architecture, such as the attempt, during and since the French Revolution, to study afresh the forms of Greco-Roman architecture without reference to the Renaissance and post-Renaissance styles.

Neo-classical style: A late eighteenth century furniture design which uses Classical forms. This style brought back the interest in Roman and Greek art.

Nervure: Same as rib in Gothic vaulting; the French term sometimes used in English.

Newel post: A post or postlike structure, used as a newel. It may be a small, simple piece of scantling, forming a part of the structural framing of the stair; or a large and elaborate pillar forming a decorative feature, as at the foot of an important principal flight.

Newel: A continuous vertical member forming the axis of a turning stair, either a post, pier, or other upright to support the inner ends of the steps, or built up of a series of circular projections, each worked in one piece with a solid step, as is common in such a stair when of stone. The term applies equally to a comparatively slender cylinder of stone as well as to a square or rectangular pier of considerable extent. By extension, an upright member set at any turning-point of a stair, or at the top or bottom of a flight; commonly forming part of the framing of the stairs, when of wood, and serving to connect, and perhaps support, the strings; and also to support the hand rails at a turn or at an end.

Niche: A recess or hollow in the upright face of a wall or pier, or a structure resembling, or in imitation of, such a form. Generally, such a feature when entirely open to the front, intended to receive a statue or other decorative object.

Nook shaft: A column or colonnette set in a square break, as at the angle of a building, or where the jamb of a doorway meets the external face of the wall. It differs from an angle shaft in standing well within the projecting corners of the wall, and usually in standing free, not as an engaged column. Sometimes there are two shafts close together, and frequently the jamb of a Romanesque or Gothic doorway has a series of shafts adorning the splay, which, if not engaged shafts, will be nook shafts in the proper sense.

Notch ornament: An ornament produced by notching the edges of a

band, fillet, or lintel. If the edge of a shelf is cut with notches alternating on the upper and the lower edges, a simple pattern of considerable effectiveness results; and this can be varied in many ways. In the simple decoration applied to the marble work of Venetian domestic architecture, this ornament is found in connection with the Venetian dentil.

O

Obelisk: (In Greek, a spit, or a painted weapon, or the like.) (A) A tall and slender decorative structure or piece of material, as a pinnacle-like ornament on a neoclassic building. More especially, a memorial or decorative piece, square in plan, or nearly so, slightly sloping, and terminated at the top by a pyramid whose sides slope more rapidly. The origin of these monuments is to be found in Egypt, where they stood commonly one on either side of the entrance to a temple or palace, their nearly vertical faces affording an admirable opportunity for hieroglyphic inscriptions, easy to read, and of decorative effect. Obelisks are known to have been put up as early as the 4th dynasty of Egyptian kings (3759-3730 B.C.), but none remain of so early a time. The largest obelisk existing is that at Heliopolis, of red granite, and stated to be 66 feet high; this also is the oldest known except some very small ones, as it belongs to the twelfth dynasty (2622-2578). It was customary to cover the pyramidion with metal, perhaps always gilded bronze, with the idea of keeping water from the grain of the stone.

Octagon: An eight equally sided figure often used as a ground-plan in Classical and subsequent architecture.

Octastyle: Having eight columns in the front or end row; consisting of a row or rows of eight columns; said of certain Classic buildings, and of architectural compositions derived from them.

Oculus: (In Latin, an eye; applied by modern archaeologists to round windows, and the like, in Roman Monuments.) A circular member, as a window or panel (compare *oeil de boeuf*); especially, the round opening in the summit of the cupola at the Pantheon, Rome; or, by extension, any opening having a similar character.

Oeil de boeuf: In French, a comparatively small round or oval window; as adopted in English usage, such a window especially when treated decoratively, as in a frieze.

Ogivale: In French, characterized by the use of the ogive; the term being applied especially to Gothic architecture, and signifying often merely pointed in style, or having pointed arches. By extension, having a form resembling in outline a pointed arch.

Ogive: In French, properly, one of the diagonal ribs in a Gothic vault. This significance has been maintained by Viollet-le-Duc, who points out that the term *croix d'augives* meant in the fourteenth century a pair of diagonal ribs. As, however, the term itself carried the idea of curves meeting one another, and as the resulting form which struck the eye was always like that of the pointed arch, it resulted that the term has been generally applied in French writing to an arch made up of two circular curves meeting in a point. The term seems to be as well established as is the adjective Gothic itself, as qualifying the pointed architecture of the Middle Ages.

Onion dome: A bulbous pointed, onion-shaped dome common on Eastern European churches.

Opaion: (A) In Greco-Roman archaeology, an opening, as in a roof, for smoke to escape. (B) In Greek architecture, same as lacunar, *B*. This is the Greek term corresponding to lacunarium in Latin.

Opisthodomos: In Grecian archaeology, a back or subordinate room or porch. A smaller division of the whole *naos* or *cella*; the treasury; the back room of the temple, sometimes opening into the larger room, sometimes opening only upon a back portico, which is then the *epinaos*.

Opus Alexandrinum: Decorative paving made up of mosaic and *opus sectile* in guilloche design.

Opus graecanium: Work done in the Greek manner; apparently a pavement, as of mosaic, or an inlay of marble, supposed to resemble in pattern or in workmanship the work done by the Greeks.

Opus incertum: A Roman wall made with a concrete face and irregularly shaped stones.

Opus interrasile: Incised ornament; made either by cutting away the pattern and leaving the ground, or by cutting away the ground and leaving the pattern in low relief.

Opum isodomum: Roman masonry done with regular courses.

Opus latericium (lateritium): Masonry of tiles, or faced with tiles.

Opus listatum: A Roman wall with alternating brick and stone block courses.

Opus pseudisodomum: In Roman masonry, a kind of stonework or ashlar in which, while the stones of each course were alike, they differed from those of other courses in respect to height, length, or thickness, so that while continuous horizontal joints were maintained, such joints were not necessarily the same distance apart in the wall.

Opus quadratum: A Roman wall made of squared stones.

Opus reticulatum: Roman masonry faced with square pieces of stone, usually very small, and set at an angle so as to cover the face of a wall with a net of joints crossing each other at right angles and making an angle of forty-five degrees with the perpendicular.

Opus sectile: Decorative paving of geometric marble slabs.

Opus signinum: Plaster or stucco stated to have been made of fragments of pottery ground up with lime; sometimes, as in Pompeii, used for floor covering, which much resembles terrazzo Veneziano. The name appears to be derived from the town of Signia in Latium.

Opus spicatum: Masonry faced with stones or tile which are arranged in herringbone fashion or in a similar pattern, producing sharp points or angles. The adjective *spicatus*, signifying having spikes or ears as of wheat, etc., is applicable to other surfaces than those of a wall. Thus, *testacea spicata* is a pavement laid herringbone fashion.

Opus tectorium: In Roman building, a kind of stucco used to cover walls in three or four coats, the finishing coat being practically an artificial marble usually polished to a hard surface to receive paintings. The distinction between this and *opus signinum* is not clear.

Opus testaceum: Masonry faced with tiles. This term, like *opus incertum* and others given above, refers to face of a wall only, the mass or body of the wall not being considered.

Opus: In Latin, work, in the sense of labor or the results of labor; the common term used in composition in the modern European languages for masonry, embroidery, and decorative work of different kinds. Some of these compound terms are taken direct from Classical authors, and are applied without a perfect knowledge of the subject to pieces of work left us by antiquity. The piece of work exists, the name is found in a Classical author; but it is often uncertain whether our modern application of the given name to the given piece of work is accurate.

Orangerie; orangery: A building of the nature of a cold greenhouse used for the storage in winter of ornamental trees in tubs. The frequent employ of orange trees in this way in connection with public and private palaces has caused the use of the term for permanent houses of the sort, which are sometimes of considerable architectural importance. The Luxembourg collection of paintings and sculpture is now housed in the orangerie of the palace, which received some modifications for the purpose.

Oratory: (A) A small chapel of any sort, more particularly one intended for solitary devotion; a place of prayer and not a place for liturgical celebration of any sort. An oratory was often erected as a memorial. At places where it was supposed that a miracle had taken place, or upon the site of the cell or other habitation of a sainted personage, an oratory was often raised, and most of these were extremely simple structures. Some few were of architectural importance. The chapel of a fortress, or a secondary or minor chapel within its walls, is often called an oratory. (B) Private home or church chapel.

Orders of architecture: The orders of architecture consist of three Greek modes and five Roman modes.

Organ gallery: In many churches, where the organ is placed high above the floor, an upper floor with a parapet, or screen, fronting toward the church, and arranged to receive the organ. It is often extended so as to afford a place for singers as well.

Organ chamber: That room or space in which the organ is placed; often, in a church, a separate structure between the choir and a transept, or beside the choir, with a large open archway between. It is often better, for the musical effect, that the organ should stand almost free under the roof of the church, in which case the space screened off to hold the actual instrument is hardly called the organ chamber.

Organ: A musical instrument in which sound is produced by the vibration of the air in pipes of wood and metal, and which is played by the keys of a keyboard opening and shutting valves of these pipes.

Oriel: A bay window; especially, one in an upper story, overhanging; carried on brackets or corbels, or upon an engaged column or pier, from which usually a corbelled structure is carried up to the floor of the oriel. This distinction is the one usually made; but in older writers the word is used for bay windows even of the largest and most massive sort.

Orientation: Primarily, the state of one who faces, or of a building which is turned, toward the east.

Orle, orlet: A narrow band, or series of small members, or units, taking the form of a border, hence a fillet forming an edging or border. Specifically, a fillet beneath the ovolo of a capital.

Orthostyle: Arranged in a straight row, as columns; rare, but used in such phrases as an orthostyle plan, or the like.

Ossature: In French, the skeleton or framework of any structure; hence, in English such a framework when of a more elaborate kind, as the steel cage construction of modern buildings.

Ossuary: A place for the deposit and preservation of the bones of the dead; especially a building for the safe keeping of bones after the desecration of the flesh, or of such as are found in excavating new graves in a cemetery.

Oubliette: In Medieval times, a pit or shaft constructed or excavated in the masonry or foundation of a castle, or similar building, and in which prisoners were confined as in the most hopeless form of dungeon, or into which their bodies were thrown.

Oundy: Wavy, or, by extension, zigzag; said of a molding, a string course, or the like.

Outporch: A porch or outer vestibule; a term having no special architectural significance.

Ovolo: A convex rounded molding, quarter round in section, or approximating that form.

Ovum: The rounded member, usually known as an egg, between the darts of an egg and anchor molding.

Oxeye: A round, or more commonly, an oval window..

P

P'ai lou: An ornamental Chinese arch.

Pagoda: A shrinelike building, often of great size, shaped as a polygonal tower, in the religious architecture of Ceylon, Burma, China, usually in the form of a tower as in China, or of a lofty stepped, pyramidal structure, as, generally, in India. The term is of disputed etymology.

Paillette: In decorative work, a bit of shining foil used in picking out relief work to obtain a jewelled effect in connection with gilding or other metallic application.

Paillon: Bright metallic foil used in decoration to show through enameling or through a glazing with transparent color, so as to modify or emphasize its brilliancy, and bring it into harmony with the general scheme of color. The term is also extended to gilding, or to parcel gilding on wood, papier-mache, etc., when the gilding is to be glazed over with transparent colors.

Pala: In Italian, anything flat and thin, as the blade of an oar. In ecclesiology, a chalice cover or chalic veil. An altarpiece.

Palace: Primarily, the official residence of any high dignitary; hence, frequently the term is applied to a residence of exceptional magnificence and extent. The name comes from the Palatium, the Palatine Hill at Rome, which there was extended to the imperial residence during the life of Augustus.

Palais: In French, a stele building; used in two general senses: (A) A palace; that is, the official residence of a sovereign, or the usual and most important residence of a prince of the blood or other great nobleman. (B) A building for the public service, especially when of size and architectural importance.

Palimpsest: (A) A parchment from which one writing has been removed to give place to another; hence, the new writing or manuscript upon such a parchment. (B) By extension, an ancient inscribed slab or Medieval brass, which has been turned and engraved with new inscriptions and devices on the other side.

Palisade: A barrier composed of long stakes driven into the earth close together, sometimes connected by horizontal beams, or bound by osiers interwoven, to form a defense against attack, or for other purposes of secure enclosure. Palisades have always been used in warfare as aids to permanent defenses, as well as for temporary defences, as in connection with fortified camps, and the like.

Palmate: Having fanlike lobes or leaves, such as characterized the Greek anthemion or honeysuckle, and its derivations in conventional architectural decoration.

Palmette: In Greek and Roman architecture, a conventional ornament, frequent in friezes, of which the most characteristic feature is an erect leaf divided into lobes, like a fan or palm leaf; a kind of anthemion. It was either carved or painted. The motive is supposed to have been developed from Oriental origins.

Pampre: A running ornament, generally in the form of a vine with grapes, used to fill cavettos and other continuous hollows in a group of moldings, as in an archivolt, in the circumvolutions of a twisted column, or wherever great luxury of decoration was required.

Panache: The triangle-like surface of a pendentive.

Pane work: The division of the exterior surface of a house into panes or panels, as constructively, in a half-timbered house by the disposition of its visible timbers, whether arranged so as to form rectangular panes, or, by branching and shaping, to enclose other and more or less decorative shapes as quatrefoils, circles, etc. The pane work of the half-timbered manor houses, inns, hospitals, etc., of the Tudor period, emphasized by the strong contrast between the white roughcast of the panes and the weathered blackness of the beams, constitutes their most distinctive characteristic.

Panel strip: A narrow piece of metal, or molded wood or batten, to cover a joint between two sheathing boards, so that several will thereby form panels; or one between a style and a panel, forming a secondary or accessory panel, as in elaborate patterns of panelling.

Panelling: (A) The making of a structure in carpentry or joinery by means of frames holding panels. (B) The breaking up of a surface by panels. (C) The structure or surface resulting from the processes *A* or *B*; thus, a room may be lined with oak panelling, or a plaster or stone surface may be broken up by panelling.

Panorama: In architecture, a building arranged to contain a large picture with or without accessories, and of the kind known as cyclorama, diorama, or panorama; those three terms being used without clear distinction in describing the representations themselves.

Papier-mache: A composition of paper reduced to a pulp, and mixed with glue, size, or other substances, so that it is readily molded or cast in any desired form. It lends itself to fine and clean modelling, and, when modelled, is conveniently applied for decorative purposes in low relief on ceilings and walls. It is often especially prepared and made waterproof, to decorate exterior work.

Parabema: In buildings of the Greek Church, a room or division closely connected with the bema, differently described by different authorities. It is probable that the signification of the term varies with different epochs and in different countries. In a regularly planned Greek church of the latter time, there were always two parabemata, one on either side of the bema.

Paradisus: In Medieval architecture, a court or atrium in front of a church, usually surrounded by cloisters.

Parapet: (A) A dwarf wall or barrier built on the edge of a terrace, platform, bridge, balcony, or other elevated place, as a protection against falling; also above the cornice of a house, whether built with a steep or with a flat roof. It is characteristically a solid construction, with a plain, straight coping; but as a feature of more or less decorated architecture, it is one of the first to be emphasized by panelling and tracery, often pierced with great richness and delicacy of detail; it is sometimes more or less broken with crenellations like a battlement, especially when used as a sky line, and in some domestic work it is corbelled out from the surface of the wall which it crowns, and takes the place of a cornice. (B) A low wall around the roof of a building or around a drop. Intended for protection. A railing that acts as a firebreak to a roof or ceiling.

Parascenium: In the ancient theater, a projecting structure or wing flanking the stage on either side, and with the scena, or background, enclosing it on three sides. It included apartments for the actors, and often the passageway, *parodos*.

Parastas (pl. Parastadae): That part of the flanking wall of the *cella* of a Greek temple which projects beyond its front or rear, enclosing walls so as to form an open vestibule; the ends of these walls were treated with bases and capitals, and the area enclosed by them with its open screen of columns became a *portico in antis*. The word *parastas* is often used to signify the *anta* itself, and Vitruvius applies the term to an isolated square pillar. The jamb of a doorway, especially when treated with shaft and capital, is called *parastas* (also written *prostas*).

Paratorium, paratory: A place where any preparation is made; particularly, in early churches, a place for the offerings.

Parclose: A screen, or other enclosing barrier, often richly decorated, to protect a tomb, as at Fifield, Berks; to separate a chapel or chantry from the main body of the church, as at Winchester, Wells, Saint Albans, Salisbury, etc.; to form the front of a gallery, or for other similar purposes. It is either solid or of open work.

Pargetting; parget work: Plasterwork of various kinds; specifically, exterior plaster facing, stamping with diapers in low relief, or in ornamental patterns raised or indented; much used in the interior, of English houses of the Tudor period. In interior work it is often delicately executed and highly finished. This sort of work is a marked characteristic in the external enrichment of some Elizabethan half-timbered houses. sometimes incorrectly called parge work.

PARGETTING, DATED 1642, BUT PRESERVING ELIZA-BETHAN MOTIVE; HIGH STREET, OXFORD.

Paris turret: A small turret built over a church porch; often occupied as a library or study.

Park: (A) A considerable extent of more or less carefully preserved woodland and pasture attached to a residence. A legally enclosed and privileged domain which is especially defined by old English law. (B) A public reservation for recreation and utility, varying in extent from great government reservations, such as Yellowstone Park, United States, to a small square, or the like, in a city. Those in, or near, cities are commonly treated with great care in some form of landscape gardening.

Parodos: In the ancient Greek theater, one of the two passages separating the stage from the cavea, or auditorium, which served also as entrances for the public. The parodos was sometimes a passageway carried through the parascenium, and sometimes distinct from it.

Parpen: A stone that passes through a wall with two smooth vertical faces.

Parqueterie, parquetry: A mosaic of woodwork for floors, composed of hardwoods of various colors or grains, tongued and grooved together in small pieces, finished flush on the surface, forming ornamental patterns, generally with borders, and always highly polished. It is sometimes composed of thin veneers glued to canvas, so that it can be put down like a carpet; but properly it is of thicker stock glued together and secured to the under flooring, so as to form a solid and permanent structure.

Parterre: The part of a theater or auditorium on the ground floor behind the orchestra. A level space in a garden, next to the main house.

Parvis, parvise: (A) an open space in front of a church or cathedral, usually surrounded by a balustrade or parapet, often slightly raised, where religious ceremonies were conducted in the open air. (B) A room or porch connected with the main entrances of a church; in this sense used very loosely.

Paschal candlestick: A massive and sometimes fixed and immovable candlestick, arranged in a church to receive the Paschal candle, which is often of great size.

Passage: In French and pronounced in the French way even in English speech, an avenue or alley connecting two thoroughfares through the intervening block, accessible to foot passengers only. Sometimes covered with glass and lined with shops.

Passage aisle: An aisle made so narrow as to serve only as a passageway, as from one end to another of a church. Such a passage allows all the width of the nave to be used for seats, or to have no more than one passage, as in the middle.

Pastophory: An early Christian church room which serves as a prothesis.

Patera: (A) The representation of a flat, round dish or disk, generally more or less decorated in low relief, to ornament a panel, frieze, etc. The term is improperly extended to rosettes and other approximately circular embellishments bearing no resemblance to disks or dishes. (B) A flat, oval or circular ornament often decorated with acanthus leaves. Common in Classical architecture.

Paternoster: An astragal, baguet, or any small round molding cut in the form of beads, like a rosary or chaplet. A molding or bead molding.

Patina: The incrustation formed on bronze by natural or artificial means. Those found originally on ancient bronzes are so admired that they have been imitated by various processes.

Patio: In Spain, and Spanish-American countries, an open court, partly or wholly surrounded by the house, but approached directly from without by a door or gateway which is frequently under the upper stories of the house.

Patten: A stand or movable support, upon a number of which a building can be set without other foundation and without breaking the ground.

Pavilion: (A) Originally, a tent or movable habitation. (B) A building more or less dependent on a larger or principal building, as a summer house; more especially, a dependent residential building.

Pedestal: (A) A support consisting of a base, dado, and a cornice used for tables. (B) The base supporting a column or colonnade or for a piece of sculpture or *objet d'art*. (C) The drawer unit supporting or suspended from the top of a desk.

Pediment: A low-pitched gable above a portico.

Pedimental: Relating to, or of the nature of, a pediment; found on a pediment; designed to be used on a pediment; thus the Niobe Group in the Uffizi Gallery is pedimental sculpture.

Pedimented: Provided with a pediment; constructed in the form of a pediment. A pedimented gable is a gable of which the foot of the coping or cornice is connected with the opposite foot by a horizontal string course, thus, in a measure, recalling the Classic original.

Pele, Pele tower: Along the Scotch and English border, a small fortified tower or keep, common from the early Middle Ages to the seventeenth century. It was the manor house of those districts, and as such formed a place of refuge for tenants and neighbors.

Pelourinho: A monument erected in a public square of the Portuguese city as a sign that the corporation has been invested with municipal rights; it has usually the form of a decorative column standing on a platform.

117

Penaria: In Roman antiquity, a storeroom; or, as some modern writers think, a small and unimportant sleeping room opening on a court.

Pendant: A boss elongated so that it hangs down.

Pendentive: A spandrel that is concave and leads from the angle of two walls to the base of a circular dome.

Penetralia : The innermost parts of a building, as the inner chambers; hence, in particular, a sanctuary; especially in Roman dwellings, the private chapel or sacred chamber in which the *penates* of a household were enshrined.

Penitentiary: (A) A place for the performance of penance; a small building in a monastic or conventual establishment in which penitents confined themselves or were confined. That part of a church to which penitents were committed during the service. (B) A prison in which convicts are confined for punishment or reformation.

Pentastylos: A pentastyle building. The term is modern, made up to correspond with hexastylos, octastylos, etc.

Penthouse: (A) Primarily, a roof of only one slope; hence, by extension, (B) A small building or shed with such a roof. In modern times used attributively, as a penthouse roof. (C) The top floor of an office or residential building, usually a living space. A subsidiary structure on top of another structure with a lean-to or other separate roof.

Pergola, Pergolo: A sort of arbor, common in formal Italian gardens or on terraces connected with Italian villas; formed of a horizontal trellis, vine-covered, and supported by columns of stone or posts of wood. A platform or balcony so protected. The Latin form, *pergula*, is sometimes used in English for such an arbor.

Peribolos: (A) In Greek architecture, a wall enclosing consecrated grounds, generally in connection with a temple. The area so enclosed. (B) In the Middle Ages, the wall enclosing the choir, the atrium, or any other sacred place; or the other walls surrounding the precinct about a church, and forming the outmost bounds allowed for refuge or sanctuary.

Peridromos: The narrow passage around the exterior of a peripteral building behind the enveloping columns.

Peripteral: Surrounded by a single range of columns. Said of a building, especially a temple.

118

Peripteros: A peripteral building.

Peristalith: A circle or cincture of upright stones, surrounding a burial mound or barrow.

Peristele: One of the monolithic upright stones in a peristalith.

Peristerium: The inner or second ciborium; the Greek term for a hanging tabernacle.

Peristylar: Surrounded by columns; having, or pertaining to, a peristyle.

Peristyle: A range or ranges of roof supporting columns enveloping the exterior of a building, as of a peripteral temple; or surrounding an internal court of a building, as in the *peristylium* of a Greek or Roman house; or forming a covered ambulatory or open screen around any large open space, partly or wholly enclosing it. Also, by extension, the space so enclosed.

Perron: A flight of steps, including platform and parapet, forming an approach, as to the entrance door of a house or public hall; usually out of doors, but occasionally in an outer vestibule, or the like.

Persienne: A shutter or window blind with slats; either hinged at the side or attached at the top and hanging loosely.

Pew chair: A hinged seat, attached to the end of a church pew, to afford accommodation in the aisle when additional seats are required. Modern usage refers to a chair designed to be used instead of, or in addition to conventional pews for seating in a church sanctuary.

Pew: Originally, an enclosed and slightly elevated place fitted with a desk and more or less complete conveniences for writing; the place for a cashier or paymaster, a clerk who had business with the public, or any one who needed a certain separation or enclosure, while still remaining accessible. Later, an enclosed space with one or more seats in a church held by one person or family, as distinguished from the open benches, which were free.

Pharos: (A) A lighthouse or beacon tower which in ancient times stood on the Isle of Pharos, at the entrance of the port of Alexandria. Hence, (B) Any lighthouse for the direction of ships; a watch tower or beacon, especially when of a more or less monumental character.

Philadelphia Chippendale: The eighteenth century furniture noted for its likeness to Chippendale furniture.

Piazza: (A) In Italian cities, an open square more or less surrounded by building; the open area made by the intersection of several streets. (B) In the United States, same as verandah.

Pict's house: In Scotland, a rude dwelling built often upon the side of a hill, so that parts of the house are excavated, while others are enclosed by walls of unhewn stones. The rude stonework was carried up in a conical or domical shape until the roof was completed; then the earth was heaped above it, or a layer of turf or peat was used to cover everything. These buildings were sometimes large, containing many chambers.

Picture gallery: A hall planned and provided with regard to wall spaces, area of floor, and lighting by day or night, for the most convenient exposition of pictures.

Piedroit: A pier partly engaged in a wall; perhaps to be distinguished from a pilaster, as having no cap and base. A term of loose application, adapted from the French *piedroit*.

Pigtail and periwig style: In German, *Zopf und Perucke Styl*, the fantastic late neoclassic of Germany, a term of ridicule corresponding to Baroqoe. The style is more commonly designated *Zopf Styl*, and this abbreviated form is rather common even in serious writing.

Pila: In Italy, a holy-water font, consisting of a bowl mounted on a shaft or foot, as distinguished from a font secured to or hanging from a wall or pier.

Pilaster mass: An engaged pier built up with the wall; usually without the capital and base of a pilaster; and undeveloped buttress, as in Romanesque work.

Pilaster strip: Same as pilaster mass, but generally applied to a comparatively slender pier of slight projection.

Pilaster: A shallow pier projecting from a wall. A column or pier with a capitol and a base.

Pilastrata: In Italian, and by adoption in English, a row, series, or order of pilasters.

Pile dwelling: A house built upon piles, especially when surrounded by water or swamp, the piles being long enough to hold the house with its platforms and accessories at some distance above the surface. Such dwellings were very common in Europe previous to the development in each region of organized society, the isolated position and the surrounding surface of water or marsh serving as a defence. They are still in use in tropical regions, as in certain of the Pacific islands. A village composed of such dwellings is known as a lake village or a swamp village.

Pilotis: (French) Pillars that support a building raising it above the ground to second story level.

Pinacotheca: In Classic architecture, a building for the preservation or exhibition of pictures; in modern use, a gallery of painting.

Pinnacle: A subordinate vertical structure of masonry, generally more or less tapering, rising above the neighboring parts of a building. It is generally used to crown a buttress, or the like, to which it gives additional weight; also, at each of the four corners of a square tower, to fill the space left by an octagonal spire above, and to complete the proportion. In some examples, the pinnacle consists of an open pavilion supporting a spire, the whole being of great relative size.

Pirca: A kind of construction found in Peruvian ruins where round stones are laid in mortar, forming a sort of rubble.

Piscina: A shallow basin, supplied with a drain pipe, generally recessed

in a niche, which is often elaborately decorated.

Pit dwelling: A residence wholly or in part under ground and formed by an excavation. Records of houses which appear to have been entirely subterranean are not uncommon, and there exist in the south of England, in several parts of Italy, and upon the sites of different Gaulish cities many pits which must have been from 4' to 6' deep and from 12' to 14' in diameter or width, all of which were evidently, from the remains within them, used for human habitation. The wall, if any was needed for greater height, was built up of rough stones, or by screens of wattle covered with mud, but the roof seems to have been in every case a pyramid or cone of boughs. It has been pointed out that there still remain many English cottages of which the floor (of beaten earth, or of stones laid upon the earth) is a foot or more below the surface, and allusions to this will be found in literature. It is claimed that houses were warmer in winter if built in this way.

Pit: In a theater, or the like, the main portion of the floor of the auditorium, situated at a lower level than the dress circle or boxes which originally enclosed it on three sides. Commonly separated from the boxes

121

by a sunken aisle. The term is now, in Great Britain, applied to the inferior seats in whatever part of the floor of the house, and in the United States has been superseded by the term orchestra or.

Placard: (A) Pargetting; parget work. (B) The decoration of the door of an apartment, consisting of a chambranle crowning its frieze or gorge. (C) In French use, a small, shallow cupboard.

Plafond: A ceiling in the sense of the underside of a floor. The French term used in English, especially when such a feature is made decorative.

Plaisance: A summerhouse near a mansion.

Planceer: The soffit or underside of any projecting member as a cornice. Also, a plank; a floor of wood; sometimes called plancher, or corrupted into plansheer.

Plane of a column: The surface of a longitudinal section made on the axis of the shaft of a column. In some Greek peristyles and porticoes the planes of the columns incline inward slightly.

Plant (on): To attach by gluing, nailing, or otherwise securing to a surface, particularly in carpentry. A

molding when not worked in the solid is said to be planted on.

Plantband: (A) Any flat or square faced molding of slight projection in comparison to its width, forming a contrast or rest in a group of moldings of curvilinear section, as a fascia in an architrave. (B) A flat arch.

Plaque: A tablet or distinctly flat plate, generally of metal, whether plain or ornamented, for exterior or interior wall decoration, or to be inserted or inlaid in a panel.

Platea: In Latin, an open space, as a street; hence, in Roman archaeology, a passage in a theater, amphitheater, or other large building.

Platform residence: A house or group of houses of American Indians built on an artificial platform, or terrace of earth. Such platforms in Florida were 20' to 50' high and sometimes nearly 2,000' in circumference, surmounted by houses of the chief and his family. The steep sides were ascended by means of steps cut in the earth and covered with wood. It is probable that some of the mounds of the so-called Moundbuilders were of this nature.

Plating: In stained glass work, the lining or doubling of one piece of colored glass by another piece with the purpose of modifying its color or diminishing its intensity.

Plaza: In Spanish, an open place in a town. The term is gradually adopted with a similar meaning in parts of the United States.

Pleasance: Historically, a garden or part of a garden intended for ornament and for enjoyment.

Plenum fan: One which supplies a current of air by forcing it from without into the given space.

Plexiform: Having the appearance of network, weaving, or plaiting, as in Romanesque and Celtic ornamentation.

Plinth block: (A) A plinth used to prevent the molding of a door or window frame from reaching the floor. (B) A block which stops the wall skirting at the base of a door or other architectural feature.

Plinth course: A course of stone, forming a continuous plinth. Specifically, the first projecting course of stones above the underpinning, forming the base or part of the base of a building.

Plinth: The base of a column or doorway; also a support for sculpture.

Plow: To cut grooves or channels, as in dadoing and housing.

Pnyx: A public place of assembly in ancient Athens; known to have had little architectural character or formal arrangement. It is generally identified with a bare rocky platform west of the Acropolis.

Podium: (A) A continuous pedestal with die, cap, and base, such as is used in elevating an order of columns or a monument above the ground, or a dome above the roof. A Roman temple was often set upon a podium, in contradistinction to the stepped platform of the Greek temple. (B) A wall, generally composed of concrete faced with marble, about 12 feet high, surrounding a Roman amphitheater; upon the platform above this wall the seats of the nobles were placed, while the other spectators occupied the ranges of seats rising behind, to the boundary walls.

Poecile: (Greek, parti-colored or painted; applied to a portico in Athens.) A portico, or by extension any public building richly adorned with paintings on its interior walls. The original structure in Athens has not been identified in modern times. It is known that it was close to the agora. It is thought that there were statues within the building, but the

123

paintings of the taking of Troy, of the war with the Amazons, of the battle of Marathon, are especially identified with the building, the pictures being by Polygnotios, Mikon, and Panainos.

Pointed architecture: That which is distinguished by the use of the pointed arch. The term seems not to have been used except in this sense, though steep roofs, spires, and the like might justify its application to buildings not furnished with pointed arches. It is not uncommon to use the term as synonymous with Gothic; and it is also not uncommon to discriminate between the Gothic style, properly so called, with its elaborate system of vaulted construction, flying buttresses, etc., and that which, having pointed arches but no Gothic construction, can only be called Gothic by a rather liberal extension of the term; such as the modern churches and halls which have wooden roofs and no provision for vaulting. The term is applied less frequently to buildings of Islamic styles.

Polygonal building: Masonry laid up with irregular polygonal-faced stones fitted together. This construction was employed in those Mediterranean lands where the earlier forms of pelasgic architecture had been previously current. It was a modifica-

tion due mainly to new implements and improved methods.

Pomel, pommel: A knob, knot, or boss; especially a ball-shaped terminal used as a finial for steep conical or pyramidal roofs, pinnacles, etc.; also for the similar decoration of furniture.

Pont: In French, a bridge; sometimes, in combination, forming the proper name of an important bridge which is not connected with the geographical name of the place.

Ponte: In Italian, a bridge.

Porch chamber: In a two-storied porch or advance projecting building, of which the ground story forms a porch, the room occupying the whole or the greater part of an upper story.

Porch: A covered place of entrance and exit attached to a building and projecting from its main mass; it may, when so projecting, be in more than one story and may form the lower story or tower or the like.

Portal: An entrance or gateway of a monumental character; specifically, an entrance which is emphasized by a stately architectural treatment, such as may make it the principal *motif* in an entire facade.

Portcullis: (A) A strong door sliding vertically, usually a grating heavily framed of wood with pointed iron bars at the bottom. It is arranged so as to be dropped suddenly and thus protect an entrance in case of a surprise. The portcullis was a constant feature in Medieval fortification, there being sometimes two or three in the same passageway. (B) An iron gate which slides vertically in grooves made in the doorway jambs. Used in castles and forts.

Porte Cochere: In French, a doorway large enough to accommodate wheeled vehicles. Such entrances are a common feature of private houses of France, and generally open into driveways which lead through the building, from the street to the interior court. From this passage the entrance to the staircase and that to the ground story is generally open, so that there is sometimes a footway or sidewalk beside the carriage road. The doorway itself, and the woodwork of the door, are often very richly decorated. The use of the term, common in the United States, to signify a carriage porch, is erroneous.

Portico: A porch or vestibule roofed and partly open on at least one side, as one section of a peristyle or a cloister; but specifically and more exactly, an ambulatory or vestibule covered by a roof supported by columns on at least one side, such as is characteristic in Greek, Roman, and neoclassic architecture. It properly includes the *pronaos* and *epinaos* of a temple, enclosed by a screen of columns between its projecting side walls (*portico in antis*); any vestibule or *pronaos* formed by one or more rows of columns standing clear of a cellar and in front of it; any one side or face of an ambulatory or *pteroma* formed by a single row of columns entirely enveloping the temple on the sides and ends; or any other form of a columnar ambulatory or vestibule, whether connected with a religious or secular building, or standing clear.

Porticus: In Latin, usually, same as portico, but employed in a somewhat larger sense.

Postern: A subsidiary door or gate; in military architecture, such a gate in a part of a work remote from the main gate; in domestic architecture, often a small door near a *porte-cochere.*

Posticum: In Roman archaeology: (A) A back door; a postern. (B) Same as *epinaos*. (C) Same as *opisthodomos.*

Pot construction: A method of constructing vaults and domes with earthen pots fitted together in a succession of rings diminishing in diameter upward to form the concave; this expedient was common in Oriental countries from the earliest times as a substitute for heavier and more costly materials, such as brick, stone, and concrete, to diminish the weight upon the supporting walls. Domes so constructed, though thin and apparently fragile, have endured the vicissitudes of centuries, and have proved as stable and permanent as fabrics much more massive and monumental. A conspicuous example of its use in Romanesque work is in the dome of S. Vitale at Ravenna.

Pourtour: In French, a circuit; a gallery or passage allowing of movement around a central hall or the like; especially, in churches, the aisle which nearly surrounds the apse or chevet, passing along the north and south sides and curving around the east end.

Powdering room: In the eighteenth century a chamber or anteroom especially adapted to powdering perukes, and, later, the hair.

Power house: A building in which steam power, water power, or the like, is generated, and from which it is conveyed for the operation of machinery or other purposes, as to the other buildings of a large factory, or

to the vehicles on a trolley or cable railway.

Poyntell, Poyntill: A pavement, generally of tiles, formed of small pieces, but differing from mosaic in that the pieces form a set pattern rather than a picture. Also written pointel or pointal.

Pozzo: (A) A well; the Italian term. Not used in English except in combination. (B) In Venice, a cistern; one of the numerous water-tight structures below the pavements of courtyards, public and private, in which is stored the water brought from the mainland. This water is drawn from the natural stream of the Brenta, on the western shore of the lagoon, and in other places.

Praecinctio: In a Roman theater, a passage running parallel with and on a level with one of the steplike seats of the *cavea*. Generally the slope of the lower ranges is broken at the *praecinctio* by a wall, from the top of which the seats slope upward to the outer wall of the of the theater. This wall of the *praecinctio* contains doors giving access to the *vomitoria*, or passages of exit and entrance. In the Flavian Amphitheater there was an intermediate *zona* or passage, parallel with seats, between the arena and the *praecinctio*. It is sometimes called *balteus*, and is equivalent to the Greek *diazoma*.

Praetorium: That part of a Roman camp or garrisoned post in which the quarters of the general were placed; the official residence of the praetor or governor of a Roman province; a hall of justice, presided over by the praetor.

Pre-Columbian: Indian, South and Central America and Mexican artifacts which pre-date the discovery of the New World.

Predella: (A) The footpace of an altar. (B) One of a series of seats or steps raised one above another; a gradin or gradine. (C) An altar ledge; one of the series of ledges or shelves surrounding an altar to accommodate a crucifix, candlesticks, vases, etc., or a painting. (D) By extension, a painting, mosaic, or bas-relief, forming the front of *B*.

Presbyterium: That part of a church in which the high altar is placed and which forms the eastern termination of the choir, above which it is generally raised by a few steps for distinction, and so that it may be visible from the nave; it is occupied exclusively by those who minister in the services of the altar, and its western boundary is the end to the choir stalls or choir proper. The use of the word choir, as including the presbyterium, is common but inexact.

Presence chamber: A reception room; especially, in modern usage, the principal hall of ceremony or state in a palace, containing the throne; an apartment for the formal reception of those entitled to admission on certain occasions.

Presidio: A frontier fort of Spanish America. This was generally the beginning of a town. A ditch was dug making a rectangular enclosure of about 500' or 600' on a side. A rampart was built around within the ditch, enclosing church, quarters, barracks, dwellings, storehouses, etc.

Press bed: A bed permanently built in a recess and more or less enclosed by woodwork, as frequently in the houses of peasants in Holland and Germany; so called from the outward resemblance of the structure to a press or cupboard.

Pricket: A vertical spike or point on which a candle is stuck and held upright; hence, such a point together with its base or stand; a candlestick; often called pricked candlestick.

Prie-dieu: A seventeenth century stand with a kneeling ledge used for prayer.

Priest's door: A door by which the priest enters the chancel or nave from the robing room or vestry. Any small, low door in the flank of the church, especially on the south side, is often called by this name.

Priory: A religious house governed by a prior or prioress.

Prism light: Prisms of glass, either made separately and set collectively in iron frames for pavement lights, or made connectedly in sheets and placed vertically or at an angle in or over window openings, or the like. The angles of the prisms are so adjusted as to intercept the rays of light from the sky, and to direct them into rooms otherwise imperfectly illuminated.

Pro-cathedral: A church used as the cathedral church of a diocese while the proper church remains unfinished or is under repair.

Prodomos: A lobby of entrance, a vestibule, usually the same as pronaos.

Profile: An outline, especially such as is revealed by a transverse section. Specifically: (A) The outline of a molding, group of moldings, or the like. (B) The outline of the surface of the ground as shown by a vertical section.

Promenade: A place suitable for walking for pleasure, as a sidewalk, a terrace, a portico, or mall, with a more of less elegant or attractive environment.

Pronaos: The open vestibule in the front to the *naos* or *cella* of a temple; usually opposed to *epinaos,* but if the treasury or rear part of the temple is under consideration, the vestibule leading to this is sometimes called the *pronaos* to the treasury, though it remains the *epinaos* of the whole structure.

Propylaea, propylaia: The name used by the Greeks to designate a porch or entrance of architectural importance; such as the one at Corinth, mentioned by Pausanias, the one at the sanctuary of Asculapius at Epidaurus, the two leading into the sacred precinct at Eleusis. By ancient writers, the name is applied almost exclusively to the building which marked the principal entrance to the Acropolis of Athens. It was a structure of singular beauty and originality, built of Pentelic marble at the time of Pericles, from the designs of the architect Mnesicles. It was begun in 473 B.C., and was provisionally completed five years later, although the original intentions of its architect were never fully carried out. Its central portion contained the portal proper, a wall pierced by five openings, of which that in the middle was wide enough to permit the passage of chariots, the others being for pedestrians only. These openings were provided with gates. Facing the open area of the Acropolis, to the eastward of this wall, was a Doric hexastyle portico of admirable proportions, but with a central intercolumniation, which for the same reason as to the middle doorway, was of unusual width. To the westward of the wall containing the gates, and therefore before, or outside of it, was a covered hall, walled on three sides, the marble roof of which, so greatly admired by Pausanius, was carried by six Ionic columns of great beauty, arranged in two rows, between which ran the roadway leading to the central entrance. The western front of this hall was formed by a portico similar to the one which faced eastward on the Acropolis. To the north and south of this portico, and at right angles with it, were smaller porticoes, of three columns in *antis*, the northern one of which had behind it a nearly square chamber, which was probably the room containing the pictures described by Pausanius, and now frequently called the *pinakotheke*, or picture gallery. This building belongs to the highest type of Athenian architecture. In ancient times, just as

today, it was esteemed a work of equal interest and importance with the Parthenon itself. The structure seems to have remained nearly as Mnesicles left it, until about the year 1656, when an explosion of gunpowder caused it partial destruction.

Propylaeum: The gateway to an enclosure.

Propylon: In ancient Egyptian architecture, a monumental gateway, preceding the main gateway to a temple or sacred enclosure. The isolated masses of masonry on both sides of the passage were built in the Egyptian manner, with battering faces, so that the whole was of the general form of a truncated pyramid, the whole being crowned with a massive cavetto cornice; or in some cases, the gateway was flanked by two solid and unpierced masses of buildings of that form, as in the pylon itself. These stood singly, or in a series of several, before the actual entrance or pylon of the temple, in order that the approach should be invested with dignity and ceremony.

Proscenium: (A) The wall in a theatre which divides the stage from the orchestra. The proscenium opening is usually framed with an arch and covered by a curtain. The stage on which the action in a Greek or Roman theatre took place. (B) The platform or *logeion* of an ancient Greek theatre, upon which the actors enacted their parts, in front of the rear wall, which was treated like a facade forming the background, the *skene*. It corresponds with the modern stage and the Roman *pulpitum*. In which lies between the curtain and the orchestra, including generally the proscenium arch.

Proscenium arch: (A) In a theater or similar building, the arch above the opening in the proscenium wall, at the front of the stage. In the United States, as usually constructed, the arch is a relieving arch above a lintel composed of iron beams; hence, (B) The imitation arch formed by means of furring, or the like, beneath such a lintel; the opening, of whatever form, which allows the performance to be seen by the audience.

Proscenium box: In a theater, or similar building, a box in or near the proscenium, as distinguished from those more removed from the stage.

Proscenium wall: In a theater, or similar building, the wall separating the stage and the auditorium; usually of masonry and very solid. It is in this wall that the proscenium arch is opened.

Prostas: An antechamber; a vestibule; according to Vitruvius, the portion of the front of a temple included between the *antae* or *parastades* of a *portico in antis*.

Prostasis: That which is put before a place to conceal it; a screen.

Prostyle: In Greek architecture, having a columnar portico in front, and not on the sides or rear.

Prostylos: A prostyle building.

Prothesis: (A) In church buildings of the Greek Church, a chapel immediately connected, generally on the north side of the *bema*. (B) The room used in an Orthodox or Byzantine church to prepare the sacraments. A sacristy.

Prothyron, Prothyrum: In Greek, something before the door. It is stated by Vitruvius that the Greeks used the term for a vestibule, but the Latin writers for a railing, or perhaps the gate itself. Commonly used in the plural, *prothyra*.

Proto-doric: Of a style apparently introductory to the Doric style; said of any building or feature of a building which is considered to have contributed anything toward its evolution, as the Proto-doric columns of the tomb at Beni-Hassan in Egypt.

Proto-ionic: Of a style apparently introductory to the Ionic style; said of any building or feature of a building which is considered to have contributed anything toward its evolution, as the footing of the columns of Nineveh in relation to the Ionic base, the Assyrian helix to the Ionic volute, the characteristic Oriental lintel of palm timber to the Greek epistyle, etc. The capital discovered by the American archaeologists at Assos in Asia Minor is an excellent example of proto-ionic style.

Prytaneium: In an ancient Greek city, the hall in which the magistrates took their meals in state at the public charge, received foreign embassies, entertained strangers of distinction, honored citizens of high public merit, and in general exercised the rites of official hospitality. It was consecrated to Vesta, and in her honor a perpetual fire was maintained in it, which, in the colonies, was originally brought from the famous Prytaneium of Athens, the mother city.

Pseudisodomum: In ancient masonry, composed of layers or courses alternately thick and thin.

Pseudo-dipteral: In Classical architecture, having an arrangement of columns similar to dipteral, but with the essential difference of the omis-

sion of the inner row, thus leaving a wide passage around the cella.

Pseudo-dipteros: A pseudo-dipteral building.

Pseudo-peripteral: In Classic architecture, having a portico in front or with porticoes in front and rear, but with the columns on the sides engaged in the walls instead of standing free, as in the case of Greek temples, that of Olympian Zeus at Girgenti, ruins of the ancient Akragas, or the nine-columned edifice at Paestum, or in the cases of Roman temples, that of Fortuna Virilis at Rome or the Maison Carree at Nimes.

Pseudoprostyle: In Classic architecture, prostyle, but without a proper pronaos, the columns of the portico being set less than the width of an intercolumniation from the front wall, or being actually engaged in it.

Pseudoclassic architecture: That phase of neoclassic architecture which marked the most stilted period of post Renaissance art, when, under the influence of Vitruvius' writings and those of his later disciples, the most formal imitation of Roman architecture prevailed, and it was the aim to revive the whole art of Rome.

Pteroma: In Classic architecture, the passage along the side of the *cella* of a temple or other building, referring generally to the space behind its screen of columns, or *pteron*. In modern practice, often used for this space on the front and rear as well as at the sides.

Pteron: (A) In Classic architecture, that which forms a side or flank, as the row of columns along the side of a temple, or the side wall itself. (B) The external colonnade in a Greek temple or other building.

Pueblo house: A communal dwelling of the village Indians called *pueblos*. These houses were, and still are, built of stone, adobe, jacal, etc., sometimes on the mesas, or clifflike hills; sometimes in clefts or hollows of the cliff face; sometimes excavated in the solid material of the cliff; sometimes on a plain or in a valley. In this article it is proposed to treat only those which are built independently of natural aid. The *pueblo* dwelling consist of a group of flat-roofed chambers combined in a single structure that resembles a pile of receding packing cases. Several of these piles, with spaces and courts between, form a village. These villages were not absolutely permanent, but were frequently abandoned, and others built elsewhere, though in some instances the same site has been built on for centuries. Ruins of these communal

dwellings extend northward in an ever narrowing region as far as the fortieth parallel, and the known area dwindles to a mere point along Green River. Southward it widens, to embrace nearly the whole of Arizona and New Mexico, and scatters into northern Mexico. Within the immense tract permanent communal dwellings were built almost everywhere, on plain and mountain slope, in valleys and canyons, and even in the bottom of the Grand Canyon of the Colorado. Single houses are common, but the majority are buildings of a semifortress type; lower stories without an entrance on the ground, and terraced upper stories reached by ladders easily removed. There was also, sometimes, a defensive wall. Before the acquisition of horse and gun, assault on one of these strongholds by predatory tribes or by a neighboring community was difficult.

The inhabited dwellings of today consist, as did the ruins, of numerous rooms built in juxtaposition, or superimposed, the upper opening on terraces formed by the roofs of those below. There is generally no prearranged plan. The beginning is in one or two single-room structures, to which others are added as required. This seems to have been a frequent method, even in many of the elaborate buildings of the Mayas and the Aztecs. Formerly the ground floor rooms in Arizona and New Mexico were entered only by a hatchway in the roof, a method still in vogue at Oraibe, which, with the other towns of the Moki, exhibits the nearest approach to pre-Columbian conditions. Frequently the house group formed a barrier around a court opening to southward, the rear wall insurmountable, and without entrance, the houses being terraced down inside to the court, and this protected by a defensive wall or a line of one story buildings. Fortresses of this kind are seen in the ruins in Chaco Canyon, in northwestern New Mexico, and at other places. The court was always a feature, and is so still. It generally has one end closed, or at least entered through a covered way or passage beneath buildings. Where adobe was not used the building support is boughs or poles, which were finally covered with earth. In the Pueblo construction tree trunks without bark and 6" or 7" diameter are laid across the tops of the walls. Outer ends when too long are permitted to project beyond the walls, sometimes being finished into a kind of portico. Smaller poles are laid across the first, somewhat separated, and then comes a layer of slender willows

or reeds, with next a layer of twigs or grass, though in some old buildings the grass was omitted. In one of the Chaco ruins thin, narrow, split boards took the place of the layer of small poles. On the grass layer a quantity of adobe mortar is spread, and then earth laid on and trodden down. The final finish is another layer of adobe mortar. Sufficient slope is given to carry off water, but not enough to create a current that would injure the surface. The walls are built up to the level of the top of the roof, and frequently somewhat above it, and a coping of thin slabs put on with their outer edges flush with the wall face. Through this parapet outlets are made for the rain, and drains are put in to carry the water clear of the walls. In the ordinary storms of the arid region these roofs answer well, but continued wet weather saturates them and causes dripping inside. Floors are constructed in the same way, the floor of one chamber being the roof of the one under it. There are no stairways within, all mounting being done outside by ladders and by steps built on end projections of walls. The ladders are easy for the inhabitants, who go up and down, even with a load, without touching the sides for the rungs with their hands, and the dogs find no barrier in them, running over the roofs at will. The original ladder, used also by other tribes, was a notched log. There was, too, another form made of a Y-shaped tree or branch. More recent ladders are similar to our ordinary kind, except that they have very long ends rising above, and held together by cross-pieces. Floors are sometimes paved with irregular slabs of sandstone, and this feature has been noted in very old ruins. When of adobe the floor is kept in repair by occasional applications of very thin adobe mortar, but moccasined feet do not injure it much. A hold is left at one corner or one side of the chamber, for a chimney, which is a modern affair, having been unknown before the appearance of the Spaniards. The chimney top is stone, adobe, or broken earthen pots placed one above the other. Within there is a hood across the corner built of sticks plastered with adobe, which begins about 4' above the floor where the hearth is laid. A mat of reeds or a slab of sandstone forms the covering for the hatchway, when necessary, and in cold weather a sheepskin is frequently placed over the top of the chimney when the fire has died out, and held there by a large stone. The end of a terrace is often roofed over, forming a sort of porch, where cooking is frequently carried on, a fireplace being built in one corner. At Zuni, the dome-shaped oven in use is often built on the roof. The house walls vary in thickness from 16" to 22", but some of the old walls were much thicker. The rooms are generally small, some used for baking being no more than 7' x 10'; 12' x 14' would be a fair average. The interior height is barely 6', and often less. In going southward rooms increase.

Pueblo: In Spanish, a town or village; especially in the United States, an Indian village (and its inhabitants) of the Southwest-Arizona and New Mexico. Village Indians have existed in many parts of the United States; indeed, except that their communal houses were of frailer material, and perished as soon as they were abandoned, the Indians of the more eastern parts of the country and of the northwest coast were as completely settled in communities as those of the so-called *pueblos*.

Pulpit: A stand, especially an enclosed stand, prepared for a speaker, generally limited to such a stand in or attached to a church. The pulpit is especially the place for the preacher of the sermon, as distinguished from the officiant who reads the Gospel or the Epistle.

Pulpitum: A stone screen in a large church separating the nave from the choir.

Pulvin: A dosseret above the capital supporting the arch above in Byzantine architecture.

Pump room: In England, in connection with a mineral spring, a room in which the waters are drunk; it is sometimes an open pavilion, and sometimes, as in the famous example at Bath, an assembly room of a more or less monumental character.

Puncheon: In carpentry, a short piece of timber especially; (A)In framing, a stud, queen post, or the like, and which is unusually short for its thickness. (B) A piece of split timber, as a slab or hewn plank roughly dressed as by the adze, such as is used in the absence of sawed boards. Architecture, a building of a peculiar type with few windows and those generally so small that bells would hardly give out their sound freely; very slender, and commonly furnished with conical stone roofs. Of these there are more than 100 in Ireland; and there are known to be more than 22 in other countries of Europe. Although it is probable that they were used rather for defense and for lookout purposes than for the placing of bells, yet a tower of this type is commonly called bell house. (C) In the Southwestern United States the work of American Indians of the *pueblo* type. Some stand alone but the greater number are near, or connected with, other ruins of rectangular form. Two or three concentric walls exist in some, separated by from 2' to 6', the outer interval being divided by transverse walls on radial lines into small chambers. The diameter of the inner circle varies from 10' to 20' or more. Walls were of roughly dressed stone. Those near other ruins are generally classed as *kivas*; isolated ones may have been lookouts.

Pycnostyle: An arrangement of columns set 1.5 times their diameter apart.

Pylon: A high, isolated structure used to mark a boundary or for decoration. A pyramidal tower which flanks an ancient Egyptian temple gateway.

Q

Quadrangle: A rectangular court-yard or mall surrounded by buildings.

Quadriga: A sculpture group composed of a four horse chariot. Used as a monument or the crown of a facade.

Quatrefoil: A decoration on Gothic furniture consisting of four flowers, petals, or leaves.

Queen Anne architecture: The architecture existing in England during the short reign of Anne, 1702 to 1714. The more important structures of the reign were generally the completion of designs fixed in all of their parts before her accession, and but little that was monumental was begun in her time. Wren's work upon Greenwich Hospital and Hampton Court was still going on, and he built many churches in London and elsewhere, of which S. Bride's, Fleet Street, is a good example. The most elaborate single building begun in Anne's reign was Blenheim, the palace by Sir John Vanbrugh, built by the nation for the Duke of Marlborough. The buildings which are especially associated with the style are the minor country houses and many houses in the suburbs of London, built frequently of red brick, and characterized by sculpture in relief, molded or carved in the same material. A certain picturesqueness of treatment, like a revival of Elizabethan, or even of Medieval styles, in mass, in sky line, and in such details as chimneys, gables, and dormer windows, is noticeable in these; and, although all is on the same moderate scale, and nothing is very massive or imposing, the style has considerable attraction when applied to dwelling houses. It was this character of the buildings of Anne's reign which caused their acceptance by some architects of the years from 1865 to 1885, in England, as types for modern designing, and country houses of this character were built in considerable numbers.

R

Rayonnant: French Gothic style from about 1270 to about 1370.

Regency style: (A) A Neo-classical style that was popular from 1811-1830 during the reign of George IV. The Chinese and Greek revival became popular and were done on mahogany or rosewood. (B) A transitional French style from 1715-1723 and comprised of the Louis XIV and Louis XV styles. During this time period the shell motif and Chinese styles became popular.

Regulus: The short band on a Doric entablature between the tenia and guttae.

Reignier work: Delicate woodwork of the nature of Marquetry, dating from the reign of Louis XIV, and named after a cabinetmaker of the time. It is not dissimilar to boule work.

Renaissance architecture: (A) That of Italy from 1420 to about 1520 A.D. (B) That of France, of Germany, Spain, and other nations of the continent of Europe, which was based upon or suggested by the Italian neo-classic style above alluded to, but which began generally at a much later period. In Spain, some buildings with neoclassic feeling date back to the second half of the fifteenth century, but in France and Germany nothing of the kind appears before 1510, except in small tomb monuments or similar pieces of decorative work which are generally thought to have been made by Italian artists.

Reredos: A wooden, metal, or stone wall or screen behind an altar.

Restoration furniture: Furniture that is richly carved with spiral turnings and scrolls. It was popular during the monarchy of Charles II from 1660-1688 and was produced in England.

Retrochoir: The space behind a high altar.

Rib, diagonal: In a ribbed vault, one of the two intersecting ribs extending from one corner of the compartment to that diagonally opposite. In Gothic vaulting, the diagonal ribs were generally semicircles; so that the wall ribs (formerets) and cross ribs (arcs doubleaux) were naturally pointed to avoid the cupola-like form which would result from too great a difference in their respective heights. When the diagonal ribs were thus pointed, the cross ribs and wall ribs were naturally given the form of a more acute pointed arch.

Rib: A molding on an arched or flat ceiling; but specifically and more properly, in Medieval vaulting, an arch, generally molded, forming part of the skeleton upon which rest the intermediate concave surfaces which constitute the shell or closure of the vault. The crowning intersections of these arches or ribs are adorned with sculptured bosses. In quadripartite vaulting the main diagonal ribs are called by that name and also *arcs ogives*; each transverse rib is called *arc doubleau*, and each longitudinal rib, *arc formeret*. To this fundamental system of ribs supplementary and subordinate ribs were afterward added, dividing the concave of the ceiling into many panels, but in general these had no function in the construction.

Rocaille: A system of decoration supposed to be founded upon the forms of rocks, or upon the artificial rock work of the seventeenth-century gardens to which were added shells sometimes of real, sometimes of imaginary shapes. The ornament soon passed into a system of scrolls combined with abundant floral and other carving, with gilding used freely, and paintings in panels. This system of ornamentation was used equally for the wood-lined interiors of handsome residences and choirs of churches and for the smallest objects of familiar ornamentation, such as the little boxes of gold, ivory, and tortoise shell used for snuff and bonbons, small toilet articles and the like. The essence of the style is that these curves shall never be continuous for more than a short distance, nor make more than one double curve like the letter *S*, without breaking off to begin again abruptly.

Rockingham porcelain: Brown and white porcelain with a purple-brown glaze that was produced in Yorkshire around 1742.

Rococo architecture: The architecture of the century beginning about 1660 A.D. in so far as it is marked by a certain excess of curvature and a lack of firm lines and formal distribution. The term is of French origin, in spite of its Italian appearance, and was apparently derived from the term rocaille. The characteristic decoration of the style is hardly seen in the exteriors of buildings, or at least hardly in the walls, porticoes, etc., but these are characterized by great boldness in deviation from the Classical orders as described and drawn by Vignola and other authorities. The capitals of columns assume new forms; wreaths and festoons adorn the Ionic capital; the entablature is sometimes cut into pieces, or wholly changed in its proportions to allow of a story of windows; there is a tendency toward setting piers and flanking buttresses, with an angle projecting in front, so that the plan of the buttress is approximately triangular; there is a disposition to use irregularly curved window heads and door heads, and to open windows of round and oval shape in unusual places; the balconies have commonly wrought-iron railings, and these are of fantastic curvature both in plan and vertically; sculpture of human figures, either complete or used as caryatids and telamones, is very much diversified in pose and gesture. The characteristic interior decoration is composed of scrolls which pass into each other abruptly, as described under rocaille. There is also in the interiors a singular indifference to the constructive character of the design, the walls passing into the flat ceilings through a very large cove, which is not limited to horizontal lines either at top or bottom, but when seen from below is difficult to determine as to size and exact location. These strange coves are often filled with very elaborate and highly finished painting, a continuation often of the composition with which the ceiling is filled. Openings also fill the wall above doors and windows.

Roman order: The peculiar system introduced by the Romans of late Republican or early Imperial times, by which an arched construction is given some appearance of Greek post-and-lintel building.

Romanesque style: An ecclesiastical style of architecture using interior bays, vaults, and round arches.

Rood loft: A gallery above a rood screen to contain images or candles.

Rood screen: A screen below the rood.

Rood: A cross or crucifix.

Roof, fan: A vaulted roof adorned with fan tracery.

Roof garden: A covered or sheltered, but otherwise open, room or series of rooms on a city roof, enabling persons to enjoy the air. In many houses of the south of France these exist; small , usually occupying part of a story, the rest of which is wholly enclosed. In some Italian palazzi are very extensive loggie, at the top, with columns carrying the general roof, but otherwise open at the sides. In American cities some attempt has been made in this direction, both by places of resort, apartment buildings and townhouses, restaurants, and clubs.

Roof: (A) That part of the closure of a building which covers it in from the sky. Upon this part of a building depends in large measure the character of its design as a work of architecture. Roofs are distinguished: (1) By their form and method of construction; as, the flat roof, characteristic of dry tropical countries, and much used in modern commercial buildings in the United States; the sloping roof, including gables, hipped, penthouse, mansard, and gambrel roofs with their varieties. (2) By the character of their covering; as, thatched, shingled, battened, slated, tiles, metal-covered, tarred, asphalted, gravelled, etc. (B) In carpentry, the term refers to the timber framework by which the external surface is supported. This, in sloping roofs, consists usually of a series of pairs of opposite rafters or couples, of which the lower ends are tied together in various ways to prevent spreading; or, where the span is too great for such simple construction and there are no intermediate upright supports, of a series of rafters supported by longitudinal horizontal purlins, which are generally carried on a system of transverse timber frames or trusses, spaced from 8' to 20' apart. In modern practice, the typical forms of these trusses have principal rafters or principals of which the lower op-posite ends are tied together by tie-beams hung in the center from a king-post, or, at two points, from queen-posts; from the lower part of these suspension members, braces or struts may be extended to stiffen the principals. To suit various conditions of shape of roof and area to be covered, these typical and elementary forms are, in modern usage, subjected to innumerable structural modifications and extensions.

One of the most marked distinctions in the historic styles consists in the pitch or inclination of the roof. Thus in the Greek temple the slope of the pediment varied from 15° to 16-1/2°; Roman roofs had a slope of from 22° to 23-1/2°; Romanesque roofs followed closely the Roman slope; the Gothic pitch was much steeper, sometimes reaching 50° or even 60°. In the Renaissance era there was in Italy a revival of the Roman pitch with the other Classic features; but the French builders of this era retained the steepest slopes of the Medieval sky lines, especially in the conical roofs of their round towers and in the pyramidal roofs with which they characteristically covered each separate division of their buildings. These lofty roofs, with their high dormers, chimneys, and crestings, constitute a distinctive characteristic of the French Renaissance, the peculiar steep roof being a development from these French traditions. The structural conditions from which the steep Medieval pitch was evolved.

Rover: In architecture, any member, as a molding, which follows the line of a curve.

Runic knot: A form of interlacing common in the ornamentation of jewels, implements, and in stone and wood carving generally among the early Northern races of Europe.

Rustic work: (A) Decoration by means of rough woodwork, the bark being left in place, or by means of uncut stones, artificial rockwork, or the like, or by such combination of these materials and devices as will cause the general appearance of what is thought to be rural in character. Where woodwork is used it is customary to provide a continuous sheathing as of boards, upon which are nailed the small logs and branches with their bark, moss, etc., carefully preserved; but these strips of wood are often arranged in ornamental patterns, causing anything but a rural appearance. (B) In cut stone; same as rusticated work.

S

Sacrament chapel: A chapel especially reserved for the preservation of the host.

Sacrament house: An ambry; used especially for the keeping of the sacred wafer.

Sacrarium: (A) In Roman archaeology, a place of deposit for sacred objects, a chapel or shrine. (B) In Christian ecclesiology, the sanctuary, the choir, the sacristy, a piscina, a sacrament house; the late Latin word being employed in various meanings.

Sacred tent; Tipi: A tent erected by American Indians to shelter some sacred object. Especially, one of three tents or *tipis*, of the Omaha, used for the Sacred Pole, a stick of cottonwood eight feet long, said to be over 200 years old, the Sacred White Buffalo-cow Skin, and the Sacred Bag consecrated to war. These sacred tents and all they contained are now in the Peabody Museum at Cambridge, Massachusetts.

Sacristy: A place reserved near the high altar and sanctuary of a church, usually a single room, but sometimes of great proportions. It is the place where priests and deacons vest for the service and unvest again, and where ecclesiastical garments are stored; and where much of the business of the church is done, as the reception and registration of requests for masses or prayers. There is of necessity a lavatory, and there should be a separate piscina for washing altar vessels and the like; also permanent presses and cupboards; and all these fittings are commonly made architectural and are often adorned very richly. In some old sacristies there were ovens for baking the bread intended for consecration; in others the church muniments are kept in a special press by themselves.

Sainte chapelle: In French, a holy chapel, that is, one of especially sacred character; a term used peculiarly for those which contain some relic of great sanctity, as any one of those which relate especially to the Passion of Christ.

Salle des sas perdus: A large hall forming a monumental vestibule or waiting room to smaller halls or apartments, as in courts of justice and other public buildings in France.

Sally: A projection; the end of a timber, as the foot of a rafter, cut with an internal angle to fit over a plate or horizontal beam.

Salutatorium: In Medieval buildings, a porch or a portion of the sacristy of a church, where the clergy and the people could meet and confer.

Sanctuary screen: Any partition which separates the sanctuary proper from the larger part of the choir.

Sanctuary: A place considered sacred, especially in connection with the idea of safety from pursuers. Thus the innermost and least public part of a temple, or of a Christian church, the separate shrine of a divinity or saint, a region within which all the trees, buildings, monuments, etc., and the soil itself was held sacred to a divinity, and there is no clear distinction between the different uses of the term. Especially, in a Christian church, the place where the principal altar is set, distinguished from the choir, or from the outer part of the chancel.

Sanctus bell: A bell hung in an exterior turret or bell cot over or near the chancel arch, which was formerly rung to fix the attention of those not in the church to the service of the mass; this notice is now usually limited to the ringing of a hand bell in the sanctuary.

Sarcophagus (pl. sarcophagi): A stone coffin. The term having been originally a Latin adjective, "flesh devouring," and applied to a certain stone from Asia Minor. It was applied substantively in later Latin to any tomb or coffin. The use of sarcophagi was common in Egypt from the time of the builder of the great pyramid. Greeks and Romans seem not to have used them often before the time of Trajan; although the famous sarcophagi of Sidon in Syria are thought to be of the time of Alexander the Great, and the Scipio tomb in the Vatican is undoubtedly of the third century B.C.; but afterward they were extremely common, and the museums of Europe contain many, very richly sculptured. In the Middle Ages the Gothic tombs of Italy often included a sarcophagus and the Renaissance brought back the use of them in a more nearly antique way, standing free. Perhaps the most celebrated are those in the smaller sacristy or Capella dei Depositi, at the Church of S. Lorenzo, in Florence, having Michelangelo's magnificent recumbent statues on their lids.

Saxon architecture: (A) Architecture of Saxony; first, as a larger state, electorate, and kingdom, down to the Napoleonic wars; second, as a smaller kingdom, following the peace of 1815, and other lands. (B) The architecture of England and southern Scotland before the Norman Conquest. There is much uncertainty as to the date of the earliest Medieval buildings existing in England and Scotland, and there is no building of which it is certainly known that it dates from the period previous to 1066.

Scabellum, scabellon: In Roman and neoclassic architecture, a high pedestal for the support of a bust, often shaped like a gaine.

Scagliola: In Italian, an interior surface decoration for columns, walls, and floors, composed of white plaster and glue, mixed in various ways with metallic oxides, or with insertions of colored stucco, generally in imitation of marble, the whole being rubbed and finely polished.

Scala cordonata, cordoni: A ramp or inclined plane formed into paved steps from 18" to 3' tread, with only 1" to 4" rise, each step being thus inclined somewhat less than the general slope. The risers or fronts of the steps are of stone, and constitute the *cordoni.* Such ramps are used for animals as well as pedestrians, and are common in Italy.

Scamillus: In Classic and Neoclassic architecture, (A) the slight bevelling of the outer edge of a bearing surface of a block of stone, making the part visible by a slight incision, as occurs between the necking of a Doric capital and the upper

drum of the shaft. (B) A plain block placed under the plinth of a column, thus forming a double plinth.

Schloss: In German, the residence of the feudal lord of the soil, a term corresponding closely to *chateau*, and containing the significance of the two English words, castle and manor house.

Sconce: (A) A candlestick or group of branches, each forming a candlestick, springing from an applique, so that the whole shall seem to project from the wall upon which the applique is hung. (B) Any construction which gives shelter by screen or roof, as a shed or covered shell. (C) A seat in an open chimney place (Scotch).

Sconcheon: The part of the side of an aperture from the back of the exterior reveal to the inside face of the wall, usually forming in the masonry a rebate or internal angle in which the wooden frame is set.

Scotch crown: The peculiar termination of the tower of S. Giles's Church at Edinburgh, consisting of eight pinnacles, from each of which a sloping bar carried on a half arch and resembling a flying buttress rises, the whole eight meeting in the middle and supporting a central pinnacle. The term is applied to other terminations of towers in which only four sloping bars occur; and this form is not peculiar to Scotland. It occurs in S. Dunstan's in East London, and elsewhere.

Scotia: A hollow molding; especially, such a molding used in the base of a column in Greco-Roman architecture and its imitations.

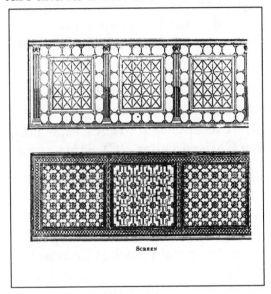

SCREEN

Screen: Any structure of any material having no essential function of support and serving merely to separate, protect, seclude, or conceal.

Screen chamber: An apartment formed by a screen separating it from a larger area.

Screen Wall: A screen of some solidity as differing from one which is pierced, especially in the intercolumniations of a colonnade.

Scroll: An ornament composed of curved lines like volutes, and sometimes of double flexure passing on from one volute to another.

Scullery: A room, generally annexed to a kitchen, where dishes are washed.

Seat: (A) A place of abode, a residence. Rarely used in modern times except in combination; though such phrases as "seat of the Marquis of Blank" are common in England. (B) Any structure affording a place for a person to sit. Especially, in architectural usage, such a structure when much larger than a chair or stool, so as to accommodate two or more persons; and commonly fixed. (C) A bed, surface, or piece of material arranged to support any member of a structure; as the bearing of a beam, the foot of a column, or the like.

Sedilia: A low-backed seat or bench within the sanctuary, to the south of the altar, for the use of the officiating clergyman at the Eucharistic celebration; wide enough not only for the celebrant to be seated, but also for the deacon and subdeacon. The back is made low in order to allow the vestments to hang over, so that the clergymen will not injure them by sitting upon them.

Sekos: In Greek archaeology, the sanctuary; a place more or less forbidden to the public. The term is sometimes used for the whole enclosure of the naos, sometimes for a part of it, this depending upon the opinion held by modern scholars as to the usage in the case of any temple or sacred enclosure. By extension, a sanctuary, shrine, holy place, or reserved chamber, as in Egyptian temples or in early Christian churches.

Semicolumn: A column half engaged in a wall.

Semidome: A half dome or Conch, such as occurs over a semicircular apse.

Seminar room: A room for study; especially, in a college library, a room provided for the pursuit of a particular line of investigation by students, under the direction of a professor.

Septa: (Latin, *septum,* an enclosure or bounding wall.) A large, enclosed and covered area or porticus, serving for a bazaar or exchange; especially, the Septa Julia near the Campus Martius, which was a magnificent building decorated with many statues and divided into seven aisles by rows and

columns, with rostra for public orations, booths for shops, etc. Its remains lie under the Palazzo di Venezia, and thence northward for 1100'.

Sepulchral: Having to do with a tomb or other burial place, or with a cenotaph.

Sepulchre light: A special lamp suspended in the Holy Sepulchre, and in all churches built to recall that sacred place.

Sepulchre: (A) A tomb; a cave or structure for purposes of interment. (B) A receptacle for relics, especially, in a Christian altar. (C) Same as Easter sepulchre.

Seraglio: (A) An enclosed or protected place; hence, a harem. (B) A palace; the Seraglio, used as a proper name, the great palace at Constantinople. Several different etymologies are given, and this term, as well as *serai* and *serail,* is used indifferently in many senses.

Serdab: A small chamber connected with an ancient Egyptian tomb.

Settle: (A) A seat or bench; specifically, a wooden bench with high back and arms for two or more people, placed near the chimney or at the foot of a bed, and often provided with a chest or coffer underneath. (B)

A part of a platform lower than another part, as one of the successive stages of ascent to the great altar of the Jewish Temple.

Severy: One bay of a vaulted structure, that is, the space within two of the principal arches. The term is evidently derived from the Latin *ciborium*, which term, from its original meaning of a covered receptacle, took first the significance of a rounded canopy, then of a covered vessel or closet to hold the host, and also of a dome-shaped structure of any kind, whence comes the present meaning of a compartment of vaulting, whether dome-shaped or not.

Sgraffito: The scratching or scoring of a surface, as of fresh plaster, with a point to produce decorating effects. Sometimes, in plaster work or pottery, the scoring is done so as to reveal a surface of different color beneath. The process is sometimes carried far, even to the decoration of large wall surfaces.

Shaft ring: In Medieval architecture, a molded band encircling a shaft; common in early English work.

Shafted impost: In Medieval architecture, an arrangement of shafts, wrought in the mass of a pier or jamb, so that corresponding groupings of archivolt moldings may start from their caps at the impost line.

Shafting: In Medieval architecture, the system of grouping shafts in a clustered pier, or in the jamb of an aperture.

Shank: One of the plain spaces between the channels of a triglyph in a Doric frieze. Called *femor* by Vitruvius. The shaft of a column; obsolete.

Shanty: A hut; a small temporary building of a rough character.

Shelf: Any ledge, wide or narrow, made of a board or other thin material, set edgewise and horizontally, for supporting small objects; as in closets for house linen, china, glass, etc. In general, a flat ledge, wherever or however occurring.

Shot tower: A high building for the manufacture of shot, which are formed by dropping molten lead from an upper story or platform into a cistern of water at the bottom. The mass of lead subdivides into drops during the descent, and the size of the shot is frequently regulated by perforated screens or sieves, having openings of various sizes, through which the lead is poured.

Shot window: In Scotland, an unglazed window, generally circular.

Shrine: In architecture, a receptacle for sacred relics, most often the body of a saint. The shrine is then a tomb in a choir, chapel or crypt, such as that of S. Edward the Confessor in Westminster Abbey. Portable shrines are made for smaller relics, often of very rich material and splendidly adorned.

Slab House: A house built of wooden slabs or rough-hewn planks. Especially applied to houses so made by the Indians of northern California and the Northwest coast. Planks were split out of cedar or other wood with elk-horn and wooden wedges driven by stone mallets. They were reduced to any required thickness by adzing. In size the planks were something extraordinary at times, reaching such dimensions as 4-1/2' x 24'. Some tribes built houses with a roof of one slope while others put up a ridge or double ridge and made two or more slopes. Several families lived under one roof, and often a whole community had but a single house. The dimensions were sometimes as great as 75' long x 40' wide and 15' high. The rafters were supported by heavy posts set in the ground, and the planks were tied horizontally on the sides between upright posts, while those on the roof ran with the slope and were grooved and overlapping. The family apartments were separated by partitions about 2' or 3' high and often higher. North of the Strait of S. Juan de Fuca the slab houses become even more massive, with carving on the posts in front and sometimes within. The totem posts set up in front are elaborately carved.

Solarium: In Roman archaeology, a part of a house exposed to the sun, generally taken to be the roof of a portico or other place serving the purpose of a modern balcony, and easy of access from the upper stories. Hence, in Medieval Latin, the second-story room or rooms. From this is derived the English solar.

Sotto portico: In Italy, a public way beneath the overhanging upper story and behind the columns of a building or a series of buildings. There are many such covered streets in Venice, especially along the water fronts.

Spandrel wall: A wall or partition erected on the extrados of an arch filling in the spandrels.

Spandrel: (A) The quai-triangular space included between the extradoses of two adjoining arches and a line approximately connecting their crowns, or the space equal to about half of this, in the case of a single arch, with whatever piece of masonry or other material fills that space. In decorative styles of architecture this is a favorite place for sculpture or inlaid ornament. (B) In steel skeleton construction, the space between the top of the window in one story and the sill of the window in the story above.

Specus: In Roman architecture, the channel of an aqueduct elevated above the ground and covered by an arch, or slabs. Sometimes the same arcade carried several of these channels, one above another.

Speos: In Greek, a cave, especially a large or deep one; hence in archaeology, a cave-temple or a large tomb; a large and architectural chamber, excavated in the rock.

Sphinx: A creature made up of parts of a lion and of another natural animal, though the artistic conception may be thought rather to include the whole nature of each. In Egyptian antiquity, the human-headed sphinx is always male; and of this nature is the Great Sphinx, which is one of the very earliest of existing monuments. It is near the great pyramids of Gizah, partly cut from the rock, partly built up of masonry, with a temple or shrine built against the breast, the path to which leads between the forepaws. The height to the top of the head is 66 feet. The name given to this image is transliterated *Hu*, or more fully, *Horemkhu*, a word having connection with the god Horus, and other androsphinxes seem to have received the same name. Such images cut out of single blocks of granite and of all sizes up to eight feet in length, were sometimes arranged along a roadway or approach to a temple, forming a double avenue. In Greek and Greco-Roman antiquity the sphinx is always female, with human head and breast. In some coins, etc., the forms are of the dog rather than of the lion.

Spina: The wall or other barrier extending along the middle of a Roman circus, and about the ends of which the contestants turned.

Spira: The moldings at the base of a column.

Spire Light: A window in a spire, generally in the form of an attenuated dormer, with a steep roof or gable, used less to give light to the interior than in conjunction with pinnacles to enrich its outlines.

Spirelet: A small spire, as of a pinnacle or turret.

Spring house: A building erected over a natural spring to protect it from injury or impurities; sometimes decorative, or large enough to contain fixed seats; or used as a place for cooling milk, or the like, in the cold water, as frequently on American farms, where the house is built of wood.

Springer: A stone or other solid which is laid at the impost of an arch.

Spur: (A) In timber framing, a diagonal brace between a post and a tie beam or rafter. (B) A buttress or similar projecting piece of walling. (C) In Medieval architecture, specifically, the carved claw or griffe projecting from the lower torus of a column, so as to cover one of the projecting corners of the square plinth beneath.

Squinch: An arch, a lintel, corbelling, or system of such members, built across the interior corner of two walls, as at the top of a tower, to serve as foundation for the diagonal or canted side of a superimposed octagonal spire or lantern. The squinch performs the functions of a Pendentive.

Sriptorium: In Medieval Latin, a writing room; specifically, the room assigned in a conventual establishment for the copying of manuscripts.

Stadhuis: In the Netherlands, a town house or city hall.

Stadium: In Roman archaeology, an open area for the foot race and for the exercises of athletes; often made architectural by its association with *thermae* or the like.

Stage: A platform in a theater, auditorium, or similar place, which is for the use of the actors and other employees.

Stalactite work: A system of corbelling of peculiar form or the imitation of such corbelling in wood and plaster. So called from a fancied resemblance to natural stalactites.

Stalactite: One of the pendent cones of lime carbonate found attached to the roofs of caves.

Stalagmite: One of the deposits of lime carbonate on the floor of caves, and which may or may not be in the form of upright pillars corresponding to pendent stalactites.

Stalk: In the Corinthian capital, the representation of the stem of a plant, sometimes fluted, from which the volutes spring.

Stall: (A) In an ecclesiological sense, a fixed seat, enclosed at the back and sides. Rows of such stalls for the use of the clergy, acolytes, and choristers are usually arranged on the north and south side of the choir; they are separated from each other by high projecting arms, and have their seats hinged so as to fold against the back when the occupant wishes to stand in the stall. On the under side of each seat there is a bracket upon which the occupant can rest when standing. In the larger churches the stalls are often surmounted by canopies; and in the monastic and some other churches the choir stalls return at the west end of each row. (B) In a stable, one of the divisions, averaging 4' to 5' wide and 9' deep, separated by partitions, open in the rear, and provided with appliances for feeding and drainage, for the accommodation of horses and cattle.

Stamba: A pillar standing alone and serving as a memorial or a votive offering. There are many of these in India, and it is found that they have been erected at all epochs from the third or fourth century B.C. down to the commencement of the European conquest and settlement of the peninsula. Some of these are elaborately built up of many courses of stone and arranged with a spreading capital to support some larger culminating structure, as a table or roofed recess for holding a lamp. The Lantern of the Dead should be compared with these. Spelled also *sthamba*.

Stanza: In Italian, a room or chamber; as the *stanze* of Raphael in the Vatican Palace.

Stencil, Stencil plate: A thin plate of metal, or sheet of paper, perforated with any desired pattern or device, so that, when held against the wall and scumbled with a brush of color, the pattern is transferred through the perforations to the surface to be decorated.

Step log: A kind of ladder made by cutting notches into the side of a log. The first ladder of the American Indians.

Stereobate: The top of a foundation or substructure, forming a solid platform upon which the columns of a Classical building are set. That part of it which comes immediately beneath the columns is distinguished as the stylobate.

Stiacciato: In Italian decorative art, very flat; said of relief sculpture.

Stinash: The Modoc term for house lodge. In Klamath it means a willow-framed lodge.

Stippling: In painting, the production of effects of gradation by fine dotting with brushpoint or other implement; a process imitated in engraving by the stipple graver.

Stoa: A portico used by the ancient Greeks as a shady promenade or meeting place, where conversation might be held or speakers heard. The *stoa* took the form of a roofed structure, the length of which was great as compared with its depth. Ordinarily, there was at the back an enclosing wall, and in front, facing the street or public square, a colonnade. The floor of the *stoa* was generally raised a few steps above the street. In early examples the depth was so slight that the space between the wall and the colonnade was covered by a single span, and the roof sloped in one direction only; but later, with greater depths, one or more lines of supports had to be introduced between the wall and the outer colonnade, to assist in carrying the roof, which then frequently had a double slope. Pausanias describes a deviation from the more usual forms in the case of the Coreyraean colonnade at Elis, of which he says, "The colonnade is double, for it has columns both on the side of the market place. In the middle the roof of the colonnade is supported, *not* by columns, but by a wall; and there are statues beside the wall on either side." Sometimes such porticoes were divided by two rows of columns into three aisles, or in one case by four rows into five aisles. The *stoa* of Attalos at Athens was, according to Vitruvius, two stories in height, the columns of the lower story being of the Doric order, those in the Upper Ionic; nor was this the only example of the two-story *stoa*, as witness those at Pergamon and Epidauros. *Stoas* were frequently adorned by statues of celebrated persons, and in certain cases the rear wall was decorated with paintings.

Stockade: (A) Same as palisade. (B) An enclosed space surrounded by a palisade. In this sense, the term carries with it the idea of a complete defensible work, however small and simple, the term palisade being limited to the line of stakes itself.

Stone setting: The art and practice of putting into permanent place the stones prepared for building, including the preparation and spreading of mortar, if used, the laying of lead joints where needed (as between bases, or shafts, and capitals), and the exact turning of arches made up of wedge-shaped solids, and similar work.

Stoneware: Potter's ware made of very silicious clay, or of clay and flint, which, when properly mixed, molded, and fired, becomes vitrified throughout. It is often molded to form copings, chimney tops, etc.

Stool: (A) Same as seat. (B) The small molded shelf under the sash of a window, serving as an interior sill.

Stoup: (A) A basin for holy water, placed in a niche or against a wall or pillar near the entrance of a Roman Catholic church. (B) Same as stoop.

Strap ornament; work: A method of ornamentation, especially characteristic of the time of Elizabeth in England, composed of a capricious interlacing, folding, and interpenetration of bands or fillets, sometimes represented as cut with foliations.

Stupa: In Indian architecture, a building erected to contain a *chaitya*, and usually of a towerlike form, with no more interior subdivisions than are sufficient to afford an adequate shrine; depending entirely upon its exterior effect.

Stylobate: In Greek architecture, that part of the stereobate upon which the peristyle stands; by extension, any continuous base, plinth, or pedestal, upon which a row of columns are set.

Sudatio: An apartment in the Roman bath or gymnasium between the iaconicum, sudatorium, or stove, and the caldarium or warm bath, where athletes retired to remove the sweat from their bodies.

Sudatory: A chamber used for the sweat bath.

Suite: A succession of connected rooms, generally on one floor. The term carries with it the double meaning of a common purpose being served by these rooms, and of their forming a sort of continuous gallery by opening into one another freely.

Summerhouse: An open ornamental pavilion in a park or garden for out-of-door rest or retirement.

Sun pole: A sacred pole made from the mystery tree with much ceremony, for use in the mystery lodge during the sun dance of the Sioux Indians. The devotees are attached to the sun pole by thongs fastened to skewers which are passed through their flesh.

Sundial: A device for indicating the time of day by means of the shadow cast by the sloping edge of a projecting point, or gnomon, set in a surface upon which the hours of the day are set forth on points radiating from the gnomon. It is sometimes in the form of a table in a garden, and sometimes it is placed conspicuously as an ornament on a wall or gable.

Suovetaurilia: In Roman antiquity, a sacrifice consisting of a swine, a sheep, and a bull; the word being compounded of the Latin names of the three beasts. Hence, in modern archaeology, a representation, as in relief sculpture, of the three creatures together.

Supercapital: A piece of stone above the capital proper of a column, perhaps recalling the ancient use of the entablature, as in Roman Imperial practice, even above isolated columns; perhaps intended rather as a constructional device to enable the capital to receive a still larger superimposed mass. The use of supercapitals is characteristic of Byzantine art and all its imitations. Also called impost.

Supercilium: In Roman architecture, the fillet above the *cymatium*, forming the topmost member of the cornice. Also, sometimes, referring to the fillets above and below the scotia of an attic base.

Supercolumniation: Superimposition in columnar architecture, with special reference to the disposition of the orders. The more elaborate orders are at the top; but where there are four or five stories the Composite in some form is commonly placed above the Corinthian.

Surbase: The molding or group of moldings forming the crowning member of a basement story, a plinth, dado, base course, or the like.

Suth door: One of the doors of a parish church, and generally the most important one. The word "suth" is most probably the old form of south, and refers to the fact that the southern door was that for the entrance of the congregation, and that where persons accused of crime might take oath that they were innocent, as well as that where notices of ecclesiastical ceremonials, feast days, and the like, were put up.

Swag: A festoon; the common English name for that form which is very heavy in the middle and slight at the points of support.

Swan neck: In stair building, a ramp terminating in a knee, as where a hand rail curves near a newel so as to be about vertical, and is then continued a short distance horizontally, entering the newel at right angles.

Syene granite: Egyptian syenite; *granito rosso*. A coarse, red granite occurring at Syene, in Egypt, and much used by the ancient Egyptians in the monoliths and temples. The various obelisks, like those in Paris and New York, are of this material.

Syenite: A rock of the nature of granite, but differing in containing no appreciable amount of quartz. Not a common stone.

Syle: One of a pair of crutches, straight instead of curved like the gavel forks.

Syrinx: In Greek archaeology, anything tubular in form; in architecture, especially a tunnel-shaped, rock-cut tomb belonging to that epoch in Egyptian antiquity which succeeded the age of the Mastaba.

Systyle: A close arrangement of columns in a peristyle, the usual systyle intercolumniation measuring two diameters from center to center of shaft.

T

Tabernacle Work: In Medieval architecture, an arcade or series of niches, highly decorated, with jamb shafts supporting carved overhanging canopies, and containing corbels for the support of figures or groups of figures.

Tabernacle frame: The frame for a door, window, or other opening, when treated as a complete design with columns or pilasters and an entablature, and also, when the opening is high in the wall, with an ornamental pendant below the window sill. Also a similar frame for a permanent work of art.

Tabernacle: (A) The portable place or worship and religious ceremonial used by the Israelites during their wanderings, as described in Exodus. (B) A house of worship, especially a building for Christian worship, but so planned and arranged as to differ from the ordinary church, as where seats for a very large congregation are provided. (C) In the Roman Catholic Church, a cupboard with doors, or similar shrine, used for keeping the consecrated bread. The use of the tabernacles is recent, dating probably from the seventeenth century; the name may, by extension, be given, as in France, to the metal

vase or hollow dove used for the same purpose, or even the suspended pyx, when made decorative in itself and kept permanently in sight. (D) A decorated recess, as a niche, or a framed space, especially when filled with figures of religious or ecclesiastical character. In this sense, any one of the niches with statues of saints, in a Medieval church porch, or the canopied open part of a pinnacle, as in Reims Cathedral, or the Eleanor Cross at Northampton.

Tablinum: In Roman architecture, a room, generally at the farther end of the atrium, in which were kept the family archives recorded upon tablets. Applied by modern archaeologists to a large and very open room in a Roman house connected with the atrium, and often serving as passage from it to the peristyle or garden.

Tabularium: At Rome, a building of the time of the Republic standing on the extreme southeastern edge of the Capitoline Hill. The upper stories have been replaced by the Palace of the Senator, but the lower stories remain almost unaltered. The building must have had one high story on the side of the Capitol, where is now the square of the Campidoglio, and two high stories crowning a very lofty basement on the side toward the Forum.

Taenia: In a Doric entablature, the fillet which separates the frieze from the architrave.

Tailloir: In French, the abacus of a capital.

Tailpiece: A short joist or rafter fitted into the Header.

Tall boy: A chimney pot of long and slender form, intended to improve the draught by lengthening the flue.

Tambour: (A) Same as drum, as of a cupola. (B) Same as bell, as of a capital. This is the French term often used in English; the original signifies also a drum of a column.

Taper: The slope or diminishing of a spire, or of a conical or pyramidal roof. Also the diminishing of a shaft of a column; but as this is very nearly always curved, it is not often called taper.

Tapestry: A fabric made by a process somewhat different from regular weaving, in which a warp is embroidered by hand with colored thread to produce a design. It is used for wall hangings. In ancient times it was the most available covering for the stone walls of halls and chambers of a strong castle or other residence of the nobility, and was usually hung from tenterhooks by means of which it was suspended at a distance of at least some inches from the face of the masonry. It was often allowed to cover the door openings in such a way that even when the door was thrown open the person entering had still no view of the interior, a parting or division between two pieces of tapestry alone serving as the entrance.

Taproom: In Great Britain, the same as barroom, as being the place where liquors are drawn from the tap.

Tarras: (A) An ancient spelling of Terrace. (B) A strong cement formerly used in hydraulic engineering.

Tarsia: The Italian inlaying of wood, usually light upon dark, common in the fifteenth century. The patterns were usually Renaissance scrollwork and arabesques, but also curious pictures with perspective effects were introduced into the larger panels. An imitation of the inlay was very commonly made by painting, as in the celebrated cupboards of S. Maria delle Grazie at Milan, known as *Lo Scaffale*, which have been well reproduced in a book bearing the same title.

Tazza: A vase having the form of a flat and shallow cup, with a high foot or stand. The term is applied to the basin of a fountain when supported by a pillar; and some fountains have two, or even three, tazzas, vertically arranged, and growing smaller as they ascend.

Tchish: The Klamath term for settlement, camp, wigwam, lodge, village, town.

Tebi: In Egyptian building, brick made of the mud of the Nile, mixed with fragments of pottery, chopped straw, or the like.

Tegula: A tile; the Latin term, and used in English for tiles of unusual shape or material, such as the marble tiles of some Greek temples.

Tel: A mound; the modern Arabic term, which enters into many compound names of sites, as in Egypt and Mesopotamia. Also written tell.

Telamon: A male statue serving to support an entablature, impost, corbel, or the like, and forming an important part of an architectural design. Telamones are generally considered the same as atlantes, which word is more usual in Classical archaeology. In the elaborate architecture of the eighteenth century, half figures of men, usually bearded, and of exaggerated muscular development and extravagant pose, are used as supports of porches, and the like. The name telamones may be extended to apply to these.

Telesterion: A place for initiation; especially the temple at Eleusis, in which were held the initiatory rites to the Eleusinian Mysteries. The building was of unusual character for a Greek temple, having 12 columns in the front, the only dodecastyle portico known in antiquity; and the interior was hypostyle, with 42 columns in six rows. Seats cut in the rock were arranged on all four sides of the building. The interior measured about 170' x 175'. The manner of its roofing and lighting is not known.

Temenos: In Greek antiquity, a piece of ground specially reserved and enclosed, as for sacred purposes, corresponding nearly to the Latin *templum* in its original signification. In some cases the temenos contains but a single shrine, or temple, in the modern sense, while in others, as in the celebrated cases of Olympia and Epidauros, many important buildings, including several temples of considerable size, are arranged within the enclosure.

Tempietto: In Rome, a small circular building designed by Bramante, and erected in 1502. It stands in the cloister court of S. Pietro in Montorio.

Templum: In Roman antiquity, a space reserved; practically the same as temenos. The idea of a building is hardly included in the term in Latin until the later times of the Republic.

Teocalli: The worship mound of the Aztecs.

Teopan: An Aztec building similar to the teocalli, and like that devoted to the service of the gods.

Tepidarium: In ancient Roman baths, a room of intermediate temperature between the frigidarium and the dalidarium and fitted with baths to correspond.

Term: A terminal figure, especially one of the sort called by the Greeks Hermes.

Terminus: In Latin, the ancient Italian god of landmarks, the guardian of property in land; hence the figure of that god, represented without legs and feet to express the irremovable nature of the landmarks, the lower limbs being replaced by a solid prism or inverted truncated cone.

Terre pleine: In French, a level platform of earth; used in English in fortification, rarely elsewhere.

Terrones work (From Spanish, *terron*, a clod of earth): A wall or building constructed of earth, mud, adobe, or similar compact and uniform material which hardens as it dries.

Tessellar: Made up of tesserae; after the fashion of mosaic work.

Tessellate: To make an inlay or mosaic of tesserae. Tessellated work is an inlay of square pieces, generally small.

Tester: A flat canopy, as over a bed, throne, pulpit, or tomb.

Testudo: In Roman architecture, an arched vault or ceiling, especially when surbased or flattened.

Tetrapylon: Something characterized by having four gateways, as a building with a nearly equal gateway in each of four sides. Such a building is the well-known arch of Janus near the Church of S. Giorgio in Velabro, Rome, and in a somewhat similar building at Constantine in Algeria.

Tetrastoon: (A) Having a porch or portico on each of its four sides, as a cloister. (B) Having four porticoes; said of any building.

Tetrastyle: Having four columns in the front or end row; consisting of a row or rows of four columns.

Thalamium: In Greek architecture, an inner room or chamber; especially, the women's apartment.

Theologeion: In Greek theater, the place where persons representing the deities of Olympus stood and spoke.

Thermae: (Latin, hot baths; a plural noun.) An establishment for bathing, of which there are many in the different cities of the Roman Empire, some of extraordinary size and importance as works of elaborate architecture. There were eleven large *thermae* in Rome in the reign of Diocletian, after the completion of the establishment bearing the name of that emperor, which was by far the largest; and more than 900 smaller ones under the control of private citizens. The peculiarity of the architectural plan is so great that it can be compared to that on no other class of buildings. The outer enclosure of the *thermae* of Diocletian measured 1,100' northeast and southwest, and nearly 1,200' in the opposite direction, without including certain projections, as of exedrae and decorative alcoves and the like, of unknown use, one of which, a rotunda, retaining its ancient cupola, is now the Church of S. Bernardo. Within this and surrounded by open spaces the great block of the *thermae* proper was about 480' x 750', and included a vaulted hall (the *tepidarium*) 80' wide, a part of which is now the nave of the Church of S. Maria degli Angeli. Here, as in other *thermae*, the tepid baths were small basins arranged around the edge of the great hall of the *tepidarium*. The caldarium or warm bath gave its name in like manner to the halls in which such baths were contained, which were in the large *thermae* circular and crowned with a cupola; but this form is not to be supposed especially fitted for that purpose, for in the Stabian baths at Pompeii the *frigidarium* is circular, the *caldarium* a rectangle with an apse, and the *tepidarium* a simple rectangle, while another cold bath, the swimming basin, is entirely out of doors in this and in the other public *thermae* of Pompeii, an arrangement which suits the much warmer climate of that city. The *iaconicum* or sweat bath differs greatly in different establishments as to size, form, and connection with the other rooms, indicating a natural difference in the habits of the people. The vast extent of the *thermae* is to be accounted for only by noting the palestrae or ground for running and for exercise, lecture rooms, libraries, rooms, and porticoes for conversation, all of which were provided within the walls, and were elaborately built and richly adorned.

Theseion: A temple or sanctuary dedicated to Theseus; especially a hexastyle peripteral Doric temple remaining at Athens, and long known by that name; but now ascertained to be a temple of Hephaestus (Vulcan).

Tholobate: The circular substructure of a dome.

Tholos: In Greek and Greco-Roman architecture, a round building. The Tholos of Epidauros in the Morea, near the eastern coast, is the most celebrated; for, although entirely in ruins, it has been theoretically restored with great appearance of authenticity, and was evidently a building of extraordinary beauty. The interior order was Corinthian, and this affords, probably, the earliest instance which we have of fine Corinthian capitals in a building of pure Greek style. One capital was found in a kind of crypt or cell, underground, and was worked with the leafage differently subdivided in different parts, as if experimentally, the capital having served to all appearance as a guide to the workmen who carved the others.

Throne room: A chief room of state containing the throne upon a dais and under a canopy.

Thymele: In Greek architecture, an altar; specifically, the altar of Dionysus, standing in the center of the orchestra of a Greek theater, and around which the chorus performed their evolutions.

Ti'pi (tee'pee): From the Dakota *ti*, a house. As *pi* is a common plural ending, it is probable that in the beginning the form *tipi*, applied to a single structure, grew out of our mistaking plural for singular. The Dakota special name for skin is *wa-ke'-ya*, and for any shelter, *wo'-ke-ya*. A conical Indian tent composed of a number of poles, with their upper ends tied together near the top, spread into a circle on the ground, and covered with skins, or in recent times with canvas. Primarily the portable *tipi* is a Dakota structure, belonging to the Plains, but the same thing is in wide use among other Indian tribes, and the term now has an equal range. As a portable skin tent it seems to have been perfected by the Dakotas, but it should be noted that other tribes (as well as the Dakotas) made bark-covered tents, and the Iroquois constructed a triangular one with a bark covering, on similar principles. The poles of the *tipi* are 7 to 20 or 30 in number, and 15' to 18' long, tied together near the small ends, while the larger ends enclose a circle 10' or 15' in diameter. The cover, being draw in around the poles is pinned together by sticks thrust crosswise through holes, or laced, for about the middle third of the distance from top to bottom, leaving the lower third open for a doorway and the upper third for a smoke outlet. The door was protected by an extra skin fastened, only by the top, to the tent outside, and spread by a stick fixed transversely near its upper end. Sometimes a loose skin was adjusted outside to the apex of the tent to form a hood that could be turned according to the wind direction; but the usual practice was to place long outside poles in pockets provided in each of the two triangular ends of the skin cover, by means of which these flaps could be arranged from below. If there was no wind, they were left open; but otherwise they were adjusted accordingly, the windward flap being set high, while the leeward one was drawn down close to the frame, leaving only hole enough for the exit of smoke. The *tipi* was fastened to the ground by pegs through holes in the edges of the skins made for the purpose, and in high winds stones or other weights were laid on the bottom portions. In travelling the poles were attached to the sides of a horse; and the long ends, trailing on the ground, furnished a vehicle for various articles of baggage.

Tierceron: In later Medieval vaulting, a secondary or intermediate rib springing from the pier on either side of the diagonal ribs or arcs doubleaux.

Tiers point: In French, the point where the two determining arcs of a pointed arch meet, the apex. The term means originally the third or culminating point of a triangle.

Tiyotipi: Among the Dakota Indians, a soldier's lodge. A sort of council tent, as well as a feasting and lounging place. Regulations for the camp, and especially for the hunt, were made in it and published by means of a crier.

Tolmen: Same as dolmen; but some attempt has been made to apply the term to a stone pierced by a hole, of prehistoric or unknown date.

Tondino: A molding of convex rounded section, especially a large one, such as a torus; the Italian term sometimes used in English.

Tope: A Buddhist monument, common in India and southeastern Asia, consisting of a tumulus of masonry, generally domical in form, for the preservation of relics, when it is distinguished as a *dagoba*; or to commemorate an event, when it is called a *stupa*. It is sometimes elevated on a square, cylindrical, or polygonal substructure built vertically or in terraces, and is nearly always crowned with a finial, called a *tee*, shaped like an umbrella.

Toran, Torana: In Buddhist architecture, a gateway, composed of from

162

one to three horizontal lintels, generally of wood, but sometimes of stone, placed one above another upon two posts, the whole being often elaborately carved. Similar gateways are, in Japan, called *torii*, and are used to give dignity to the approach to a shrine or sacred place.

Torch: In architectural decoration, an emblem founded upon sculptured representations; in Greco-Roman work, usually, of a bundle of strips held together by occasional withes or bands. This feature is generally repeated without a clear understanding of its significance. The torch inverted is used to symbolize death, probably because of the obvious idea of turning the burning torch downward in order to extinguish the flame against the ground.

Torso: An imperfect statue, of which the body alone, or the body with parts of the limbs is in place and tolerably perfect. By extension, the body of a complete statue. The adjectival term applied to a twisted or spiral shaft is founded on confusion between a French and an Italian term of wholly different meanings, and should be avoided.

Totem pole: A wooden post set up in front of a dwelling by some North American Indians, carved with totemic emblems. The most remarkable are those of the tribes of the Northwest coast, like the Haida.

Tower: A structure, of any form in plan, which is high in proportion to its lateral dimensions; or which is an isolated building with vertical sides and simple character, even if not high in proportion; or a part of a structure higher than the rest, but always having vertical sides for a part of its separate and detached altitude; or, in buildings erected for defense, a projecting part, nearly equivalent to a bastion, often, but not always, higher than the curtain. Towers include the ancient pharos and the modern lighthouse; the keep, the gateway tower and other projecting breaks in the walls of Medieval castles; the pele tower, and other isolated towers of defense, observation, or refuge of feudal times; the round tower in its limited and its more general sense; the *lat, stamba, vimana, sikra,* and the so-called *pagoda,* in all its meanings, and often the *tope* and *stupa;* the campanile of Italy; the bell tower of the Christian world, including the central tower, the spire-topped tower or steeple; the minaret of Islam; the shot tower; the water tower; the clock tower in all its forms, and the *beffroi;* and, in modern times, such engineering works as the uprights set to carry

163

the anchorage of the suspension bridge; also, in fact though not in name, the high many-storied office buildings or sky scrapers of the United States, when assuming the form of a shaft of uniform width and depth, high in proportion to horizontal dimensions, and rising above surrounding structures. The general rule is that towers stand upon the ground, and rise from it without serious break in their verticality; but there are important exceptions. The whole class of central towers are without continuous vertical lines, except as the reentrant angle of nave and transept is carried up by the projecting angle of the tower. The church towers of London are, in some notable instances, set upon the roofs of the columnar porticoes of their fronts; and this, though an obvious anomaly, has been followed elsewhere, and makes an important feature of a subordinate style of neoclassic art.

Trabeated: Constructed with horizontal beams or lintels.

Trabeation: Lintel construction as contrasted with any form of arched construction; hence, by extension, an entablature.

Trachelium: In a Grecian Doric column that part of the necking which comes between the hypotrachelium and the capital proper.

Transenna: In early Christian architecture, a carved open lattice work, or screen of marble, or of fine metal work, used to enclose shrines.

Transept: Any large division of a building lying across, or in a direction contrary to, the main axis. In a Christian basilica the large and high structure immediately next to the apse, on the side nearer the main entrance; usually so high that the nave and aisles stopped against its wall; and also more open and larger within than any other part of the church. In a cruciform church the transept is commonly of the same section as the nave; it may have two aisles, like the nave, or one, or none. That part which is to the north when the sanctuary is at the east is the north arm of the transept, often called simply north transept, and that to the south, similarly, the south transept, the bay of the nave lying between being known as the crossing. Occasionally, in England, there are two complete transepts, and the nomenclature then is, northeast transept, southwest transept.

Trascoro: In Spanish church architecture, a part of the choir, or enclosed space for the clergy or choristers, which part is separated from the main choir, as by the open passage at the crossing of the nave and transept. This separation is made in Seville and Santiago cathedrals, where the names given are *coro* (choir) for the western half, and *capilla mayor* (greater chapel) for the eastern part; but sometimes the eastern part is called the *coro* and the western part the *trascoro*.

Tre Cento: In Italian art, the fourteenth century.

Trecentisti: In Italian art, the people of the fourteenth century, used especially of literary men, scholars, and artists.

Treenail: (A) A large pin of hard wood used in Medieval woodwork and in modern use, for fastening together timbers, as especially in shipbuilding. It is now little used in architecture, at least in the United States. (B) Same as Gutta, in Greek architecture, because of the theory that the guttae represent the heads of nails, or pins.

Trefoil: A panel, an opening, or a division of tracery, having three foliations, or lobes, separated by cusps.

Trellis: (A) Screenwork made of strips crossing one another, either at right angles or in a more elaborate

pattern. The most usual form is that made of thin laths of wood. By extension, (B) An arbor or framework, for the support of vines.

Triapsidal: Having three apses. The two more usual dispositions of a triapsidal church are, that with three apses at the eastern end, as one at the end of the choir and two terminating the side aisles; and that with three apses on the east, north, and south sides of a central tower, or central square, into which the nave and its aisle open on the western side.

Tribunal: (A) In Roman archaeology, that part of a basilica used to receive the seat of the magistrates, and also, by extension, the raised seat or post of any person of authority. (B) A platform from which speeches are delivered, or where a presiding officer sits. In this sense used very loosely and applied also to the court or magistracy itself, or to any body or individual to which important matters are referred.

Triclinium funebre: In Roman archaeology, an arrangement of three couches and a table in connection with a tomb, for the purpose of occasional banquets in honor of the dead. One such near Pompeii is an open-air structure of masonry, enclosed by a low wall, the interior of which is decorated as if in a private house.

Triclinium: (A) A couch upon which persons recline while at meals; the name implying the division of it into three parts, nearly separate, enclosing the table on three sides, the fourth side being left open for service. (B) By extension, a dining room in a Roman house, furnished with a low table, surrounded on three sides by couches. In general, each couch accommodated three guests reclining, the total number of guest being thus limited to nine.

Triforium: In Medieval church architecture, the space between the vaulting and the roof of an aisle, when opened into the nave over the nave arches and under the clearstory windows by an arch, or two arches, in each bay, or, more characteristically, by three arches (hence the name), the whole forming a gallery.

Triglyph: In Greek architecture, one of the vertical blocks in a Doric frieze, suggesting, in stone, the outer ends of the ceiling beams of the primitive wooden construction; it has two vertical grooves or triangular channels with a corresponding chamfer on each side, behind which is a groove or rebate, into which are fitted thin slabs which fill the me-

topes, and often called by that name. One triglyph is set over and on the axis of each column, except those of the corners, which, however, are set nearer to the adjoining columns than the width of the regular intercolumniation; one over each intercolumniation on its axis, and one at each corner of the frieze, showing two faces. The arrangement in Roman Doric is nearly the same, but the last triglyph of each range is sometimes placed, like the rest, over the center of the column and not on the corner.

Trilith, Trilithon: A structure composed of three stones, especially, in prehistoric architecture, a monument or part of a larger structure so built up.

Triplet: A group of three; especially, in Medieval architecture, such a group of windows; also in combination, as a triplet window.

Tripod: Any object standing on three legs, specially a table, a seat, or a stand for a vase or caldron, such as were common in Classical antiquity, when it was sometimes used as a sort of portable altar. It was used extensively as a decorative symbol.

Trompe: In French, a piece of vaulting of conical or partly spherical shape, or resembling one corner of a cloistered vault, the essential thing being that it supports a weight imposed upon it on one side or irregularly. Thus, if a projecting angle of a building is cut off below, the overhanging piece, triangular in plan, may be carried on corbelling; but if carried on an arched structure, that structure is a *trompe*. A turret-like building in a reentrant angle may be carried in a similar way. A pendentive is of the nature of a *trompe*.

Trunk: (A) Same as shaft; that is, of a column; obsolete or obsolescent. (B) A large and central or principal spout, conductor, or hollow shaft, as in ventilation, the delivery of grain, and the like.

Tudor architecture: The accession of Henry VII to the throne of England marked the beginning of a period so distinct in the architectural history of England that it has been customary to describe it by the name of Henry's Welsh family, Tudor. No one period of English history is more interesting than this, covering the reigns of Henry VII, Henry VIII, Edward VI, Mary, and Elizabeth I, a long and eventful period reaching from 1485 to 1600. The later work is often separately designated as Elizabethan, but there is hardly sufficient change in character to make a real division. With Tudor times an enormous im-

petus was given to house building by the general tendency toward more comfort and luxury, and this was further accelerated by the dissolution of the monasteries, which put land and wealth in the hands of the layman. The great lord and landowner was not only the head of his family, but the head of a host of retainers of every description, from lesser nobles and knights down to the artificers in the various trades. The keeping up of such a retinue and establishment bred hospitality, and also led to a demand for apartments for the family, where some retirement from the motley turmoil was possible. The plan of the house had developed from two directions toward a similar end. The buildings grouped about the irregular castle court grew into the group which surrounded the regular quadrangle. The great hall of the manor or grange was extended laterally, and then at right angles on the two ends, until it also enclosed a quadrangle, or at least bounded it on three sides. Modifications of this plan gave the E and the H plans. These then, the quadrangle, the E, and the H, are the general types of Tudor house plans. The climate called for substantial material, light on the south, shelter on the north, steep roofs, many fireplaces, and abundant admission of sun. Thus the

English characteristics of Tudor work have their natural explanation, building structures which were long and low, with steep roofs and gables, many tall chimneys, and great glazed bays. Of the rooms, the hall, although no longer so all-important as in early days, was still the most important feature, and the stairs, but recently mere squared logs going up between walls, were now an especial object of decoration. Oak was almost invariably the material. The stairs had close strings, and the balusters and panels forming the balustrade were often profusely carved in a manner which suggested the influence of the Italian Renaissance, and yet was distinctly English. Indeed, up to the time of Grinling Gibbons, there was no carving in England which approached in skill and dexterity the work of Italy and France. It is coarse, often grotesque, but generally well-placed, effective, and well understood in relation to the architecture (this latter an especially valuable quality, and one liable to be overlooked when the technical skill of the carver attracts too much attention). Although Gothic work was now a thing of the past, in nothing is its influence so clearly seen as in the windows, which, throughout the Tudor period, remained subdivided by mullion and transom, and thus permitted the retention and development of the many-sided bay so characteristic of the English country house, both as an external feature and as a marked characteristic of the hall and dining room, in which it was most frequently found. With the growth of the arts and the new learning more space was required for pictures and books, and this may have in part accounted for the long galleries which were so striking a feature. These rooms, or corridors, were generally on an upper floor, often running the length of the house under the roof, and of such size and importance that the English artist loved here to display fine panelling, marble mantles, and richly modelled ceiling. In the reign of Elizabeth I, Italian influence was more clearly felt, and Classic detail was pretty generally adopted, but the main lines were still Tudor. Under her successor, Classic really began to rule, and a distinct style arose known from the Stuart family as Jacobean.

Tudor flower: An ornament of late English Gothic art; a trefoil flower developed from the upright points of the crossing or the cusps of the foliated arch.

Tumulus: An artificial mound of prehistoric or unknown antiquity; especially a barrow or grave mound;

168

but applied, as the origin of the word warrants, to artificial hills intended for sacrificial purposes, the ruins of fortifications, and the like.

Tupik: From the Eskimo; a tent. In the milder Arctic weather the *iglu* and *iglugeak* become uninhabitable, the former because of the dampness, and the latter because the dome meets and falls in. The Eskimo then resort to tents. Some of these resemble the ordinary *tipi*, but have no smoke hold, the fire being built outside. While others are of a horseshoe shape, and still others are similar to our "A" tents, but with rounded ends. These variations belong to different localities. Skins are the usual covering. Sometimes two or more tents are placed together.

Turret: A small tower; especially one attached to a larger tower, as where an *echauguette* or stair turret rises above the platform of a fortified tower, or where a circular stair is built at an angle of a church tower to lead to the belfry.

Tuscan order: One of the three Roman orders of architecture according to Vitruvius; one of the five recognized by sixteenth century writers. It resembles the Roman Doric, but has fewer and bolder moldings, no triglyphs, and no decorated details. In Neo-classic work the shafts are sometimes built with rusticated bands, and, in a superimposition of orders, its place is in the basement.

Tuscan architecture: (A) That of the ancient Etruscans. (B) That of modern Tuscany at any epoch, especially any style taking shape in this region and not extending much beyond it. The most important of such styles is the round-arched Gothic, exemplified by the Loggia dei Lanzi and the Bargello, or Palace of the Podesta, both in Florence, and the Cathedral of Lucca, and other buildings; a style which was mainly Gothic in structure with its system of building received from the north, but which protested against the northern style as a decorative system.

Tympanum: The triangular recessed space beneath the coping of a pediment and between the raking cornice of the roof and the horizontal geison below. Also the slab or piece of walling which is used to fill up the space between an arch and the square head of a door or window below. This may be a single stone, or, if of small parts, it may rest upon a lintel. It is often used for rich decoration, and in large Gothic churches it may receive the richest relief sculpture. The term having merely the general significance of a smooth, thin plate or membrane is applied also to a panel by writers who take the word in this sense direct from Vitruvius.

Tzompantli: An Aztec building erected for the purpose of receiving and executing prisoners of war, and for dividing their flesh among the proper recipients.

U

Unburnt: Not baked, or fired, in a kiln; said of articles of clay such as in most cases are so completed by exposure to heat. Unburnt bricks are very common in Egyptian and Syrian building.

Uncoarsed: Masonry not laid up in courses or layers with continuous horizontal joints, but irregularly.

Unctorium: In the Roman baths, an apartment used by the bathers for anointing the bodies with oil or some unguent, which was then scraped off with a *strigil*.

Undercroft: Any vault or secret passage underground.

Underpitch groining: The groining and also the groined vaulting resulting from the intersection of a larger and higher vault by smaller ones. It is generally assumed that the larger and the smaller vaults spring from the same plane and have the same, or nearly the same shape; the smaller vaults will then intersect the larger one but will not reach above its haunches.

Underthroating: The cove of an outside cornice when so treated as to serve as a drip.

Upper croft: The triforium gallery or other upper gallery of a church, a term, perhaps, obsolete.

Urn: A receptacle for the ashes of the dead; usually a large vase with a rounded body and a foot. When of this special shape, it is employed as a symbolic decoration or finial in modern work, especially in mortuary monuments.

V

Vase: A hollow vessel of decorative character and various form, with or without ears or handles; hence the resemblance of such a vessel, in solid material, as marble, much used in the art of the Renaissance to decorate balustrades, pedestals, gate posts, and monuments of all sorts.

Vasistas: A small opening in, or by the side of a door of entrance; usually fitted with a wicket to shut and a fixed grating or the like through which to look or to speak. Its purpose is to ascertain, before the door is opened, the character of the person asking for admission.

Vault, groin: A curved line that forms when two vaults intersect.

Vault, rear: A vaulted space between window glass and the inner face of a wall.

Vaulting tile: A light piece of baked clay, intended to serve as a part of the filling of a vaulted cell, or of a groined vault built on centers.

Vaulting course: A horizontal course made up of the abutments or springers of a vaulted roof; generally made of stones set in projection or corbelled out, with horizontal beds.

Vaulting shaft: In ribbed vaulting, the vertical upright, in one or several rounded members, which leads to the springer of a rib or group of ribs. This shaft may rise from the ground, or from a corbel at a greater height in the face of the masonry.

Vaulting cell: One compartment of a vault which is so planned that one part can be built at a time, as in ribbed vaulting.

Velarium: In the roofless Roman theater and amphitheater, a great awning which was often spread to protect the spectators from the sun or rain.

Veneer: A thin facing of hard wood, which has desirable ornamental qualities under polish, glued upon a more common wood, usually pine, as in doors, wainscoting, cabinet work, etc.

Veranda, Verandah: An open gallery or portico covered by a roof supported by pillars, and attached to the exterior of a building.

Vermiculation: The act or art of producing vermiculated ornament; the roughening so produced.

Vestiary: A room or place for the keeping of vestments, garments, or clothes; a wardrobe.

Vestibule: A lobby or passage intermediate between the entrance and the interior of a building; a place of shelter or accommodation to those awaiting entrance to a building; and in northern climates the area between outer, storm, or front doors and inner, or vestibule doors, by which the house is protected from the cold drats. Less properly, an anteroom to a larger apartment or suite.

Vestibulum: In Roman archaeology, the outer vestibule, a recess or sheltered place outside of the outer doors of a building, as distinguished from the *fauces*. It was sometimes large and adorned with columns, forming an important architectural member, and a place where many persons could find shelter; but this must have been unusual, as only one of any elaborateness has been found in Pompeii. The Villa of the Papyri at Herculaneum seems to have had a perfectly plain, square vestibule within an outer columnar portico; it is possible that some allusions in ancient writers may be explained in this way.

Vestry hall: In England and in some of the English colonies, a hall in which the inhabitants or ratepayers of a parish, or their representatives, met for the dispatch of the official business of the parish.

Vestry: A sacristy. A room adjoining the choir of a church, and sometimes behind the main altar, where the sacred vessels and vestments are kept, and where the priest puts on his robes. In Protestant churches, a waiting room, next to the chancel or pulpit, for the accommodation of the clergy. A choir vestry is a robing room for the choir.

Viaduct: An elevated roadway supported by arches of masonry, or by trestles of iron or wood, carried over a valley or any low-lying district where an embankment would be inexpedient or impracticable.

Vicarage: (A) In England, the home or residence of a vicar. (B) The benefice and office or functions of a vicar.

Victorian architecture: That of the reign of Queen Victoria; the term may be applied, therefore, to any building commenced or planned since the accession of the queen, but is used more especially for buildings of any characteristic style unknown previous to the year 1837. During Victoria's reign the Gothic Revival began, culminated, and declined; and there were several other important movements, fashions, or attempts at creating a new style, such as the revived style of Queen Anne. Buildings, such as those which, belonging to the later years of the Gothic Revival, contain French and Italian elements freely used in connection with English, together with a free use of party-colored materials, are commonly called Victorian Gothic.

Vihara: A Buddhist monastery. Structures of this sort were often excavated from the solid rock; the halls, the ceilings of which were supported by sculptured pillars, being surrounded by small sleeping cells.

Vista: A view or prospect provided by nature or art, as through an avenue of trees in a park, or through a series of arches or other openings in a building. One of the leading *motifs* of design in the planning of important works, as palaces, temples, or gardens, especially in Classic or Renaissance architecture, is the establishment of continuous center lines through openings in adjacent halls and chambers, or through corridors or alleys, by which vistas are obtained terminating in some feature of especial interest, such as a statue, fountain, etc. This device tends to order, symmetry, and coherence in architectural composition.

Vitruvian scroll: A scroll of great simplicity, without leafage or the like, but generally having the section of a flat band.

Vitruvian: Of or pertaining to Marcus Vitruvius Pollio, a Roman architect of the first century B.C., the author of an important treatise which preserves much that is valuable in regard to Greek and Roman art, and is our principal authority for facts and practice in the building arts of the Classic period. The term "Vitruvian" is used to distinguish principles and practices of the architecture of ancient Rome as revealed to us by this author.

Vivarium: A place where animals are kept alive, and as far as practicable in their natural state, as a zoological garden. When adapted especially to fish, it is called an aquarium; to birds, an aviary; to frogs, a ranarium, etc.

Volcanic stone: Stone which has been formed by volcanic agency, including lava, peperino, pumice, tufa, tufo, etc.

Volute: A spiral scroll; especially that which forms the distinctive feature of the Ionic capital, which is repeated in the horns of the Corinthian and Composite capitals.

Vomitorium: One of the passages arranged to give direct ingress to, or egress from, the various tiers of seats in a Roman theater or amphitheater.

Voussoir: One of the stones used to form an arch or vault, being cut on two opposite sides to converging planes, in what is generally a wedge shape, though in some forms of vault four faces converge as in a truncated pyramid.

W

Wagon-headed: Having a continuous round arched vault or ceiling, as in barrel vaulting.

Wall tower: A tower built in connection with, and forming an essential part of, a wall; especially one of a series occurring in a mural fortification, as a city wall.

Wall chamber: A chamber built in the thickness or mass of a wall, as often in a Medieval castle in the upper stories.

Watch tower: A lofty structure intended to enable the approach of enemies to be detected, as by sea or though a mountain pass. The term is often applied loosely to any high building whose use is not known.

Watching loft: A lookout chamber in a tower, steeple, or other high building for police or military purposes, or for fire service.

Water tower: A tower constructed to hold a column of water at a level high enough to supply fountains or to afford a head for the distribution of water through a system of pipes for fire service, etc.; sometimes movable, and even light enough to be dragged by horses to a conflagration.

Wattle and dab; Watle and daub: Building with wattle work plastered with clay or mud.

Wattle: Basket work; a framework composed of interwoven rods or twigs.

Wattling: A method of construction by the interweaving of boughs, rods, canes, withes, vines, etc.

Wave scroll: Same as Vitruvian Scroll. So called because of a suggestion of sea waves in regular succession.

Weathercock: A vane; especially a vane in the form of a cock, as an emblem of vigilance, often associated with a horizontal cross bearing on the ends of its arms the letters *N., S., E.* and *W.,* to denote the points of the compass.

Well curb: A parapet or low wall built at the mouth of a well to prevent persons or beasts from falling into it, and so arranged as to allow the drawing of the water under proper conditions. The term may be taken to cover also the appliances for drawing the water, so far as they are constructive in character and not mere pieces of machinery. The well curb of common wells at farmhouses in America and largely in England is of wood, and often has a slight roof overhead. This is sometimes enlarged into decorative piece of architecture, especially for a well on the village green, or the like, or when a memorial purpose is attached to it. The well curbs of the Middle Ages have generally perished. There are, however, some elaborate wrought-iron canopies and herses existing, as notably in Nuremberg and cities of Belgium, some of which have come down but little altered from the fifteenth century. Very splendid well curbs of architectural character exist in some towns of Italy. Pienza, attached to the Palazzo Piccolomini, has two columns upon which rests a trabeated structure treated on either side like a Classical entablature, and from the under surface or soffit of this trabeation is suspended the wheel and other machinery for the buckets of the well. Another at San Gimignano in Tuscany is much more simple and probably earlier. In character it is still somewhat Medieval and probably dates from the early fifteenth century. The horizontal beam of stone in this case is supported on simple uprights which are carried out on the inner side with corbels, so as to diminish the free bearing of the lintel, which is loaded with a small ornamental superstructure.

Wicker: A pliant twig, osier, or withe used in making wickerwork or basketwork, also work done and any fabric made in this way. As applied to the making of closures with mud or clay, wickerwork is generally called wattle.

Wicket: A small door, gate, window, or trap; especially a small door or gate forming part of a large one, usually specified as wicket door, wicket gate, etc., according to use.

Wickyup: (A) An American Indian hut or shelter composed of brush, rushes, boughs, or bark; especially one of the dwellings of the Paiute, which are built of the tule rushes woven over a conical framework of poles 8' or 10' high, and also in some localities of rough cedar (juniper) or pine branches covered with boughs and twigs from the same trees, and open to the sun for a third of their circumference. (B) Throughout the Western United States any rude, temporary shelter or habitation. The derivation is from the Algonquin, or possibly an origin in the Dakota word *wakeyapi*, the plural of *wakeya*, a form of skin tent. The word is found in many of the Algonquin dialects. In the Sac-and-Fox-Algonquin it occurs as *wigiap* and *wikiapi*, being their form of the word *wigwam*. In the Menomone-Algonquin it is *wikiop*, a habitation of bark, brush, or wood. This may be a corruption of *wikomik*, which in turn may derives from *wigiwam (wigwam)*. It would appear, however, that inasmuch as *wiki* is a word for home and *wekop* is basswood bar, that a probable derivation is from a compound of these two, *wikiwekop*, denoting a home covered with basswood bark (or with mats of basswood bark) as distinguished from one covered with another material. This would be contracted according to Indian habit into *wikiop*.

Wigwam: An Algonquin house, built of poles and bark or mats, varying in size and shape according to locality and tribe. It was generally either circular or a flattened ellipse. It was made by planting poles in the ground and bringing their tops together. The Ojibwa brought them to a point with a curve outward, that is each pole was bow-shaped, the convex side out. The Menomone form was a flattened ellipse with the poles forming an arched roof; and when the wigwam was quadrilateral its roof was arched. The covering was of various kinds of bark, and also mats of woven basswood bark, and skins. The covering was held in place by a second series of poles tied through to the first; and on the inside horizontal poles were added for bracing. A hole was left in the top for a smoke outlet. The size on the ground was about 10' x 14' for the oblong, and 10' to 16' for the circular. The height was from 6' to 10'. The quadrilateral were much larger, being sometimes 50' long. Term may derive from *wikomik*, another Algonquin name for house, also from *wigiwam*, but this would appear rather to be contracted from something like *wikimatik*; *wiki*, home, and *matik*, tree or wood, and meaning a house of wood or logs, as distinguished from *wigiwam*, derived from *wigi (wigwas)*, birch bark, a house of birch bark. The derivation of *wigwam* is also given from *wek*, his house, or *wekowan*, their house.

Wilderness: In ornamental gardening of the formal sort, a part of the grounds less regular in treatment, and supposed to have some of the wilderness of nature.

Windbreak: An arrangement of vertical poles, bushes, boughs, bundled rushes, or of stones, in a semicircle or in a straight line, as a shelter from wind. Used by American Indians to protect tent entrances. The windbreak in winter is often extended entirely around the *tipi*.

X,Y,Z

Xenodocheum, Xenodocheion: In Classic architecture, a room or building devoted to the reception and accommodation of strangers or guests.

Xyst, Xystus: In Greek and Roman architecture, a long covered portico for exercise in bad weather. In Roman villas, a garden walk or avenue planted with trees.

Zaccab: An earth used in ancient and modern times by the natives of Yucatan as stucco, plaster, etc. It is mixed with lime in place of sand. The color is white, and it occurs abundantly in pockets. The cement used by the ancient Mayas is said to have been composed of one part slaked lime to two parts zaccab.

Zeta: A closed or small chamber; a room over a church porch where documents were kept.

Zigzag: Making short and sharp turns; in architecture said especially of the moldings in arched door heads and the like of Romanesque style.

Zoophoric column (or pillar): A pillar supporting the figure of a beast, usually symbolic, like that which carries the lion of S. Mark in the Piazzetta at Venice, and the similar one in the Piazza Signoria at Verona. Such columns were set up by the Venetian Republic in some, at least, of the cities subject to its rule.

Zoophoric: Carrying the figure of an animal.

Zoophorus, Zophorus: A representation of living things; in Classical archaeology, a frieze or other band or panel filled with human figures and animals; especially the cella frieze of the Parthenon.

Zwinger: In old German, a fortress or strong place in or adjoining a city; also an outer court or bailey; a popular term, from which, by extension, comes the modern name of several palaces, or parts of palaces, in German cities.

Aalto, Hugo Alvar Henrik:
1898-1976. One of the foremost contemporary architects, Aalto studied at the Technical University in Helsinki from 1916-1921. Originally a Neoclassic designer, in 1927 he evolved stylistically into international modern. In 1924 he married the architect Aino Marsio, who was to become his associate for the next 25 years until her death. Their most important collaboration came in 1935 with the establishment of the ARTEK furniture design company. Bent plywood furniture was invented by Aalto in 1932. Between 1922 and 1976, his exhibitions included Industrial Exhibition (Finland, 1922), 7th Centenary Exhibition (Finland, 1929), Forestry Pavilion (Finland, 1938) ARTEK Exhibition Pavilion (Sweden, 1945), and Finnish Pavilion (Venice, 1956). Aalto developed his own style, evident after World War II His originality derived in part from his use of roofs with a single-pitch, curvilinear walls, and the use of interior fittings as part of the overall design. His love of using brick and wood together is reflected in many of his buildings. Major works include the Library at Viipuri, Finland (1927), The Finnish Pavilion at the Paris Exposition (1935), the Experimental City (1941), the Senior Student's Dormitory at Massachusetts Institute of Technology (1947), and the Town Hall in Saynatsalo (1949). Later works include the Vogelweidplatz in Vienna (1953) and Helsinki's Cultural Center in (1955), Scandinavian Bank Building (1962), and the "Finlandia" conference center and concert hall (1970). Other major works are located in Imatra, Lapland; Jyvaskyla, Otaniemi, and Muuratsalo, Finland; Alborg, Denmark; New York City, New York; Lucerne, Switzerland; Mount Angel, Oregon; and Bologna, Italy. An accomplished writer as well, his works include *An Experimental Town* (1940); *Post-War Reconstruction* (1941); *Alvar Aalto: Synopsis* (1970); and *Alvar Aalto: Sketches* (1971). In 1952, after Anino Marsio's death in 1949, he married Elissa Maakiniemi. She was an architect also, and their collaborations produced many projects. After his death in 1976, she continued his work, completing projects which had been in the planning stages. [ARCHITECT]

Abadie, Paul, the Younger:
1821-1884. A son of Paul Abadie the Elder. In 1835 he entered the *Ecole des Beaux Arts* (Paris) under the direction of Achille Leclere. In 1848 he was made architect of the dioceses of Angouleme, Perigueux, and La Rochelle, and in 1861 *inspector general*

des edifices docesains. Abadie was interested in the restoration of many Medieval monuments, especially the Church of S. Front at Perigueux and the Cathedral of Angouleme. He built also the Hotel de Ville at Angouleme. In 1874 he replaced Viollet-le-Duc as architect of Notre Dame (Paris). He began the Church of the Sacre Coeur on Montmartre (Paris) but did not finish it. [ARCHITECT]

Abbondi, Antonio: (called lo Scarpagnino) d. 1549. Abbondi was chief architect of the Proveditori del Sale in Venice. On Oct. 13, 1505, he was appointed superintendent of the reconstruction of the Fondaco dei Tedeschi (Venice), from the model of Girolamo Tedesco, which was finished in 1508. In 1506, his name appears in the records of S. Sebastiano (Venice), of which church he is supposed to have been the supervising architect. After a Jan. 10, 1514, fire destroyed many buildings of the Rialto quarter in Venice, Alessandro Leopardi, Giovanni Celest, Fra Giovanni Giocondo, and other architects were called before the Doge and Signoria to make proposals for reconstruction. On July 18, 1514 four models were presented. Abbondi's design was selected Aug. 26, 1514. The work of reconstruction was finished about 1522. The buildings are called the Fabbriche Antiche to distinguish them from the Fabbrice Nuove, added later by Jacopo Sansovino. This reconstruction included the Church of S. Giovanni Elemosinario. In 1520 with Francesco Lurano he finished the Ponte della Pietra at Verona. On Oct. 6, 1527, Abbondi succeeded Santo Lombardo as *proto-maestro* of the Scuola di San Rocco. He built the upper story of the main facade, one of the finest in Venice. His name occurs in the accounts of the Doge's Palace, but not in a prominent way. [ARCHITECT]

Adam, James: d. 1794. James Adam was one of the four sons of William Adam, and appears to have ranked next to Robert Adam in reputation. It is not possible now to separate the work of the brothers. His name appears with that of Robert in the title of their *Works in Architecture.* [ARCHITECT]

Adam, William (I): d. 1748. William was the father John, William, Robert and James Adam. He designed many of residences in Scotland, the library and University of Glasgow, the town hall of Dundee, the royal infirmary, and orphan's hospital, of Edinburgh, etc. William Adam held the office of King's Mason at Edinburgh. [ARCHITECT]

Adam, William (II): d. 1822. One of the four sons of William (I) Adam. He outlived his brothers and concluded their undertakings. [ARCHITECT]

Adam Robert: 1727-1792. Robert Adam was the second son of William Adam and the most eminent of the four brothers Adam: John, Robert, James, and William. He was educated at Edinburgh University and visited Italy in 1754. He visited also Dalmatia and published the *Ruins of the Palace of the Emperor Diocletian at Spalatro in Dalmatia* (London, 1764). In association with his brothers he began in 1768 to build the Adelphi (London), a vast terrace constructed on arches that contain warehouses and support streets and houses. The brothers, especially Robert and James, seem to have originated the practice of grouping unimportant London houses into masses having the appearance of single imposing edifices. They were especially successful in designing the interior arrangement, decoration, and furniture of residences. They commenced the publication of their works in 1773. The second volume was completed in 1778. A posthumous third volume was added, and the whole published in 1822 with the title, *Works in Architecture of the late Robert and James Adam, Esqs., complete in three vols. with 125 plates engraved by Bartolozzi, Piranesi, etc.* Robert Adam was buried in Westminster Abbey. [ARCHITECT]

Alavoine, Jean Antoine: 1778-1834. Alavoine served with Napoleon's army in Italy. In 1804 he returned to France and entered the *Ecole d'Architecture*. He rebuilt the central spire of the Cathedral of Rouen after the original burned Sept. 15, 1822. Alavoine was charged with the construction of the Colonne de Juillet in the Place de la Bastille (Paris). After his death his design was modified by his successor Louis Joseph Duc. [ARCHITECT]

Alberti (Leone Battista degli): 1404-1472. Alberti assumed the literary name Leo (Leon) in Rome. He was born at Venice during the banishment of the Alberti, one of the most distinguished Florentine families. Although a natural son, his father Lorenzo educated him with extreme care. He possessed great strength and was devoted to horsemanship and athletic sports. He excelled in mathematics and mechanics and is said to have invented the *camera oscura*. The Alberti were restored to Florence in 1428, and became closely allied to the Medici family. Leone Battista was appointed to the office of *scrittore ed abbreviatore delle lettere apostoliche*, in which he served six popes (Martin V to Paul II). He lived in Rome and conducted his work in other cities by visits, correspondence (some of his letters still exist), and the assistance of competent persons. The documentary evidence about his buildings is meager. Vasari lists his works in Rome which have disappeared. He was doubtless associated with B. Gambarelli (Rosselino) in the attempted reconstruction of S. Peter's. The reconstruction of the Church of S. Francesco in Rimini (*il Tempio Malatestiano*) was begun on the inside at the chapels near the door by Matteo Pasti. Alberti appears to have been called in by Sigismondo Malatesta about 1447 to design the marble exterior and especially the facade, suggested by the arch of Augustus at Rimini. In May, 1459, Alberti followed the court of Pius II (Pope from 1458 to 1464) to Mantua, where he built for Lodovico Gonzaga the little Church of S. Sebastiano. The more important Church of S. Andrea in Mantua was begun in 1472, the year of his death. Its plan, undoubtedly by Alberti, shows an interesting treatment of intersecting barrel vaults, which seems to have been copied by Bramante in his design for S. Peter's. He probably continued for Gonzaga the choir

of the Church of the Nunziata in Florence, begun by Michelozzi. Alberti is supposed to have built in Florence for Giovanni Rucellai the Rucellai Palace about 1445-1451. A manuscript in the library at Florence, however, ascribes this building to B. Gambarelli (Rosselino), who probably acted as Alberti's associate. He built the Chapel of S. Pancrazio (before 1467) and the main front of the Church of S. Maria Novella (about 1470). Alberti's *De Re Aedificatoria Lib. X*, the first great book of the Renaissance on architecture, was begun in 1449 and published after his death in 1485. Alberti's *Della Pittura libri tre*, (1435) dedicated to Brunellesco, and *I Cinque Ordini Architettonnici* and *Della Statua* (after 1464) are published by Janitscheck in *Kleinere Kunsttheoretische Schriften* (Vienna, 1877). A complete edition of his works has been published (*Opere Volgari di Leon Battista Alberti*, 1845). [SCHOLAR AND ARCHITECT]

Albini, Franco: 1905 -1977 Albini studied in Milan at the Polytechnic University, where he later became a professor. His early work reflects the reductivist style, while later it moves to combine form and structure in the style of dogmatic rationalism. His display projects are extremely noteworthy in the history of architecture and include the Palazzo Bianco Museum in Genoa and the treasury of Genoa Cathedral. Other major projects involve the La Rinascente department store in Rome, The Villa Pestarini in Milan, the Museo del Palazzo Bianco in Genoa, and the municipal museum in Padua. [ARCHITECT]

Alessi, Galeazzo: 1512-1572. Probably a pupil of Giambattista Caporali, the translator and commentator of Vitruvius, Alessi went to Rome about 1536, where he appears to have been associated with Michelangelo. In 1542 Alessi went to Perugia and built the chapel and loggia of the Cittadella Paolina. Other buildings in Perugia are ascribed to him. His most important works are in Genoa, the earliest being the Church of S. Carignano, for which the contract was made Sept. 7, 1549. He enlarged the port and built the arsenal, which he adorned with a Doric portico. Alessi is best known by the street of palaces which he built in Genoa, the Strada Nuova (now Garibaldi), in which are his palazzi Cambiaso, Gambaro, Parodi (begun 1507), Spinola (1560), Giorgio Doria, Adorno, Serra, and Rosso. He built the Palazzo Grimaldi near the Church of S. Luca, another Palazzo Grimaldi in the Borgo S. Vincenzo, the two Palazzi Lomellini, and many villas near Genoa. The cu-

pola and choir (1567) of the Cathedral of Genoa and the Loggia de' Banchi are by him. In Milan Alessi built the Palazzo Marini, now the Municipal Palace, the facade of the Church of S. Maria presso S. Celso, the hall of the Auditorio del Cambio and the Church of S. Vittore di Capo. Like the San Gallo, Scamozzi, and other architects of the time, Alessi enjoyed a large practice in Italy and designed many buildings in France, Portugal, and Flanders. The architecture of Flanders, which was then in close commercial relation with Genoa, was much influenced by him. [ARCHITECT]

Ammanati, Bartolommeo: 1511-1592. He began as a pupil of the sculptor Bandinelli, but afterward went to Jacopo Sansovino in Venice whom he assisted with Cattanco, Alessandro Vittoria, and others at the Library of S. Mark. Returning to Florence, he formed his style on the Medici tombs by Michelangelo. Ammanati went to Rome during the reign of Paul III (Pope 1534-1549) and assisted Vignola and Vasari at the Villa di Papa Giulio. Returning to Florence in 1557 and the service of the Duke Cosmo I de' Medici, Bartolommeo made the fountains of Pratolino and Castello and the beautiful bridge of S. Trinita (Florence,

1567-70). In 1559 he won the commission of the fountain of Neptune in the Piazza della Signoria, Florence, in competition with Benvento Cellini, Gian Bologne, Vincenzo Danti, and Il Moschino. He built the garden facade of the Pitti Palace, the second cloister of S. Spirito, and the Palazzi Guigni and Ramirez di Montalvo in Florence. Ammanati began the immense Ducal Palace at Lucca, Italy, which was continued by Pini and Juvara. The Palazzo Micheletti in Lucca is also attributed to him. [SCULPTOR AND ARCHITECT]

Ammonios: Supposed to have restored the celebrated Pharos (lighthouse) of Alexandria (Egypt), probably during the reign of the Emperor Anastasios. [ARCHITECT]

Andrea da Pisa (Andrea Pisano): 1270-1349. He received his training in Pisa, Italy, probably from Giovanni da Pisa. Before going to Florence, Andrea worked in Venice, where he is supposed to have assisted in the decoration of the Church of S. Marco and the Doge's Palace. The only work that can with certainty be ascribed to him is the first bronze door that was made for the Florentine Baptistery between 1330 and 1336. At the death of Giotto in 1337, Andrea was appointed architect of the Campanile and built the two stories of

niches above the work of Giotto. From 1347 to 1349 he was chief architect of the Cathedral of Orvieto. The beautiful reliefs of the Genesis on the facade of that building are supposed to show his influence. [SCULPTOR AND ARCHITECT]

Androuet (alled du Cerceau) Baptiste: ca. 1544-ca. 1602. Baptiste is supposed to have been the son, probably the oldest, of Jacques (I.) Adrouet du Cerceau. A document of 1577 mentions him as *"architecte a Charieval,"* where it is supposed that his father was then at work. After the death of Pierre Lescot in 1578, Baptiste succeeded him in the superintendence of the royal buildings in Paris, especially the Louvre. He probably continued the work on the southern side of the great quadrangle. In May, 1578, *"un jeun e du Cerceau architecte du Boi,"* probably Baptiste, began the construction of the Pont Neuf (Paris). In 1582, Baptiste succeeded Jean Bullant as architect of the Chapel of the Valois at Saint Denis, near Paris. For the King of Navarre, afterward Henri IV, he fortified the towns of Melun and Pontoise (France). [ARCHITECT]

Androuet (du Cerceau), Jacques (II): d. 1614. A son of Jacques (I) Androuet du Cerceau. Jacques (II) first appears in the accounts of Francois d'

Alencon in 1577 as an attache of that Duke. In March, 1595, he was charged with the superintendence of the construction of the Louvre and the other royal palaces. It has been assumed that he designed and constructed the Louvre's Pavillon de Flore (remodeled under Napoleon III), that portion of the long gallery that lies between Pavillon Lesdiguiere and the Pavillon de Flore, and that portion of the Tuileries that stood between the Pavillon de Flore and the pavilion built by Jean Bullant. There is no proof of this. The work may have been done by Etienne de Perac. [ARCHITECT]

Androuet (Endrouet) (du Cerceau) Jacques (I): ca.1510-ca.1584. Founder and chief of an important family of French architects. The surname du Cerceau came from the *cerceau* or circle that served as a sign over the door of his atelier. It became inseparable from his name and was afterward used as a title, his descendants being called Sieurs du Cerceau. Although a leader in the propaganda of the Italian Renaissance in France, the only evidence that he studied in Italy is in the character of his works, and especially of certain drawings ascribed to him in the royal library of Munich. The only building that can be attributed to him with certainty is the choir of the little Church of Montargis, France. He is supposed to have built parts of the Chateaux of Montargis, Verneuil, and Charleval, all destroyed. He is known only by his books on architectural subjects and his splendid engravings. The large number of drawings and engravings attributed to him have been catalogued by Von Geymuller. His principal books are *Recueil de Vingtcing Arcs de Triomphe*, (Orleans, (1549); *Liber de eo picturae genere quod grottesche vocant Itali*, (Orleans, 1550), dedicated to Renee de France; reprinted by Wechel in 1566, with the title *Livre de Grotesques; Livre d'architecture de Jacques Androuet du Cerceau contenant les plans et dessaigns de cinquante Bastimens tous differens, etc.*, (Paris, Benoist Prevost, 1559), dedicated to the King; *Lecons de perspective positive*, (Paris, Mamert-Pattison, 1576), dedicated to Catherine de' Medici; *Le premier volume des plus excellens Bastimens de France*, Paris, Gilles Beys, 1579), also dedicated to Catherine de' Medici; and *Livre des edifices antiques Romains*, (1584), dedicated to the Duke of Nemours. (The two volumes dedicated to Catherine de Medici compose the most important of Jacques Androuet's works. Because many of the buildings represented in them have been destroyed or mutilated, their historical interest is very great). [ARCHITECT AND ENGRAVER]

Antimachides: Associated with Antistates and others in the commencement of the temple of Zeus at Athens under Peisistratos. [ARCHITECT]

Antiphilos: Antiphilos is mentioned by Pausanias as one of the architects of the Treasury of the Carthaginians at Olympia, the others being Pothaeus and Megacles. This was probably the fourth from the west in the series of treasuries discovered on the northern side of the Altis at Olympia (Greece). It was built by the Syracusans and was popularly called Carthaginian because of the spoils from the Carthaginians which it continued. [ARCHITECT]

Antistates: The architects Antistates, Kallaeschros, Antimachides, and Porinos laid the foundation of the temple of Olympian Zeus at Athens during the reign at Peisistratos. According to Aristotle, the work was interrupted by the banishment of Hippias, the son of Peisistratos in 510 B.C. [ARCHITECT]

Architect's Co-Partnership: (Estab. 1939) This consortium was founded in 1939 by 11 English architects. Though not all of the original group remained with it, the initial purposes for which the group was formed re-

main viable today. ACP prefers to be known as an anonymous association of architects dedicated to designing architecture which not only fills a need socially but also provides enjoyment aesthetically. Some of the major projects that have demonstrated the group's purpose are, the new rubber factory at Brynmawr in South Wales; a school at Ripley, Derbyshire, England; and the biochemistry building at Imperial College in London. [ARCHITECT]

Argelios: A writer on architecture mentioned by Vitruvius. He quotes him on the Doric and Corinthian order, and on an Ionic temple of Aesculapius at Tralles, of which he seems to have been the architect (Vitruvius,). He flourished probably about 376 B.C. [ARCHITECT]

Arnolfo di Cambio (di Lapo Vasari): ca. 1232-ca. 1303. Arnolfo was not the son of Lapo, as supposed by Vasari. In a document of 1266 they are mentioned as associated in the atelier of Niccolo da Pisa at Siena . In the *provisione* of 1300 (Florentine Cathedral) he is mentioned as *Magister Arnolfus de Colle, filius olim Cambii, Capud Magister laborarii et operis*. In 1295 he began the Church of S. Croce (Florence). Vasari credits him with the marble facing of the Baptistery (Florence.) In 1294 the citizens of

Florence decided to rebuild the Cathedral Church of S. Reparata built in 407. The work was begun by Arnolfo in 1296 at the western end. His name appears in an inscription on the wall opposite the campanile, *ISTVD AB AR-NOLFO TEMPLVM FVIT EDIFICATVM.* He probably had charge of the building for six or seven years and built a part of the outer wall of the nave. His plan was much changed and enlarged by later architects. The name Santa Reparata was afterward changed to the present Santa Maria del Fiore. The construction of the Palazzo Vecchio (Florence) is attributed to Arnolfo by Vasari without corroboration. The fine monument of the Cardinal de la Braye in the Church of S. Domenico at Orvieto with its mosaics and sculpture is by Arnolfo. [ARCHITECT AND SCULPTOR]

Artaude (Artaudus), Guillaume: With the title *operarias* he began the construction of the great bridge called the Pont Saint Esprit over the river Rhone (France) in 1265. Associated with him were Clarius Tharanus, Jascobus Bengarius, and Pons de Gainaco. This great bridge, begun in 1265 and completed in 1309, is 5.40 meters wide, and 840 meters long, and has 26 arches. [ARCHITECT AND ENGINEER]

Artorius Primus: The inscription found upon the greater theater at Pompeii, *M. ARTORIVS, M. L. PRIMVS AR-CHITEVS,* undoubtedly refers to the architect who restored the theater after the earthquake of 63 A.D. His name is found also on the basilica at Pompeii, which he probably restored at the same time. [ARCHITECT]

Arup, Sir Ove: b. 1895. Although he studied philosophy and mathematics first, Arup found his niche in civil engineering. Although he was not an architect, the firm that he established in 1949 has grown from an original 45 employees to more than 1,600, located in the United Kingdom and more than 1,000 more in other offices around the globe. The firm underwent many changes from its inception. Arup collaborated with many of the fine architects of his time. He produced or collaborated on such projects as the Penguin Pool at the London Zoo, Pompidou Center in Paris, and the Sydney Opera House. [ARCHITECT]

Asam, Cosmas Damian: 1686-1742. The brothers, Cosmas Damian Asam and Aegid Quirin Asam, were sons of the painter Hans Georg Asam, who decorated the Church of Benedikt Beuren, Germany, in 1693. They were trained in Rome at the time when the reputation of Andrea Pozzo was at its height and were contemporaries of the elder Tiepolo. Cosmas decorated (about 1724), the stairway and Chapel of the Palace of Schleissheim near Munich. He does not appear to have been much employed at the Residenz in Munich, which was then in process of construction under Francois Cuvillies. The most important work of the brothers Asam is the Johanneskirche in Munich (1733-1746), which is undoubtedly the finest specimen of the Baroque style in Germany. [PAINTER AND ARCHITECT]

Atwood, Charles B.: b. 1849. Atwood was educated at the Lawrence Scientific School of Harvard University. He worked for several years in the office of Ware and Van Brunt (Boston) and in 1872 began his own business. In 1875 he took charge of the architectural work of the firm of Herter Brothers in New York City and in that capacity designed much of the detail of W. H. Vanderbilt's house on Fifth Avenue. Atwood was chosen designer in chief to the World's Fair in Chicago and designed the Peristyle and Art Building for that exposition. [ARCHITECT]

Aubriot, Hugues: *Prevot de Paris.* Before 1369 he completed the second wall of the city of Paris (*l'enceinte de*

Charles V) begun by his predecessor Etienne Marcel. He laid the first stone of the historic Bastille (Paris) April 22, 1370. The building was finished in about four years. This work brought upon him the animosity of the people. He was condemned by the Bishop of Paris and himself imprisoned in the Bastille, March 1, 1382. He escaped to Dijon, where he died soon after. [ARCHITECT]

Baglioni, Baccio (Bartolomeo) d' Agnolo: 1462-1543. The Baglioni conducted a *botega* in Florence where many kinds of decorative work were done. The organ of the Church of S. Maria Novella (Florence), one of Baccio's earliest known productions, has been removed. The lower part, or cantoria, is at the South Kensington Museum, London, the upper part in the Church of Rueil, near Paris. After 1495 he assisted Il Cronaca and later Antonio da San Gallo in the construction of the great hall of the Palazzo Vecchio, Florence. He built the Palazzo Bartolini (begun about 1520). Ascribed to him, also, are the villas Bartolini and Borgherini and the Palazzi Ginori, Taddei, and Borgherini. In 1498 he became *capomaestro* of the Palazzo Vecchio. He made a model of the facade of S. Lorenzo from the drawings of Michelangelo. In 1506-1515 he built a section of the cornice gallery of the dome of the Florentine Cathedral and in 1516, with Antonio da San Gallo, began the loggia opposite Brunellesco's Spedale degli Innocenti. [ARCHITECT, SCULPTOR, AND WOODWORKER]

Baglioni, Giuliano di Baccio d' Agnolo: 1491-1555. The four sons of Baccio d' Agnolo continued his work. Of these, the two oldest, Giuliano and Domenico, attained eminence as architects. Vasari employed Giuliano to execute work from his designs and attributes many buildings to him. For Baldasare Turini he built the Capella Turini in the Cathedral of Pescia (1540), which was intended to contain a picture by Raphael. He also built the Casetta Campana at Montughi, near Florence, and the Palazzo Grifoni at San Miniato al Tedesco (between Florence and Pisa). [ARCHITECT, SCULPTOR, AND WOODWORKER]

Bahr, Georg: 1666-1738. Of his early life nothing is known. It is not probable that he visited France or Italy. Bahr held the office of *Rathsbaumeister* in Dresden (Saxony), and devoted his life to the development of the architecture of Protestant churches. His most important building is the monumental Frauenkirche in Dresden, built between 1726 and 1740, one of the most notable domical buildings of the time. [ARCHITECT]

Baker, Sir Herbert: 1862-1946 Baker moved to Johannesburg, South Africa and virtually changed the course of South Africa's architecture by designing buildings that preserved the traditional heritage of England, Italy, and France. In addition, his buildings extended the arts and crafts movement. Many of the homes in the Dutch Cape were rundown. Through Baker's efforts, groups of citizens became interested in and active in the restoration of these dwellings. After Baker left the Cape in 1902 for Transvaal, he discovered quite different conditions there. There were no quaint buildings to restore; rather there were mud or stone huts. As Baker's practice grew, so did the number of buildings built in the traditional forms, using readily available local materials. Major works attributed to Baker are the Government House and Union Buildings in Pretoria, the Secretariat and Legislative Buildings in New Delhi, the Bank of England and India House in London, and the War Memorial Cloister at Winchester College in England. [ARCHITECT]

Ballu, Theodore: 1817-1885. Ballu was a pupil of Louis Hippolyte Lebas at the *Ecole des Beaux Arts* from 1834 to 1840. In 1840 he won the *Grand Prix de Rome*. His *envoi de Rome* was a remarkable restoration of the Erectheum at Athens. Returning to Paris, he was employed on many important works, notably the completion of the Church of S. Clotilde, the restoration of the *Tour de S. Jacques de la Boucherie* (1854-1858), and the restoration of the Church of S. Germain l'Auxerrois (1858-1863). In 1860 he was made architect in chief of the fourth section of the public works of the city of Paris (religious edifices). Between 1861 and 1867 he built the Church of the Trinite with its presbytery. From 1871 to 1876 he was inspector general of the public works of the city of Paris. In 1874, with de Perthes, Ballu won the first prize in the competition for the new Hotel de Ville (Paris), which they constructed. [ARCHITECT]

Baltard, Louis Pierre: 1764-1846. Baltard was a pupil of A. F. Peyre and Pique. Between 1788 and 1791 he studied in Rome. In 1792 he was made architect and designer of decorations at the Opera (Paris). In 1793 he served as engineer with the army in Calvados (France). In 1796 he was appointed professor of architecture at the *Ecole Polytechnique* and was employed as engraver on the great work undertaken to illustrate Napoleon's Egyptian expedition. Baltard was architect of the Pantheon under the Empire and between 1815 and 1818 served as supervising architect of the prisons and markets of Paris. In 1818 he was made professor at the *Ecole des Beaux Arts*, and from 1837 until his death was inspector general of the public works of the city of Paris. At Lyons (Rhone, France) Baltard built the Prison of the Quartier Perache (1830), the Arsenal for Artillery (1840-1846), and other buildings of importance. He exhibited paintings in the salons of 1810, and 1812, and 1814. He published *La Colonne de la place Vendome* (1810), *Recueil des Monuments antiques* (1801), *Grands Prix d' Architecture* (with Vaudoyer, 1818-1834). [ARCHITECT, PAINTER AND ENGRAVER]

Baltard, Victor: 1805-1874. A son of Louis Pierre Baltard. He was educated at the *Lycee Henri IV* and studied architecture and painting with his father and at the *Ecole des Beaux Arts*, Paris. In 1833 he won the *Grand Prix de Rome*. In 1850 he was associated with Lassus and Viollet-le-Duc in the preservation of diocesan buildings. Between 1852 and 1859, with F. E. Callet, he designed and built the great market (*Halles Centrales*) of the city of Paris. In 1853 he was made architect of the Hotel de Ville, Paris. With Max Vauthier he designed and built the famous stairway of the Couer d'Honneur of this building, afterward destroyed (1871). March 30, 1860, Baltard was made architect in chief of the city of Paris. Between 1850 and 1871 he built the Church of S. Augustine. In 1847 he published his monograph *Villa Medicis a Rome* and in 1863, with F. E. Callet, the *Monographie des halles centralles de Paris* (2d ed., 1873). [ARCHITECT]

Barozzio, Giacomo (Vignola): 1507-1573. Giacomo was the oldest son of one Clemente Barozzio of Milan, who, forced to leave that city by political disturbances, settled at the village of Vignola near Modena, Italy. He went to Bologna to study painting and later turned his attention to architecture. About 1535 he went to Rome. Vignola was commissioned by Primaticcio, who visited Rome in 1539-1540, to superintend the casting of antique statues for Francois I of France. A visit to France about this time did not produce any important results. Returning to Rome, he was charged by the Vitruvian Academy, which was founded in 1542 by Marcellus Cervinus (afterward Pope for 21 days as Marcellus II), Bernardino Maffei (afterward cardinal), Alessandro Manzuola, and others, including probably Michelangelo, with the investigation and measurement of the Roman monuments.

He was about this time much occupied with important works at Bologna. Gaye publishes a long letter from Vignola to the officials of the Church of S. Petronio at Bologna defending his design for the facade of that church. (The facade was never built.) He made the canal at Bologna at this time, and designed the fine Palazzo Isolani at Minerbio (now destroyed). The famous Portico dei Banchi at Bologna was built by him later, in the pontificate of Pius IV (Pope 1559-1565). Vignola was made chief architect of Julius III (Pope 1550-1555) and directed the reconstruction of the Aqua Virgo aqueduct at Rome (built 48 B.C.). He also built at the Villa di Papa Giulio at Rome the larger casino with the semicircular colonnade. For Alessandro Farnese, second cardinal of that name, he built the great pentagonal palace of Caprarola, seven miles southeast of Viterbo, Italy (begun 1547, finished 1559), the famous del Gesu Church at Rome and laid out the Farnese gardens on the Palatine Hill. The fine gateway that he built for these gardens was removed for the recent excavations in the Forum. For Ottavio Farnese (1520-1585) Vignola planned the Ducal Palace of Piacenza, now nearly destroyed. He is supposed to have been employed by Michelangelo Buonarroti, and some of the characteristics of that artist's work as architect are ascribed to Vignola. He built the Porta del Popolo in Rome. In 1564 he succeeded Michelangelo as architect of S. Peter's. He wrote two books: the *Regola delli cinque ordini d'architettura* (1563), and *Le due Regola della Porspettiva Pratica*, published by Ignatio Danti after his death in 1583. Vignola had a large professional practice. A partial list of his buildings is published in the *Architectural Publication Society's Dictionary*. The *Oeuvres complets de Vignole*, ed. Lebas and Debret, was published in Paris in 1815. [ARCHITECT]

Barry, Sir Charles, R. A.: 1795-1860. Barry was articled to Middleton and Bailey, surveyors, at Lambeth, London. He exhibited his first drawing, a "View of the Interior of Westminster Hall," at the Academy in 1812. In 1817 he visited Italy and in 1818, Greece, Palestine, and Egypt. Barry built the Sussex County Hospital and the Manchester Royal Institution. In 1832 he completed the Travellers' Club in London, one of his most successful buildings. S. Stephen's Chapel (Westminster, London), which had been used for the sittings of the Houses of Parliament, was destroyed by fire Oct. 16, 1834. July 17, 1835, a royal commission was appointed to select a site and designs

for a new building. Barry entered the competition. His designs were accepted Feb. 29, 1836. He laid the first stone of the new building of the Houses of Parliament April 27, 1840. That portion which was intended for the House of Lords was completed in time for the session of 1847, and the House of Commons for the session of 1852. In 1837 Barry won the competition for the building of the Reform Club, London. In 1840 he made additions to University College, Oxford. Barry was elected associate of the Royal Academy in 1840, a Royal Academician in 1844, and knighted in 1852. He was a Fellow of the Royal Society, a member of the Royal Institute of British Architects, and won the gold medal of the Institute in 1850. He published *Illustrations of the new Palace of Westminster*, one vol. fol., London, 1849, and *The Travellers' Club House*, 1839. [ARCHITECT]

Basevi, George: Basevi entered the office of Sir John Soane in 1810. In 1818 he went to Italy for three years. In 1825 he designed Belgrave Square, London, and in 1835 the Fitzwilliam Museum, Cambridge. With Sidney Smirke he built the Conservative Club in Pall Mall, London. Basevi was killed by a fall from a scaffold while inspecting the tower of Ely Cathedral. [ARCHITECT]

194

Bayeux, Jean De (I): d. 1398. On May 29, 1388, he succeeded Jean des Perriers (Sesperriers, or Perier) as *maitre macon* of the Cathedral of Rouen, France, and Aug. 5, 1389, became *maistre des oeuvres de maconnerie* of the city of Rouen. In 1390 he made plans for the reconstruction of the Beffroi at Rouen. He built a large part of the city wall, including the tower called Guillaume-Lion, and the Porte Martainville, for which he made the plans in 1394. [ARCHITECT]

Beauchamp, Richard: d. 1481. Beauchamp, Bishop of Hereford, and afterward of Salisbury, England, was made master and supervisor of the works of S. George's Chapel, Windsor. The designs for this building were probably made by him, or under his direction. After his death, Sir Reginald Bray succeeded to this office. Beauchamp built the great hall of his episcopal palace and a handsome chapel at Salisbury Cathedral to contain his monument. [BISHOP AND ARCHITECT]

Beazley, Samuel: 1786-1851. Samuel Beazley was a nephew of Charles Beazley, also an architect of note. In 1816 he rebuilt the Royal Lyceum Theater, London, in 1822. This building was destroyed by fire, and again rebuilt by him in 1831-1838. He remodelled Drury Lane Theater, London, in 1822 and added the portico in 1831. Before Aug. 14, 1820, he rebuilt the Theater Royal, Birmingham, retaining the facade designed by George Saunders in 1780. Beazley designed the Theater Royal, Dublin, in 1821, the facade of the Adelphi Theater, London, in 1841, the Soho Theater, London, in 1834, the S. James Theater, London, in 1836-1837, a theater in Brazil, and another in Belgium. He made additions to the University of Bonn, Germany. He was a successful dramatist and author. [ARCHITECT AND DRAMATIST]

Becquet, Robert: d. 1554. The old wooden spire of the Cathedral of Rouen was burned in 1514. A new one was begun soon after by Martin Desperroys, *maitre charpentier* of the Cathedral. The work was long delayed, and at the death of Desperroys was assumed by his assistant, Robert Becquet. He was directed to present a new plan. The spire was completed in 1544. This splendid spire of wood upon a stone base was destroyed by lightning Sept. 15, 1822. It has been replaced by an iron structure designed by J. A. Alavoine. Becquet executed the carpentry of the choir of the Cathedral. He was a poet of ability, and in 1545 won the prize of the "Rose" on the *Concours des Palinods*. [ARCHITECT]

Benedetto da Maiano: 1442-1497. A younger brother of Giuliano da Maiano and, according to Perkins, a pupil of Luca della Robbia in sculpture. Benedetto was associated with Giuliano in their *botega* (atelier) in Florence, and the architectural portion of the works attributed to him probably belongs to Giuliano. He made the altar of S. Savino in the Cathedral of Faenza about 1471 (Bode). Before 1481 he made the marble doorway at the Palazzo Vecchio, Florence. His sculpture at Loreto, including the fountain of the sanctuary, dates from 1484-1487 (Gianuizzi). For Pietro Mellini he made the fine pulpit in the Church of S. Croce, Florence. About 1488 he appears to have visited the court of Matthias Corvinus, King of Hungary. Benedetto's reputation as an architect rests mainly upon the assertion of Vasari that he designed and built the first story of the Palazzo Strozzi in Florence (begun 1489). The documents indicate, however, that Giuliano da Sangallo was the designer of the building. The extremely delicate portico of the Church of the Madonna delle Grazie at Arezzo is ascribed to Benedetto by Vasari. About 1490 he made the bust of Antonio Squarcialupi in the Florentine Cathedral. After the death of Giuliano da Maiano in 1490, Benedetto entered the service of Alfonso, Duke of Calabria, afterwards King Alfonso II, for whom he made, in the Church of Mont Olivetto, Naples, a retable with a bas-relief of the Annunciation and other works. The black marble monument of Filippo Strozzi in the Church of S. Maria Novella, Florence, was made by him about 1493. Probably after this date, he made at San Gimignano, near Florence, the altar of S. Bartolo at the Church of S. Agostino. [SCULPTOR AND ARCHITECT]

Benedikt (Benesch): Benesch, an architect of Laun, Bohemia, built for Wladislaw II, King of Bohemia (d. 1516), the *Residenz on the Hradschin* in Prague. One wing of this palace with the great vaulted hall, Kronungssaal, his most important work, is still in existence. He built also the Church of S. Barbara at Kuttenberg near Laun. Benesch was essentially a constructor, building on Gothic lines. In the decoration of his buildings, Renaissance details appear. [ARCHITECT]

Benezet (Benoit), Saint: According to the *Chronicle of Frere Robert d'Auxerre*, Benoit came to Avignon in 1177, *le disant envoye de Dieu pour construire un pont sur le Rhone.* He collected the necessary money as alms in various parts of France and built the bridge of Avignon on the model of the Pont du Gard, built by Hadrian in the second century A.D. near Nimes, France. Of his structure only the chapel, in which he is buried, and portions of the piers remain. The rest has been rebuilt at different periods. He founded the order of *freres pontifs* who built many Medieval bridges in France. [ARCHITECT AND ENGINEER]

Benjamin, Asher: He published *Town and Country Builder's Assistant* (1797), *The Practical House Carpenter* (4th ed., 1835) and *Elements of Architecture*, books much used by early American architects. He built numerous residences in western Massachusetts. [ARCHITECT]

Bere, Richard: Bere was installed as Abbot of Glastonbury, Somerset, England, in 1493. He built King Edgar's Chapel at the eastern end of the church of that abbey, which was finished by Abbot Whiting. Bere strengthened with arches both sides of the east end of the abbey, which was beginning to "cast out." In 1503 he was sent on an embassy to Rome, and on his return built a chapel to Our Lady of Loretto on the north side of the abbey church. He built also the Chapel of the Sepulchre in the south aisle, in which he was buried. His initials and cognizance, a cross between two beer mugs, may be seen in S. Benedict's Church in Glastonbury. [ABBOT AND ARCHITECT]

Bernard da Venezia: He is described as *tagliatore e magistro a lignamine* and was the favorite architect of Gian Galeazzo Sforza (d. 1402), Duke of Milan. Bernardo was the first architect of the Certosa at Pavia, his name appearing in a document dated a month before the first stone of that building was laid (Aug. 27, 1396). He was frequently consulted during the construction of the Cathedral of Milan (begun at the close of 1396). He built the castle of Pavia and the Church of the Madonna del Carmine in Milan (1400). [ARCHITECT AND SCULPTOR]

Bernardo Di Lorenzo, of Florence: An important architect who appears frequently in the accounts of the buildings of Nicholas V (Pope 1447-1455) and Pius II (Pope 1458-1464) in Rome. He was admitted to the guild of stonecutters in 1447 and first appears in the pontifical records of Nicholas V, Dec. 31, 1451. He is easily confounded with Bernardo Rossellino, as they both appear under the same name, *Bernardus Fiorentinus*. [ARCHITECT]

Bernini, Giovanni Lorenzo: 1598-1680. Bernini was the son of a Tuscan sculptor, working in Naples. His talent developed early. While still a youth, he made the beautiful group, "Apollo and Daphne" at the Villa Borghese, Rome, and the "Rape of Proserpina" at the Villa Ludovisi. In the reign of Urban VIII (Pope 1623-1644) he made his earliest important work of architecture, the Baldachino of S. Peter's in Rome. After the death of Carlo Maderna in 1629, Bernini succeeded him as architect of S. Peter's. He continued the construction of the Palazzo Barberini, Rome, begun by Maderna. The facade and the staircase are ascribed to him. In 1642 he began the monument of Urban VIII at S. Peter's. During the reign of Innocent X (Pope 1644-1655), Bernini appears to have suffered from the intrigues of his pupil Boromini, who superseded him as architect of S. Peter's. At this time he built the Capella Cornaro at the Church of S. Maria della Vittoria, Rome, and the fountains of the Piazza Navona, of the Piazza Barberini, and the Piazza di Spagna, Rome. Bernini's most appreciative patron was Alexander VII (Pope 1655-1667), who made him *architetto alla camera apostolica*, a position which he held for the rest of his life. For him he built his most famous work, the great colonnade of the Piazza of S. Peter's, Rome, and the Scala Regia at the Vatican. Bernini built the Palazzo Ludovisi and many other public and private buildings in Rome. He was requested by Colbert to make designs for the completion of the Louvre, and by let-

ter of Louis XIV, dated April 11, 1665, was invited to Paris. Bernini was treated like a prince in France, but, his design for the Louvre being inferior to that of Claude Perrault, it was not executed, he returned to Rome in the autumn. He made the monument of Pope Alexander VII in S. Peter's. [SCULPTOR AND ARCHITECT]

Berretini, Pietro (Pietro da Cortona): 1596-1669. He is best known by his work as a decorator, which is to be found in Rome, Florence, and many other Italian cities. To him is largely due the fully developed style of the late Renaissance. His most important works are the decoration of the great hall of the Palazzo Barberini, Rome, and of the galleries of the Pitti Palace, Florence. He also decorated the Church of S. Carlo al Corso, all in Rome. Examples of his purely architectural work are the Church of SS. Luca e Martina in Rome, and the beautiful facade of the Church of S. Maria della Pace, Rome, before 1659. The facade of S. Maria in Via Lata, Rome, was built from his designs about 1680. Many of his drawings are in the Uffizi. [PAINTER, DECORATOR, AND ARCHITECT]

Biard (Biart), Nicolas (Colin): b. 1460. Biard is said to have directed the construction of the Chateau of Amboise, France, after March 3, 1499.

In association with Jean de Doyalc, Didier de Felin, and Andre de Saint Martin, he worked on the Pont Notre Dame, Paris, begun March 28, 1499. Soon after this he was charged by Louis XII with the erection of that part of the Chateau of Blois which was built during his reign. While occupied with this building he was invited, in 1504, by the Cardinal Georges d'Amboise, the minister of Louis XII, to inspect the works at the Chateau of Gaillon near Rouen. He visited Gaillon in 1505 and 1506, and seems to have been a general inspector, or supervisor, of the construction there. On Dec. 14, 1506, he was called to Rouen to advise concerning the completion of the Tour de Beurre at the Cathedral. On Dec. 4, 1507, he was consulted concerning the dangerous condition of the tower of the Cathedral of Bourges which fell Dec. 31. He began the reconstruction of this tower Oct. 19, 1508. [ARCHITECT AND BUILDER]

Bindesboll, Michael Gottlieb:
1800-1856. A Danish architect. In 1822-1823 Bindesboll studied in Germany and France. Having won the travelling stipend at the Academy of Copenhagen, he went in 1835 to Italy and Greece. In August, 1835, he presented his design for the projected Thorwaldsen Museum at Copenhag-

en, which was finished in 1847. In March, 1856, he was made professor at the Academy in Copenhagen. [ARCHITECT]

Bischoff, Peter (Von Angelsheim):
On April 25, 1473, Peter attended the reunion of architects and builders at Regensburg, Bavaria, Germany, of which Jost Dotzinger was the leading spirit. He appears as architect of the Cathedral and city of Strasbourg in a document dated May 1, 1473, which bears his name and seal. His work included the supervision of the streets, pavements, bridges, and all public works of the city. [ARCHITECT]

Blondel, Francois: 1617 or 1618-1686. In 1652 Blondel was appointed tutor of the son of Henri Auguste de Lomenie, Secretary of State to Louis XIV and travelled with him in Germany and Italy. He was afterward employed in several negotiations with foreign governments, notably at Constantinople. On his return he received a brevet as counsellor of state. He was also made tutor of the dauphin and professor of mathematics at the *College Royale.* His knowledge of architecture was acquired during his travels. Blondel's first practical work was the reconstruction of the bridge at Saintes (Charente Inferieure, France). In

1670 he built the triumphal arch of the Porte S. Bernard, Paris, which was destroyed in the Revolution. In 1673 he rebuilt the arch of Porte S. Antoine, Paris. Blondel's greatest monument is the triumphal arch in Paris called the Porte S. Denis, which was begun in 1674. The sculpture was begun by Girardon, and finished by Michel Anguier. In 1672 he was made director of the *Academie de l'Architecture*, established in 1671. On account of his knowledge of fortifications he was made *marechal-de-camp* in 1675. His published works are *Cours d'Architecture enseigne dans l'Academie Royale* (Paris, 2 vols., 1675-1683); *Cours de Mathematique pour le Dauphin* (1683); *L'art de jeter les bombes et nouvelle maniere de fortifier les places; Une Histoire du Calendrier Roman* (1682) [ARCHITECT]

Blondel, Jacques Francois:
1705-1774. He is supposed to have been the son of Jean Francois Blondel. On May 6, 1743, with the approval of the *Academie de l'Architecture,* he opened one of the earliest of the French private schools of architecture. The success of this school won for him the position of *architecte du roi* and, in 1756, a membership in the *Academie de l'Architecture.* In 1762 he was made professor at the Louvre. In 1773 he presented a plan for the improvement of the city of Metz. In 1768 he planned the Hotel de Ville and Salle de Spectacle at Strasbourg,. He planned the reconstruction of the abbey of S. Armand near Valenciennes, Nord, France, and the restoration of the Cathedral of Chalons-sur-Marne. In 1765 he was a member of the commission charged with the conservation of the Cathedral of Strasbourg. Blondel was an accomplished engraver. He completed the *Architecture Francaise* begun by Jean Marot and published, 1737-1738, *De la distribution des maisons de plaisance et de la decoration des edifices en general*, and after 1771 the *Cours d'Architecture* (Paris, 1771-1777), which was continued after his death by Pierre Patte. [ARCHITECT]

Boffrand, Germain: 1667-1754. The son of Germain Boffrand and architect and sculptor of Nantes, France. He went to Paris quite early and studied architecture, probably under Jules Hardouin-Mansart. In 1690 he was made custodian of the drawings in the *cabinet du roi*. In 1706 he assisted in the decoration of the Hotel Soubise, Paris. In 1708 he was admitted to the *Academie de l'Architecture*. Between 1715 and 1718 Boffrand rebuilt a great part of the arsenal, Paris, where he decorated a *salon.* Between 1725 and 1727 he repaired the southern portal of the Church of Notre Dame, Paris, with the rose window. On Nov. 29, 1711, he was made chief architect for the Duke of Lorraine at Nancy, where he built the great altar of the Cathedral and the Hotel de la Monnaie. He was architect of the Duke of Bavaria, for whom he erected a hunting lodge, and worked also on the episcopal palace at Wurzburg, Germany. In France, Boffrand held the position of *architecte du roi* and *premier ingenieur et inspecteur general des ponts et chaussees du royaume.* In 1745 he published the *Livre d'Architecture contenant les principes generaux de cet art, ect.* [ARCHITECT AND DECORATOR]

Bologne (Boulogne), Jean (Giovanni Bologna, Fiammingo): 1524-1608. Jean was the son of a sculptor of Douai in French Flanders. Bologne is his family name and has no connection with the city of Bologna in Italy. In 1540 he entered the atelier of the sculptor Jacques Dubroeucq at Antwerp. He spent several years in Rome and about 1553 was invited to settle in Florence by Bernardo Vecchietti, at whose villa, Il Riposo, he lived for several years. The Grand Duke Francesco I de'Medici became his principal patron. On April 28, 1563, Bologne was commissioned by

Pius IV (Pope 1559-1565) to make the famous fountain of Neptune at Bologna (finished 1567). His Flying Mercury, made in 1574, was first placed in the Acciajuoli gardens in Florence, and it was transferred to the Villa Medici, Rome, before 1598. When the Villa Medici was sold to the French government about 1769 the statue was brought back to Florence. About 1577-1581 Bologne made the colossal statue called "L'Appenino" (25 meters high) at the villa of Pratolino near Florence. He was also employed in the decoration of the Boboli gardens, Florence, his most important works there being the fountain of the Isoletto and the fountain of the Grotticella. There is a charming fountain by him at the villa of Petraia, near Florence. His equestrian statue of Cosimo I. was placed in the Piazza della Signoria, Florence, in 1594. His group of "Hercules and the Centaur" in the Loggia dei Lanzi, Florence, was made between 1594 and 1599. In 1596 he began the three bronze doors of the facade of the Cathedral of Pisa to replace those by Bonano da Pisa which had been destroyed by fire Oct. 24, 1595. He was assisted by Pierre Franqueville, his favorite bronze-caster, Fra Domenico Portigiani, and others. The fine statue of S. Luke at Or S. Michele, Florence, dates from 1602. In 1604 he began the equestrian statue of Henri IV, which, completed by Pietro Tacca, was placed in position at the Pont Neuf, Paris, Aug. 23, 1614 (destroyed Aug. 11, 1792). His figurines and smaller works are especially fine, among the best being the crucifix in the new sacristy of S. Lorenzo, Florence. [ARCHITECT]

Bolton, William: d. 1532. The prior of S. Bartholomew, London, is mentioned in the will of King Henry VII as "Maister of the Works" of the Chapel of the Virgin Mary, now called Henry the Seventh's Chapel, at Westminster Abbey, London. The actual prior at this time was William Bolton. It is extremely probable that he designed the chapel, although it has usually been credited to Sir Reginald Bray. The first stone of the building was laid Jan. 24, 1503. The greater part of it was built in the reign of Henry VIII (1491-1547). [ECCLESIASTIC AND ARCHITECT]

Bonanno (Bonannus) of Pisa: The great bronze doors of the Cathedral of Monreale are signed "*Bonnanus civis Pisanus*," with the date 1186. The doors which were made for the Cathedral of Pisa in the latter part of the twelfth century are ascribed to him. Those of the front were destroyed in

1596. That of the transept remains. An inscription found in excavating at the base of the Leaning Tower of Pisa gives the name of "Bonnanus," who is supposed to have been the architect of the building. His work appears to have been suspended at the third gallery on account of the increasing inclination. [ARCHITECT AND SCULPTOR]

Bonneuil, Etienne or Pierre: Bonneuil worked on the Cathedral of Notre Dame in Paris. In 1287 he went to Upsal in Sweden to build the Church of the Trinity (Cathedral) on the model of Notre Dame. [ARCHITECT]

Bono, Bartolomeo (Bergamasco): d. 1529. On Aug. 20, 1492, he was appointed *Proto al'ufficio del sale*. As such he must have been involved in many public buildings erected in Venice about that time. The earliest work attributed to him is the great chapel and two lateral chapels of the Church of S. Rocco, built about 1495. In 1510 he built the upper part of the campanile in the Piazza di S. Marco. He began the Scuola di S. Rocco in 1516 and had charge of the work there until June 3, 1524. He laid the foundation and built the hall in the lower story. He began the Procuratie Vecchie which was continued by J. Sansovino. He was succeeded in his office of *proto* by Jacopo Sansovino at the same salary, 80 ducats a year. All the buildings mentioned are in Venice. [ARCHITECT AND SCULPTOR]

Bono, Bartolomeo Di Giovanni: Bartolomeo Bono is the greatest of the sculptor-architects of the later Gothic period in Venice. He assisted his father in his work on the facade of the Ca' d' Oro, begun in 1421. He is mentioned with him in the contract of Jan. 18, 1422, and elsewhere in the records of the building. He also appears in the contract of Nov 10, 1438, between his father and the *Provveditori del sale* for the construction of the Porta della Carta between the Doges' Palace and the Church of S. Marco. This portal was called *della Carta* from the *carte* or notices posted there and *Porta dorata* from the gilding and color employed upon it. It was finished in 1441. The relief of the tympanum of the great door of the Scuola di S. Marco is undoubtedly by Bartolomeo. The Arco Foscari at the Doges' Palace is attributed to Bartolomeo, although documentary proof is lacking. Its statues are among the finest in Venice, and the peculiar use of Renaissance motives with Gothic details is very interesting. [ARCHITECT AND SCULPTOR]

Bono (Buono), Giovanni (Zane Bon): Giovanni was the founder of an important family of Venetian architects and sculptors of the fifteenth century. The customary attribution to the Bono of the northwestern portion of the Doges' Palace, on the Piazetta, is without foundation in the documents. The Domus Magna Contarini a S. Sofia, now called the Ca' d' Oro on the Canal Grande, was begun in 1421. A copy of the contract, dated Jan. 18, 1422, between Marino Contarini and Zane Bon Taiapiera for work to be done on this building still exists. Giovanni's name appears frequently in the Contarini records and other contracts. The chief work of the Bono is the Porta della Carta between the Doges' Palace and S. Marco. The contract made between Giovanni Bono and the *provveditori del Sale,* dated Nov 10, 1438, is given by Paoletti. His will is dated March 25, 1442. Other works in Venice are ascribed to him conjecturally. [ARCHITECT AND SCULPTOR]

Borromino (Borromini), Francesco (Castelli): 1599-1667. His father, Giovanni Domenico Castelli, afterward called Borromino, was an architect in the service of the Visconti at Milan, Italy. Francesco studied sculpture at Milan and was first employed at Rome as a sculptor. He afterward entered the service of Carlo Maderna as draftsman. He was associated with Bernini in his work at S. Peter's and at the Palazzo Barberini. During the reign of Innocent X (Pope 1644-1655) he superseded Bernini as architect of S. Peter's. His earliest important building is the curious Church of S. Carlo alle quattro fontane (1640-1667), a good example of the fully developed Baroque style in Rome. He built also the cupola and other portions of the Church of S. Agnese in the Piazza Navona. About 1650 Borromino built the cloister and oratory of S. Filippo Neri. He built the Palazzo Falconieri with the interesting loggia overlooking the Tiber. He remodelled the Palazzo Spada, where he designed the curious perspective corridor. All the works mentioned here are in Rome. Borromino died by suicide. [ARCHITECT AND SCULPTOR]

Boyle, Richard, third Earl of Burlington and fourth Earl of Cork: 1695-1753. Richard Boyle succeeded to his father's titles and estates in 1704. On Oct. 9, 1714, he became a member of the Privy Council and August 1715 was made Lord High Treasurer of Ireland. He grew up under the influence of Sir Christopher Wren, spent several years in Italy, and became an enthusiastic admirer of Palladio. He was a skillful architect and had a strong influence upon the architectural work of his time. In 1716 he undertook the reconstruction of the family mansion, Burlington House, in Piccadilly, London, which was originally built by his great-grandfather, the first earl. Walpole attributes the fine colonnade of the court to Burlington himself. In 1730 he rebuilt his villa of Chiswick from a design suggested by La Rotonda of Palladio and laid out the park in the Italian style. Burlington designed General Wade's house, Cork Street, London (destroyed), a dormitory for Westminster school, London, and the Assembly Rooms at York. His principal helper was William Kent, who lived at his house until his death in 1748. Burlington spent much of his wealth upon the preservation and restoration of important public monuments, among others the church in Covent Garden, London, designed by Inigo Jones. He bought in Italy many of the original designs of Palladio, which he published under the title *Fabriche Antiche* (London, 1730). [ARCHITECT]

Bramante (Donato D'Agnolo), incorrectly called **Bramante Lazari**: ca. 1444-1514. The surname Bramante comes from *bramare*, to desire ardently, doubtless derived from some family peculiarity. Donato, the son of Angelo, was born at Asdrualdo, near Urbino, Italy. There is no proof that he assisted Luciano da Laurana on the Palace of Urbino, but the influence of that work upon his style was very great. He began as a painter and, according to Fra Castiglione, had for teachers Piero della Francesca and Mantegna. In 1477 he decorated the Palace of the Podesta at Bergamo, Italy, and there are still fragmentary frescos in Lombardy which are ascribed to him. He appears to have gone to Milan about 1472 in the reign of Galeazzo Maria Sforza (1468-1494) and to have remained there until the fall of the Sforza dynasty under Lodovico Sforza. Bramate's Milanese differs so much from his Roman work that it has been ascribed to a fictitious Bramante of Milan. He built at the Church of S. Maria presso S. Satiro the transept with its curious apse in perspective low relief, and the famous sacristy. He appears in the records of the Canonica (the interesting cloister of S. Ambrogio) in 1492 as director of the works. He is supposed to have worked on the Ospedale Maggiore. Bramate's chief work at Milan is the dome and sacristy of S. Maria dei Grazie (1492). The lower parts of that building show his influence especially. On June 27, 1490, he made an interesting report, which has been preserved, on the competition for the central tower of the Cathedral. Of his buildings near Milan the most important is the facade of Abbiate Grasso, dated 1477, which suggests the Nicchione of the Belvedere, Vatican. He probably planned the Cathedral of Pavia and built the nave of the Cathedral of Como. Bramante seems to have settled in Rome after the capture of Milan by Louis XII On Oct. 6, 1499. The Classic surroundings developed at once an entire sympathy with antique style and proportion. This is shown in his first building, the Tempietto of S. Pietro in Montorio, finished before 1502. (The upper part was added later.) The Cancelleria is commonly ascribed to Bramante, but the facade bears the dates 1489 and 1495, and it was undoubtedly begun by the Cardinal Raffaello Riario as early as 1486. Vasari's words *"rizoluzione di gran parte"* may refer to extensive additions by Bramante. The case of the Giraud Torlonia Palace, a replica of the Cancelleria, is similar. In the letter of gift of this palace to Henry VII of England, dated March, 1504, it is described as *"nondum perfecta."* Bramante built the cloister of S. Maria della Pace in 1504. The immense palace which he built for the offices of Julius II was famous for its magnificent use of rustication. A few fragments remain in the Via Giulia. He began the Santa Casa and the palace at Loreto. One of Bramante's most interesting works was the palace bought by Raphael in 1517 and preserved to us by a sketch of Palladio. Bramante does not appear at the Vatican until the reign of Julius II (Pope 1503-1513), who wished to unite the old Vatican with the Belvedere of Innocent VIII (Pope 1484-1492). Bramante planned an immense quadrangle, the shorter sides formed by the two palaces and the longer by galleries copied from the theater of Marcellus. This court led by three levels up to a great apse, the Nicchione of the Belvedere. He finished the eastern gallery only. In the old Vatican, Bramante built the *loggie* which received Raphael's decorations. The reconstruction of the Basilica of Constantine (S. Peter's) was attempted in the reign of Nicholas V (Pope 1447-1455) and again in the reign of Paul II (Pope 1464-1471). Julius II resumed the work April 18, 1506, and placed it under the direction of Bramante. At his death the four piers of the dome had been raised to the cornice and the apse opposite the main entrance had been vaulted. His design was a Greek cross with towers in the open angles and a central dome. Bramante is sup-

posed to have been illiterate, but there are several sonnets and other poems and some fragments of manuscripts which are attributed to him. [ARCHITECT]

Breton, Gilles le: d. 1552. Three architects of this name, probably brothers, appear in France during the first half of the sixteenth century. Gilles le Breton was charged with the transformation of the Chateau of Fontainebleau (Seine et Marne, France), probably from the commencement of the work about 1528 until his death in 1550, and to him are due the most interesting parts of that building. He built at Fontainebleau, about in the order given, the pavilion of the Porte Doree with the buildings near it in the *Cour Ovale* and the so-called gallery of Francois; in the main structure of the Cour du Cheval blanc, the Chapel of la Trinite and the *rez-de-chausse* of that portion nearest the pool; and, later, in the *Cour Ovale*, the Tour du Peristyle, the Chapel of S. Saturnin, and the great hall called the Galerie Henri *II* The splendid wooden ceiling of the Galerie Henri *II* is the work of Philibert de l'Orme, who succeeded Le Breton as architect of the building in 1550. [ARCHITECT]

Breuer, Marcel: 1902-1981. Originally born in Hungary, Breuer's family moved to the United States when he was 25. He became a naturalized citizen and spent the next 15 years teaching at Harvard University. He quickly established his own practice as well, and he is considered by some to be one of the greatest architects of all time. His famous chairs, the Wassily and Cesca, were designed many years before they were finally produced by Knoll Furniture. His designs were strong statements linking light, texture, space, power, and detail. In spite of the last statement however, it is extremely difficult to classify or label Breuer's work. At best, it should be said that he was a form-setter, an artist who set the pace, a man who transformed his personal beliefs into his designs in a way no one has matched. Major projects include the office designs of Unesco in Paris, the IBM Research Center in France, the Abbey of St. John in Minnesota, the Lecture Hall for New York University, and the Whitney Museum of American Art in New York City. [ARCHITECT]

Briosco, Andrea (Riccio): 1470-1532. The son of one Ambrogio Briosco, a Milanese goldsmith in Padua. He was a pupil of the sculptor Bartolomeo Bellano. In 1500 he designed the Capella del Santo in the Church of S. Antonio, Padua. About 1505-1507 he made two bas-reliefs for the choir of S. Antonio. The contract, dated June 19, 1507, for his great candelabrum at S. Antonio is given by Gonzati. This work was finished in 1516 and is 3.92 meters high and 1.12 meters in extreme width. For the Church of S. Fermo in Verona he made the tombs of Girolamo and Antonio della Torre. Eight bas-reliefs from Girolamos's tomb are now in the Louvre (Paris). On Nov 12, 1516, Briosco was commissioned to make the model for, and direct the works at, the Church of S. Giustina at Padua. [SCULPTOR AND ARCHITECT]

Brosse, Salomon (Jacques) de: ca.1560-1626. The baptismal name of the great De Brosse was Salomon, and not Jacques as formerly supposed. He was probably a Son of Jehan de Brosse and a nephew of Jacques (II) Androuet du Cerceu. He was appointed architect to Maria de' Medici, queen of Henri IV (1553-1610). In 1615 he began for her the Palace of the Luxembourg (Paris), which was nearly completed in 1620. The principal characteristics of the Luxembourg are usually supposed to have been derived from the garden facade of the Palazzo Pitti in Florence. They were probably rather suggested by the old Chateau of Verneuilsur-Oise (destroyed), which is supposed to have been designed by Jacques (I) Androuet du Cerceau. Between 1613 and 1624 Salomon built the new aqueduct of Arcueil to supply the Luxembourg with water. He also built the fountain of the Medici in the Luxembourg garden. Between 1616 and 1621 he built the portal of the Church of S. Gervais (Paris) and between 1618 and 1620 the *Salle des Pas-Perdus* at the *Palais de Justice* (Paris) to replace the Medieval hall burned in 1618. De Brosse was a Huguenot. In a register of burials of an old Protestant cemetery in Paris is found the entry, *Salomon de Brosse, inegnieur et architecte des bastimens du roy, natif de Verneuil, enterre a Saint-Pere, le 9. Decembre 1626.* [ARCHITECT]

Brown, A. Page: 1859-1896. He was educated at Cornell University. After working for three years in the office of McKim, Mead, and White (New York City) he spent two years in Europe. On his return he designed the Art Museum and several other buildings for Princeton University. He is best known by the California state building which he designed for the World's Fair in 1893. He designed several important buildings in California. [ARCHITECT]

Brunellesco; Brunelleschi (Filippo di Ser Brunellesco): 1377-1446. Filippo's father received the name Brunellesco from his own mother's family, the Brunelleschi, of Florence. Filippo was born in Florence, and apprenticed to a goldsmith. He was early interested in mechanics and made many practical inventions. Two statuettes of prophets in the silver retable of S. Giacomo at Pistoia are supposed to be by him. He made, also, a wooden crucifix at S. Maria novella. He entered the competition for the doors of the Florentine Baptistery, in 1401. From 1401 to 1417 Brunellesco appears to have lived in Rome with Donatello, making occasional visits to Florence. In 1404 he joined the corporation of jewellers and, in the same year, served on a commission at the Cathedral of Florence. In 1415 he again appears at the Cathedral. The general scheme of the dome was, undoubtedly, established by the model made about 1367. In 1417 the work had proceeded as far as the oculi in the eight sides of the drum. The cupola itself was begun in 1425. Ghiberti and Brunellesco, both members of the guild of goldsmiths, of Florence, were associated at first on equal terms. Filippo superseded Ghiberti and became *capo maestro* about 1438 and *provisore a vita* in 1445. The lantern was finished in 1461 (after his death) from Brunellesco's model. All Brunellesco's work is in Florence or vicinity. The reconstruction of S. Lorenzo was begun not later than 1420. Filippo finished the old sacristy and transept of that church before he died. The nave was built from his plans after his death, by Manetti Ciacheri. He built the Badia at Fiesole, near Florence, after 1439. The second cloister of S. Croce was built from his designs. The Church of S. Sprito was begun by Brunellesco, and finished after his death. The Chapel of the Pazzi, at S. Croce, Filippo's most perfect building, was begun not earlier than 1429. The unfinished Church of the Camaldoli, or degli Angeli, was begun after 1426. The plan is an interesting example of 8 sides on the inside, changing to 16 on the outside. The Spedale degli Innocenti was commenced in 1419. The Loggia, with sculpture by Andrea della Robbia, is well known. He began the Pitti Palace for Luca Pitti, about 1444. Many drawings of this building, after the end of the fifteenth century, show the three stories of the facade with only seven windows in the second and third. The rest has been added since. The Pazzi Palace is attributed to Filippo without documentary evidence. He built a large part of the Palazzo della parte Guelfa. Brunel-

lesco is credited with having discovered the modern science of perspective. [ARCHITECT]

Bruce, Sir William: d. 1710. Sir William Bruce, Scottish architect, was the second son of the third baron of Blairhall. By letter of Charles I, dated June 3, 1671, he was appointed general overseer and superintendent of the reconstruction of the Palace of Holyrood (Edinburgh, Scotland). [ARCHITECT]

Bulfinch, Charles: 1763-1844. The earliest native architect of Boston, Bulfinch graduated at Harvard College in 1781 and between 1785 and 1787 travelled in Europe. He visited Paris while Thomas Jefferson was minister to France and spent three or four months in Italy. After his return his first work was the Doric column erected to take the place of the old woodeN beacon on Beacon Hill (Boston). In 1796 he undertook the Franklin Place improvement in which his entire fortune was lost. On July 4, 1795, Bulfinch laid the corner stone of the State House in Boston (finished 1798). He finished the McLean Hospital, Somerville, in 1818, and in the same year received the commission for the General Hospital in Boston. On Jan. 8, 1818, Bulfinch succeeded B. H. Latrobe as architect of the Capitol in Washington. He built the rotunda according to Latrobe's plans and added, from his own designs, the portico and approaches on the western side. He finished the Capitol in 1830. [ARCHITECT]

Bullant, Jean: 1515-1578. In his *Reigle Generalle,* Bullant asserts that he measured the antique in Rome. He very early entered the service of the Constable Anne de Monmorency. The result of their cooperation was the more interesting part of the Chateau of Ecouen, France. The original design and the older work are doubtless by another person. The classical influence of Bullant appears gradually and becomes predominant in the wing to the right of the main entrance built about 1550. He built the main entrance (destroyed), and the portico, copied from the temple of Castor and Pollux at Rome, which was added to the left wing, the first appearance of the colossal order in France. This work especially marks the transition from the early Renaissance to the clearly defined French Classic style. On Oct. 25, 1557, Bullant was appointed *controleur des batiments royeaux* but, like Philibert de l'Orme, lost his office after the death of Henri II (July 10, 1559). A period of about 10 years follows in which no building of importance can with certainty be ascribed to him. It is believed that during this time he was occupied with the Petit Chateau of Chantilly, the reconstruction of the Chateau of Fere-en-Tardenois, and the improvement of various churches in the vicinity of Ecouen, as at Bellay, Sarcelles, Villiers-le-Bel, etc. The great Constable Anne de Montmorency was killed at the battle of Saint-Denis, Nov 10, 1567. The mausoleum for himself and his wife, Madeleine de Savoy, in the church at Montmorency, was begun by Bullant soon after. The work continued a long time and appears never to have been completed. Fragments of this monument, which was destroyed in the Revolution, are now in the Louvre. In 1570 Bullant superintended the works at the Chapel of the Valois, at Saint-Denis, near Paris. Jan. 8, 1570, he succeeded Philibert de l'Orme as architect of the Tuileries and built the pavilion connecting with De l'Orme's work on the south side. In 1572 Catherine de' Medici abandoned the Tuileries, and Bullant began for her the great Hotel de la Reine, which afterward came into the possession of Charles de Bourbon, Compte de Soissons, and was called Hotel de Soissons, Paris. In the eighteenth century it was destroyed, except the great column built in imitation of Trajan's column at Rome, which still remains. Bullant's first book appeared in 1561 under the title *Recueil d'Horlogiographie*, quarto, with engravings on wood. The second part followed the next year and with the first formed a volume entitled *Petit Traicte de Geometrie et d' Horlogiographie pratique*, (1562). His second work, *Reigle generalle d'Architectture*, came from the press May 27, 1564. A second edition was printed in 1568. In 1619 an edition was issued by N. Pilouet, *reveue et corriglee par Monsieur de Brosse, architecte du roi*. Bullant died at Ecouen, Oct. 10, 1578. [ARCHITECT]

Buonarroti-Simoni, Michelangelo: 1475-1564. The Buonarroti-Simonis were an old burgher family of Florence. Michelangelo was born at Caprese in the Casentino (Tuscany), while his father Lodovico (d. 1534) was *podesta* of that village. April 1, 1488, he was apprenticed to the painters Domenico and David Ghirlandaio for three years. He was one of the boys selected to study from the antique statues collected in the gardens of the monastery of S. Marco, Florence and there attracted the attention of Lorenzo de' Medici, who invited him to his palace, where Michelangelo lived and worked until his patron died.

In 1491 Michelangelo came in contact with Savonarola (1452-1498), whose influence upon him was very great. Through the assistance of the prior of the convent of S. Spirito, for whom he made a crucifix, he had abundant opportunity for dissection and began that exhaustive study of anatomy to which he devoted a large part of his life. Just before the expulsion of the Medici (Nov. 8, 1494), Michelangelo went to Bologna, where he made one of the kneeling angels of the Arca of S. Domenico. Returning to Florence in 1495 he made a statue of "S. John," and a sleeping "Cupid" which was sold to the Cardinal Riario in Rome as an antique. Going to Rome, June 25, 1496, he made there at this time the "Bacchus" of the Museo Nazionale, Florence, a "Cupid," probably that of the South Kensington Museum, and the beautiful "*Pieta*" of S. Peter's, Rome, for which the contract was signed Aug. 26, 1498. Michelangelo returned to Florence in 1501 and began the colossal statue of "David" in August of that year. It was placed in position before the Palazzo della Signoria, June 8, 1504, and is now in the Accademia, Florence. The "Madonna of Bruges" was probably made at about this time and a bronze "David," which was sent to France and drifted to the Chateau of Villeroy, where it disappeared. The two rondels of the Royal Academy, London, and the Museo Nazionale, Florence, and the picture of the "Holy Family" at the Uffizi doubtless belong to this early period. In 1504 he began the famous cartoon representing soldiers alarmed while bathing in the Arno (the so-called "Battle of Pisa"). It was made as a companion to Leonardo da Vinci's "Battle of Anghiari," begun 1503. This cartoon, which influenced the art of the Renaissance more than any other work, was finished in 1506, but abandoned a few years later and finally destroyed.

In 1505 Michelangelo was called to Rome by Julius II (Pope 1503-1513), and in April of that year began the mausoleum of the Pope, a work that extended through many years of his life and was the source of endless irritation and disappointment. A part of the design, with the statue of "Moses," was finally set up in the Church of S. Pietro in Vincolo, Rome, after 1542. Disturbed by some misunderstanding with the Pope about the mausoleum, Michelangelo abandoned Rome for Florence before May 2, 1506. In December of the same year he made peace with the Pope at Bologna and executed a bronze statue of him which stood over the door of the Church of S. Petronio (Bologna)

until Dec. 30, 1511, when it was destroyed. At Bologna, Michelangelo came in contact with the work of Giacomo della Quercia, which had a powerful influence upon his compositions for the ceiling of the Sistine Chapel (Vatican, Rome). This ceiling, begun in the summer of 1508, represents scenes from the Creation, surrounded by a superb setting of architecture and figures. It was finished in October, 1512. Julius II was succeeded by Giovanni de' Medici, Leo X (Pope 1513-1521). Leo found little for Michelangelo to do in Rome. In 1515 the Pope conceived a scheme for the construction of a facade for the Church of S. Lorenzo in Florence, for which designs were made by Michelangelo, Giuliano da San Gallo, Andrea and Jacopo Sansovino, and others. That of Michelangelo was preferred. From 1516 to 1520 Michelangelo was occupied in the mountains of Carrara and Serravezza, building roads, opening quarries, and preparing marbles for this facade, which was never built. Leo X was succeeded by Adrian VI (Pope 1522-1523), and he in turn by Giuliano de' Medici, Clement VII (Pope 1523-1534). Clement employed Michelangelo in the construction of the new sacristy of S. Lorenzo, Florence, and the tombs of the two dukes, Giuliano and Lorenzo de' Medici. The sacristy was finished before 1524. The magnificent sculpture of the two tombs was kept in hand for a long period and not actually placed in position until after 1534. Michelangelo began the Laurentian library in Florence in 1526. During the siege of Florence in 1530, he was made controller general of the works of defence.

In 1534 Michelangelo settled in Rome for the remainder of his life. Under the patronage of Paul III (Pope 1534-1549) he completed the decoration of the Sistine Chapel by painting the picture of the "Last Judgment" (begun 1534, finished 1541). The decorations of the Pauline Chapel were painted between 1542 and 1549. About 1544 he was called to complete the Farnese Palace (Rome), which had been placed in charge of Antonio (II) da San Gallo. The third story, with the cornice and much of the court, are attributed to Michelangelo. He had, however, from this time until his death very able assistants, such as Vignola and Giacomo della Porta, and it is impossible to separate their work from his. After the death of Antonio (II) da San Gallo, in 1546, Michelangelo became architect of S. Peter's and worked on that building until his death without compensa-

tion. He returned to the main features of the design of Bramante and, in 1557, made a model of the cupola, according to which it was built after his death by Giacomo della Porta. The dome as constructed doubtless represents Michelangelo's conception very perfectly. The *Porto Pia* (Rome) is also ascribed to him. The reconstruction of the Capitol was begun with the placing of the statue of "Marcus Aurelius," in 1538. Michelangelo designed the main features of the present buildings, which were carried out after his death. He rebuilt the great hall of the Thermae of Diocletian (now the Church of S. Maria degli Angeli), which was again remodelled in 1749 by Vanvitelli.
[SCULPTOR, PAINTER, ARCHITECT AND POET]

Buontalenti, Bernardo: 1536-1608. A pupil of Vasari and of Giulio Clovio, the miniaturist. For the dukes Francesco I. (1541-1587) and Ferdinando I (1541-1609) de' Medici he designed the villas of Pratolino, Artiminio, Mariguolle, and Magia, near Florence. He built the additions to the Palazzo Vecchio, Florence, on the Via dei Leoni, the Tribuna of the Uffizi, and the gallery connecting the Uffizi with the Pitti Palace. He continued the arrangement of the Boboli Gardens, begun by Trobolo, and built the grotto and other architectural adornments there. Buontalenti fortified Porto Ferraio, Livorno, and Grosseto. The Palazzo Reale in Siena and the Palazzo Nonfinisto in Florence, are attributed to him. [SCULPTOR, PAINTER, LANDSCAPE ARCHITECT]

Burges, William: 1827-1881. He was educated at University College and King's College, London, was also a pupil of Edward Blore and Digby Wyatt, and applied himself especially to Medieval architecture. In 1856 he won the first award in the competition for Lille Cathedral. Burges designed the Cathedral of Brisbane in Queensland (1859) and the Cathedral of Cork (Ireland), his most important work (1862). In 1865 he restored Cardiff Castle. He prepared designs for the new law courts in the Strand and for the decoration of S. Paul's Cathedral (London), which were not executed. He designed Trinity College in Hartford, Connecticut. [ARCHITECT]

Burklein, Friedrich: 1813-1872. Burklein came to Munich (Bavaria) about 1828 and entered the atelier of Gartner. He held the offices of *bauconstructer regierungs-inspector* and professor in the *Polytechnische Schule* in Munich. He went with Gartner to Greece, and assisted him in the construction of the royal palace at Athens. He assisted the King Maxi-milian II (1811-1864) in his development of the city of Munich. Burklein's chief work was the laying out of the Maximilianstrasse and construction of the Mazimilianeum. He worked in a style peculiar to himself (*Neuer Baustil*), a combination of Romanesque and Renaissance. [ARCHITECT]

Burnham, Daniel Hudson: 1846-1912. Burnham was (along with J. W. Root) an important part of the founding of the Chicago School of architecture. He was greatly influenced by H. H. Richardson during the last 30 years of the nineteenth century, the neo-classicist   (where is the rest?) [ARCHITECT]

Buschetus (Busketus, Buschetto): The first architect of the Cathedral of Pisa. The date, 1006, in the inscription on his monument, which still stands in the Cathedral, is probably that of the commencement of the building. The inscription on the facade, with the date 1063, is supposed to refer to a subsequent enlargement (*Mothes*, Vol. I., p. 722). In a contract of Dec. 2, 1105, Buschetto is mentioned as one of four architects who had worked on the Cathedral; the others were Uberto, Leone, and Signoretto. He was probably a Byzantine Greek. [ARCHITECT]

Butterfield, William, F.S.A.:
1814-1900. He devoted himself to the study of Gothic architecture and was especially successful in the introduction of color by the help of brick, stone, marble, and mosaic. The earliest of his more important works is the Church of All Saints, Margaret Street, London, begun in 1849. He designed S. Augustine's College, Canterbury; all the buildings of Keble College, Oxford; the Cathedral of Perth; Balliol College Chapel, Oxford; S. Michael's Hospital, Axbridge; the school buildings at Winchester College; the chapel, quadrangle, and other buildings at Rugby School; Rugby parish Church ; S. Alban's, Holborn; S. Augustine's, Queens's Gate; and churches at Enfield, Winchester, Dover Castle, and Tottenham. All the work mentioned is in Great Britain. There are several important buildings by Butterfield in Australia. [ARCHITECT]

Candela, Felix: b. 1910. Candela was born in Madrid, but in 1939 he emigrated to Mexico, where he lived and practiced until 1971 at which time he emigrated to the United States. Both builder and designer, he has made considerable contributions to the field through the use of concrete and steel. He built his first shell structure in 1949 in Mexico. His Cos-

mic Ray Pavilion at the Mexico University threw him into the vanguard of the design world. The Church of the Miraculous Virgin in Mexico City was designed in 1953 by Candela. This project showed that concrete could be turned and twisted without losing the sense of the design structurally. Now known throughout the world for his designs, Candela's client base spread quickly from England to Saudi Arabia. His career also included professorships at such institutions as the National University of Mexico, the University of Illinois, Cornell University, the University of Virginia and Harvard University. [ARCHITECT]

Canina, Luigi: 1794-1856. About 1826 Canina was commissioned by the Prince Camillo Borghese to enlarge and restore the Villa Borghese (Rome), which was built for Paul V (Pope 1605-1621). He directed the excavations undertaken by Leo XII (Pope 1823-1829), Pius VIII (Pope 1829-1830), and Gregory XVI (Pope 1831-1846) in the Roman Forum, the Appian Way, and the Campagna. The results of his archaeological investigations were published in numerous works, which are almost wholly discredited because of the large part that conjecture had in their preparation. The tendency of modern investigation has been to prove them erroneous in almost every respect. [ARCHITECT AND ARCHAEOLOGIST]

Caristie, Augusin Nicolas: 1783-1862. The earliest-known Caristie was Michel Ange, an Italian, who built the college of the Jesuits at Autun (France) in 1709 and rebuilt the Church of the Celestins at Amiens (1726-1732). The father of Augustin Nicolas was an architect in Dijon at the end of the 18th century. A. N. Caristie went from Lyons to Paris to study with A. L. T. Vaudoyer and Ch. Percier and won the *Grand Prix de Rome* in 1813. In 1824 he was commissioned by the minister of the interior to examine the condition of the Roman triumphal arch at Orange, and to report concerning the means required to restore and preserve it. He investigated also the Roman theater at Orange. Caristie published his results in two works, *Notice sur l' Etat Actuel de l' Arc d' Orange et des Theaters Antiques d' Orange et d' Arles*, etc. (Paris, 1839), and *Monuments Antiques a Orange; Arc de Triomphe et Theater* (Paris, 1856). He completed the restoration of the arch in 1829 and exhibited his drawings in the Salon of 1831. In 1824 he was charged with the design and construction of the Mausoleum to the victims of Quiberon and in 1827 appointed architect of

the presbytery of the Madeleine (Paris). In 1842 he undertook the restoration of the Chateau of Anet, especially the great portal and chapel. [ARCHITECT AND ARCHAEOLOGIST]

Castellamonte, Amadeo Conte di: An architect of the school of Pellegrino and Domenico Tibaldi. He entered the service of Carlo Emmanuele II, Duke of Savoy (1634-1675), and for him planned the *Piazza di S. Carlo* (1638), the *Palazzo Reale* (begun 1646), and the *Ospedale Maggiore* (1675), all at Turin (Italy). For the Duke also he built the hunting seat and park near Turin called *Veneria Reale* (now destroyed). Castellamonte published a description of his park in the form of a dialogue entitled *Veneria Reale* (Turin, 1674). [ARCHITECT]

Cattaneo, Danese (da Carrara): ca. 1509;-1573. He was established first in Rome, but went to Venice with Giacomo Sansovino after the sack of Rome in 1527. He assisted Sansovino at the Dodge's Palace, the Libreria di S. Marco, the loggia of the Campanile and the Zecca (mint). Cattaneo wrote a poem in 24 cantos entitled *L' Amor di Marfisa*. [ARCHITECT, SCULPTOR, AND POET]

Caus (also **Caux**), **Salomon De:** 1576-1626. He probably derived his name from the *Pays de Caux* (of the department of *Seine Inferieure,* France). He made a special study of mechanics and architecture, travelled extensively, and drifted to England where he became architect and "engineer in ordinary" to Henry, Prince of Wales. He was also drawing master to the Princess Elizabeth, and followed her to Heidelberg (Germany), where she married (April 1612) the Elector Palatinate, Friedrich V. Salomon laid out the great garden of the castle at Heidelberg and probably made additions to the castle itself. He returned to France about 1620, and acquired the title *ingenieur et architecte du roi.* In his *Raisons des forces mouvantes,* Salomon describes a machine for raising water by means of the expansive power of steam, thus taking the first step toward the invention of the steam engine. His principal works are *La Perspective avec la raison des ombres et miroirs* (London, 1611-1612); *Institution Harmonique* (Heidelberg, 1614); *Les Raisons des forces mouvantes* (Frankfurt, 1615); *Hortus Palatinus,* etc. [ENGINEER, ARCHITECT, AND LANDSCAPE ARCHITECT]

Chalgrin, Jean-Francois Therese: 1739-1811. Chalgrin was a pupil of Servandoni and Moreau. He won the *Grand Prix de Rome* in 1757. On his return from Italy he was made inspector of public works of the city of Paris, under Moreau. About 1777 he rebuilt the northern tower of the Church of S. Sulpice in Paris and designed the organ loft of that church. Chalgrin is famous as the designer of the Arc de Triomphe de l'Etoile (Paris). Napoleon I (1769; d. 1821) originally intended that this monument should be called Arc de Triomphe de la Grande Armee, and be placed on the Italian boundary. When work upon it was undertaken in 1806, he changed the location to the Place de la Bastille (Paris) and the name to Arc de Marengo. The location was objected to by the *Academie de l'Architecture* in association with Jean Armand Raymond. Raymond retired in 1808, leaving Chalgrin in charge, who planned the arch much as it now appears. At his death the monument had been carried to the height of about 18 feet. [ARCHITECT]

Chamberlin, Powell and Bon: (Estab. 1952) This London partnership was formed in 1952 by Peter Hugh Girard Chamberlin (1919-1978), C. Hamilton Powell (b. 1920), and Christopher Bon (b. 1921). The firm made important donations to the field of urban renewal planning with its design and subsequent building of the Barbicon development, in which it was shown that a housing project could not only provide shelter but also aesthetically pleasing and functional living areas as well. Additionally, the firm's design of Bousfield Primary School in England won the London Bronze Medal for Architecture in 1956. The design and development of Leeds University (project from 1963) is a perfect example of how a city center can be mixed with an academic format. [ARCHITECT]

Chambiges (Sambiches, Cambiches), Martin: d. 1532. Martin Chambiges was called from Paris to Sens (Yonne, France) in 1489 to design the new transept of the Cathedral. He began the construction on Nov. 8, 1490, and in 1494 transferred the superintendence to Hugues Cavelier, afterward making occasional visits of inspection. He appears to have modified his plans in 1598. On Nov. 7, 1499, Martin was invited to attend consultations in Paris concerning the reconstruction of the Pont Notre Dame, which had fallen during the preceding month. In 1501 he commenced the doorway called "Portail d'Abraham" and in 1513 the northern portal of the Cathedral of Sens. In 1502 Martin was invited to Troyes (Aube, France), to advise concerning the construction of the facade of the Cathedral. He designed the facade with its two towers and portal in 1502-1503, but did not commence

building until the autumn of 1506. In 1500 he made the plans for the transept of the Cathedral of Beauvais (Oise, France). He began construction at once and continued in charge until his death. He was assisted by Jean Wast. [ARCHITECT]

Chelles, Jean de: From the commencement of the Cathedral of Notre Dame (Paris) in 1163, the name of no architect connected with the work is known until 1257, when the southern arm to the transept was enlarged and the southern portal built, which bears the inscription, ANNO * DNI * M.CCLVII MENSE * FEBRVARIO * IDVS * SECVNDO * HOC * FVIT * INCEPTUM * CRISTI * GENITRICIS * HONORE * KALLENSI * LATHOMO * JOHANNE * MAGISTRO. The rose window above appears to belong to the thirteenth century. The chapels of the nave, built between 1245 and 1250, may be his work. The northern portal has been ascribed to him but was probably built about 1313. A Jean de Chelles was working of the old Louvre in 1265 under the direction of Raymond du Temple. [ARCHITECT AND SCULPTOR]

Chillenden, Thomas: Chillenden, prior of Canterbury Cathedral from 1391 to 1411, is supposed to have built, or to have superintended the building of, the nave, choir, and part of the chapter house of Canterbury Cathedral. Archbishop Arundel contributed also to this work. [ECCLE-SIASTIC]

Chrodegand, Saint: In 757 Chrodegand, Bishop of Metz, reestablished the *monasteria clericorum,* or communities of clergymen in the service of the cathedral churches. The cloister that he built about his Cathedral at Metz, Lothringen, Germany, was the pattern from which buildings of this class were afterward constructed. This cloister, which probably retained many of its original features, was destroyed in 1754 by the Marechal de Belle-Isle. Chrodegand rebuilt the Cathedral of Metz and designed the abbey of Gorze. [BISHOP AND ARCHITECT]

Churriguera, Don Josef: d. 1725. A native of Salamanca (Spain), he went to Madrid in 1688. At Madrid he designed the great catafalque for the obsequies of the Queen Maria Louisa (d. 1689), built the now portal of the Church of S. Gayetano, a palace for Don Juan de Goyeneche, and executed various pieces of sculpture for altars of churches and convents. He was succeeded by his sons Geronimo and Nicolas. The term Churrigueresque is applied to the extravagant style which he affected. [SCULPTOR AND ARCHITECT]

Cleomenes (Kleomenes): Cleomenes is mentioned by various authors as the builder of the city of Alexandria (Egypt). [ARCHITECT AND ENGINEER]

Cockerell, Charles Robert: C. R. Cockerell was the second son of Samuel Pepys Cockerell and in 1809 became an assistant of Sir Robert Smirke during the reconstruction of Covent Garden theater, London. In 1810 he commenced a tour of Greece, Asia Minor, Sicily, and Italy. On April, 1811, with Baron Haller von Hallerstein, architect for the King of Bavaria, Baron Stackelberg, and others, Cockerell went to the Aegina and excavated the ruins of the temple of Minerva, which were bought by the British Museum in 1813. Cockerell published the results of his investigations under the title *The Temple of Jupiter Panhellenius at Aegina and of Apollo Epicurius at Bassae, near Phigaleia in Arcadia* (London, 1860,). His studies of the *Temple of Jupiter Olympus at Agrigentum* were published in 1830 with other monographs by W. Kinnard, T. L. Donaldson, W. Jenkins, and W. Railton in a volume supplementary to the *Antiquities of Athens* by Stuart and Revett. He was appointed surveyor of S. Paul's Cathedral in 1819. About 1830 he began the National Monument in Edinburgh, which was never completed.

In 1833 he succeeded Sir John Soane as architect of the Bank of England. He was elected associate of the Royal Academy in 1829 and in 1836 Royal Academician. From 1840 to 1857 he was professor of architecture at the Royal Academy, London. In 1847 he succeeded Harvey Lonsdale Elmes as architect of S. George's Hall, Liverpool. Cockerell was president of the Royal Institute of British Architects in 1860-1861, *Chevalier* of the *Legion d'Honneur*, member of the American Institute of Architects, etc. He was buried in S. Paul's Cathedral. Much of his success was due to his skill in drawing the human figure. [ARCHITECT AND ARCHAEOLOGIST]

Coducci, Mauro (Moretto) of Bergamo, "Moro Lombardo": In a document dated July 1476, the design and construction of the fine Church of S. Michele in Isola at Venice is ascribed to "Moretto di Lorenzo da Venezia." In 1482 Moretto took charge of the works at the campanile of S. Marco and on June 12, 1483, was chosen *protomaestro* of the new Church of S. Zaccaria (Venice) begun by Antonio Gambello. He built the great stairway of the Scuola di S. Marco. In the memoranda of a lawsuit between his heirs and the authorities of the Church of S. Maria Formosa (Venice), in 1506, Mauro di Coducci is mentioned as the architect of that building. The names Moro, Moretto, Moreto, appear frequently in the Venetian records at this time, but they do not always refer to the architect Coducci. [ARCHITECT AND SCULPTOR]

Contini, Antonio: Contini was a nephew of Giovanni da Ponte. He built the Bridge of Sighs between the Doges' Palace and the prison in Venice. [ARCHITECT]

Contreras, Rafael: 1824-1890. His father, Don Jose Contreras, architect of the city of Granada (Spain), had charge of the Alhambra Palace near Granada. Rafael succeeded him and on Nov. 23, 1847, was commissioned to restore the palace. He was succeeded by his son, Don Mariano Contreras. Rafael published *Estudio descripto de los monumentos arabes de Granada, Sevilla y Cordoba, etc.* (3d ed. 1885); *Recuerdos de la Dominacion de los Arabes en Espana* (1882), etc. [ARCHITECT]

Cooley, Thomas: 1740-1784. Cooley won first premium for a design for the Royal Exchange, Dublin (Ireland), 1769, and completed that building in 1779. He built several other public buildings in Dublin. [ARCHITECT]

Cossutius: The construction of Olympian Zeus at Athens, begun by Antistates and his associates under Peisistratos and discontinued at the time of the banishment of Hippias, the son of Peisistratos (510 B.C), was taken up by Antiochos IV (Epiphanes), King of Syria (reigned 176-164 B.C.). The architect employed by him, Cossutius, continued the building in the Corinthian style. The name Cossutius is inscribed upon a base in Athens, which probably carried a statue of the architect. The temple of Zeus was finished during the reign of Hadrian. [ARCHITECT]

Costa, Lucio: 1902-1963 Born in France of Brazilian parents, Costa completed his early education in France. His later education was in Brazil, however, the country where his most famous work was completed. Costa was a planner as well as an architect and is probably best known for his collaboration with Le Corbusier and Niemeyer on the Ministry of Education and Health in Rio de Janeiro from 1937-1943. This work, along with the Brazilian Pavilion at the New York World's Fair in 1939, firmly established Costa as a major influence in Brazilian architectural history. As well, the collaborations with Niemeyer were paramount in the rise of Niemeyer to his fore-most position in later years. Costa's design for the new capital of Brasilia, however, is his most noted work. Shaped like a bow and arrow, the plan is stylistically simple, combining classic elegance with modern utilitarianism. This master plan provides as well an excellent backdrop for Niemeyer's public buildings. [ARCHITECT]

Cotte, Robert de: 1656-1735. Robert was the son or grandson of Fremin de Cotte, architect of King Louis XIII, who served as engineer at the siege of La Rochelle (1627-1628). He was a pupil of Jules Hardouin-Mansart, whose wife's sister he married. Mansart confided to him the direction of the works at the *Invalides* and other important buildings. He was made a member of the *Academie Royale d' Architecture* in 1687 and *architecte du roi* in 1689. Between 1700 and 1702 he directed, under the supervision of Mansart, the works at the Hotel de Ville at Lyons, France. About 1707 he rebuilt the central tower of the Cathedral of Orleans. At the death of Mansart in 1708 he succeeded him as *premier architecte du roi*. The portal of the Church of S. Roche (Paris) was designed by Robert in 1734 and finished by his son Jules Robert de Cotte. Robert de Cotte built the peristyle of the Grand Trianon at Versailles. He made designs for the royal palace and Buen Retiro at Madrid. [ARCHITECT AND DECORATOR]

Craig, James: d. 1795. Craig was a nephew of James Thomson, the poet, and a pupil of Sir Robert Taylor. In 1767 he won a competition for a plan for the construction of new streets and squares in the city of Edinburgh (Scotland). The New Town of Edinburgh was built according to this plan. [ARCHITECT]

Cronaca, Il (Simone del Pollajuolo): 1457-1508. Simone was called Cronaca, the chronicler, from his endless stories about the Roman monuments. He was brought up as a woodworker, *intarsiatore*, spent much time in Rome, and acquired a thorough knowledge of the antiquities. The buildings that can with certainty be credited to him are in Florence and not very numerous. In 1489 he superintended work upon the roofs of the Duomo. In 1490 he was appointed *maestro dei scarpellini* at the Palazzo Strozzi and in 1497 became architect of that building. Cronaca substituted plain stone for rustication in the last three courses and designed the celebrated cornice of the Strozzi. At about this time he built the sacristy of Santo Spirito from the model by Giuliano da San Gallo. The fine

Church of S. Salvatore al Monte (consecrated 1504) is attributed to Simone by Vasari. It was much admired by Michelangelo. June 23, 1495, Cronaca was made *capomaestro* of the Duomo and after July 15, 1495, built the great hall of the Palazzio Vecchio, entirely remodelled by Vasair. Milanese publishes a *Prospetto Cronologico dell vita e delle opere di Cronaca* in his Vasari. [ARCHITECT]

Crundale, Richard de: d. 1292 or 1293. Richard de Crundale built, and probably designed, the Eleanor Cross which was situated in the village of Charing, now the region called Charing Cross in London. After his death the work was continued by Roger de Crundale. Richard de Crundale did the marble work of the monument of Queen Eleanor in the Chapel of Edward the Confessor in Westminster Abbey and was employed on the works at the Palace of Westminster. [ARCHITECT]

Cuvillies, Francois De (I): 1698-1767. He came to Paris in 1714 and entered the atelier of Robert de Cotte. On Sept. 15, 1725, he was appointed *Hoffbaumeister* to the Elector Karl Albrecht (of Bavaria). On Dec. 13, 1763, he assumed the direction of all the Elector's constructions. When Karl Albrecht became emperor as

222

Karl VII (Jan. 24, 1742), Cuvillies was made *Hofkammerrath* and *Hofbaumeister* at the imperial court. He built the Lustschloss at Nymphenburg near Munich. It is probable that he designed the *Residenz-theater* in Munich, which was begun April 15, 1751, and is one of the finest examples of the French Baroque style in Germany. He made extensive additions to the Residenz (Royal Palace) at Munich. Cuvillies excelled in the arrangement of parks and gardens. [ARCHITECT, DECORATOR, AND ENGRAVER]

Cuypers, Petrus Josephus Hubertus: 1827-1921. Cuypers was born in the Netherlands and is considered by some to be the greatest Dutch architect who ever lived. Cuypers studied at the Antwerp Academy prior to becoming the architect for the city of Roermond. His most famous buildings are the Rijksmuseum and the Central Station, both of which are built in the Dutch Renaissance style. Cuypers adapted the Gothic manner to design many Roman Catholic Churches. [ARCHITECT]

Cyrus: d. 52 B.C. A Greek architect employed by Cicero. He made Cicero and Clodius joint heirs of his estate. He died on the day when Clodius was murdered. [ARCHITECT]

Dammartin (Dampmartin), Andre de: d. ca. 1400. Andre was employed at the Old Louvre in the year 1365. On January 28, 1380, he was called to Troyes (Aube, France) to inspect the works at the Cathedral. In 1383, by letters patent of Philippe le Hardi, Duke of Burgundy (1342-1404), he was appointed chief architect of all his constructions and especially of the church and monastery of the Chartreuse near Dijon. In 1384, with Raymond du Temple, he inspected the works at the Chateau of Rouvres (France). [ARCHITECT]

Damon, Captain Isaac: Damon studied architecture with Ithiel Town of New York and was from 1812 to 1840 the leading architect in western Massachusetts. Among his works were the first church of Northampton (built 1811, burned in 1878), the first church of Springfield (about 1818, still standing), the church and county courthouse in Lenox (about 1814, still standing). [ARCHITECT]

Dance, George (I): 1695-1768. In December 1735, Dance was appointed clerk of the city works by the corporation of the city of London. Between 1739 and 1753 he designed and built the Mansion House (the official residence of the lord mayor of the city of London), which was altered somewhat by his son George Dance. He built many London churches. [ARCHITECT]

Danckerts de Rij, Cornelis (the younger): 1561-1634. A son of Cornelis Danckerts de Rij the elder, in 1595 he succeeded his father as city architect of Amsterdam (Holland). According to Immerzeel, he built the Haarlemmer port, the Zuiderkerk, and the Noorderkerke in Amsterdam. He also built the fine tower of the Westerkerke. [ARCHITECT]

Daphnis: Daphnis was one of the architects of the temple of Apollo near Miletus. [ARCHITECT]

de l'Orme, Philibert: ca. 1515-1570. De l'Orme's father was Jehan de l'Orme, architect at Lyons, France, possibly related to Pierre and Toussaint Delorme, master masons at Gaillon. Various passages in his works point to 1515 as about the date of his birth. He went to Rome at 19 or 20 and in 1534 became a protege of the learned Marcellus Cervinus, who was elected Pope in 1555 as Marcellus II. He was also employed by Paul III (Pope 1534-1549) at S. Martino del Bosco in Calabria. In 1536 De l'Orme returned to Lyons with the famous General Guillaume du Bellay and his brother, Jean du Bellay, the cardinal. The portal of S. Nizier at Lyons is as-

cribed to him. He followed the Cardinal du Bellay to Paris and began for him the Chateau of Saint-Maurles-Fosses. In 1546 he entered the royal service charged with the inspection of fortresses in Brittany and distinguished himself by defending the city of Brest against the English. Jan. 29, 1548, he was designated *architecte du roi* and April 3 was appointed *inspecteur des batiments royaux* at Fontainebleau, Saint-Germain, etc. He also directed the manufacture of tapestry at Fontainebleau. Becoming the preferred architect of Henri II and Diane de Poitiers, he was endowed by them with the benefices of five abbeys having a revenue of 6000 livres and Sept. 5, 1550, was made a canon of Notre Dame (Paris). After the death of Henri II (July 10, 1559) he was superseded in the office of *inspecteur* by Primaticcio. He retained his benefices, however, and his will, published in the *Archives de l'art francais*, shows a considerable fortune. The Palace of the Tuileries was begun by de l'Orme in 1564 under the personal direction of the queen dowager, Catherine de' Medici (1519-1589). His design contemplated an immense rectangle 188 meters long by 118 meters wide. Of this only the garden front was built, and of this front only the central pavilion with its connecting wings was by de l'Orme. His work was almost entirely remodelled by Jacques Lemercier, Louis Levau, and D'Orbay in the reign of Louis XIV, and by the architects of Napoleon III. The palace was destroyed by the Commune on the night of May 23-24, 1871.

The Chateau of Anet was the chief glory of Philibert de l'Orme. An inscription over the main portal dates the work between 1548 and 1552. The Chateau was spared by the Revolution but was sold Feb. 1, 1798 for 3,200,000 francs without its movables. Much of the architectural decoration was bought for the government by Alexandre Lenoir, assisted by Napoleon Bonaparte, then first consul. The portal of the main building stands now in the court of the *Ecoles des Beaux Arts* in Paris. The palace was then broken up for building material, except the left wing, partially restored in 1828. The chapel was restored by A. N. Caristie and reopened Sept. 3, 1851. The tomb of Francois I at Saint-Denis is the only work of de l'Orme which is now intact. The architecture is ascribed to him exclusively in the *Comptes des batiments du roi*. He became superintendent at Fontainebleau after the death of Francois I and in the Salle

du Bal substituted a fine ceiling of wood for the vault projected by Gilles le Breton. At the Chateau of Monceaux he first used the *couverture a la Philibert de l'Orme,* a method of building wooden roofs which substituted for single heavy beam planks bolted together "so that the junction in each case took place upon the center of the piece by which it was doubled." There is a record of a contract with him dated Jan. 27, 1557, for the construction of the bridge and gallery at Chenonceau. In 1561 De l'Orme published, a*vec privilege du roi* (Charles IX), *Nouvelles inventions pour bien bastir et a petite fraiz,* etc., and in 1567, *Le premier tome de l'architecture, etc.,* dedicated to Catherine de' Medici. The second volume never appeared. In 1858 M. Leopold Delisle discovered in the *Bibliotheque Nationale* a manuscript entitled *Instruction de Monsieur d' Ivry dict De l'Orme,* a personal defence of about 1560 which throws much light upon his career. It is printed in Berty, *Les grands architectes francais.* [ARCHITECT]

Deane, Sir Thomas: 1792-1871. Deane was the son of a builder of Cork (Ireland). He made a fortune in his father's business, became mayor of Cork, and was knighted in 1830. He then commenced practice as an architect and built at Cork the Bank of Ireland, the Savings Bank, the Queen's College, the portico of the Courthouse, etc. With his son Thomas Deane he built the Museum at Oxford (England). [ARCHITECT]

Debret, Francois: 1777-1850. Debret was a pupil of Charles Percier. In 1813 he replaced Cellerier as architect of the abbey Church of S. Denis, where he accomplished numerous restorations. He was himself replaced by Viollet-le-Duc in 1846. After 1822 Debret laid the foundations of the building of the *Ecole des Beaux Arts* (Paris), which was continued by his pupil, Jacques Felix Duban. [ARCHITECT]

Deinocrates: The architect appears under various names; Dinokrates (Vitruvius), Dinochares and Timochares (Pliny), Cheirokrates (Strabo), Stasikrates (Plutarch), etc. The place of his birth is also variously given, Macedonia, Rhegion, and Rhodes. He was the favorite architect of Alexander the Great (356-323 B.C.), whose attention was attracted by his scheme for transforming Mt. Athos into a colossal statue. Deinocrates was employed to lay out the city of Alexandria (Egypt). He rebuilt the temple of Artemis at Ephesus. [ARCHITECT]

Delorme, Pierre: Pierre was one of the three principal architects of the Chateau of Gaillon (Eure, Normandy), the others being Pierre Fain and Guillaume Senault. About 1502 he was employed by the Cardinal Georges I d'Amboise (d. May 25, 1510) to make additions to the episcopal palace at Rouen. His name first appears in the accounts of the cardinal's chateau at Gaillon, Jan. 1, 1507. He built the so-called *Maison Pierre Delorm*, (destroyed) on the south side of the main court facing the *grande maison* of Guillame Senault. The *comptes* show that he was constantly employed at Gaillon during the life of the first cardinal. It is supposed that he was related to Philibert de l'Orme. [ARCHITECT]

Demetrios: A priest of the temple of Artemis at Ephesus and one of the architects of that building. [ARCHITECT]

Dinzenhofer, Kilian Ignatz: 1690-1752. The family of Dinzenhofer came originally from Bamberg in Bavaria, where there were several architects of that name. His father, Christoph, was an architect practicing in Prague (Bohemia). Kilian went to Vienna in his twentieth year and worked with Fischer von Erlach. He travelled in Italy, France, and England, and settled in Prague after the death of his father in 1722. He was employed on nearly all the most important buildings undertaken at Prague at this time. His chief work is the cupola of the Church of S. Nicholas at Prague. [ARCHITECT]

Dolci, Giovanni (Giovannino) di Pietro dei: d.ca. 1486. He first appears in the records of the reign of Nicholas V (Pope 1458-1455), and was employed by Pius II (Pope 1458-1464). Under Paul II (Pope 1464-1471) he held the office of *soprastante delle fabbriche*, and worked at the Vatican and the Palazzo di S. Marco (Rome). Under Sixtus IV (Pope 1471-1484) he built the Sistine Chapel (Vatican, Rome), which has been incorrectly attributed by Vasari to Baccio Pontelli. Two bulls of Sixtus IV, dated Nov. 14, 1481, are in existence, which confide to Giovannino the reconstruction of the citadel of Civita Vecchia. Oct. 17, 1482, he was created chatelaine of that fortress. [SCULPTOR AND CIVIL AND MILITARY ARCHITECT]

Dosio, Giovan' Antonio: 1533-ca. 1609. Dosio began as a goldsmith in Rome, where he spent three years in the atelier of Raffaello da Montelupo. He was employed by Pius IV (Pope 1559-1565) to restore antique marbles at the Belvedere. Returning to Florence about 1574, his first work was the Capella Gaddi in the Church of S.

Maria Novella. He built also the Giacomini-Laderel Palace (begun 1580), the residence of the Florentine Bishop Alessandro de' Medici (begun 1582), and the Capella Niccolini (begun 1585) in the Church of S. Croce. In the competition of 1586 he made a design for the facade of the Duomo, Florence. [ARCHITECT AND SCULPTOR]

Dotzinger, Jost (Jodoque, Jodocus): d. 1472. After the death of Hans Hultz, in 1449, Dotzinger succeeded him as supervising architect of the Cathedral of Strasbourg. The Cathedral was practically finished at this time. His most important work is the baptismal font now in the northern wing of the transept. In 1455 he undertook the restoration of the choir. Dotzinger was especially connected with the reorganization and consolidation of the Masonic corporations of Germany. Before his time the architects and stonecutters had formed isolated lodges (*Bauhutte*) which had originated in the Benedictine monasteries and were secularized at the same time as the art of architecture itself. On April 25, 1459, he called together a general convention at Ratisbon (Regensburg, Bavaria), which consolidated the scattered lodges in one order and established statues and regulations for its government. Nicholas Dotzinger, probably a son of

Jost, was also an architect and attended the convention at Regensburg. [ARCHITECT]

Duban, Jacques Felix: 1797-1870 (at Bordeaux). Duban was a pupil of Francois Debret and the *Ecole des Beaux Arts* and in 1823 won the *Grand Prix de Rome* in architecture. After acting as assistant of Debret at the *Ecole des Beaux Arts* he became chief architect of that building in 1832. He constructed from his own plans the main building of the school, containing the hemicycle, the library, etc. He also arranged the interesting collection of architectural fragments in the open court. He occupied himself with the improvement and decoration of this building until his death. In 1840 he undertook the restoration of the Saint-Chapelle, Paris, but gave up this work to Jean Baptiste Lassus in 1849. In 1845 Duban began the restoration of the Chateau of Blois, with which he was occupied 25 years. About 1845 he restored the Chateau of Dampierre for the Duc de Luynes. Duban began the reconstruction of the Chateau of Chantilly, for the Duc d'Aumale, but was interrupted by the political disturbances of 1848. In 1849 he was appointed architect in charge of the Chateau of Fontainebleau and of the Louvre. He made extensive restorations at the Louvre, but was superseded by Louis Visconti as architect of that building in 1853. [ARCHITECT]

Dudok, Willem Marinus: 1884-1974 Dudok was an engineer as well as an architect. Having first been educated at the Royal Military Academy in Breda, Netherlands, Dudok then went on to become the city architect for the town of Hilversum. Influenced by Frank Lloyd Wright to some degree, Dudok's most renowned building is the Hilversum Town Hall which was completed in 1930. His personal style was imitated by many albeit not very successfully; most of his work was contained within Hilversum, and he did not really leave any successors. [ARCHITECT]

Durandus (Durand): The inscription *Durand me fecit* is found on one of the vaults of the nave of the Cathedral of Rouen. On account of similarity of workmanship, it is supposed by some authorities that all the vaults of the nave were built by him. [ARCHITECT]

Eames, Charles: 1907-1978 Charles Eames could be considered a Renaissance man. He designed furniture, made toys and films, designed exhibitions and built his own house. With Eero Saarinen, he won the competition for a chair which was designed for the Museum of Modern Art in New York City. Eames did not leave a large inheritance of buildings bearing his design skills to the world of architecture. Rather, he left his indelible mark with his chairs and personal residence, which reflected his love of comfort and whimsy, color and form, fun and light, all contributions which have never been equalled in the design field. [ARCHITECT]

Eginhard: Eginhard was director for construction of the Emperor Charlemagne (b. ca. 742-814). He is supposed to have made the plan of the monastery of S. Gall (Switzerland), which is still preserved in the archives of the suppressed monastery. [ABBOT AND ARCHITECT]

Egle, Joseph von: 1818-1899. He was educated at the polytechnic schools of Stuttgart, Nuremberg, and Vienna, and attended (1839-1841) the Academy of Architecture in Berlin. In 1847 and 1848 he served as the correspondent of the *Allgemeine Bauzeitung* in North Germany, England, and Italy. He was made professor at the polytechnic school in Stuttgart in 1850, in 1857 was appointed *Hofbaumeister*, and in 1884 *Hofbaudirector* in Wurtemberg (Germany). He built the Polytechnikum (1860-1865),

remodelled the royal palace (1864-1867), built the Gothic Marienkirche and a Catholic church, all in Stuttgart (Germany). [ARCHITECT]

Eiffel, Gustave: 1832-1923 Of course Eiffel is best known for the Eiffel Tower in Paris. Notwithstanding this legacy, however, it should be noted that his bridges are equally important, as well as his engineering contributions to the Bon Marche store in Paris and the Statue of Liberty in New York. Built in 1889 for the Paris Exhibition, the Eiffel Tower remained the highest building in the world until the Chrysler and Empire State Buildings were erected in New York City. Thanks to Eiffel, metal finally achieved its prominent place in architectural design. [ARCHITECT]

Eigtved, Nikolai: 1701-1754. Eigtved began as a gardener in Germany. In 1729 he served in the Saxon army as lieutenant of engineers. In 1732 he was sent by Christian VI of Denmark (d. 1746) to study architecture in Italy. On his return he was made court architect, inspector of the Academy at Copenhagen (1745), and finally director of the Academy (1751). He built the palace of the crown prince (1745), the four palaces of the Amalienborg place, the old Royal Theater, the palaces of Christianborg, Fredensborg, Sophienberg and Bregentved. Eigtved began the Marble Church at Copenhagen, which was continued by Nicolas Henry Jarin. [ARCHITECT]

Einhart: He came to the school of the monastery of Fulda in Germany in his youth and was later attached to the court of Charlemagne (742-814) as general superintendent of the imperial buildings. He built the palace at Aix-la-Chapelle (Aachen), Germany, of which the chapel remains and has given its name to the town. [ARCHITECT, PAINTER, SCULPTOR]

Erwin Von Steinbach (I): When Conrad von Lichtenberg became Bishop of Strasbourg, in February 1273, his cathedral still lacked the facade. An inscription that existed on the left portal until 1720 ascribes the commencement of the work to Erwin von Steinbach. The first stone was laid May 25, 1277. His plan included only the two lower stories of the facade with the rose window. The great screen of the third story was a later addition. The spire was finished by Hans Hultz of Cologne in 1439. Erwin restored the nave after the great fire of Aug. 14, 1298. He designed the Chapel of the Virgin (finished 1361, destroyed 1681) and probably designed the tomb of Bish-

op Conrad. He was succeeded by his sons, Erwin (II) and Han (Jean) called Winlin. [ARCHITECT]

Etienne: Supervising architect (*maitre de l'eglise*) of the Cathedral of Rodez (Aveyron, France), the reconstruction of which he began between 1289 and 1294. [ARCHITECT]

Eupalinos: According to Herodotus Eupalinos, son of Naustrophos, of Megara, Greece, constructed the aqueduct of Samos about 630 B.C. [ENGINEER]

Eupolemos: Eupolemos built, about 420-416 B.C., the temple of Hera at Argos in place of the old building which was destroyed in 423 B.C. [ARCHITECT]

Fain, Pierre: In 1501-1502 Fain worked on the archepiscopal palace at Rouen. On December 4, 1507, he contracted with others to build the chapel of the Chateau of Gaillon (Eure, France). In 1509 he completed the portal leading from the outer to the inner court at Gaillon, which is now at the *Ecole des Beaux Arts*, Paris. [SCULPTOR AND ARCHITECT]

Fieravanti (Fioravanti), Ridolfo Dei (Aristotele): ca. 1418-ca. 1480. A son of Fieravante dei Fiervanti. He entered the service of Nicholas V (Pope 1447-1455) in Rome and moved the great monolithic columns from the Church of S. Maria Sopra Minerva to the Vatican. He suggested to Nicholas V and Paul II the transportation of the obelisk of the Vatican to the piazza di S. Pietro, which was finally accomplished by Domenico Fontana in 1586. He served the Sforza in Milan and in 1467 was invited to Hungary by the King Mathias Corvinus, for whom he built bridges over the Danube. In 1472 he was in the service of Ferdinand I, King of Naples. In 1475 he went to Russia and for Ivan III built the Cathedral of the Assumption at Moscow and probably also portions of the Kremlin. He probably designed the facade of the Palazzo del Podesta in Bologna. [ARCHITECT, ENGINEER, AND MATHEMATICIAN]

Filarete (Antonio di Pietro Averlino, Averulinus): ca. 1400-ca. 1465. The surname Filarete (*phil-arete*, lover of virtue) is given by Vasari but is not found in contemporary sources. He assisted Ghiberti on the second gate of the baptistery. Filarete made of Eugenius IV (Pope 1431-1447) the bronze doors of S. Peter's Church at Rome (1445). Soon after the accession of Nicholas V (Pope 1447-1455) he went to Milan, where he held the position of cathedral architect from February, 1452 to July 5, 1454. Filarete's chief work is the Ospedale

Maggiore at Milan, of which the first stone was laid April 12, 1457. He undoubtedly made the plans and carried out the southwestern short side and the adjacent portions of the long side as far as the main court. He left the work in 1465. Filarete began the Cathedral of Bergamo in 1457. His famous *Trattato dell' Architettura*, written for the instruction of the Duke Francesco Sforza, was begun about 1460 and finished in 1464. [ARCHITECT]

Fingini, Luigi: b. 1903. Fingini was born in Milan and received his architectural training at the Polytecnic in Milan. Along with Gino Pollini and Giuseppe Terragni, he then established Gruppo 7 (Group Seven) in 1927. This partnership became the first Italian group of architects to develop the rational architecture in Italy. Best known for their design of the Church of the Madonna of the Poor in Milan in 1954, they also did extensive design work for Olivetti, which included not only the factory itself, but also the nursery school, the housing project for workers, and the social services center. [ARCHITECT]

Fischer von Erlach, Johann Bernhard: 1650-1723 Fischer Von Erlach was a contemporary of Andrea Pozzo and was educated in Rome. Returning to Vienna, he began the Schloss Schonbrunn, the construction of which was interrupted by the death of the Emperor Joseph I, and built the Church of S. Carlo Borromeo (begun 1715), the Peterskirche, the palace of the Prince Eugen, now Finanzminis-terium (1703), the Trautson Palace (1720-1730), the Hofbibliothek (1722-1726), all in Vienna, the Kolle-gienkirche in Salzburg (1696-1707), the Kurfursten Kapelle in the Cathe-dral of Breslau, Germany (1722-1727), the Clam-Gallus Palace in Prague, Bohemia (1707-1712), and other buildings. He published *Entwurfe historischer Baukunst* (1725). [ARCHI-TECT]

Fontaine, Pierre Francois Leonard: 1762-1853. Fontaine was a pupil of Antoine Francois Peyre. In 1785 he went to Rome, where he was joined by Charles Percier. He was asso-ciated with Percier in Paris, and to-gether they were made directors of the decorations of the opera house. When Napoleon became First Consul they were made his architects and retained that position under the Em-pire. Percier and Fontaine restored the Chateaux of Malmaison, Saint-Cloud, Compiegne, Versailles, and other imperial residences. They re-stored the buildings of the court of the Louvre, and designed and built the Arc de Triomphe du Carrousel. They laid out the Rue de Rivoli and built additions to the Palace of the Tuileries in that street. In 1814 Perci-er retired from their association. Fontaine was court architect of Louis XVIII, for whom he built the Cha-pelle Expiatoire in the Rue d'Anjou, Paris. During the reign of Charles X he was architect to the Duke of Or-leans, for whom he restored and en-larged the Palais Royal. He was chief architect of Louis Philippe. During this reign he remodelled the garden in front of the Tuileries, thus contrib-uting to the defacement of the monu-ment of Philibert de l'Orme. Fontaine was architect in charge of the Louvre, the Tuileries, and the royal buildings until 1848. From 1831 to 1833 he was architect of the Theater Francais, Paris. In 1849 he was chosen president of the *Conseil des batiments civils*. Fontaine pub-lished alone a *Histoire du Palais Royal*. [ARCHITECT]

Fontana, Carlo: 1634-1714. It is not known that Carlo was related to ei-ther Domenico or Giovanni Fontana. He was a pupil of Bernini. He built the facade of the Church of S. Marcel-lo in the Corso (Rome, 1683), the monument of Queen Christina of Sweden in S. Peter's Church (1689), the facade of the Church of S. Maria in Trastevere (1702), the cupola of the Cathedral of Montefiascone and the Cathedral of Fulda (1696). The villa of the princes of Lichtenstein at Vienna was built from his designs between 1697 and 1700. He built the Palazzo Bolognetti (now Torlonia), Rome, 1680, the Palazzo Grimani, Rome, the Villa Visconti at Frascati, and the great portal of the Palazzo Reale at Genoa. Fontana succeeded Mattia de' Rossi as architect of S. Peter's Church in the reign of Innocent XII (Pope 1691-1700) and published his descriptive monograph, *Templum Vaticanum*, in 1694. He published also works on the Flavian Amphitheatre, the aqueducts, and the innundations of the Tiber. Fontana designed several fountains in Rome. His nephews, Girolamo and Francesco Fontana, assisted him in his work. Girolamo built the Cathedral and fountains of Frascati. [ARCHITECT]

Fontana, Domenico: 1543-1607. Domenico was born in Lombardy near Lake Como and came to Rome during the lifetime of Michelangelo. He was a *protege* of the Cardinal Montalto (Pope Sixtus V, 1585-1590). About 1580 he built this cardinal's villa (later Villa Negroni, Rome). When Montalto became Pope he made Domenico pontifical architect (1585). He built the lantern of the main cupola of S. Peter's Church according to the designs of Michelangelo. Fontana moved the obelisk of Nero's circus from its old position to the Piazza di S. Pietro (1586). He also placed the obelisk of the Piazza del Popolo (1587) and that of the Piazzi di S. Giovanni in Laterano (1588). About 1586 he began the facade of the northern transept of the Church of S. Giovanni in Laterano, Rome. He also built the Palazzo Laterano and the palace of Sixtus V at the Vatican. The fountain of the Acqua Paola, Rome, is usually credited to his brother Giovanni. Domenico designed the similar fountain of the Termini, Rome. He built the facade of the Palazzo Quirinale in the Via Pia. In 1592 Domenico removed to Naples and built there the Palazzo Reale. [ARCHITECT]

Fontana, Giovanni: ca. 1540-1614. Giovanni came to Rome with his younger brother Domenico, whom he assisted in many of his undertakings. He was an engineer and contractor rather than architect and was especially concerned with the restoration and construction of aqueducts, laying out streets, and the like. He arranged the water works in the Vatican gardens and at the Villa Mondragone, at Frascati. The design of the fountain of the Acqua Paola, Rome, is attributed to Giovanni, although it is doubtless quite as much the work of his brother Domenico and his nephew, Carlo Maderna. When Domenico went to Naples in 1592 Giovanni succeeded him as papal architect under Clement VIII (Pope 1592-1605). [ENGINEER, CONTRACTOR]

Freyssinet, Eugene: 1879-1962. Freyssinet, born in Paris, studied at the *Ecole Polytechnique* and the *Ecole Nationale des Ponts et Chaussees*, also in Paris. His reinforced concrete structures are considered to be some of the most beautiful ever designed. Of particular note were the hangars at the Orly Airport in Paris. Unfortunately, they were destroyed during World War II. Although not an architect *per se*, Freyssinet's designs of bridges and the Basilica of St. Pius at Lourdes combined aesthetic style and economical techniques. [ARCHITECT]

Frontinus, Sextus Julius: d. ca. 106 A.D. He first appears about 70 A.D. as *praetor urbanus* under the Emperor Vespasian, 75 A.D. he was appointed governor of Britain and was superseded in that office by Agricola in 78. In 97 he was appointed *curator aquarum*, or superintendent of the aqueducts. He was succeeded about 106 A.D. by the Younger Pliny. Two of his works are extant: *Strategematicon, Li-*

bri IV and De Aquaeductibus Urbis Romae, Libri II. [ENGINEER]

Fulbert: d. 1029. The Cathedral of Chartres, probably the fourth church erected on the site of the present building, was burned Sept. 7, 1020, during the reign of Robert le Diable, Duke of Normandy. The Bishop Fulbert devoted himself to the immediate reconstruction of the church. The crypt of the church was completed about two years after the conflagration. The Cathedral was completed during the administration of his successor, the Bishop Thierry and dedicated Oct. 17, 1037. The towers were added after 1115. This church, with the exception of the towers which still stand, was destroyed by fire in 1194. The present Cathedral was built on its ruins. [BISHOP AND ARCHITECT]

Fuller, Thomas: 1822-1898. Fuller was articled to an architect in London, and assisted J. R. Brandon in the preparation of his works on Gothic architecture. He practiced in the West Indies and in Canada and in 1863 took charge of all government buildings at Ottawa. In 1868 Fuller and Laver were chosen (by competition) architects of the capitol at Albany, New York, and held that position until they were superseded by H. H. Richardson, Eidlitz, and Olmsted. In 1881 he was appointed chief architect of the Dominion Government and held that office until 1897. [ARCHITECT]

Fuller, Richard Buckminster: 1995-1983. Fuller, who was born in Massachusetts, never received more than two years of college training, but his radical designs were efficient combinations of arrangement for maximum utilization of space and resources. An author, inventor, mathematician, engineer, philosopher, poet, and teacher as well, Fuller achieved notoriety first with his Dymaxion House, a model for low-cost mass production and a virtual machine for living. This design led to the design of the geodesic dome, for which he is perhaps most famous. The geodesic dome was designed not only for living space but also for large industrial applications. The achievement of combining a rigid structure while using a minimum amount of materials was a rare breakthrough in the architectural world and has never been duplicated. There are now more than 100,000 geodesic domes in the world. Fuller is considered to be a true universal man. His philosophies and moral attitudes regarding the sharing of natural resources are reflected in his writings, his designs, and his forward thinking ideas. He lectured at all major Eastern universities, including Harvard and Cornell. [ARCHITECT]

Furness, Frank: 1839-1912. Eccentricity was Furness's style. He has been compared to Teulon and Keeling (English architects). Although some of the features of his work are original, his style would best be defined as Gothic. Designs included the Provident Institution in Philadelphia which was destroyed in 1879 and the Pennsylvania Academy of Fine Arts, also in Philadelphia. [ARCHITECT]

Gabriel, Jacques (II): d. 1686. Jacques (II) was a nephew by marriage of Jules Hardouin-Mansart. He was the principal constructor employed at the Chateau of Versailles, where he built the canal, reservoir, etc. In 1667 he built the establishment of the Gobelins. In 1675 Gabriel undertook the construction of the new buildings of the Chateau of Clagny. In 1685 he began the construction of the Pont Royal. [ARCHITECT]

Gabriel, Jacques Ange: 1698-1782. Jacques was the son of Jacques Jules Gabriel and assisted his father in many undertakings. At the death of his father in 1742 he succeeded him as *premier architecte* of Louis XV, and continued and completed many of the buildings begun by him. In 1745 he was made *inspecteur general des batiments royaux*. In 1751 he made the plans for the buildings of the Ecole Militaire, Paris, which was built mainly by Alexandre Brongniart between 1752 and 1787. In 1752 he took part in the famous *concours* for the creation of the Place Louis XV, now Place de la Concorde, Paris. His plans were accepted in 1753. Work was begun in 1754 and the Place was opened in 1763. The Colonnades in the Rue Royale were not completed until 1772. Between 1753 and 1774 Gabriel rebuilt the central pavilion, the right wing and Salle de Spectacle of the Palace of Versailles. Between 1762 and 1768 he built the Petit Trianon in the gardens of Versailles. In 1755 he was intrusted with the restoration of the Louvre, principally the eastern portion with the colonnade designed by Claude Perrault. This part of the palace had never been roofed over and was much injured. About the same time he rebuilt the Chateau of Compiegne. [ARCHITECT]

Gabriel, Jacques Jules: 1667-1742. Jacques Jules was a son of Jacques Gabriel (II). In 1709 he was created *controleur des batiments* at Versailles and *architecte ordinaire du roi*. Between 1728 and 1733 he built the Ho-

tel Dieu at Orleans (Loire, France) and in 1727 made plans for the reconstruction of the public buildings of the city of Rennes which had been burned in 1720. In 1730 he made plans for the Palais Royal at Bordeaux (Gironde, France), which was completed in 1749. He began also the exchange and customhouse in that city, which were finished by his son Jacques Ange. In 1738 Gabriel commenced the restoration of the Hotel des Comptes, Paris. This building, remodelled by Louis Joseph Duc for the prefecture of police, was destroyed by the Commune in 1871. [ARCHITECT]

Galli da Bibiena, Ferdinando: 1657-1743. Ferdinando was the son of Giovanni Maria Galli, a painter. The family took the name Bibiena from a little town in Tuscany. Ferdinando entered the service of Ranuccio Farnese II, at Parma. He was called to Spain by King Carlos III. At the coronation of the Emperor Charles VI in 1711 he went to Venice where he remained until 1716. Returning to Parma, he built the Church of S. Antonio Abate. The extraordinary decorations of the double ceiling of this church were painted by him also. One of his last works was the Teatro Reale in Mantua. Like the other members of his family he was especially interested in the construction and decoration of theaters and in some scene painting. His *Architettura Civile* was published in 1711. [ARCHITECT]

Galli da Bibiena, Giuseppe: 1696-1757 (at Berlin). Giuseppe was the son of Ferdinando Galli da Bibiena. He went to Vienna with his father and spent his life in the service of the various German courts. He was especially interested in theater construction, scene painting, the decoration of processions, and the like. In 1723 he arranged an imperial fete at Prague. He built a theater at Bayreuth, Bavaria, in 1747 and in 1750 rebuilt an opera house at Dresden, now destroyed. [ARCHITECT]

Gambarelli, Antoni Di Matteo (Rossellino): 1427-1479. Antonio was the youngest of five brothers Bambarelli who had a shop on the corner of the Via del Proconsolo in Florence. The others were Domenico (b. 1407), Bernardo, Giovanni (1417-1496), and Tommaso (b. 1422). His principal work, the monument of the Cardinal Jacopo of Portugal, in S. Miniato near Florence, was ordered in 1461. According to Vasari he built also the chapel in which it is placed. Antonio designed the tomb of the Duchess of Amalfi in the Church of Monte Olive-

to at Naples. He was assisted by Antonio Barocci da Milano on the tomb of Roverella in the Church of S. Giorgio at Ferrara (finished 1475) at Pistoia, which was begun by his brother Bernardo before his death. [SCULPTOR AND ARCHITECT]

Garnier, Tony: 1869-1948. Garnier was born in Lyons, France, the child of working-class parents. He received his degrees from the *Ecole Nationale des Beaux-Arts* in Lyons and the Ecole de Beaux-Arts in Paris and was awarded the *Prix de Rome* in 1899. Garnier's conception of a *Cite Industrielle* is a model of large scale urban planning and modern architecture, with all buildings out of concrete. This project, designed by Garnier from 1904 onward, reflected the socialist thinking of Emile Zola, the French author, who had a strong influence upon all of Garnier's works. Garnier believed that architecture should be inspired by the beauty of antiquity while at the same time meeting current social needs. And so, along these lines, his *Cite Industrielle* design incorporates housing, transportation, industrial, and recreational needs, while remaining aesthetically pleasing and meeting the moral and material needs of the individual. Later in life, Garnier was given the opportunity by Edouard

Herriot, the radical mayor of Lyons, to bring some of his designs into partnership. They specialized in office and administration buildings, which distinctively identify post-war architecture in Germany even today. Their best known work is the Thyssen Building which looks like a monolithic box and was built in Dusseldorf in 1960. The first covered shopping center in Berlin, the Europa Center, was also designed by the pair. The firm has won many international awards over its life. [ARCHITECT]

Gartner Friedrich von: 1793-1847. In 1809 Gartner entered the academy in Munich and in 1812 went to Paris, where he studied under Percier (see Percier). He later travelled in Italy and Sicily. In 1820 he was appointed professor of architecture in the academy at Munich and was at the same time director of the porcelain manufactory. In Munich he built most of the large buildings of the Ludwig-strasse; i.e., the Feldhern-Halle (1841), the Ludwigskirche (finished 1845), the library (1831-1842), the university (1835-1840), the Siegestor (1844), and the Blinden Institut. He also built in Munich the Wittelsbacher Palace (1843), the arcades of the New Cemetery, and other works. In 1836 he visited Athens, where he

built the royal palace, In 1840 he built the Pompejanum near Aschaffenburg. Gartner restored the cathedrals of Bamberg, Regensburg (Ratisbon), and Speier (Spires). [ARCHITECT]

Gau, Franz Christian: 1790-1854. Gau was naturalized as a French citizen and became a pupil of Debret and Lebas. He undertook the completion of the great work concerning Napoleon's expedition to Egypt and also finished the third and fourth volumes of Francois Mazois's book on the ruins of Pompeii. From 1831 to 1844 Gau was architect of the prisons and hospitals. He published *Antiquities de la Nubie* (Paris, 1820). [ARCHITECT]

Ghiberti, Lorenzo de: 1378-1455. The earliest of the three pairs of bronze doors of the baptistery of Florence was made by Andrea da Pisa. In 1401 a competition was opened for another. According to Vasari the competitors were Ghiberti and Brunellesco of Florence, Giacomo della Quercia and Francesco Valdambrini of Siena, Nicolo Spinelli and Nicolo Lamberti of Arezzo, and Simone of Colle in Val d' Elsa. The competitive panels of the "Sacrifice of Abraham," executed by Brunellesco and Ghiberti are both in Museo Nazionale, Florence. Ghiberti was successful, and the work began in December, 1403. It was finished in April 1424. In a document of April 16, 1420, Ghiberti is mentioned as associated on equal terms with Brunellesco in building the cupola of the Cathedral of Florence. He appears occasionally in the records but had little to do with the actual construction. On Jan. 2, 1424 (before the completion of his first doors), Ghiberti received a commission for another pair for the Florentine baptistery. This, the most celebrated work of its kind in existence, was finished in 1452. It is composed of 10 panels in relief representing subjects from the Old Testament. In the framework are busts and figures in high relief. Ghiberti modelled also the beautiful framework of birds and foliage. The cartoons for many of the painted glass windows in the Florentine Cathedral were drawn by Ghiberti. He was succeeded by his son Vittorio; there were sculptors of the Ghiberti family in the sixteenth century. [GOLDSMITH, SCULPTOR, ARCHITECT]

Ghini, Giovanni di Lapo: Ghini first appears in the records of the Cathedral of Florence in 1355 as a member of the commission appointed to consider the model of Francesco Talenti and in 1364 superseded him as chief architect of the Cathedral. About

1360, Ghini appears to have made a model called *chiesa piccola* in the records) which called for five bays in the nave and five chapels about the rotunda. On Aug. 13, 1366, this model was superseded by that of the commission of architects and painters, according to which the church was built essentially as it stands. On August, 1371, Ghini's name appears in the records for the last time. [ARCHITECT]

Giacomo Della Porta: 1541-1604 in Rome. The most important of the pupils of Vignola. Between 1564 and 1573 he was occupied at Genoa, his principal work there being the completion of the Church of S. Annunziata. After the death of Vignola in 1573, he returned to Rome and finished the church called Il Gesu, begun by that architect. Before his death in 1564, Michelangelo and his assistants had made a model for the cupola on S. Peter's Church (Rome) and had completed the construction as far as the cornice of the drum. The cupola itself was built by Giacomo della Porta. He also built the Palazzo Paluzzi, the Palazzo Chigi in the Piazza Colonna, the Palazzo Serlupi, the Palazzo d' Este, and the facade of the Church of S. Maria in Monte (1579), the facade of the Church of S. Luigi de' Francesi (1589), all in Rome.

He was very successful in designing decorative architectural accessories. He made several fine fountains in Rome, the most important of which is the Fontana delle Tartarughe (of the Turtles), the figures of which were modelled by the sculptor Taddeo Landini. Della Porta's Villa Aldobrandini near Frascati, his last work (1598-1603), with its fine garden and casino, is especially characteristic. [ARCHITECT]

Gibbs, James: 1682-1754. He was the son of Peter Gibbs, a Roman Catholic merchant of Aberdeen, and took his M.A. degree at Marischal College, Aberdeen. After the death of his parents he entered the service of a builder in Holland. He was discovered by John Erskine, eleventh Earl of Mar, who sent him to Rome, where he entered the school of Carlo Fontana, surveyor general to Pope Clement XI. Returning to London in 1709, he won the friendship of Sir Christopher Wren. The Church of S. Mary le Strand was begun by Gibbs on Feb. 15, 1714. In August 1721, he began for Harley, Earl of Oxford, the Church of S. Peter, Vere Street, London, and a little later the tomb of Matthew Prior in the south transept of Westminster Abbey. On March 19, 1722, the first stone was laid for his famous Church of S. Martin's in the Fields, and on June 22, 1722, he began the Senate House in Cambridge. In 1723-1725 he built the Church of Allhallows in Derby (except the tower). Gibbs prepared a scheme for rebuilding the quadrangle of King's College, Cambridge. Only the western side was carried out. The quadrangle of S. Bartholomew's hospital was begun by him June 9, 1730. The first stone of the Radcliffe Library at Oxford, his best building, was laid June 16, 1730. [ARCHITECT]

Gilly, Friedrich: 1771-1800. A son of David Gilly, *oberbaurath* in Berlin. Gilly was one of the most talented German architects of his time. His early death, however, prevented the accomplishment of any very important results. There are a few buildings in the vicinity of Berlin which are ascribed to him, but he is best known by his sketches and designs, of which there are three portfolios in the Technische Hochschule at Charlottenburg, near Berlin. He had great influence upon the development of the architect Schinkel. [ARCHITECT]

Ginain, Paul Rene Leon: 1825-1898. Ginain was a pupil of Lebas and won the *Premier Grand Prix de Rome* in 1852. He built in Paris the Church of Notre Dame des Champs, the library of the Faculte de Medecine, the Musee Brigole-Galiera, and other works.

He was professor of architecture in the *Ecole des Beaux Arts*, member of the *Institut*, and *architecte honoraire* of the French government and the city of Paris. [ARCHITECT]

Giocondo (Jocundus), Fra Giovanni: ca. 1515-1519. Fra Giocondo was a Franciscan monk and one of the most learned men of his time. He made a collection (begun 1477) of 2000 Latin inscriptions, which was dedicated to Lorenzo de Medici, *Corpus Inscriptionum Latinorum.* He published a celebrated critical edition of Vitruvius, in 1511, dedicated to Pope Julius II. The charming Loggia del Consiglio at Verona (1476-1492) is attributed to him without documentary evidence. In 1489 Giacondo entered the service of Ferdinand I, King of Naples. After the capture of Naples by Charles VIII in 1495, he followed the French King to Paris and in 1497 was established at Amboise. Jehan Jocundus, *deviseur de Bastimens* is mentioned twice in *Archives de l' Art Francais.* The Chateau of Gaillon, the Pont Notre Dame, the old Chambre des Comptes, and other works in France have been ascribed to him. In fact, however, his name is not found on the records of any important structure of the time, except the Pont Notre Dame at Paris (1499-1512). In 1513 Giocondo was associated with Raphael and Giuliano da San Gallo in the construction of S. Peter. A design for that building, attributed to him by Antonio da San Gallo is in the Uffizi. [ARCHITECT]

Giovanni da Pisa: ca. 1240-ca. 1320. Son of Niccolo Pisano (see Niccolo da Pisa). In 1274 he went to Perugia to superintend the construction of the fountain of the great piazza from his father's designs. The bas-reliefs of the lower story are especially ascribed to him. Between 1278 and 1283 he built the cloister which surrounds the Campo Santo at Pisa. The Church of S. Maria della Spina, Pisa, ascribed to him by Vasari, was not built before 1323. Between 1302 and 1311 he made a pulpit for the Cathedral of Pisa, which was ruined by the conflagration of 1596. Fragments of this pulpit are now in the museum of the city of Pisa. In 1289 he began the facade of the Cathedral of Siena. His design was modified by the architects of the next century. The pulpit of S. Andrea at Pistoia is one of his most important works (1303). He commenced the enlargement of the Cathedral of Prato in 1317. [ARCHITECT, SCULPTOR]

Girardon, Francois: 1628-1715. Girardon was a pupil of Francois Anguier. He studied in Rome and on his return became the favorite sculp-

241

tor of Charles Lebrun. His earliest known work is the tomb of the Duke d'Epernon and his wife in a chapel of the Church of Cadillac (Goronde, France). In 1690 Girardon contracted to build the great altar of the Church of S. Jean-au-Marche in Troyes, which still exists. About 1699 he began the equestrian statue of Louis XVI which stood in the Place Louis le Grand (now Place Vendome), and was melted down for cannon in the Revolution. Perhaps his most famous work is the monument of the Cardinal Richelieu in the Church of Sorbonne, Paris. Many of his works are in the garden of Versailles. [ARCHITECT, SCULPTOR]

Giuliano da Maiano: 1432-1490. A brother of Benedetto da Maiano. In ascribing the Palazzo di S. Marco and other important buildings in Rome at this period to Giuliano da Maiano, Vasari probably confused him with Giuliano da San Gallo. His name does not appear in the Roman records. Saint Gemignano near Florence. In 1472 he designed the Palazzo del Capitano at Sarzana near Spezia, Italy. On May 26, 1474, he began the Cathedral of Faenza, and at about this time built the place of the Cardinal Concha at Recanati. On April 1, 1477, he was elected *capomaestro* of the Cathedral of Florence.

Between 1475 and 1480, with Francione, he made the wooden doors of the Sala d'Udienza at the Palazzo della Signoria, Florence. He also assisted Baccio Pontelli at the Ducal Palace of Urbino. In July, 1487, Giuliano was paid through the bank of the Gondi in Florence 200 ducats for the models of the palaces of Poggio Reale and of the Duchesa near Naples. On Feb. 17, 1488, he entered the service of Alfonzo II, and constructed for him these two palaces. Of the Poggio Reale, Giuliano's most important work, nothing remains except a drawing by Serlio. [ARCHITECT, ENGINEER, WOODWORKER]

Gonzalez-Velasquez, Alexandro: 1719-1791. Gonzales received his training in Paris and travelled in Italy, Sicily, and Greece. In 1764 he entered the service of Friedrich II (Frederick the Great). He built at Potsdam, near Berlin, the offices of the Neues Palast, the Freundschaftstempel, and Marble Palace. He built in Berlin the Konigsbrucke with its colonnade, the two towers of the Gensdarmen Markt and other important buildings. [ARCHITECT, PAINTER]

Goujon, Jean: Goujon appears first in Normandy. It is supposed that he was born there. It is not known that he ever studied in Italy. He is first mentioned in a contract dated Aug. 9,

1541, for two columns supporting the organ loft of the Church of S. Maclou at Rouen. The two sculptured wooden doors in the porch of this church are always ascribed to Goujon without evidence, except such as is derived from their style -- in this case, very convincing. A third door on the side of the church is later and may be by another hand. From about 1542 until 1544 he was associated with the architect Pierre Lescot and the sculptors Laurent Regnauldin and Simon Leroy in the construction and decoration of the choir screen (jube) of the Church of S. Germain l'Auxerrois, Paris. The jube was destroyed in 1745. The records of this work have been preserved, and two of its bas-reliefs by Goujon are now in the Louvre. About 1544 he became architect to the Constable Anne de Montmorency and was associated with Jean Bullant in the decoration of the Chateau of Ecouen. The chimneypiece by Goujon at Ecouen is extremely fine. In the dedication of Jean Martin's translation of *Vitruvius*, published in 1547, for which Goujon drew many plates, he is mentioned as Architect to the King, Henri II. After this time, and probably until his death, he was occupied in association with Pierre Lescot in making the splendid sculpture on the facade of the Louvre at the southwest angle of the old court. The pairs of figures about the *oeils-de-boeuf* over the doors are especially fine. The contract for the music gallery, supported by four caryatides in the lower hall of this building, one of his most famous productions, was made in 1550. The so-called Fountain of the Innocents in Paris was originally a loggia built at an angle of the old cemetery of the Innocents on the corner of the Rue Saint-Dennis and the Rue aux Fers, Paris. On June 10, 1786, the cemetery was suppressed. The fountain, with Goujon's bas-reliefs, was rearranged in the square that replaced the cemetery. Goujon's decorations of the Chateau of Anet date from about 1553. Of these, the most important is the group of "Diana with a Stag," which is now in the Louvre. The sculptured decoration of the Hotel Carnavalet, Paris, is attributed to Goujon by Sauval. After 1562, Goujon's name disappears from the meager records of the works at the Louvre. He was probably a Protestant, and it has been supposed, without proof, that he was killed in the massacre of S. Bartholomew (Aug. 24, 1572). A "*Giovanni Goggeon francese, intaliotore dirilieve,*" who died in Bologna, Italy, between 1564 and 1568, is supposed to have been the great French sculptor. [ARCHITECT, SCULPTOR]

Grandjean de Montigny, Auguste Henri Victor: 1776-1850. A pupil of Dellannoy and Percier at the *Ecole des Beaux Arts*, in 1799 he won the *Premier Grand Prix d'Architecture*, with Gasse. About 1814 he went to Brazil and erected at Rio de Janeiro the Palace of the Fine Arts, the Exchange, and other important buildings. Grandjean de Montigny published *Recueil des plus beaux Tombeaux executes en Italie pendant les XV et XVI siecles and Architecture de la Toscane*, in association with Auguste Famin. [ARCHITECT]

Grimaldi, Fra Francesco: Grimaldi's first work in Naples was the convent and Church of S. Apostoli. In 1608 he built the fine Capella del Tesoro at the Cathedral, Naples. He built the Church of S. Maria degli Angeli at Pizz-Falcone near Naples. The reconstruction of the Church of S. Paolo Maggiore, Naples was accomplished from his designs after his death. [ARCHITECT]

Guarini, D. Guarino: 1624-1685. Guarini was a Theatine monk who carried the Baroque style in Italy to its extreme development. In 1674 he became the court architect to Duke Carlo Emmanuele II of Savoy. He served also his successor, King Vittorio Amadeo I. His most extraordinary buildings are the domical Church of S. Lorenzo and the sanctuary of the Maddona della Consolata, both in Turin. He built about 1657 the mortuary chapel of the house of Savoy at the Church of S. Giovanni. Buildings were erected from Guarini's designs at Lisbon and Prague. He built the Theatine Church of S. Anne on the Quai Voltaire, Paris, which has been destroyed. Guarini was a speculative writer on philosophy and mathematics. His last work was an *Architettura civile*. [ARCHITECT]

Gumpp, Georg Anton: 1670-1730. Gumpp was one of the most important architects of the Baroque style in Germany. His best works are the S. Jacobskirche (1717-1724), the S. Johanniskirche (1729), the Landhaus (1719-1728), the Turn and Taxis Palace, all at Innsbruck in the Tyrol. [ARCHITECT]

Gundulf: ca. 1024-1108. Born in France, and became about 1060 a monk of the Abbey of Bec. In 1077 he was appointed Bishop of Rochester, England, by Lanfranc. He built, or caused to be built, the Cathedral of Rochester. Of his work, a part of the west front, and the tower on the north side remain. For William the Conqueror, he built the Great White Tower in London. [ARCHITECT, BISHOP]

Halfpenny, William: Alias Michael Hoare, architect. He is known by his numerous practical works on architecture; *Multum in parvo, or the Marrow of Architecture* (1722-1728), *Practical Architecture* (London, 1730), *Perspective Made Easy* (1731), *Modern Builder's Assistant* (1742-1751), and other works. He was assisted by John Halfpenny. [ARCHITECT]

Hamilton, Sir James, of Fynnart: d. 1540. A natural son of James, first Earl of Arran and Master of the Works to King James V of Scotland. He built the northwest portion of Holyrood House, Edinburgh, and was employed on the castles of Edinburgh, Sterling, and Rothesay, all in Scotland. [ARCHITECT]

Hamilton, Thomas: In 1820 he designed the memorial to Robert Burns at Ayr, Scotland, and April 28, 1825, laid the first stone of the High School, Edinburgh. He had a large practice in Scotland. [ARCHITECT]

Hansen, Hans Christian: 1803-1883. A brother of Theophilos Hansen. In 1831 he won a stipend at the academy in Copenhagen which enabled him to travel in Italy and Greece. He was made court architect at Athens. Hansen designed the university at Athens and in association with Schaubert and Ludwig Ross rebuilt the temple of Nike Apteros on the Acropolis, putting into place the ancient blocks of marble, which had been recovered when the Turkish fortifications were destroyed. [ARCHITECT]

Hansen, Theophilos: 1813-1890. Hansen was educated at the academy of Copenhagen. In 1838 he visited Italy and Greece and practised for eight years in Athens, building at this time the observatory near that city. Reaching Vienna in 1846, he built the Waffen Museum of the Arsenal and other buildings in a Medieval style. He again went to Athens in 1860-1861 to build the Academy, one of his most successful works. In the reconstruction of the city of Vienna (begun in 1857) Hansen built the Fine Arts (1874-1876), and the Parliament House (1883). [ARCHITECT]

Hardouin-Mansart, Jules: 1646-1708. Jules Hardouin was the son of Raphael Hardouin, *peintre ordinaire du roi* and Marie Gauthier, a niece of Francois Mansart. He added his grand-uncle's name to his own and was known as Hardouin-Mansart, frequently signing himself Mansart. He studied architecture with Francois Mansart and Liberal Bruant. While assisting Bruant in the construction of the Hotel de Vendome, Paris, he was presented to the King, Louis XIV, who requested him in 1672 to design the Chateau of Clagny for Madame de Montespan. In 1674 he was commissioned to enlarge the new Chateau of Saint-Germain-en-Laye (finished under Henri IV but destroyed in 1776). Oct. 22, 1675, Hardouin-Mansart was appointed *architecte du roi* and later *controleur general des batiments du roi*. In 1675 he was admitted to the Academie de l'Architecture. His name appears for the first time in the accounts of the Palace of Versailles, Feb. 26, 1677. He was occupied with that building during the remainder of his life. At this palace he built between 1679 and 1681 the great southern wing. He finished in 1684 the Grande Galerie, overlooking the park in the central pavilion, and the garden facade of the central pavilion. Between 1684 and 1688 he built the great northern wing, thus completing the entire length of 580 meters. He built the grand stairway, and in 1698 began the beautiful Orangerie. The chapel of the chateau was begun in 1696, but was not finished until 1710 (after Mansart's death) by Robert de Cotte. In 1685 he approved the plans of Francois Romain for the Pont Royal. In 1686, he was appointed *premier architecte du roi*, and in the following year sold the office of *controleur general des batiments du roi* to his grand-

nephew, Jacques Jules Grabriel. In 1688 Mansart built the two wings of the Grand Trianon in the Park at Versailles, which were afterward connected with a colonnade by Robert de Cotte. He continued the work of Liberal Bruant at the Hotel des Invalides, building the portal of the church in 1693. He designed the dome, which was well under way when he died, but was not finished until 1735. Mansart was assisted in is work by Robert de Cotte, who succeeded him as *premier architecte* in 1708, by Charles Daviler, and by Cailleteau called L'Assurance. [ARCHITECT]

Harrison, Henry G.: 1813-1895. He designed several important buildings in New York City, and became prominent in connection with the architectural schemes projected by Mr. A. T. Stewart for Garden City, Long Island. Of the proposed buildings only the Cathedral, designed by Harrison, was carried out. [ARCHITECT]

Harsdorf, Caspar Frederik: 1735-1795. Educated in France and Italy, and was chief royal architect at Copenhagen, Denmark, and director of the Academy of Sciences in Stockholm, Sweden. He built the propylaea of the royal palaces in Copenhagen and other important buildings. [ARCHITECT]

Hasenauer, Karl, Freiherr (Baron) von: 1833-1894. He was educated at the Collegium in Braunschweig, Germany, and at the academy of Vienna, and travelled in Italy, France, and England. In 1854 he won first prize in architecture at the academy of Vienna. He won also second prize in the competition for the new facade of the Cathedral of Florence. In association with Semper he designed at Vienna the Museums of Art and Natural History, built between 1872 and 1884, and the new Imperial Palace. He designed also the Hofburg Theater at Vienna. He published *Das K. K. Hofburgtheater* in Wien (1890). [ARCHITECT]

Hawksmoor, Nicholas: 1661-1736. At the age of eighteen he became the scholar and domestic clerk of Sir Christopher Wren and was employed by him from 1682 to 1690 as deputy surveyor at Chelsea Hospital, and after 1705 as deputy surveyor at Greenwich Hospital, London. He assisted Wren in the construction of S. Paul's Cathedral from June 21, 1675, until its completion. Hawksmoor was associated with Vanbrugh at Castle Howard, 1702 to 1714, and at Blenheim Palace, 1710 to 1715. At Oxford he designed the library of Queen's College, 1692, and the two towers of All Soul's College, both of which buildings have been ascribed to Wren. Jan. 6, 1716, he was appointed surveyor to the committee in charge of the construction of churches for them, the best being those of S. Mary Woolnoth, 1716-1719, and S. George Bloomsbury, 1720-1730. He was made surveyor of Westminster Abbey at the death of Wren, and completed the towers. His excellence lay in his attention to details and thorough knowledge of construction. [ARCHITECT]

Here de Corny, Emmanuel: 1705-1763. Supposed to have received his training from Germain Boffrand and was made architect in ordinary to Stanislas I, King of Poland, and Duke of Lorraine. At Luneville, France, then a city belonging to the Duke, he built the towers and the tribune of the organs of the Church of S. Remy, the Hotel des Carmes, and many other important buildings. At Nancy, France, then the capital of Duke Stanislas, he built the Church of Bon Secours, the convent of the Minimes, and the important constructions of the Place Royale, commenced in 1751, which include the Hotel de Ville, the episcopal palace, the Hotel Alloit, the theater, the College Royale de Medicine, the Hotel Jacquet, and the Arc de Triomphe. Here de Corny published

Recueil des plans et elevations des chateaux, jardins, et dependances que le roi de Pologne occupe in Lorraine (Paris, 1753); *Plans et Elevations des batiments de la place Royale de Nancy, etc.; Recueil des fondations et etablissments faits par le roi de Pologne* (Luneville, 1762). [ARCHITECT]

Hittorff, Jacques Ignace: 1793-1867. Hittorff was born at Cologne and naturalized as a French citizen. He was a pupil of Charles Percier. Between 1819 and 1823 he visited England, Germany, Italy, and Sicily. After 1825 he built with Lepere the Church of S. Vincent de Paul, Paris. About 1831 he was architect of the Parisian prisons. In 1833, as the result of a competition, he was made architect of the Place de la Concord, the Champs Elysees, and the Place de l' Etoile. In the Place de la Concord he built the pedestal of the obelisk, placed the statues of the cities of France, and completed the decoration, lamps, fountains, etc. From 1844 to 1866 Hittorff was architect of the Column of the Place Vendome, Paris. The Neo-Grec movement received much help from him; and the Church of S. Vincent de Paul is often spoken of as a monument of the style. In 1864 he was made general inspector of the *Conseil des batiments civils*. He won a first-class medal at the ex-

position of 1855. In association with Zanth Hittorff published *Architecture Moderne de la Sicile* (Paris, 1835), and *Architecture Antique de la Sicile, recueil des monuments de Segeste et de Selinonte* (Pais, 1870). He published alone *Restitution du Temple d'Empedocle a Selinonte; ou l' Architecture polychrome chez les Grecs* (Paris, 1851). [ARCHITECT]

Hoban, James: He was a native of Ireland and settled in Charleston, South Carolina, before the Revolution. July, 1792, he came to Washington and was employed on the public buildings there for more than a quarter of a century. His plan for the President's mansion (the present White House) was accepted, and this building was built by him. He rebuilt it after its destruction by the British in 1814. He superintended the construction of the old Capitol from the designs of Dr. Thornton. [ARCHITECT]

Holabird and Roche: (Estab. 1880.) This partnership, formed in 1880 between William Holabird (1854-1923) and Martin Roche (1855-1927), was influenced by W. Jenney and H.H. Richardson, the founders of the Chicago School of Architecture. Holabird, after spending a few years in the employ of Jenny, teamed up with Roche and designed the Tacoma Building in Chicago. They went beyond the Home Insurance Building's design and virtually established steel skyscraper construction. Their Marquette Building was important in its elegance of design. [ARCHITECT]

Holden, Charles: 1875-1960. An English architect born of poor parents, Holden joined the firm of C.R. Ashbee in 1897. However, the bulk of his work was accomplished within the partnership of Percy Adams. Hospitals were the focal specialty of the firm. Of particular note is the King Edward VII Sanatorium in Midhurst, England. Later on, the Bristol Public Library and the British Medical Association offices were projects undertaken by them. Holden's work evolved into a new phase beginning in 1924. His main interest was in the design of station buildings and other aspects of public transportation, from benches to platforms. London University engaged him to design its new buildings in 1932. He and William Holford spent the last years of his practice concentrating on planning. [ARCHITECT]

Holford, Sir William: 1907-1975. Holford was born in Johannesburg. He later emigrated to England, where he spent the rest of his life as an urban planner. He was active in helping to formulate town planning legislation and designed houses, industrial buildings and public buildings. His most important building is St. Paul's Cathedral in London. As well, many universities used his services. In addition, Holford taught at Liverpool University, and University Town College in London. His fourteen story building of flats at Kensal, London was the first large modular building. [ARCHITECT]

Holland, Henry: ca. 1746-1806. He designed Claremont House, Surrey, England, for Lord Clive, and directed the construction of Battersea Bridge, London, etc. His chief work was the reconstruction of Carlton House, Pall Mall, London. This palace was begun in 1788, and destroyed in 1827. In 1791 he designed Drury Lane Theatre, London, for R.B. Sheridan. [ARCHITECT]

Holt, Thomas: d. 1624. He was a native of York, England, and a carpenter. He is supposed to have come to Oxford about 1600, when Sir Thomas Bodley was beginning his New Schools. Holt is credited with the design of these buildings, especially the great tower, the facade of which is decorated with the five orders superimposed. [ARCHITECT]

Hood, Raymond Mathewson: 1881-1934. Born in Rhode Island,

Hood spent the first years of his practice as an architect working with others and designing no buildings of note. However at the age of forty-one, he and John Mead Howells won one of the most important competitions to date, that of the Chicago Tribune Building. They competed against architects from all over the world and this project catapulted Hood into fame. The Tribune Building was designed in the Beaux Arts Neo-gothic style. His practice began to grow at an amazing rate. The Daily News Building in New York City is another example of his designs; however it is very different stylistically from the Tribune building. Rockefeller Center in New York was also designed in part by Hood, in collaboration with Fouilhoux. [ARCHITECT]

Horta, Baron Victor: 1861-1947. Horta, born in Brussels in 1861, studied at Ghent Academy and later at *Academie des Beaux-Arts* in Brussels. His first important design was that of the Hotel Tassel in Brussels. This building, done in Art Nouveau, threw Horta into the forefront of European architecture and ushered in modern architecture in Europe. It was the first private house in which iron was used a great deal and two-dimensional forms were used exten-

sively. The Hotel Solvay in Brussels was built one year later. This lavish hotel took Art Nouveau to its peak. It combined Baroque and Classical architecture, style and color, aesthetics and practicality. Later on, Horta returned to a more Classical style, as evidenced in the Palais des Beaux-Arts in Brussels. [ARCHITECT]

Howard, Sir Ebenezer: 1880-1928. Howard was born in London and began his auspicious career as a stenographer. On a trip to the United States, he met Walt Whitman and Ralph Waldo Emerson, both of whom had a tremendous influence. His main contribution lies in his idea for a Garden City, as delineated by him in his book, *Tomorrow: A Peaceful Path to Social Reform* (1898). The book's second edition was entitled *Garden Cities of Tomorrow* (1902). Howard's vision for garden cities were as independent and not as suburbs. The earliest garden city based on his ideas was Letchworth, which was designed under the direction of Parker and Unwin in 1903. [ARCHITECT]

Howe, George: 1886-1955. Howe was born in Massachusetts and studied at Harvard and the *Ecole des Beaux-Arts*. His partnership with the Swiss architect, William Lescaze was formed in 1929. Together they designed the Philadelphia Saving Fund Society building, which issued in the International Modern period. He also designed many residences, his own home "High Hollow" being particularly noteworthy. Other buildings of repute are the Chrystie-Forsythe Building Housing Development and the Wasserman House. [ARCHITECT]

Hugh of Lincoln, Saint: ca. 1135-1200. The son of a Lord of Avalon near Grenoble, France, and brought to England by King Henry II to build the Carthusian monastery at Witham. In 1186 he was made Bishop of Lincoln in England, and built the choir, called S. Hugh's Choir. of Lincoln Cathedral, one of the earliest specimens of Gothic architecture in England. Some of his work still remains in the choir, which has, however, been much rebuilt. In is probable that the entire Cathedral was built according to his scheme. He was not himself an architect, but employed others, especially Geoffrey du Noyer. [BISHOP OF LINCOLN]

Hunt, Richard Morris: 1828-1895. His early training was received at a private school in New Haven and at the Latin School in Boston. At the age of fifteen he went abroad with his family and settled in Geneva, where he studied architecture and

drawing with Samuel Darier. In 1848 he entered the *Ecole des Beaux Arts* in Paris under the direction of Hector Martin Lefuel. For several years Hunt travelled about Europe, visiting also Asia Minor and Egypt. In 1854 he returned to Paris and rejoined Lefuel, who had succeeded Visconti as architect of the extension of the Louvre and Tuileries undertaken by Napoleon III. He was appointed inspector of works and had charge of the details of the Pavillon de la Bibliotheque in the new Louvre. In 1853 Hunt came to America and was associated with Thomas U. Walter, who was then occupied with the extensions of the capitol in Washington. He afterward established himself in New York and opened an atelier for architectural students, where many prominent architects received their training. Hunt was for many years the best-known architect of America, although his practice did not include many public monuments of importance, Among his principal works are the Tribune building and the Lenox Library in New York, two buildings at West Point, the National Observatory in Washington, the Administration Building of the World's Fair in Chicago (1893), the Fogg Museum at Harvard University, "Marble Hall" (a residence) at Newport, "The Breakers" (a residence) at Newport,

251

the houses of Mr. W. K. Vanderbilt, Mr. F. W. Vanderbilt, Mr. E. T. Gerry, and Mr. John Jacob Astor in New York, and "Biltmore House" (a residence) at Asheville, North Carolina. In 1888 he was elected president of the American Institute of Architects, and in 1893 received the gold medal of the Royal Institute of British Architects. He was honorary and corresponding member of the *Academie des Beaux Arts* of the Institute of France (1882), and chevalier of the *Legion d' Honneur*. [ARCHITECT]

Huyot, Jean Nicolas: 1780-1840. Huyot was the son of a builder. He began the study of architecture at the school of design in the *Rue de l' Ecole de Medicine*, and afterward entered the atelier of Antoine Francois Peyre who employed him in the restoration of the Chateau of Ecouen. In 1807 he won the *Premier Grand Prix de Rome*. He made an extended tour in 1817 of the Mediterranean countries, visiting Constantinople (Istanbul), where he designed several buildings. In Egypt he attempted a new classification of the monuments and a restoration of the ancient city of Thebes. Huyot made a special study of the topography of Athens. In 1822 he was appointed by the Institute to a professorship in the history of architecture. In 1823 he was charged in

association with Goust with the completion of the Arc de Tiomphe de l' Etoile, at that time raised to the spring of the arch. He presented a scheme introducing four columns on each side. The ministry preferred, however, the original design of Chalgrin. On the retirement of Goust in 1829 Huyot assumed superintendence of the work until 1832, when he was superseded by Abel Blouet. The entablature and the decoration of the vault of the arch were at this time completed. [ARCHITECT]

Isidorus of Miletus: He was employed with Anthemius of Thalles in the construction of the Church of S. Sophia at Constantinople (532-537 A.D.). Another Isodorus of Miletus, probably his nephew, erected important works on the banks of the Euphrates. [ARCHITECT]

Jacob von Landshut: d. ca. 1509. He became architect of the Cathedral of Strasbourg in 1495, and built the chapel and portal of S. Lorenz at the Cathedral before 1505. [ARCHITECT]

Jacquet, Jean: According to Sauval, the brothers Jacques, Jean, and Mathieu Jacquet were among the most skillful builders in Paris in 1530. Jean, a son of Mathieu, was architect of the Church of S. Gervais, Paris, from 1580 to 1603. [ARCHITECT]

Jefferson, Thomas: 1743-1826. Thomas Jefferson, third President of the United States, was much interested in art, especially architecture. He was intimately associated with the construction of several private and public buildings of importance, and it is probable that much of the actual design and superintendence of these works were due to him. About 1770 Jefferson began the mansion at Monticello, Virginia. In 1784 he was appointed minister to France, and made use of the opportunity to improve his knowledge of architecture. He returned to Monticello in 1787, and completed his house. Jefferson was doubtless the chief architect of the buildings of the University of Virginia, which was established in Charlottesville, Virginia, in 1818. During his official residence in Washington he was largely concerned in the erection of the national Capitol. [ARCHITECT, STATESMAN]

Johnson, A. E.: 1821-1895 (England). He was a pupil of Sir Gilbert Scott and Philip Hardwicke. In 1852 he went to Melbourne, Australia, and obtained an extensive practice. Among other works in Melbourne he built the General Post Office and the Church of England Grammar School, and remodelled the Customhouse. He was diocesan architect, and had charge of all the public buildings in the Melbourne district. [ARCHITECT]

Johnson, Philip Cortelyou: b. 1906. Johnson was born in Cleveland, Ohio and studied under Gropius and Breuer at Harvard. Along with Henry Russell Hitchcock, Johnson published a most influential book, *The International Style* (1932). As well, it was Johnson who arranged Mies van de Rohe's and Le Corbusier's first trip to New York City. Van de Rohe's influence is very evident in the home which Johnson built for himself, "The Glass House". His design of the Kneses Tifereth Israel Synagogue in Port Chester, New York, spread his fame further, with its eclectic style. Additionally, Johnson is responsible for designing the New York State Theater at Lincoln Center and several notable museums, including the Amon Carter Museum in Fort Worth and the Art Museum of South Texas in Corpus Christi. His Pennzoil Building in Houston, Texas features two mirrored administration towers and a huge public glass hall. His capricious Crystal Cathedral in Los Angeles is filled with dazzling light effects. The AT&T Building in New York combines Gothic, Renaissance, Neo-classical and Art Deco and is just another example of his unparalleled, flamboyant, mixed styles of architecture which have left an un-equalled influence. [ARCHITECT]

Johnston, Francis: d. 1829. He erected many important buildings in Dublin, Ireland. In 1824 he commenced, at his own expense, the erection of the building of the Royal Hibernian Academy, which he presented to that institution. He held the office of architect of the Dublin Board of Works. [ARCHITECT]

Jones, Inigo: 1573-1652. He was christened at the Church of S. Bartholomew the Less, London, July 19, 1573, as "Enigo Jones the sonne of Enigo Jones." His artistic inclination developed early, especially in "Landskip Painting." A picture at Chiswick is ascribed to him. He went to Italy about the end of the sixteenth century, probably at the expense of the Earl of Pembroke, and after passing several years at Venice was invited to Denmark by Christian IV, brother-in-law of James I of England. Jones returned to England before 1605, and from that time to 1613 was employed in arranging a brilliant series of masks and entertainments for the court. Two volumes of his costume designs are at Chiswick. To this period have been ascribed, without much reason, the garden front of S. John's College, Oxford, and other works in a Medieval

style. From 1610 to 1612 he was Surveyor of the Works to Henry, Prince of Wales. In 1613 Jones made another visit to Italy and again in 1614. His copy of Palladio's *Architettura* with manuscript notes, at Worcester College, Oxford, bears the date Jan. 2, 1614. In 1615 he returned to England to become the King's Surveyor of Works. In 1618, for Charles I, Jones planned an immense palace at Whitehall to extend 950 feet along the Thames and 1280 feet from the river to S. James's Park. Of this design an unimportant part of one court was built and still stands, the famous Banqueting House. Jones served on the commissions for the renovation of old S. Paul's Cathedral, and in 1633 began the facade with the splendid Corinthian portico which was one of his favorite works; destroyed in 1666. Lindsey House still remains in Arch row, Lincoln's Inn Fields. It was the beginning of a large scheme of improvement undertaken in 1620, which was never carried out. George Villiers, Duke of Buckingham, employed Jones to build the Water Gate of York House, which still stands. The Church of S. Catherine Cree, London (1628-1630), is ascribed to him without documentary evidence. The porch of S. Mary's at Oxford is also ascribed to him. Jones's additions to Somerset House were destroyed in 1775. Shaftesbuy House, Physicians' College, London, and other important works have disappeared. Ashburnham House in Little Dean's Yard, Westminster remains. He designed the villa at Chiswick, the facade of Wilton, the Ionic bridge at Wilton, and other works. The little monument to his "Ancient poor friends," George Chapman, the poet, is in the yard of the Church of S. Giles-in-the-Fields, London. About 1613 he began for Francis Russell, fourth Earl of Bedford, the famous piazza and church of Covent Garden, London. Inigo Jones was Royalist in the Civil War and was captured at Basing House, October, 1643. He was buried in S. Bennett's Church , Paul's Wharf, London, June 26, 1652. Many of his drawings of unexecuted schemes remain at Chiswick, in the British Museum, and elsewhere. In 1620 Inigo Jones was commissioned by the King to write an account of Stonehenge, which he supposed was a Roman ruin, and left notes on the subject which were published by John Webb in 1655. [ARCHITECT]

Jones, Owen: 1809-1874. Son of Owen Jones (1741-1814), a Welsh antiquary. He studied at the Royal Academy, London. In 1830 he visited France and Italy; and in 1833,

Greece, Egypt, and Constantinople. In 1834 and again in 1837 he went to Granada, Spain, and made numerous drawings of the Alhambra. In 1851 he was appointed superintendent of the works at the Great Exhibition in London, and 1852 designed the Egyptian, Greek, Roman, and Alhambra courts at the Crystal Palace. Jones published *Plans, Elevations, Sections, and Details of the Alhambra* (1842-1845); *The Illuminated Books of the Middle Ages* (1844); *The Polychromatic Ornament of Italy* (1846); and *The Grammar of Ornament* (London, 1858). [ARCHITECT, DESIGNER]

Juan Bautista de Toledo: Studied in Rome, especially under the influence of Michelangelo Buonarroti. He was recalled to Spain by Phillip II His most important work is the Palace of the Escorial which was begun by him in 1563 and finished by Juan de Herrera. He built the facade of the Church of Descalzas Reales at Madrid, and other important works. [ARCHITECT]

Juan de Badajoz: Juan designed and, about the year 1537, directed the execution of the plateresque work of the cloister of S. Zoil de Carrion de los Condes, Spain. He was architect of the Cathedral of Leon, Spain, and completed the principal facade of the monastery of S. Marcos in that city. [ARCHITECT, SCULPTOR]

Juvara (Ivara), Filippo: 1685-1735 in Madrid. Juvara was a pupil of Carlo Fontana. His work, although done in the Baroque period, is marked by simplicity and much Classical refinement. His life was spent mainly in the service of the dukes of Savoy at Turin, Italy. Juvara's chief monument is the monastery of the Superga near Turin, which shows the influence of contemporary French practice. The Villa Stupinigi, near Turin, was probably designed by him. Many villas in Piedmont were built by him. One of his most characteristic works is the facade of the Palazzo Madama, Turin, 1710, with its fine stairway. He continued the construction of the Ducal Palace at Lucca, begun by Bartolommeo Ammanati. At Mantua, Juvara built the cupola of the Church of S. Andrea, designed by Leon Battista Alberti two centuries before. Juvara's last years were spent in Spain and Portugal. [ARCHITECT]

Kayser, Karl: d. 1895. An architect of Vienna, Austria, who went to the Mexico City, and was employed by Maximilian, Emperor of Mexico, in the reconstruction and restoration of palaces there. After the death of Maximilian he returned to Vienna,

and modernized several Medieval and Baroque palaces. [ARCHITECT]

Kent, William: 1685-1748. He went to London in 1704, and in 1710 to Rome. Returning to England in 1719, he became a protege of Lord Burlington. He assisted Lord Burlington, and built Devonshire House, Piccadilly, and the Horseguards, Whitehall; and altered and decorated the great country houses of Stowe, Houghton, and Holkham. Kent was successful as a designer of gardens, his most important work being the park at Stowe. [ARCHITECT, PAINTER, LANDSCAPE GARDENER]

Keyser (Keiser), Hendrick Corneliszoon de: 1565-1621. One of the most important Dutch architects. He was a pupil of Cornelis Bloemaart and studied in France. He established himself with Bloemaart at Amsterdam in 1591. July 19, 1594, he was appointed sculptor and architect to the city of Amsterdam, and in this capacity had general supervision of the artistic work done by the city. De Keyser made the cartoons for the windows in the Church of S. John at Gouda, Holland, which were presented by the city of Amsterdam. He made the monument to Erasmus in the Groote Markt at Rotterdam, and the monument to William, Prince of Orange, in the Groote Kerk at Delft. He built many of the ornamental gates in the fortifications of Amsterdam. De Keyser built also the court of the East India House and the Exchange at Amsterdam. At Hoorn, Holland, he built the Hoogerbeerts monument, and the front of the Oosterkerk, 1615. His son Pieter de Keyser succeeded him and finished many of his works. [ARCHITECT, SCULPTOR]

Klenze, Leo von: 1784-1864. Klenze studied at the University and at the Academy of Architecture in Berlin. In 1803 he went to Paris to study with Durand and Percier and in 1805 visited Italy. In 1808 he was appointed court architect of King Jerome of Westphalia. In 1816 he became court architect at Munich, Bavaria, and began in that city the Glyptothek, his most important building (finished 1830). Among his many works in Munich are the Schloss Pappenheim, the Leuchtenberg Palace, 1818, the Hoftheater, rebuilt 1823-1825 from the plans of Karl von Fischer, the new facade of the Residenz, the southern building called Konigbau in imitation of the Palazzo Allerheiligen-Hofkirche, 1826, the Odeon, 1826, the Propylaen, and other works. Klenzebuilt also the Wallhalla near Regensburg. In 1834 restoration of the Acropolis which were not executed. In 1840-1850 he

built the Hermitage in Saint Petersburg, Russia. [ARCHITECT]

Klint, Peder Vilhelm Jensen: 1853-1930. Danish born Klint began his career as an engineer and then a painter. He practiced as an architect the last thirty-four years. His principal contribution was the Grundtvig Church in Copenhagen, which shows a melding of the northern European Gothic style and Expressionism. It features a gabled brick front and a massive pipe organ. [ARCHITECT]

Knobelsdorff, Hans George Wenceslaus: 1699-1753. Knobelsdorff entered military service, and in 1720 was quartered in Berlin, where he became interested in the work of Andreas Schliter and others. In 1736 he travelled in Italy and, returning to Berlin, was appointed overseer of buildings to Friedrich II. He built the Opera House in Berlin, the Palace of Sanssouci near Potsdam, and the new wing of the Palace at Charlottenburg. Knobelsdorff laid out the Thiergarten in Berlin and the Lustgarten at Potsdam. He painted excellent portraits and landscapes. [ARCHITECT]

Langhans, Karl Gotthard: 1733-1808 (Germany). He designed the Regierungs Gebaude in Breslau, Silesia, and in 1774 was called to Berlin. His reputation rests mainly upon the

Brandenburger Thor in Berlin, built in imitation of the Propylaea at Athens, between 1789 and 1793. He built also in Berlin the Herkulesbrucke, 1787, and the Colonnade in the Mohein Strasse. About 17898 Langhans designed the Schloss theater and Belvedere in the park at Charlottenburg. [ARCHITECT]

Langley Batty: 1696-1751. He was the son of gardener, and practised the profession of landscape gardening. He made an attempt to arrange Gothic architecture under five orders, and organized a school mainly for the training of carpenters. Langley is best known by his extensive series of practical works on matters pertaining to architecture, such as, *Practical Geometry applied to Building, Surveying, Gardening, etc.* (1726) ; *New Principles of Gardening etc.*, 1728, and the like. [ARCHITECT]

Lassus, Jean Baptiste Antoine: 1807-1857. Lassus was one of the chiefs of the modern Gothic school in France. He was a pupil of Lebas and Henri Labrouste and entered the *Ecoles des Beaux Arts* in 1828. Influenced by the general romantic movement led by Victor Hugo, he devoted himself entirely to the study of Gothic architecture, especially that of the period of King Philippe Auguste. From 1841 to 1849 he was as-

sociated with Duban in the restoration of the Sainte Chapelle, Paris, and after 1849 had charge of that building. He built the spire and cleared away the buildings from the south side of the chapel. In 1841 he won a gold medal in the competition for the tomb of Napoleon I. In 1845 he was associated with Viollet-le-Duc in the restoration of the Cathedral of Notre Dame, Paris, and in 1848 succeeded E. H. Godde as architect of the restoration of the Church of S. Germain l'Auxerrois, Paris. Lassus was appointed *conservatuer* of the buildings of the diocese of Paris in 1849, and of the diocese of le Mans and of Chartres in 1852. He restored the spires of Chartres Cathedral. Lassus designed much ecclesiastical furniture, bronzes, and the like. He contributed frequently to the *Annales Archeologiques*. In 1837 he was chosen to direct the illustration of the *Monographie de la cathedrale de Chartres*, published under the direction of the *Ministere de l' Instruction Publique*. He prepared an edition of the *Album* of Villard de Honnecourt which was completed after his death by Alfred Darcel, and published by the French government. [ARCHITECT]

Latrobe, Benjamin Henry: 1762-1820. The son of the Rev. Benjamin Latrobe, superintendent of the

Moravians in England. He entered the Stamp Office in London in 1783. He afterward studied architecture and built several residences in England. In 1796 he emigrated to Virginia and met President Washington. He was appointed engineer to the state of Virginia. He afterward went to Philadelphia, where he undertook the superintendence of the water supply. By letter of Thomas Jefferson, dated March 6, 1803, Latrobe was appointed surveyor of public buildings in Washington with the especial charge of the Capitol. He was directed to retain the main features of the design of Dr. Thornton, but nevertheless made very considerable changes. In 1806 his general conduct of the work was defended by Latrobe in a letter to members of Congress. Work on the Capitol was suspended in 1811, and on Aug. 24, 1814, the building burned by the British. Feb. 15, 1815, Congress authorized President Madison to borrow $500,000 for the completion of the Capitol, and on April 20 of that year Latrobe was reappointed architect of the building. He resigned his position Now. 24, 1817. Between 1811 and 1815 he was interested in steamboat navigation at Pittsburgh. On his retirement in 1817 he went to Baltimore, and in 1820 to New Orleans. [ARCHITECT]

Le Corbusier, Charles-Edouard: 1887-1966. Born in French Switzerland and trained at the arts and crafts school and by apprenticeship rather than formally educated, Corbusier stands alone in the field of architecture. From 1920 to 1960, Corbusier is the dominant figure in his field. He was also a painter, author, journalist, lecturer, urban planner, wood sculptor, and furniture designer. Although tremendously unconventional and not an easy man to work with, his artistry commanded a huge following which has not been equalled. Frank Lloyd Wright's work influenced him, as did the authors Charles Blanc and Auguste Choisy. Early in his career he developed Purism, as shown in the Villa Schwob, built in 1916. Corbusier's desire for harmony is reflected in everything he did. In 1925, he designed the Esprit Nouveau exhibition building at the Paris Exhibition, which featured a tree growing through the building. His designs for the League of Nations Building in Geneva (1927), although never built, and the Centrosojus in Moscow had a large influence on many modern architects. Corbusier was asked to advise on the Ministry of Education Building in Rio de Janeiro. It was later built by Costa and Niemeyer, as well as some others.

His Salvation Army Hostel in Paris featured a long curtain wall. Later, Corbusier began to leave his glass and metal period and entered into a period that showed much sculptural aggression, as evidenced by the Unite d'Habitation in Marseille (1947-52). This building typified his Anti-Rational designs. His influence spread all over the world. Japan was greatly impacted by his Law Courts and Secretariat, part of his plan for the town of Chandigarh, France. This building featured heavy concrete forms. Corbusier designed the Museum of Modern Art in Tokyo following this pattern as well (1957-59). Honorary doctorates were awarded to him by the University of Zurich and Cambridge University, and in 1959, he was awarded the Gold Medal from the Royal Institute of British Architects. Among his most famous published works are *Le Modulor* (1948) and *Le Modulor 2* (1955). These books discuss his Modulor system, which is a complicated scheme of proportions based on the Fibonacci series and using human figures as its basis. His *Oeuvre Complete* is a collection of his works and represents one of the most forceful books in modern architecture. [ARCHITECT]

Lebas, Louis Hippolyte: 1782-1867. Lebas was a pupil of the elder Vau-

doyer of Charles Percier and of the *Ecole des Beaux Arts*, Paris. In 1806 he won the *Second Grand Prix de Rome*. From 1806 until 1808 he served as a soldier in Italy. He was appointed inspector of the construction of the Bourse, Paris, which comprised the Pont Nuef, the *Institut*, the Biblioteque Mazarin, and the *Ecole des Beaux Arts*. In 1840 he was appointed professor of the history of architecture at the *Ecole des Beaux Arts*. For many years he conducted the most important private architectural schools in Paris. [ARCHITECT]

Lechner, Odon: 1845-1914. Lechner represents Art Nouveau architecture. His town hall in Kecskemet and his Museum of Decorative Art in Budapest are Gothic in style. Later, he leaned toward Moorish and folk-art designs, as evidenced in the Postal Savings Bank in Budapest. [ARCHITECT]

Leclere, Achille Francois Rene: 1785-1853. A pupil of Jean Nicolas Louis Durand and Charles Percier. In 1808 he won the *Premier Grand Prix de Rome*. While in Rome he made a famous restoration of the Pantheon. In 1815 he opened an architectural school in Paris, which developed many prominent architects. Leclere built many residences in Paris, and restored many chateaux in the provinces. He was appointed *inspectuer general* of the *Conseil des batiments civils* in 1840. [ARCHITECT]

Lefuel, Hector Martin: 1810-1880. Lefuel was trained in architecture by his father and Jean Nicolas Huyot, and won the *Premier Grand Prix de Rome* in 1839. In 1845 he was appointed inspector of the works at the *Chambre des Deputes*, Paris, and in 1853 architect of the Chateau of Fontainbleau, where he built for Napoleon III the new Salle de Spectacle in the right wing. In 1854 he succeeded Visconti as architect of the buildings connecting the Louvre with Tuileries. Lefuel made important changes in Visconti's designs. He finished the inner fronts of the buildings enclosing the Place du Carrousel, and remodelled, from his own plans, the Grande Galerie of the Louvre from the Pavillon Lesdiguieres to the Pavillon de Flore. Between 1860 and 1870 he remodelled the Pavillon de Flore itself and between 1871 and 1876 the Pavillon de Marsan. He was made *Inspectuer general des batiments civils* in 1866. [ARCHITECT]

Legeay, Jean: In 1732 Legeay won the *Grand Prix* in architecture. He was called to Berlin in 1754, and became Architect to the King, Friedrich II (Frederick the Great). He designed the Palace of Sans Souci, and other buildings in and near Potsdam and Berlin. [ARCHITECT]

Lemercier, Jacques: ca. 1590-1654. Jacques is supposed to have been a son of Nicolas Lemercier. He studied in Rome. About 1617 he built the old Chateau of Louis XIII, the small building of brick and stone which forms the principal facade of the Cour de Marbre at the Palace of Versailles. In 1624 Lemercier was commissioned by Cardinal Richelieu to continue the construction of the old court of the Louvre. He built, adjacent to the wing erected by Pierre Lescot on the western side, the pavilion called Tour de l'Horloge, and the building next to this pavilion on the north, thus completing the western side of the old quadrangle. The Tour de l'Horloge, with its famous caryatides by Jacques Sarrazin may be considered the best example of his work. In 1629 he commenced the Palace of Cardinal Richelieu, Paris, which was afterward transformed into the Palais Royal. Of this there remains only a gallery of the second court, which is decorated with marine emblems. In 1629 also he was commissioned to build the college of the Sorbonne, founded by Robert de Sorbon in 1252. His famous Church of the Sorbonne was begun in 1635. In 1631 he began the Chateau of Richelieu in Poitou, now nearly destroyed.. He commenced in 1633 the Church of S. Roch, Paris, completed by Jules Robert de Cotte and his son. In 1633 he succeeded Francois Mansart as architect of the Church of Val de Grace, Paris, which was then built about 10 feet above the soil. Lemercier carried the walls to the spring of the vault. Between 1639 and 1641 he built the first Salle de Spectacle of the Palais Royal. He built the famous stairway of the Cour du Cheval Blanc at Fontainbleau. [ARCHITECT]

Lemercier, Pierre: The founder of an important family of French architects and the earliest architect of the great Church of S. Eustache in Paris, the first stone of which was laid Aug. 19, 1532. The interesting adaptation of Renaissance details to Gothic forms which characterizes this building originated with him. Sept. 25, 1552, he was commissioned to finish the high tower of the Church of S. Maclou at Pontoise, Seine-et-Oise, France. His work at Pontois and Paris was continued by his son, Nicolas Lemercier. The architects of S. Eustache were of the same family, and preserved the unique style of the building throughout. The facade is later. [ARCHITECT]

Leonardo da Vinci: 1452-1519. Leonardo da Vinci was a pupil of Verrocchio. In 1483 he settled in Milan and began the equestrian statue of the Duke Francesco Sforza. Many sketches for this work have come down to us, but the actual form which it assumed is uncertain. The model, nearly 8 meters high, was finished in 1493, and still existed in 1501. It is not known when Leonardo's most celebrated picture, the "Last Supper," in the refectory of the Church of L. Maria delle Grazie, Milan, was begun. He was still working upon it in 1497. Very little of the original painting is now to be seen. He left Milan in 1499 at the fall of Lodovico Sforza, and entered the service of Cesare Borgia as engineer. After the fall of Cesare in 1503 Leonardo went to Florence, and was commissioned by the Gonfaloniere Piero Soderini to paint a picture of the battle of Anghiara for the hall of the Council at the Palazzo Vecchio. The central group of horsemen fighting has been preserved to us in a sketch by Rubens and an engraving by Edelinck. In 1515 he went with the King, Francois I, to France, and spent the last years of his life at the little manor of Cloux, near Ambroise. Leonardo left numerous architectural drawings and notes among his manuscripts, but no practical work in architecture can now be attributed to him. [ARCHITECT, PAINTER, SCULPTOR, ENGINEER]

Leoni, Leone: ca. 1509-1509. Leoni appears to have worked at first in Venice. Like his enemy, Benvenuto Cellini, he was a man of violent temperament. He was imprisoned in the galleys for murder, but was liberated by the great admiral, Andrea Doria, at Genoa, and was placed in charge of the imperial mint at Milan. He became the preferred sculptor of the Emperor Charles V, at one time having his atelier in the Imperial Palace at Brussels. The greater part of his life was spent at Milan. His palace at Milan, built himself, is famous for the colossal half-length figures of its facade. One of Leoni's finest works is the statue of Terrante Gonzaga at Gustalla, Lombardy. [ARCHITECT, SCULPTOR, GOLDSMITH]

Lepautre (Le Paultre), Antoine: 1621-1691. Antoine was a brother of Jean Lepautre. He built between 1646 and 1648 the church of the abbey of Port Royal, Paris. His chief work is the Hotel de Beauvais, in the Rue Saint-Antoine, Paris, of which the cour d'honneur and the grand stairway remain in their original condition. Lepautre designed the Hotel des Gardes at Versailles and

built the two wings of the Chateau of Saint-Cloud. He was a member of the Academie Royale d'Architecture at its foundation in 1677. In 1652 he published his *Oeuvres d' Architecture*. [ARCHITECT, ENGRAVER]

Leroux, Roulland: d. 1527. Roulland was a nephew of Jacques Leroux. He was associated with his uncle in his work on the Tour de Beurre at the Cathedral of Rouen. April 24, 1509, he presented a new plan on parchment for the portal of the Cathedral of Rouen, which he built with the assistance of many sculptors, especially Pierre Desobeaulx, who carved the great bas-relief of the "Tree of Jesse" in the tympanum of the main door. In 1516 he made the plans for the mausoleum of the Cardinal d'Amboise in the Cathedral of Rouen, which was finished in 1525. On Oct. 4, 1514, the central wooden spire of the Cathedral was destroyed by fire. Leroux designed a new spire, of which he completed the first story. [ARCHITECT]

Lescot (L'escot),Pierre: ca. 1510-1578. Lescot was equivalent in the old French to *l'ecossais*, "the Scotchman." Pierre is supposed to have belonged to an ancient Parisian family of this name which was probably of Scottish origin. He was born at about the same time as Jacques (I) Androuet

Du Cereau, Philibert de l'Orme, and Jean Bullant. In Jean Goujon's epistle to the readers, published in Jean Martin's translation of Vitruvius in 1557, Lescot is called *Parisien*. He was *Seigneur de la Grange du Martroy* and *Seigneur de Clagny*, was created *Abbe commendatiore de Clermont*, and, Dec. 18, 1554, canon of the Cathedral of Notre Dame, Paris. The details of his life are known mainly from the poetical epistle which was addressed to him by the poet Ronsard. Lescot was the earliest architect to develop the use of the pure Classic orders in France. His first known work was the roodscreen (jube) of the Church of S. Germain l'Auxerrois, Paris, which was built between 1541 and 1544. The sculptural decoration of this work was by Jean Goujon, Laurent Regnauldin, and Simon Leroy. He was also associated with Jean Goujon in the construction of the fountain of the Nymphs. He is supposed to have made the plans for the Hotel Carnavalet, Paris. Lescot's greatest work is the wing of the Louvre Palace which is situated on the western side of the old quadrangle at its southwestern angle. This building was projected in 1540 by Francois I, but the building was not begun until 1546. Lescot was occupied with this building until his death. [ARCHITECT]

Lethaby, William Richard: 1857-1931. Born in England, Lethaby took his training at the Royal Academy Schools in London. For the first twelve years, he worked under R.N. Shaw. Although Shaw acted as mentor for Lethaby, including setting him up in his own independent practice in 1889, he was principally influenced by Morris and Phillip Webb and wrote a book about the latter. Lethaby was a thinker and teacher as well as an architect. In fact, his buildings are few. The Avon Tyrell in Hampshire, Melsetter on Orkney, the church at Brockhampton in Herefordshire, and the Eagle Insurance Building in Birmingham, England are his principal contributions to architecture. The church is considered to be extremely original in design. He was the first Director of the Central School of Arts and Crafts in London, which was the first architectural school featuring individual workshops for arts and crafts, and therefore, a forerunner to the Bauhaus. [ARCHITECT]

Levau (Leveau), Louis: 1612-1670. The son of Louis Levau, general inspector of the buildings at the Chateau of Fontainebleau. About 1650 he built his first important work, the Hotel Lambert de Thorigny on the Isle Saint Louis, Paris. For Nicholas

Fouquet he built the Chateau of Vaux-le-Vicomte, between 1653 and 1660. In 1655 he succeeded Christophe Gamart as architect of the Church of S. Sulpice, Paris, and was himself superseded at that work by Daniel Gittard in 1670. In 1656 Levau succeeded Jacques Lemercier as *architecte ordinaire du roi,* and continued the works at the Louvre. He completed the northern side of the old quadrangle and rebuilt a large part of the southern side, making a new facade upon the river. This front was afterward rebuilt by Claude Perrault. Levau also designed a facade for the eastern front which was never executed. In 1664 he began to remodel the Tuileries. He rebuilt the central pavilion, removed the grand stairway, and replaced the circular cupola by a larger square one. He destroyed the pretty roofs of the side wings with their dormer windows and built a story in the Corinthian order with an attic in their place. He also rebuilt the upper part of the pavilion designed by Jean Bullant and completed the Tuileries by building the Pavillon Marsan on the north. In 1662 Levau began the palace of the College des Quatre Nations, called also Palais Mazarin opposite the center of the southern side or the Louvre quadrangle on the other side of the river. In 1664 he commenced the Church of S. Louis-en-l'Ille, Paris, which was continued by Gabriel le Duc. To the old Chateau of Louis XIII, at Versailles, he added a front court with two pavilions and an orangerie. [ARCHITECT]

Lippi, Annibale: Lippi built the Palazzo Salvati alla Longara and the Palazzo de Spagna in Rome. His chief work was the completion in 1590 of the Villa Medici, Rome, begun by the French Academy in Rome. [ARCHITECT]

Lissitsky, Eleazar Markevich: 1890-1941. This Russian architect was educated at the College of Technology and received his diploma in 1915. He collaborated with Malevich and contributed "Prouns" to the field of architecture. Prouns are a combination of painting and architecture. In 1921 he taught at the Moscow Academy, later in both Germany and Switzerland. Along with van Doesburg and Mies van der Rohe, Lissitsky was a co-creator of Constructivism. His 1920 design of the spiral-shaped monument to the Third International is well-known. His Lenin Tribune project was the precursor to constructivism. Lissitsky's contribution was primarily a linking between the Eastern Constructivism and the Western avant garde schools in the 1920's. His Proun Cabinet, designed originally for the 1923 Berlin Exhibition and his Abstract Cabinet were reconstructed after he died. The Soviet Pavilion for the 1939 World's Fair in New York was also designed by him. [ARCHITECT]

Lombardo, Antonio (Solaro): d. 1516. A son of Pietro Lombardo, whom he assisted in much of his work. In 1595 he finished one, the finest, of the reliefs in the Capella des Santo in Padua. After 1504 he was associated with Alessandro Leopardi, Alberghetto, and Campanato in the erection of the altar and monument of the Cardinal Zeno in the Church of S. Marco. In 1506 a payment of twenty gold ducats was made to Antonio on account of Alfonso d' Este, Duke of Ferrara, probably for the decoration of the Cameribi d' Alabastro in his palace. Antonio spent the last eleven years of his life at Ferrara. [ARCHITECT, SCULPTOR]

Lombardo, Pietro(Pietro Solaro): ca. 1433-1515. The son of one Martino of Carona in Lombardy, probably also an architect. The earliest notice of Pietro Lombardo is in a document dated Sept. 8, 1479. He was probably employed on the presbiterio and door of S. Giobbe at Venice, as well as the tomb of Cristoforo Moro in

that church. The Palazzo Vendramin-Calergi, in Venice, is ascribed to Pietro. In the contract of March 4, 1481, for the erection of the Church of the Miracoli, Pietro is mentioned as the architect of the monument of the Doge Pietro Mocenigo at the Church of SS. Giovanni e Paolo, which was finished in 1481. A contract was made with Pietro, March 4, 1481, for the construction of the Church of S. Maria dei Miracoli at Venice. The work was begun at once and finished in 1489. The little monument to Dante at Ravenna was erected by Pietro in 1482. May 1, 1489, the *procuratiri* of the Scoula de S, Marco at Venice contracted with Pietro Lombardo and Goivanni Buora for the reconstruction of that building, which had been ruined by fire. After November, 1490, they were superseded by Mauro Coducci. Pietro also rebuilt the Church of S. Andrea della Certosa, Venice which was destroyed early in the nineteenth century. After the flight of Antonio Rizzo in 1498, Pietro was appointed *protomaestro* of the Doges' Palace, May 16, 1498. Owing to the loss of documents it is impossible to determine how much of the building was designed by him. In 1500-1506 he built the wings of the Torre dell' Orologio in the Piazza de S. Marco, Venice, and in 1502 rebuilt the Duomo of Cividale in Friuli, which had fallen in. Pietro Lombardo conducted a *botega* in the quarter of S. Samuele, Venice, where a large business was done in decorative sculpture. The figures were usually cut by his sons, Antonio and Tullio. [ARCHITECT, SCULPTOR]

Lombardo, Tullio (Solaro): d. 1532. A son of Pietro Lombardo. He assisted his father in many of his undertakings. Tullio made the bas-reliefs of the Apostles in the Church of S. Giovanni Grisostomo in Venice. According to Temanza he assisted Leopardi on the monument to the Doge, Andrea Vendramini, in the Church of SS. Giovanni e Paolo are ascribed to him. In 1501, Tullio undertook two of the bas-reliefs in the Capella del Santo at Padua, which were not finished before 1525. The Capella del SS. Sacramento in the duomo, and the transept of the Church of S. Maria Maggiore at Treviso are also ascribed to him. Oct. 29, 1507, he was associated with his father in the construction of the Church of S. Salvatore in Venice. In 1523 he carved a door for the studiola of Isabella d' Este Gonzaga, in the Palazzo at Mantua. [ARCHITECT, SCULPTOR]

Longhena, Baldassare: 1604-1682. The last architect of the great Vene-

tian school. His understanding was formed by the work of Scamozzi, Palladio, and Jacopo Sansovino. His earliest important undertaking was the Church of S. Maria della Salute, Venice, which was begun in 1631, but not finished until 1656. In 1640 he was appointed *Proto della procuratia di Sopra,* or state architect of Venice. The splendid Church of S. Maria agli Scalzi, which Longhena built about 1646, is also famous for the ceiling of the nave by G. B. Tiepolo. Longhena built the Capella Vendramini in the Church of S. Pietro di Castello, the ancient Cathedral of Venice, and the great altar of the Church of S. Francesco della Vigna. The most perfect expression of his skill is the Palazzo Pesaro, built about 1644. He built also the Palazzo Battaglia, the Palazzo Flangini, the Palazzo Giustinian-Lolin, the Palazzo Zanne, near Sant' Agostino, the Palazzo Lezze, the Palazzo Morosini, near San Casciano, the Palazzo Marcello (now Papadopoli), near Santa Marina, and the Palazzo Widmann, near San Casciano. He built also the great stairway of the monastery of S. Giorgio Maggiore, and the monument to the Doge Giovanni Pesaro in the Church of the Frari. All the work mentioned here is in Venice. [ARCHITECT]

Loos, Adolf: 1870-1933. Loos was born in Austria and educated at the *Technische Hochschule* in Dresden. In 1893, at the age of 23 and his education completed, Loos decided to travel to the United States, where he stayed for three years. These three years were spent doing odd jobs and studying American architecture. Most impressed by the Chicago School of Design, Loos was especially impressed by Sullivan's theory that buildings should be designed without ornamentation. Upon returning to Europe, Loos incorporated that theory into his architectural designs, as shown in one of his early designs (1898) of the Goldmann Shop interior. He published a series of articles espousing his newly found theories, which also had been affected by Otto Wagner. He founded a Free School of Architecture in 1906. His renovation of the Villa Karma at Clarens (1906), the Karntner Bar in Vienna (1907), the Steiner House, also in Vienna (1910) were further putting his style into practice. The Steiner House was one of the first private residences to be built from reinforced concrete and is considered a major architectural benchmark. Loos became well-known for his article "Ornament and Crime," first published in 1908. The Muller House in Prague influenced architects such as Lurcas, Mendelsohn, Neutra, and Schindler. [ARCHITECT]

Louis, Louis Nicolas Victor: 1731-1800. Victor Louis was a son of a mason of Paris. In 1746 he entered the *Ecole royale d' Architecture*. In the competition for the *Prix de Rome* in 1755 he was granted a special prize with a gold medal and a pension at Rome. He returned to Paris in 1759. In 1765 Louis was appointed architect to Stanislas Auguste Poniatowsky, King of Poland, with permission to reside in Paris. He restored and decorated the royal palace at Warsaw but left no monuments in Poland. His chief work is the great theater of Bordeaux, built to replace one burned in 1755; this was inaugurated April 7, 1780. The main features of its arrangement have been adopted in the Grand Opera in Paris. In 1780 Louis Philippe Joseph d'Orleans, Duke of Chartres, commissioned him to rebuild his residence, the Palais Royal in Paris, originally designed for the Cardinal Richelieu by Jacques Lemercier. The restoration included a new theater to take the place of the old Salle de l' Opera. This theater, long celebrated as the Theater Francais, was injured by fire. Louis published a monograph on the *Salle de*

Spectale de Bordeaux Paris, 1782. [ARCHITECT]

Louis Kahn: 1901-1974. Kahn was born in Estonia in 1901 and emigrated to the United States in 1905. He was educated at the University of Pennsylvania and opened his own partnership with George Howe in 1941. In later years he taught at Yale University, Massachusetts Institute of Technology, and the University of Pennsylvania. The partnership with Howe (and later Oscar Stonorov) was strongly influenced by Buckminster Fuller. Their Carver Court Housing Estate in Coatesville, Pennsylvania, is much acclaimed, as is the Richards Medical Research Building in Philadelphia and the Yale University Art Gallery. His style was a blend of Brutalism, post-modernism and Rational architecture, and his buildings reflect his metaphysical beliefs and search for the perfect architectural form. His work paved the way for later architects such as Aldo, Rossi, James Stirling, and Mario Botta. The laboratory buildings of the Jonas Salk Institute in La Jolla, California, allowed free working space and provided a spiritual place where the employees could think creatively. In later years, Kahn's design for the government center of Dacca, Bangladesh allowed his style to come to maturity. Additionally, the house-within-a-house idea which Kahn had is clearly shown in the Central Building of the Assembly in Dacca. [ARCHITECT]

Luciano da Laurana: d. 1483. Luciano came from Laurana or Lovrana, a little city in Istria, then Venetian territory. Frederico III, Count of Montefeltro and first Duke of Urbino, issued letters patent (now in the Vatican Library) dated June 10, 1468, creating Luciano chief architect and engineer of the palace which he had begun to erect at Urbino. According to Baldi, Luciano had worked on the Poggio Reale, near Naples, and was recommended to Montefeltro by the Neapolitan court. Associated with him were Baccio Pontelli and probably Francesco di Giorgio Martini. The principal sculptor employed was Barocci of Milan. The palace is also attributed to Luciano. [ARCHITECT]

Ludwig, Meister: An important German architect of the Gothic period. From 1275 to 1306 he conducted the works at the Cathedral of Regensburg in Bavaria. Associated with him were his sons Weichmann and Konrad. [ARCHITECT]

Lunghi, Martino (the elder): Architect of the school of Giacomo della Porta in Rome. He designed the

Church of S. Maria della Vallicella, the facade of S. Girolamo degli Schiavoni, after 1585, the Palazzo Ceri, and the Palazzo Altemps, all in Rome. Lunghi's most important work is the Palazzo Borghese, Rome, 1590. [ARCHITECT]

Lunghi, Martino (the younger): d. 1657. A son of Onorio Lunghi. He built about 1650 the Church of SS. Vincenzo ed Anastasio near the fountain of Trevi for the Cardinal Mazarin and the little Church of S. Antonio de' Portoghesi, about 1652. Less important are the facades of S. Adriano and S. Maria dell' Orto and the altar of S. Carlo al Corso. All are in Rome. [ARCHITECT]

Lutyens, Sir Edwin: 1869-1944. Lutyens, born in England, opened his own practice at the age of 20. His country houses were designed in the Arts and Crafts school and included Deanery Garden in Sonning (1899), Orchards in Godalming (1899), Tigbourner Court (1899), and Folly Farm in Sulhampstead (1905 and 1912). Later on, he turned to neoclassicism in style, as evidenced by the plan for New Delhi (1912) and the commercial buildings Britannic House (1920-1924), as well as the Midland Ban headquarters in London (1924-1930). He designed the British

Embassy in Washington, D.C. in 1925-1928). He was greatly influenced by Phillip Webb. He was traditional in his designs, being one of the last of his generation. His New Delhi Viceroy's House features a huge dome and is considered his most famous work. His later buildings were not designed within the mainstream of European architecture. [ARCHITECT]

Luzarches, Robert de: The Carlovingian Cathedral of Amiens, France, was burned in 1218. The Bishop, Evrard de Fouilloy, determined to rebuild it at once on a magnificent scale. The plans for this building, the present Cathedral, were made by a layman, Robert de Luzarches. At the death of Evrard in 1223, the foundations were completed. During the bishopric of his successor, Geoffroy d'Eu, the work was pushed with the greatest activity. Thomas de Cormont succeeded Luzarches and built the nave and transept according to the plans of his predecessor. In the labyrinth of the pavement of the Cathedral, destroyed about 50 years ago, were to be seen the figures of Bishop Evrard and of the three architects, Luzarches, Thomas, and Renaud de Cormont, with a commemorative inscription which is now in the Musee de Picardie. [ARCHITECT]

Mackintosh, Charles Rennie: 1868-1928. Born in Glasgow and educated at the Glasgow School of Art, Mackintosh was one of the forerunners of the twentieth century school of rationalism. This Scottish architect was a leader of the Art Nouveau movement in Britain. Along with his friend Herbert MacNair and the MacDonald sisters, one of whom he married later, Mackintosh was the fourth member of "The Four" as they are called. They designed the Scottish Section of the International Exposition of Decorative Arts in Turin in 1902. Mackintosh was excited about the work of the critic John Ruskin and began keeping notebooks filled with sketches of works in progress. The notebooks have gained much recognition. Mackintosh designed the Glasgow School of Art, and that school is his most famous design. He had won a competition for the design, which featured rational plan and a center piece of complex originality. The interior was a unity of rectangles and refined curves. The Viennese were deleting Art Nouveau from their architectural style, and Mackintosh inspired them with his designs. His interior work had developed into his own style and featured white lacquered chairs and cabinets, which were decorated with metal inlays and colored enamel. Some of the works which showed this interior design clearly were the tea rooms for Mrs. Cranston, which have unfortunately been destroyed, houses at Windyhill in Kilmacolm, Hill House in Helensburgh, and a school on Scotland Street. His furniture designs linked the Scottish fashions with the Viennese School. A difficult, erratic man, he made several geographical moves beginning in 1913 and virtually left the architectural field, designing furniture and fabrics, and painting landscapes for the rest of his life. [ARCHITECT]

Mackmurdo, Arthur Heygate: 1851-1942. Born into a wealthy family in 1851, Mackmurdo built his first house in England beginning in 1880. The house at 8 Private Road in Enfield is quite refined in its sophistication. The Century Guild, a collection of artists, architects, and designers, was formed by Mackmurdo in 1882. This group took its inspiration from Ruskin and Morris and started off by publishing a magazine called *The Hobby Horse* in 1884. Mackmurdo designed covers for books, one of which was for a book of Wren's city churches in which he introduced tendrils that were long and curved. This style was taken up by architects 10 years later, influencing Belgian architects to Art Nouveau. From 1886 on, Mackmurdo was the only pioneer in Art Nouveau. His designs were clearly elegant and basic in breaking from the prior styles. Beginning in 1904, Mackmurdo left the architectural field to become an economic thinker and author. [ARCHITECT]

Maderna (Maderno), Carlo: 1556-1629. A Lombard architect who followed his uncles, Domenico and Giovanni Fontana, to Rome. He was associated with them in their work and completed several undertakings commenced by them, among others the Fontana dell' Acqua Paola. He was for many years the leading architect in Rome. His earliest independent work appears to be the facade of the Church of S. Susanna (1595-1603). He built also the Palazzo Mattei di Giove (1602). The idea of applying the long nave of the Church of Gesu, by Vignola, to the great Church of S. Peter originated with Domenico Fontana. The execution of the scheme was the work of Carlo Maderna, who built also the facade as we now see it, the design for which was based on the model left by Michelangelo. The vestibule is one of Maderna's best works. The interior of the Church of S. Maria della Vittoria dates from 1605. Maderna continued the construction of the Palazzo Quirinale, designed the stairway of the Palazzo Chigi (1587) in the Piazza Colonna, and built the Palazzo Odescalchi in the Piazza dei SS. Apostoli. One of his most important works is the Palazzo Barberini (begun 1624), which was continued by Bernini and Borimini. Maderna designed the fountains of the Piazza di San Pietro. All the works mentioned are in Rome. [ARCHITECT]

Maillart, Robert: 1872-1940. This Swiss engineer was a primary force in bringing reinforced concrete design from its early days to its place as a considerable force in material for structure. Maillart studied at the Polytechnic College in Zurich and, prior to establishing his own firm in 1902, worked for other engineering firms. His work with reinforced concrete brought about a fresh style, which allowed it to extend over curves instead of the previous straight construction. The Tavenasa Bridge, built in 1905, was the prototype where curves blend with road. He began playing with Mushroom Construction in 1908, and although United States architects were also using this type of construction, his warehouse in Zurich (1910) is a prime example of this style. [ARCHITECT]

Malevich, Kasimir: 1878-1935. Born near Kiev in 1878, this Russian painter and architect studied at the School of Art in Kiev. He moved to Moscow in 1908 and was a pioneer in Suprematism, a style which he named. His painting Black Square on White Ground is the first example of Suprematism. He was highly influenced by the postimpressionists, the Fauvists and later the Cubists. In the 1920's he moved from painting to sculpture and architecture, worked with Lissitsky, and visited the Bauhaus, where he was a definitive force on the Modernists. [ARCHITECT]

Manetti, Antonio (Ciaccheri): (15th century.) A Florentine architect who continued and completed several of the buildings undertaking by Brunellesco. He built the nave of the Church of S. Lorenzo in Florence after Brunellesco's death. He is not to be confounded with Antonio di Tuccio Manetti. [ARCHITECT]

Mansart, Nicolas Francois: 1598-1666. Francois was the son of one Absolon Mansart, a master carpenter. At the age of 24 he constructed the portal of the Church of the Feuillants in the Rue Saint-Honore (Paris), now destroyed. In 1632 he began the church of the convent of the Filles de la Visitation (Paris), which was dedicated in 1634 as Notre-Dame-des-Anges (now used as a Protestant church). In 1634 he began extensive additions to the Hotel Carnavalet in Paris, and in 1635 built the hotel of the Marquis de la Vrilliere, occupied by the Banque de France since 1811. In 1635, also, he was commissioned by Gaston, Duke of Orleans, to erect the great building at the rear of the court of the Chateau of Blois (Loir-et-Cher). His scheme, interrupted by the death of Gaston, contemplated the entire reconstruction of the Chateau. In 1645, Mansart began for Anne d'Autriche, queen of Louis XIII, the great Church of the Val-de-Grace (Paris). When the walls had reached a height of about 10 feet above the ground the work was transferred to Jacques Lemercier. Mansart afterward built for the Chateau of Fresnes a chapel from the plans which he had made for the Val-de-Grace, reduced to one third. At the invitation of Colbert (d. 1683), he made designs for the completion of the Louvre, but his intractable temperament prevented their execution. He built many residences in Paris and chateaux in the provinces, which still exist. [ARCHITECT]

Marchand (Marchant), Guillaume: ca. 1530-1605. In 1578 he was commissioned with Guillaume Gullying, Thibaut Metezeau, and Jean and Francois Petit, to design and build the Pont-Neuf (Paris). He was charged by Henri IV to continue the construction of the Pont-Neuf, which was not finished until 1608. Between 1594 and 1596, he was associated with others in the construction of the eastern half of the Grande Galerie of the Louvre. On March 27, 1600, he undertook, with Pierre Chambiges and others, the construction of the western half of the Grande Galerie. For Henri IV he began the new Chateau of Saint-Germain-en-Laye, which was finished in 1610 (destroyed about 1775). [ARCHITECT AND BUILDER]

Mardargent (Marc D'Argent), Jean Roussell: d. 1339. He became abbot of S. Ouen at Rouen in 1303. Mardargent augmented the revenues of the abbey and designed its church. He built the choir with its chapels, the pillars of the central tower, and began the transept and nave. [ABBOT AND ARCHITECT]

Marot, Daniel: Daniel was probably a son of Jean Marot. He was a Protestant, and at the Revocation of the Edict of Nantes, Oct. 22, 1685, took refuge in Holland and became architect to the Prince of Orange, later King William III of England. He went with William to England in 1688 and is supposed to have designed the gardens of the Palace of Hampton Court. After the death of William in 1702, Marot returned to Holland. He published *Ouvres de Sieur Daniel Marot, architecte de Guillaume III de la Grande Bretagne,* (Amsterdam, 1712). [ARCHITECT AND ENGRAVER]

Marot, Jean: ca. 1620-1679. Marot built the portal of the Feuillantines and numerous residences in Paris. With Lemercier, he made plans for the completion of the Louvre, which were never executed but are engraved in his book. Marot is known by his architectural engravings, the greater part of which were collected in his *Architecture francaise ou Recueil des plans, elevations, coupes et profiles des eglises, palais, hotels et maisons particuliers de Paris, etc.* He published also *Le Magnifique chateau de Richelieu.* [ARCHITECT AND ENGRAVER]

Martini: 1439-1502. Besides his work on fortification, he was a student of antiquity; a manuscript of his translation of Vitruvius, bound up with other essays of his, is preserved in Florence. In 1476 he became attached to the court at Urbino and from 1491 was in Naples. The only building of importance which is certainly by him is the Church of the Madonna del Calcinaio, near Cortona, of which the first stone was laid in 1485, but this is one of the most valuable churches of the Renaissance. The cupola was added by Pietro di Domenico Nozzi. [ARCHITECT AND MILITARY ENGINEER]

Martinus: The fine Romanesque port of S. Erasmo at Veroli (Italy) is signed by Martinus: MANIBVS FACTVS MARTINI QVEM PROBAT ARCVS. The work belongs to the middle of the twelfth century. [ARCHITECT]

Mascherino, Ottavio (Ottaviano): ca. 1530-ca. 1610. Mascherino rebuilt the Church of S. Salvatore, Rome, which had been destroyed by fire in 1591. His most important work is the Palazzo Quirinale, Rome, which he designed for Paul V (Pope 1605-1621). The facade on the Piazza di Monte Cavallo and the court are his work. [ARCHITECT]

Masegne, Giacomello di Antonio Dalle: His work shows Tuscan influence decidedly. In 1338 the Frati Minori of the Church of S. Francesco at Bologna contracted with Masegne to make the great altar of that church. It is adorned with statuettes of the Virgin and saints, bas-reliefs of the Coronation of the Virgin, and other subjects. In 1400 he made the tomb of Antonio Venier at the Church of SS. Giovanni e Paolo in Venice. A brother called Pietro Paolo dalle Masegne is stated to have worked with him. The Septo, or low screen enclosing the choir of S. Mark's Church, Venice, with numerous statuettes, was made by the Masegne in 1394-1397. [SCULPTOR AND ARCHITECT]

Massari, Giorgio: An architect of the eighteenth century in Venice. One of his most important works is the Church of S. Maria del Rosario (called Gesuati) in Venice (1726-1743), which was decorated by G. B. Tiepolo. He built also, in Venice, the upper order and staircase of the Palazzo Rezzonico. [ARCHITECT]

Mathias (Mathieu) D'Arras: Mathias d'Arras was brought from Avignon (France) by the Emperor Charles IV to plan and construct the Cathedral of Prague. He laid the foundations of the choir and built the surrounding chapels. The choir was completed, probably after his plans, by his successor, Pierre Arler of Peter Parler. [ARCHITECT]

Mathias von Ensingen: d. 1463. Mathias was the son of Ulrich von Ensingen. In 1420 he was called to superintend the construction of the Cathedral of Berne in Switzerland. In 1446 he went to Ulm and in 1451 was made architect of the Cathedral of that city. An inscription on the northern portal of the Cathedral of Ulm gives the date of his death. He was succeeded by his son Moriz von Ensingen. [ARCHITECT]

Matthew, Sir Robert Hogg:
1906-1975. This Englishman is well known for his work as architect to the London County Council between 1946 and 1953. The Council started commendable work on housing and schools. Beginning in 1953, he taught at Edinburgh University and played a considerable part in the progressive style of the buildings there. Varying heights, the arrangement of the buildings, and the landscaping made these I.C.C. buildings and estates an example for the rest of Europe. He established his own firm, Robert Matthew, Johnson-Marshall and Partners. The firm's designs were not in keeping with Matthew's style. Examples of the buildings designed by the firm are the New Zealand House, an International Modern building; the Commonwealth Institute in London, which featured a hyperbolic parabolic roof; and York University, which is austere and elegant. The Hillingdon Civic Center, which was designed by

Andrew Derbyshire, a member of Matthew's firm, is made of brick with very atypical roofs. It is of the anti-modern movement, aiming to speak the language of the heart. [ARCHITECT]

Maybeck, Bernard Ralph:
1862-1957. This California architect was born in New York and was educated at the *Ecole des Beaux-Arts* in Paris. The work of Viollet-le-Duc impacted on Maybeck. Beginning in 1894, he established an office in Berkeley, moving that practice to San Francisco in 1902. He was a professor at the University of California in Berkeley and the Mark Hopkins Institute of Art in San Francisco. Maybeck's style was that of the Bay region and he was a pioneer in the promulgation of that design school. Maybeck experimented with prefabricated units, shown clearly in his design of the First Church of Christ Scientist in Berkeley. He loved working with wood, shown in First Church and the Faculty Club on the university's campus in Berkeley. He was also influenced by the Gothic and Japanese styles. He designed many private homes, although the interiors of these homes were more impressive than the exteriors. His most exciting home design was that of the Wynton House, located on the Russian River in northern California.

His most famous design is that of the Palace of Fine Arts in San Francisco. [ARCHITECT]

McComb, John: 1763-1853. His family was Scotch and settled in New York. He designed the front of the old government house in New York, 1790, S. John's Church, the Murray Street and the Bleeker Street churches, and many public and private buildings in New York, Philadelphia, and the Eastern states. McComb was supervising architect of the city of New York during the erection of the City Hall, and is supposed to have been its designer. [ARCHITECT, ENGINEER]

McKim, Charles Follen: 1847-1909. McKim was an engineer first, having studied at Harvard University. Between 1867-1870, he educated himself in architecture at the *Ecole des Beaux Arts* in Paris. He worked with H. H. Richardson upon his return to the United States. His private practice was started in partnership with William Rutherford Mead, later adding Stanford White. Colonial architecture was of interest to the firm, although it was not a usual practice for architects of the period. As well, the Italian Renaissance played an important part in their designs. The Villard Houses on Madison Avenue in New York reflect their Renaissance influence. McKim designed the facade. In 1893, McKim designed the Agricultural Building for the Chicago Exhibition. Later on, works included the Cricket Club (1891), Madison Gardens (1891) the Washington Triumphal Arch in New York, and Columbia University in New York, whose library rotunda was inspired by the Pantheon in Rome. Also designed by McKim were the Morgan Library and the Pennsylvania Railway Station, both located in New York. [ARCHITECT]

Mendelsohn, Erich: 1887-1953. This German-born architect studied economics at the University of Munich and architecture at the Technische Hochschule in Berlin. In 1919 Mendelsohn's sketches won attention at an exhibition in Paul Cassirer's gallery in Berlin. One of these drawings was later to be translated into Mendelsohn's most famous work, the Einstein Tower in Potsdam (1920). It was completed in 1921, made from masonry, but looked like reinforced concrete. The Einstein Tower is one of the best examples of the Expressionist School. The exterior and interior are square shafts, but the tower and base are curvilinear with deep recesses. His principle desire in designing the tower was the achievement of organic unity, a principle to which he adhered in all future works. Among Mendelsohn's other notable works are the Mosse Building in Berlin (remodeled 1921), which carried the spirit of the International Modern style. In the Schocken stores for Stuttgart (1926) and Chemnitz (1928), horizontal lines are combined with spiral staircases to form an elegance of design which was Mendelsohn's trademark. He was influenced early by Greek art, and that influence can be seen in the Columbus Haus in Berlin, his own house also in Berlin, the Hadassah University Medical Center and Schocken House, both in Jerusalem. Mendelsohn emigrated to Israel and later to the United States. He was impressed with the skyscrapers he had seen on a trip to the United States in 1924. Upon emigration to the United States, his main works consisted of a series of Jewish temples and community centers, one of the more beautiful of which is the Temple in Cleveland, Ohio, which features a 100' dome. He also built the Maimonides Hospital in San Francisco (1946). [ARCHITECT]

Meo (Bartolomeo) del Caprino: 1430-1501. Meo was undoubtedly one of the leading architects of his time in Italy. About 1462 he entered the service of Pius II (Pope 1458-1464)

and assisted in the construction of the loggia of the Benediction at the Vatican. He was employed by Paul II (Pope 1464-1471) at the Vatican and at the Palazzo di S. Marco, Rome. Meo built the Cathedral of Turin, probably between 1471 and 1491. [ARCHITECT]

Metezeau, Clement (II): 1581-1652. He was a son of Thibaut Metezeau, and grandson of Clement (I). He enjoyed the protection of Marie de' Medici, queen of Henry IV of France and was associated with Salomon de Brosse in the construction of the Palace of the Luxembourg, Paris. In 1624 he had already become architect to Louis XIII. His name is especially associated with the great dike which was built across the harbor of La Rochelle, Charente-Inferieure, France, to secure the reduction of that city, besieged by Louis XIII. The dike was designed by Metezeau in association with Jean Theriot, an engineer, and built by Jean Theriot. [ARCHITECT]

Michael of Canterbury: *Magister Michael de Cantuaria cementarius* contracted to build the Eleanor Cross at East Cheap, London. During the years 1291, 1292, and 1293 he was paid 226 pounds 13 shillings for this work. No one else is mentioned in connection with it. The construction of S. Stephen's Chapel, Westminster, begun about 1292, burned in October 1834, is also attributed to him. S. Stephen's, Westminster, was for a long period the Parliament House of Great Britain. [ARCHITECT]

Michelozzi, Michelozzo di Bartolommeo de: ca. 1396-1472. Michelozzo was trained as a goldsmith and assisted Ghiberti on both doors of the Florentine Baptistery. He built for Cosimo de' Medici the famous Palace in the Via Larga, Florence, which was bought by the Riccardi in 1659 and, enlarged by them, is now the Prefetura. He built the library, finished 1441, and convent and cloister of S. Marco in Florence (1437-1452). About 1444 he began the works at the Church of SS. Annunziata, Florence. He built the chapel, sacristy, *Chiostro del Antiporto*, and began the Tribuna or choir of this church. He remodelled the interior of the Palazzo Vecchio, Florence, especially the main court and the Hall of the Two Hundred. At Milan he remodelled the Palace of Cosimo de' Medici, now Vismara, and built the Chapel of the Portinari at the Church of S. Eustorgio, famous for frescoes by Vincenzo Foppa (both between 1456 and 1462). The arcade of the Palazzo Rettorale at Ragusa in Dalmatia is ascribed to him. July 14, 1428, Michelozzo

signed the contract for the exterior pulpit at Prato, the records of which still exist. The sculpture is by Donatello. They also made together the Brancacci monument at Naples and that of ex-Pope John XXIII at the Florentine Baptistery. The Aragazzi tomb of Montepulciano is ascribed to Michelozzo alone. [SCULPTOR AND ARCHITECT]

Mies van der Rohe, Ludwig: 1886-1969. Although born in Germany, Mies emigrated to the United States in 1938. He was educated at the *Domschule* and the Trade School in Aachen, and he served as an engineer in the German Army from 1914-18. Along with Frank Lloyd Wright, Le Corbusier and Walter Gropius, he is considered one of the four most influential architects of the twentieth century. His training included nothing formal in architecture and he learned much of his craftsmanship from his father, a stonemason and carver. He became an apprentice to Paul Brune in Berlin. In 1908 Mies joined forces with Peter Behrens, one of the more productive architects in Germany. By the end of the first World War, he was extremely excited about the Expressionist School of design and designed his famous glass skyscrapers between 1919 and 1921. The discipline and purity with which he designed buildings has rarely been equalled in modern architecture. De Stijl, and the Dutch movement, helped him define his style for the German Pavilion of 1921 in Barcelona, his courtyard house projects of the 1930's, and the campus of the Illinois Institute of Technology in Chicago from 1938 to 1959. The German Pavilion was an open floor plan with precious materials such as marble, travertine, onyx, polished steel, and bottle-green glass. Between 1930 and 1933, Mies was director of the Bauhaus. He once said in an interview that "I don't want to be interesting, I want to be good." Mies was invited to teach at the Illinois Institute of Technology. He had emigrated to the United States because of the Nazis in 1937, and he accepted the teaching position in 1938. The Farnsworth House in Plano, Illinois (1950) is another of his noteworthy buildings and features an open pavilion design. This glass and metal home included three floating slabs, which were lifted off the ground with metal I-beam supports. [ARCHITECT]

Mills, Robert: After 1829, when Charles Bulfinch retired, the office of supervising architect of the Capitol at Washington was vacant until July 6, 1836, when President Jackson appointed Robert Mills, a former assistant of Benjamin Latrobe. He held the office until 1851. [ARCHITECT]

Montferrand, Auguste Ricard de: 1786-1859 (at Saint Petersburg, Russia). De Montferrand was a pupil of Charles Percier. In 1816 he went to Saint Petersburg and assumed the position of architect of the Czar Alexander I. In 1817 he was successful in a competition of the reconstruction of the old Cathedral of S. Isaac at Saint Petersburg. The present Cathedral was designed by him and completed in about 40 years. He published *L'eglise catedrale de Saint Isaac, description architecturale, etc.* (Paris and Saint Petersburg, 1845) [ARCHITECT]

Montorsoli, Fra Giovanni Angiolo da: 1507-1563. He received his name from the village of Montorsoli, near Florence, where he was born. He was attached to the works at S. Peter's, where he attracted the attention of Michelangelo, whom he assisted in the completion of the Medici tombs in the new sacristy of S. Lorenzo at Florence. The statue of S. Cosimo, now in the sacristy, was made by him. In October, 1530, he entered the religious order of the Servi dell' Annunziata, in Florence. Returning to Rome, he was employed by Clement VI (Pope 1523-1534) to restore antique statues at the Belvedere, Vatican. Montorsoli also assisted Michelangelo on the tomb of Julius II. A visit to Paris was without important results. About 1543, for the great admiral Andrea Doria, he began the decoration of the Church of S. Matteo, Genoa, including the altar and the tomb of the admiral. He assisted also in the decoration of the Doria Palace. In September, 1547, Montorsoli was called to Messina, Sicily, to construct the great fountain of the Piazza del Duomo. This was followed by the fountain of the port of Messina. [SCULPTOR AND ARCHITECT]

Montreuil, Pierre de: (13th century.) A layman, and the principal architect for Louis IX (S. Louis). The Saint-Chapelle of the Chateau of Saint-Germain-en-Laye, near Paris, is supposed to have been one of his earlier works, but the attribution is discredited by Viollet-le-Duc. He built the refectory (1239-1244) and the Chapelle de la Vierge (begun 1244) at the monastery of S. Germain des Pres, Paris, which were destroyed during the Revolution. Some of the glass of the chapel has been placed in the Church of S. Germain de Pres; the carved doorway with the statue of the Madonna is in the Church of Saint Denis, near Paris. The tomb of Montreuil existed in the Chapel of S.

Germain des Pres until the Revolution. In 1240 Montreuil was commissioned by S. Louis to build the Sainte-Chapelle of the royal palace (later in the Palais de Justice), Paris. This building, one of the finest works of the thirteenth century, was built to contain the Crown of Thorns, a fragment of the true Cross, and other relics, which were secured from Baudouin de Courtenay, Emperor of Constantinople. It was dedicated April 25, 1248. The chapel of the Chateau of Vincennes, near Paris, is also attributed to Pierre de Montreuil. [ARCHITECT]

Montreuil (Montereau), Eudes de: d. 1289. Probably related to Pierre de Montreuil. In 1248 he went with King Louis IX of France (S. Louis) on the seventh crusade and assisted in the fortification of the city of Jaffa, in Palestine. On his return, in 1254, he built the church of the great asylum for the blind, established by S. Louis, which was called the Hospice des Quinze Vingts (destroyed 1779). He built also, in Paris, the churches of the Blancs Manteaux, of the Val des Ecoliers, of the Mathurins, of the Cordeliers, of S. Catherine, and of the Hotel Dieu. His epitaph was to be seen in the Church of the Cordeliers until its destruction in 1580. [ARCHITECT]

Morard: d. 1014. Morard was elected abbot of the monastery of S. Germain des Pres, Paris, in 990. He rebuilt the church of his abbey, which had been repeatedly sacked by the Normans. Of his work only the interior porch and the base of the tower remain. The rest of the church belongs to the second half of the eleventh and first half of the twelfth century. It was consecrated April 21, 1163. [ABBOT AND ARCHITECT]

Morris, William: 1834-1896. Morris was born in Essex, England, and first studied theology, then architecture, although not formally for the latter. He trained under the Gothic revivalist G. E. Street, where he was to meet Shaw and Webb. Morris, although he designed no buildings, influenced future architects tremendously. He worked with Webb to produce his own home, the Red House, located at Bexley Heath in Kent. He did not like the housing designs of his contemporaries; his own home was a benchmark in the English domestic revival. His house was red brick and its design exerted considerable influence on other architects. In 1861 he, along with some friends, started the firm of Morris, Marshall & Faulkner. Morris executed many designs for wallpaper, ornamentation, stained glass, textiles, carpets, tapestries, and other woven furnishing materials. Between 1890 and 1896, the firm also designed books. Morris' designs are two-dimensional and they also played a major role in creating a following. Beginning in 1877, he started lecturing, which continued until his death in 1896. He pleaded with his students to consider their designs carefully and to do away with unattractive towns and buildings. He asked them to reform the ugliness contained within the local communities. Morris was also one of the founders of organized socialism in England and believed that all art should be "by the people for the people." Morris started the movement toward mass production of designer fabrics, wallpaper, etc., and he desperately believed that the common people should have access to these designs, not just the upper classes. [ARCHITECT]

Mullet, A.B.: d. 1890. Mullet came to Washington from Ohio soon after the close of the Civil War at the invitation of Secretary Chase and was made supervising architect of the Treasury. An immense number of public buildings were carried out under his administration in New York, Boston, Chicago, Cincinnati, and other great cities of the United States. [ARCHITECT]

Mutius, Caius: Mutius is mentioned by Vitruvius as having built the temple of Honos and Virtus in Rome with great skill. [ARCHITECT]

Mylne, Robert, F.R.S.: 1734-1811. He was a descendant of John (IV) Mylne. Mylne travelled in France and Italy and in 1758 won the gold and silver medals in architecture at the Academy of S. Luke in Rome. He competed successfully for the construction of Blackfriars' Bridge in London, of which he was appointed architect Feb. 28, 1760. This structure was removed in 1868. In 1767 he was appointed surveyor to Canterbury Cathedral. [ARCHITECT AND ENGINEER]

Nash, Sir John: 1752-1835. He was a pupil of Sir Robert Taylor. His name is especially associated with the transformation of the old Marylebone region in London into Regent's Park, with its terraces and surrounding streets, which was begun in 1811. Regent Street, Park Crescent and Square, Albany, and other adjoining streets were laid out and built from Nash's designs. He completed Saint James's Park and transformed Buckingham House into Buckingham Palace. [ARCHITECT]

Nervi, Pier Luigi: 1891-1979. Born in Sondrio, Italy, Nervi belongs to the small group of engineers and archi-tects who used reinforced concrete to its fullest potential. Nervi was educated at the University of Bologna. His degree was in civil engineering, and he had to wait quite a long time before he achieved his elevated position among designers. He was also an entrepreneur and a university professor, an interesting combination considering the fact that such a blending was not allowed in Britain. Nervi's stadium in Florence, Italy, was built between 1930 and 1932. Its cantilevered roof is 70' deep, and the building features a flying spiral staircase. He won a competition for airship hangars, which were subsequently built at Orbetello starting in 1936. These hangars were based on the idea of a vault with diagonally intersecting concrete beams and huge angle supports. Unfortunately, the hangars were destroyed during World War II. In 1943 and 1950 Nervi built two great exhibition halls in Turin, considered to be his greatest architectural designs in reinforced concrete. They featured diagonal grids. Between 1953 and 1960, Nervi's notoriety won him the commission to do the Unesco Building in Paris. In 1958, Nervi designed the Exhibition Hall on the Rond-point de la Defense in Paris. This building was a triangle, the sides were 710' long, and the rood consisted of three triangular sections of warped concrete. Other well-known structures are the Pallazzo dello Sport and the Palazzeto dello Sport, both located in Rome and built in the late 1950's and early 1960's. [ARCHITECT]

Neumann, Johann Balthazar: 1687-1753. In 1711 he entered the artillery service in Wurzburg, Germany. He attracted the attention of the Prince-Bishop, Johann von Schonborn, who sent him to Italy, France, and the Netherlands to study. Neumann built the fine palace at Wurzburg decorated by Tiepolo, and the palaces of Bruchsal and Werneck. [ARCHITECT]

Neutra, Richard Josef: 1892-1970. Born in Austria, Neutra took his education at the Polytechnic School in Vienna and graduated with honors. Influenced greatly by Loos and Wagner, Neutra emigrated to the United States at the age of 25, believing that the future of architecture would be determined there. He joined the firm of Holabird and Roche, where he met Sullivan during his last days. He met Frank Lloyd Wright at Sullivan's funeral and decided to go to southern California as a result of that meeting. In Los An-

geles he met Rudolph Schindler, whose firm he joined and with whom he would later collaborate on several projects. Most of Neutra's work is residential; his clients were wealthy, and his designs reflect that wealth. His modern designs were meant to join the house with the environment and used primarily post and beam construction. He achieved a blending of the interior and exterior of the houses with large amounts of glass and infiltrations of the interior and exterior. In later years, Neutra designed schools, religious and commercial buildings. [ARCHITECT]

Niccolo da Pisa: ca. 1207-1278. At about 15, he went with Emperor Frederic II to Naples, where he was employed on the Castel Capuano and Castel del Ovo. In 1233 he made the bas-relief of the Deposition over one of the side doors of the Cathedral of S. Martino at Lucca. Niccolo's chief works are the pulpits of the Baptistery at Pisa and the Cathedral of Siena. The Pisan pulpit is signed *Nicola Pisanus*, with the date 1260. It is the first important work of modern sculpture which is based on a study of the antique. The models were found in certain Roman remains at Pisa. About 1265 Niccolo began the Area di S. Domenico at Bologna. The contract for the great pulpit of the

Cathedral of Siena is signed Sept. 29, 1266. In 1274 Niccolo went to Perugia to design the fountain of the Piazza. The 24 statuettes about the basin are attributed to him. Many important buildings are ascribed to Niccolo by Vasari without corroboration. [SCULPTOR AND ARCHITECT]

Niemeyer, Oscar: b. 1907. Born in Brazil, Niemeyer studied at the *Escola Nacional de Belas-Artes* in Rio de Janeiro. He joined the firm of Locio Costa in 1934. In 1936, Niemeyer had the opportunity to work with Le Corbusier as part of a team of architects to design the new building for the Ministry of Education in Rio. He built the Brazilian Pavilion at the New York World's Fair in 1939 with Costa. His own style was fully evident in his casino, club and Church of St. Francis at Pampulha, Belo Horizonte, built between 1942 and 1943. These buildings' highlights included parabolic vaults, bending walls, and a porch cover with a double-curving form. He became chief architect for NOVA-CAP, the governmental building authority in 1956 and later was an adviser to them. This organization was responsible for the design of Brasilia, Brazil's new capital. The president's palace, with its original screen supports in front of the glass front, was designed by Niemey-

er in 1957. The Square of Three Powers, which housed the Houses of Parliament, was the height of Niemeyer's designs. One building had a dome, one a saucer-shaped roof, and there is a skyscraper in between the two. One of Niemeyer's gifts was that his style reflected the purpose of the buildings he designed. [ARCHITECT]

Olmsted, Frederick Law: 1822-1903. Olmsted studied engineering; however, he is principally known for his landscape architecture. He travelled worldwide and is considered the main landscape architect after Downing died and America's foremost park designer. He was made superintendent for Central Park in New York. Among his other designs are the parks system of Boston and Stanford University in Palo Alto, California. As well, he designed the landscaping for the Niagara reserve and very wealthy homes and estates. [ARCHITECT]

Omodeo (Amadeo), Giovanni Antonio: 1477-1522. Antonio was born near the Certosa at Pavia and was attached to the works at that building at the age of 19 with his brother Protasio. About 1470-1471 he built the Chapel of the Colleoni at the Church of S. Maria Maggiore in Bergamo.

He designed the monuments in this chapel to Bartolommeo Colleoni and his daughter Medea. About 1478 he returned to Pavia, and in 1490 succeeded Guiniforte Solari as architect of the Certosa. The facade of the Certosa was carried out by himself, his associates Benedetto Briosco, the Mantegazza, and about 30 others whose names are known. He was at the same time supervising architect of the Cathedral of Pavia. From 1499 to 1508, with Giovanni Jacopo Dolcebuono, he directed the work on the central tower of the Cathedral of Milan, which they carried to the summit of the octagon. [ARCHITECT AND SCULPTOR]

Organi, Andrea Degli (da Modena): (Late 14th-early 15th century.) The first architect (*ingegnere*) employed on the Cathedral of Milan (begun 1386). His name appears in a memorandum of Jan. 15, 1387. On April 13, 1387 he is mentioned as *ingegnerio domini* (ducal engineer). In October of this year he was appointed to superintend the laborers at the Cathedral. In a letter dated Jan. 3, 1400, of the Duke Gian Galeazzo Visconti, he is mentioned as the father of Filippino degli Organi. [ARCHITECT]

Organi, Filippino Degli (da Modena): d. 1450. Son of Andrea degli

Organi. He is first mentioned in a letter of the Duke Gian Galeazzo Visconti, dated Jan. 3, 1400. He was at this time appointed to a position on the force employed in the construction of the Cathedral of Milan and on Oct. 12, 1404, became a regular architect (*ingegnere*) under the direction of Marco da Carona. On Sept. 16, 1410, he served on the commission that determined the form of the vaulting and flying buttresses. The upper part of the Cathedral was built from the drawings which he made at this time (*secundum disignamentum magistri Filippini*). In 1417 Filippino became chief architect and retained that position until 1448. He made the monument of Marco Carelli (now in the nave of the Cathedral), probably with the assistance of Jacopino Tradate. [ARCHITECT AND SCULPTOR]

Orsini, Giorgio (da Sebenico): Giorgio appears to have been born at Zara, Dalmatia. His family was a branch of the noble Roman house of Orsini. On April 23, 1441, he superseded Antonio di Pietro Paolo as architect of the great Cathedral of Sebenico, Dalmatia. This building is an important example of the transition from the Gothic style to the Renaissance. In 1444 Orsini built a chapel in the Church of S. Rainerio at Spalato, Dalmatia, and in 1448 the

Gothic altar of S. Anastasio in the Cathedral of that city. Between 1451 and 1459 he built the Loggia dei Mercanti and the facade of S. Francesco della Scala at Ancona in Italy. In June 1464, he was associated with Michelozzo Michelozzi in the reconstruction of the Palazzo del Rettore at Ragusa. In 1470 Giorgio was sent on a special mission to Rome. In his contract with the cathedral authorities at Sebenico he was bound to do some of the carving with his own hand. The door of his house at Sebenico, with the bear of the Orsini carved on the lintel, is still in existence. [ARCHITECT AND SCULPTOR]

Ostberg, Ragnar: 1866-1945. Ostberg took his studies in Stockholm between 1884 and 1891. Shortly after he graduated, he travelled widely throughout America and Europe. His chief contribution to architecture is considered to be the Stockholm City Hall, which was started in 1909 and completed in 1923. This transitional building covered Nineteenth Century Historicism and Twentieth Century Modernism. Ostberg was successful in combining the Swedish past, Romanesque, and the Renaissance in his detailing of this structure. The way he accented his detail work is characteristic of the Arts and Crafts movement in Europe. The

building influenced architects in England during the 1920's. [ARCHITECT]

Otto, Frei: b. 1925. Otto, was born in Germany, and studied at the Technical University in Berlin. He is most famous for his pioneering suspended roofs, which he first presented in his thesis in 1954. His first one was built a year later in 1955. Many more exhibitions were to show his work, including Cologne (1957), Berlin (1957), Lausanne (1961), Hamburg (1963), and Montreal (1967). The Montreal building was the German Pavilion and achieved him world notoriety. Otto's roofs were made of steel or polyester web and suspended on cable nets, which are then extended between heavier cables, then fastened to masts and ground anchors. An author as well, Otto's *Tensile Structures*, published in 1967, is considered the authoritative work in its field. A member of the Rational School, Otto's designs and breakthroughs were extremely important in revival of the tent as structurally viable. [ARCHITECT]

Oud, Jacobus Johannes: 1890-1963. Born in Holland, this Dutch architect was educated at the Quellinus School of Arts and Crafts, the State School of Drafter in Amsterdam, and the Delft Technical College, which presented him with an honorary doctorate after the end of World War II. After meeting the van Doesburg and Rietveld, Oud became the founder of the Di Stijl group, which advanced Cubism. From 1918 until 1927, Oud was Housing Architect to the City of Rotterdam. One of his major bequests was the development of inexpensive and mass-produced housing for the working class. He was influenced by Frank Lloyd Wright and Berlage. Examples of his work include the Cafe de Unie in Rotterdam (1924-1925); terraced housing at Scheveningen (1917), and a factory designed in Purmerend in 1919. Later, the Shell Building at The Hague, built between 1938 and 1942, and various homes were built by him. [ARCHITECT]

Palladio, Andrea: ca. 1518-1580. Palladio is supposed to have been the son of a carpenter named Pietro, employed by the scholar and poet, Gian Giorgio Trissino. He became the protege of Trissino, who gave him the name Palladio (from Pallas, goddess of wisdom), and educated him as an architect. Palladio's first work was the Palazzo Godi Lonedo in 1540. He visited Rome first with Trissino in 1541 and again in 1544. In 1545 he presented four designs for the reconstruction of the basilica of Vicenza. Work was begun from his

model in 1549. Palladio built the Palazzo Pisani at Bagnolo, near Vicenza; the Palazzo Porto, now Colleoni, in Vicenza, 1552; the Palazzo Thiene (Banca popolare), Vicenza, 1556; the Palazzo Foscari on the Brenta before 1561; the Palazzo Pisani, near Padua, 1565; the famous Palazzo Valmarana, Vicenza, after 1566; and the Palazzo Porto Barbarano, Vicenza, after 1570. The famous villa, called the Rotonda, which he built for Paolo Almerico, near Vicenza, was begun before 1570 and finished about 1591. The facade of the Church of S. Francesco alla Vigna (Venice) was designed by him in 1562. In 1561 he built the cloister of the Convento della Carita (now the Accademia, Venice) on the plan of a Roman house. It was nearly destroyed by fire in 1650. Palladio built the refectory of the Church of S. Giorgio Maggiore, Venice, about 1560, and in 1565 the church itself with its fine facade. In 1570 he designed the cloister of the same building. He began the Church of the Redentore, Venice, in 1576 (finished (1592). In the third book of his *Architettura* is given a splendid design for a bridge supposed to have been intended for the Rialto, Venice. In 1571 the loggia of the Piazza Maggiore, Vicenza, was begun from his designs. In February, 1580, he began the celebrated Teatro

Olimpico, which was finished after his death by his son Silla and Vincenzo Scamozzi. Palladio's treatise on architecture was first published complete, in Venice in 1570 with the title, *I quattro Libri dell' Architettura*. Many of his drawings were published by Lord Burlington in 1730 and those on the Roman baths by Bertotti Scamozzi. A collection of his buildings was published by Bertotti Scamozzi in 1776. [ARCHITECT]

Paris, Pierre Adrien: 1747-1819. He was a student at the *Ecole royale d' Architecture* and studied in Rome as *pensionnaire du roi*. In 1778 he was appointed *dessinateur du cabinet du roi,* and in 1780 was admitted to the *Academie d' Architecture*. In 1787 he was appointed architect of the Cathedral of Orleans and finished the towers of that church in 1790. In 1787 he was commissioned to install the Assembly of Notables in the Palace of Versailles. He designed the Hotel de Ville at Neufchatel, Pas-de-Calais, France. In 1806 he was appointed director of the French Academy at Rome. During his administration he bought the antiques of the Villa Borghese for the Louvre. [ARCHITECT]

Parler, Peter: ca. 1333-ca. 1397. Parler came of a stonecutter's family in Cologne (Germany). He was architect of the choir and nave of the Cathedral of Prague, in Bohemia, begun 1392. He was assisted and succeeded by his sons, Nicolaus, Johann, and Wenzel. His bust stands in the triforium gallery of the Cathedral of Prague. He is also known as Peter von Gmund. [ARCHITECT]

Pasti (or Basti), Matteo de: Pasti came from Verona (Italy) and was a pupil of Pisanello, the painter and medalist. About 1446 he attached himself to the court of Sigismondo Malatesta at Rimini, Italy. The remarkable reconstruction of the Church of S. Francesco at Rimini, undertaken by Sigismondo, was undoubtedly executed under the direction of Pasti so far as the interior is concerned. A letter to him from Leon Battista Alberti, dated Nov. 18, 1454, indicates that the exterior was built by Pasti from drawings and directions sent by Alberti from Rome. As medalist he ranks next to Pisanello. [ARCHITECT, PAINTER, SCULPTOR]

Patryngton, Robert de: On January 5, 1368, he was appointed master mason of York Cathedral (England) and built a great portion of the present choir. He succeeded W. de Hoton and was himself succeeded by Hugo Hedon. [ARCHITECT]

Paulus: He made the altars, pavement, and mosaics of the Cathedral of Ferentino, Italy (1106-1110) and a pavement in the Vatican gardens, which is supposed to have come from the first basilica of S. Peter on the Vatican Hill. He probably built the Cathedral of Ferentino, Italy. An altar in the church of S. Lorenzo at Terra di Cave, near Rome, bears his name and the date 1093. [ARCHITECT AND MOSAICIST.]

Paxton, Sir Joseph: 1801-1865. The son of a farmer, in 1823 he entered the service of the Horticultural Society, which had leased the gardens at Chiswick (England) from the Duke of Devonshire. In 1826 he was appointed by the Duke superintendent of the gardens of Chatsworth. In 1836-1840 he built the great conservatory at Chatsworth. Paxton built the Crystal Palace of the great Exhibition of 1851 on the principle of a very large greenhouse, and deserved the credit of the bold innovation. He was knighted in 1851. He designed several important buildings and published many works on botany and gardening. [LANDSCAPE GARDENER AND ARCHITECT]

Pei, Ieoh Mine: b. 1917. Born in China in 1917, Pei emigrated to the United States in 1935. He took his degrees from Massachusetts Institute of Technology and Harvard. He worked with the urban developer William Zeckendorf for a few years and designed several excellent buildings with him, including the Mile High Center in Denver, Colorado, built between 1952 and 1956. In 1955, Pei formed his own firm, I.M. Pei and Partners in New York City. Pei's firm has designed many major buildings, some of which are the biggest civic and corporate projects. Among his projects are the National Airlines Terminal at Kennedy Airport in New York City (1970), the John Hancock Tower in Boston (1973); and the John F. Kennedy Library at Harvard (1979). His designs are clear and consistent; his buildings integrate Classical design with contemporary construction techniques. [ARCHITECT]

Pennethorne, Sir James: 1801-1871. He was a nephew of Sir John Nash and studied also with A. Pugin. He visited France and Italy. In 1832 he was employed by the commissioners of metropolitan improvements (London) to devise plans for New Oxford Street, Kensington Palace gardens, Victoria, Kennington and Battersea parks, the Chelsea embankment, etc. He built in London the Museum of Economic Geology, the Stationer Office, Westminster, the west wing of

Somerset House, and made many improvements in Buckingham Palace. His most notable work is the building for the University of London. [ARCHITECT]

Pennethorne, John: 1808-1888. A younger brother of Sir James Pennethorne. In 1830 he made a journey through Europe to Egypt. He was the first to observe the curvature and optical refinements of the Parthenon and he also observed the curvatures of the temple of Medinet Haboo in Egypt. In 1844 he published privately a pamphlet entitled *The Elements and Mathematical Principles of the Greek Architects and Artists*, in which he set forth a theory of optical corrections. Mr. F. C. Penrose continued these investigations in 1846 and published his *Principles of Athenian Architecture* in 1851 (1 vol. folio). Pennethorne's great work on *The Geometry and Optics of Ancient Architecture* was not published until 1878. He published also a paper in the *Transactions of the Royal Institute of British Architects* (1878-1879) on "The Connection between Ancient Art and the Ancient Geometry." [ARCHITECT]

Percier, Charles: 1764-1838. Percier was a pupil of Antoine Francois Peyre, in whose atelier his association with Pierre Fontaine began. He was

employed also by Chalgrin and Pierre Paris. In 1786 he won the *Premier Grand Prix de Rome* in architecture. He supported himself during the Revolution by designing furniture and decorations, introducing antique motives from Rome and Pompeii This may be thought the beginning of the so-called *style empire*, popular throughout Europe in the early years of the nineteenth century. In 1794 Percier and Fontaine acting together, replaced Pierre Paris in the direction of the decoration of the Opera in Paris. Between 1802 and 1812 they had charge of the Louvre and Tuileries. They restored the colonnade of the Louvre and completed the upper story of the buildings on the court. At the Tuileries they constructed the chapel and theater, and the buildings adjacent to the Pavillon Marsan in the newly opened Rue de Rivoli. They designed the Arc de Triomphe du Carrousel and the great stairway of the Museum of the Louvre, which was removed by Napoleon III They designed residences in Antwerp, Brussels, Venice, Florence, and Rome. Percier retired from the association with Fontaine in 1814. He published *Restauration de la Colonne Trajane* (1788) and, in association with Fontaine, *Palais, Maisons et autres edifices de Rome Moderne* (Paris, 1802); *Recueil de decorations executees dans l'eglise Notre Dame et au Champs-de-Mars* (Paris, 1807); *Choix des plus celebres Maisons de plaisance de Rome et de ses environs* (1809-1813); *Recueil des decorations interieurs* (Paris, 1812), etc. [ARCHITECT]

Perrault, Claude: 1613-1688. Claude Perrault was a mathematician, scientist, and practicing physician, who acquired a taste for architecture. In 1664 Louis XIV undertook the construction of the eastern facade of the quadrangle of the Louvre (Paris). The designs made by Levau not being acceptable, a scheme was elaborated by Bernini, which was begun Oct. 17, 1665, and soon afterward abandoned. Before the arrival of Bernini, Perrault had presented a plan for the building, which was rejected at the time but this was presented again in 1667 and accepted. This building, forming the eastern side of the great court, and having on its outer face the famous colonnade of the Louvre, was completed in 1674. The southern facade (the river facade) was also built by Perrault. These buildings were not actually roofed over until 1755. [PHYSICIAN AND ARCHITECT]

Perreal, Jean (Jehan de Paris): 1463-ca.1529. As early as 1486 he resided at Lyons, France. On March 25, 1493, he commenced the Church of the Cordeliers in that city and in the same year was charged with the restoration of the arches of the *Pont du Rhone* at Lyons. In 1494 he accompanied the expedition of Charles VIII into Italy. In 1499 he was *controleur general des batiments* of the city of Lyons. For Anne, queen of Louis XII, he designed the monument of Francois II, Duke of Brittany, for the Cathedral of Nantes, which was executed by Michel Colombe, 1502-1556. In 1505 he was commissioned by Marguerite d' Autriche to make the plans of the monastery and Church of Brou at Bourg-en-Bresse (Eure-et-Loire) and in 1510 was made *controleur* of the works. In 1513 he was replaced at Brou by the Flemish architect, van Boghem. (ARCHITECT)

Perret, Auguste: 1874-1954. Born in Brussels, Belgium, Perret studied at the *Ecole des Beaux Arts* in Paris. Between 1879 and 1905, Perret worked for his father's building and construction firm in Paris. His teacher, Julien Guadet, greatly influenced Perret, as did his own father. Neoclassicist in style, Perret used modern technology, especially reinforced concrete, to carve a name for himself and to forge a new era in concrete construction. 22 Rue B. Franklin in Paris was constructed on a lot which precluded other types of apartment construction and featured Art Nouveau faience tiles. After his father died in 1905, Auguste and his brother Gustave renamed the firm Perret Freres. A large war memorial church built near Paris at Le Raincy in 1922 features an interior and exterior entirely of concrete with a thin shell for a roof. The Museum of Public Works in Paris (1937) and the reconstruction of Le Havre (begun 1945), a harbor destroyed by the Germans in World War II, are further examples of Perret's original and creative design style. [ARCHITECT]

Perronet (Peronet), Jean Rodolfe: 1708-1794. He was educated as a military engineer but abandoned this profession for architecture. In 1745 he rebuilt the choir and spire of the Cathedral of Alencon (France), which had been destroyed by fire in 1744. In 1747 he was made director of the *Ecole des Ponts et Chaussees*, Paris, founded in that year. In 1748 he began with Hippeau the great bridge at Orleans, France. In 1763 he replaced Hippeau at his death as *premier ingenieur du roi*. He designed the bridge at Nantes in 1764, the bridge at Nogent-sur-Seine in 1766, the bridge at Neuilly (Paris) in 1768, and the Pont Louis XVI (now Pont de la Concorde) in 1786. Perronet held the office of *inspecteur general et premier ingenieur des ponts et chaussees du royaume*. He published *Description des projets de la construction des ponts de Neuilly, de Nantes, d' Orleans et autres*, etc. (Paris, 1782-1783; supplement, Paris, 1789.) [ENGINEER AND ARCHITECT]

Peruzzi (Petrucci, Perucci), Baldassare: 1481-1556. Peruzzi was probably born at Volterra, Italy, the son of a Florentine weaver, and was brought up in Siena. He went to Rome about 1503 and, under the patronage of the famous Sienese banker, Agostino Chigi, devoted several years to study. One of his earliest buildings was Chigi's villa, now called the Villa Farnesina, finished about 1510. After the death of Raphael, Peruzzi was associated with Antonio (II) da San Gallo in the superintendence of the works at S. Peter's Church and held that position intermittently from Aug. 1, 1520, until his death. During the reign of Adrian VI (Pope 1522-1523) he was invited to Bologna by the *presidenti* of the Church of S. Petronio to design a facade for that church. A drawing in the Gothic style now in the sacristy is attributed to him. Peruzzi in 1525 built the Ossoli Palace in Rome. At

Siena he was twice made *architetto del publico* on petition of citizens. The little court of the oratory of S. Caterina and the Villa Belcaro date from this time; and in 1529 he was made *capomaestro* of the Cathedral. He began the famous Palazzo Massimi (*Alle Colonne*) at Rome in 1535, the year before his death. He began also the Palace of Angelo Massimi (now Palazzo Orsini). In painting, Peruzzi was at first a pupil of Pinturicchio. He afterward assisted Raphael in Rome. Among his many works are the painting of the choir of S. Onofrio (Rome), much of the decoration of the Farnesina, and the decoration of the Capella Pozzetti at S. Maria della Pace (Rome, 1516). He frequently designed fetes and processions and painted many facades. His notes and designs were used by Serlio in preparing his books. Peruzzi was buried in the Pantheon near Raphael. [PAINTER AND ARCHITECT]

Peter of Colechurch: d. 1205. London Bridge was destroyed and rebuilt in 1091, 1136, and probably at many other times. All these early structures were of wood. According to some authorities, the last wooden bridge was built by Peter, curate of S. Mary Colechurch (London), in 1163. The first stone bridge was begun by Peter of Colechurch in 1176 and fin-

ished in 1209. It was constructed on 20 arches with 19 piers, and houses were built upon it. [PRIEST AND ARCHITECT]

Pietrasanta, Giacoma da: Many of the buildings in Rome that are attributed to Vasari, Giuliano da Maiano, and Baccio Pontelli, were probably built by Pietrasanta, among others, the Church of S. Agostino, built in the reign of Sixtus IV (Pope 1471-1484). In 1452 he made several marble doors for the Capitol, and in the records of Pius II (Pope 1458-1464), he is mentioned as superintendent of the construction of the loggia of the Benediction, with the title *Superstes fabricae pulpiti*. In 1467 and 1468 he appears as director of the works at the Vatican and the Palazzo di S. Marco (Rome). [ARCHITECT]

Pippi, Giulio (Giulio Romano): 1492-1546. As the principal assistant of Raphael he was associated with him in executing the frescoes of the Stanze of the Vatican. He also superintended the execution of the frescoes in the loggia of the Farnesina (finished about 1518). He assisted in the decoration of the Loggia of the Vatican and of the Villa Madama, near Rome. In 1525 he designed the Palazzo del Te (abbreviation for Tejetto, a sluiceway or canal) at Mantua (finished 1528). Giulio built his own palazzo, which still stands in Mantua, and the tomb of Baldassare Castiglione in the Church of S. Maria delle Grazie (Mantua). [PAINTER AND ARCHITECT]

Piranesi, Giovanni Baptista: 1720-1776. He was the son of a mason and went to Rome at the age of 18 to study architecture. His plates were published under the following titles, *Monumenti degli Scipioni* (1785); *Sciographia quatuor Templorum Veterum,* dedicated to Pope Pius VI (1776) (Part II contains the Pantheon); *Della Magnificenza ed Archittura de' Romani,* dedicated to Clement XIV; *Il Campo Marzio dell' Antica Roma* (Rome, 1762); *Antichita d' Albano e di Castel Grandolfo,* dedicated to Clement XIV; a volume of plates on the column of Trajan, a volume of plates on the ruins of Paestum, various engravings of Roman vases, candelabra, etc. [ARCHITECT AND ENGRAVER]

Poelzig, Hans: 1869-1936. Poelzig was born in Berlin and educated at the Technical College there. In addition to establishing his own office, he served as professor of architecture in the School of Arts and Crafts at Breslau and later became its director (1903), where he remained for the next 13 years. In 1920 he was ap-

pointed city architect of Dresden and later taught at the College of Technology and the Academy of Arts in Berlin. During this whole period he was busy designing buildings as well. The water tower at Posen (1910) is a fine example of Poelzig's Expressionist style. During and after World War I, Poelzig's designs included the House of Friendship (Istanbul, 1916), the town hall in Dresden (1917), and the Festival Theater for Salzburg, Austria (1919-1920). Unfortunately, his visionary designs for these buildings were never built. However, the foremost example of his work is the conversion of the Grosses Schaupielhaus in Berlin. Its vault, corridors, and foyer clearly exhibit his abilities and is often used as the primary example of Expressionism. [ARCHITECT]

Polyclitus (the younger): Polyclitus, the son of Patrocles, flourished between 370 and 336 B.C., and built the Tholos (round temple) and theater at Epidauros, in Greece. He is not to be confounded with the great sculptor Polyclitus or Argos. [ARCHITECT and SCULPTOR]

Pons: He rebuilt the abbey of Montierneuf at Poitiers (France), which was dedicated Jan. 24, 1096. [MONK AND ARCHITECT]

295

Pontelli (de Puntellis) or Pintelli, Baccio (Bartolomeo): d. ca. 1492. Pontelli was a pupil of Francione. The earliest notice of him is as *intarsiatore* at Pisa (Italy), where he was employed in 1471. In 1475-1477 he made the stalls in the choir of the Cathedral of Pisa. In 1479 he went to Urbino, where he came under the influence of Francesco di Giorgio Martini. After the death of Federigo da Montefeltro, Duke of Urbino, in 1482, he went to Rome. On July 27, 1483, he was sent to inspect the work of Giovannino dei Dolci at Civita Vecchia and in 1484 himself directed the construction of that citadel. During the reign of Innocent VIII (Pope 1484-1492) he was placed in charge of all the fortresses in the Marches. Nothing is known of him after 1492. [ARCHITECT, ENGINEER]

Ponti, Bio: 1891-1979. This Italian designer studied at the Milan Polytechnic School of Architecture, where he later taught between the years 1936 and 1961. In 1928 he started the Italian journal of architecture, *Domus*, a periodical which was to have lasting influence on many architects. His most well known buildings, the Mathematics Building at Rome University (1934), the Montecatini Building in Milan (1936), and the Pirelli Tower in Milan (1956) are distinctly International Modern in style but are additionally extremely original in design. Ponti's legacy to the design world did not begin or end with his architectural skills; he was decidedly a universal man, expressing his artistic talents in the fields of interior, theatrical, furniture, lighting, and industrial design, as well as ceramics and painting. Ponti believed that art, architecture, and life were inseparable, and that belief is expressed in all of his designs. [ARCHITECT]

Pontifs, Guillaume: On May 27, 1462, he succeeded Geoffray Richier as *maitre d' oeuvre* of the Cathedral of Rouen. Between 1463 and 1467 he completed the Portal de la Calende and the Tour Saint Romain. In 1484 he built the portal of the Cour des Libraires and in 1485 commenced the Tour de Beurre, of which he built one story. He built the screen of the choir and the sacristy. [ARCHITECT]

Poppelmann, Matthaus Daniel: 1662-1736. Poppelmann held the offices of *Baukondukteur* (1696), *Landbaumeister* (1705), and *Oberlandbaumeister* (1718) in Dresden, Saxony. In 1711 he began the famous Baroque palace called the Zwinger (Dresden). He built also the Schloss Moritzburg near Dresden (1722-1730) and the old Hollandische Palast (1715-1717), which was transformed by von Bodt and was later called the Japanische Palast (Dresden). Poppelmann built numerous fine residences. [ARCHITECT]

Portigiani, Pagno di Lapo: 1406-1470. Pagno assisted Michelozzo at the Church of the Annunziata in Florence. In 1428 he worked on the front of S. Giovanni at Siena and in 1460 made the plans for the Bentivoglio Palace at Bologna. His best work is the monument of Giovanni Cellini in the Church of S. Jacopo at S. Miniato al Tedesco, between Florence and Pisa. [SCULPTOR AND ARCHITECT]

Post, Pieter: 1608-1669. The architect of Prince Maurice of Orange. He went with the prince to Brazil. He erected a church and other buildings at Olinda and rebuilt the fortifications of Pernambuco. Among his principal works in Holland are the Huis ten Bosch at The Hague, the Sael van Oranje, the Swanenburg situated between Amsterdam and Haarlem, the Palace at Rijxdorp, the Stadhuis at Maestricht, and the Waag (weighing house) at Gouda. A collection of engravings of his buildings was published at Leyden in 1715. [ARCHITECT]

Post, George Browne: 1837-1913. Post was trained as a civil engineer. He worked in Hunt's office for a time before opening his own practice in 1860. He did not subscribe to a particular school of design. for he was a planner as well, and is somewhat credited with founding the American-style hotels, where each room has its own bath. Post's Statler Hotel in Buffalo, New York, is an example of this style, which is, of course, now the standard. Post was also responsible for designing Cornelius Vanderbilt's residence, along with other homes for the extremely wealthy. Office buildings designed by Post include the Equitable Building in New York (1869), the New York Times and Pulitzer Buildings (1889), and the St. Paul Building (1897-1899), which was the highest building in New York at the time it was built. [ARCHITECT]

Powell and Moya: (Estab. 1946.) The partners in this English architectural firm are A. J. Philip Powell (b. 1921) and John Hildalgo Moya (b. 1921). Both of them were educated at the Architectural Association School of Architecture under Frederick Gibberd, who influenced them greatly. The firm entrenched itself into the architectural establishment when it won a competition for Churchill Gardens, originally called the Pimlinco Housing Competition, which was built in 1946. Other examples of their work include the Mayfield School in London (1956), the Princess Margaret Hospital in Swindon (1957), the Festival Theater in Chichester (1961), the additions to St. John's College in Cambridge (1967), Christ Church in Oxford (1968), Wolfson College, Oxford, (1974), and the London Museum (1976). The firm, although not necessarily original in its design style, has consistently produced high quality work and has won many different awards over the years. [ARCHITECT]

Primaticcio (Primatice), Francesco: 1490-1570. Primaticcio was associated with Giulio Romano at Mantua and in 1531 was called to France by Francois I and employed at Fontainebleau. He was at first associated with Il Rosso, at whose death he assumed sole charge of the decoration of the palace. In 1554 he was made *abbe* of S. Martin de Tours. On Aug. 3, 1559, he replaced Philibert de l'Orme as superintendent of the royal buildings. About 1562 he assumed direction of the construction of the monument of Henri II at Saint Denis. The construction of portions of the Palace of Fontainebleau is ascribed to him. In 1562 he assumed the title

commissaire general des batiments du roi and had large power over the artistic productions of his time in France. [PAINTER, SCULPTOR, AND ARCHITECT]

Pudsey, Hugh: He was Bishop of Durham from 1153 to 1194 and built the unique chapel called the Galilee at the western end of that Cathedral, an interesting specimen of late Norman architecture, erected for the use of women, who had been hitherto excluded from the church. It was altered in the early English and perpendicular periods. [BISHOP]

Puget, Pierre: 1622-1694. Puget was born at Marseilles (France). He was apprenticed to a shipbuilder and was at first employed to decorate galleys. He came especially under the influence of Pietro da Cortona, Jean Bologne, Algardi, and Bernini. In 1655-1657 he made the famous caryatids of the portal of the Hotel de Ville at Toulon. In 1660 he settled in Genoa, where, among other works, he made the colossal statues of S. Sebastien and S. Ambrose in the Church of the Carignan. His practice as an architect was considerable. About 1664 he was occupied with the Arsenal, the Halle de ola Poissonnerie, the Chapelle de l' Hospice de la Charite, and the Portail des Chartreaux at Marseilles, the Hotel d' Aiguilles at Aix, and with the decoration of galleys at Toulon. Some of these decorations of ships are in the Louvre. He is best known as a sculptor of full statues and groups. [SCULPTOR, ARCHITECT, AND PAINTER]

Quesnel, Francois: With Claude de Chastillon he made the plans of the hospital of S. Louis (Paris), which was built in 1607. Quesnel was the author of the first geometrical plan of the city of Paris. [ARCHITECT AND PAINTER]

Raimond (Raimondus): Raimond, *maitre d'oeuvre* of Carcassonne (France), planned the Cathedral of Lugo (Spain) and commenced its construction in 1169. [ARCHITECT]

Rainaldi, Carlo: Carlo was a son of Girolamo Rainaldi. He was the leading architect of the great Church of S. Agnese in the Piazza Navona, Rome. One of his best buildings, and a fine example of the Baroque style, is the Church of S. Maria in Campitelli (1665). He also built the facade of the Church of S. Andrea delle Valle and the twin churches of S. Maria de' Miracoli and S. Maria di Monte Santo in the Piazza del Popolo (about 1662). All the works mentioned are in Rome. [ARCHITECT]

Rainaldi, Girolamo: 1570-1655. A pupil of Dominico Fontana. He was much employed as engineer, especially in laying out the harbor of Fano (Italy). About 1623 he built the Church of S. Luca at Bologna. Rainaldi was one of the many architects called upon to make designs for the facade of the Church of S. Petronio (Bologna). He was also employed by the Farnese and Este families at Parma, Modena, and Piacenza. He returned to Rome in 1650 and built the Palazzo Pamfili in the Piazza Navona. [ARCHITECT]

Rainerius (Ranucius): He made the central window of S. Silvestro in Capite, Rome. Works of his sons Nicolaus and Petrus are dated 1143 and 1160. [ARCHITECT]

Ranconval or Ranguevaux, Jehan: A son or pupil of Henri Ranconval, *maitre des oeuvres* in the city of Metz (Lothringen, Germany). In 1468 he was architect of the Cathedral and about 1473 succeeded his father as *maitre des oeuvres* of the city of Metz. In 1477 he designed the tower of La Muette at the Cathedral. In 1481 he commenced the Church of S. Symphorien at Metz. [ARCHITECT]

Raymond, Jean Armand: 1742-1811. Raymond was a pupil of Jacques Francois Blondel and Leroy and in

1766 won the *Grand Prix de Rome* in architecture. In 1787-1788 he was appointed architect of the province of Languedoc. He went to Paris after the Revolution and was associated with Chalgrin in designing the Arc de Triomphe de l'Etoile. His design was accepted at first but was afterward replaced by that of Chalgrin. Raymond retired from the association with Chalgrin Oct. 31, 1808. He was employed on the Louvre, the Bibliotheque Nationale, and the Opera. [ARCHITECT]

Raymond du Temple: d. ca. 1404. He seems to have been employed on the old Louvre (Paris) as early as 1364. At that date he built a stairway on the south side of the north wing of that building. He made extensive additions to the palace in the reign of Charles V, which included the Tour de la Librarie, where the King's manuscripts were stored. Within the palace he built the Salles du roi et de la reine. In 1370 he appears as *maitre macon* of the Cathedral of Paris, probably succeeding Jehan le Bouteillier; in 1370-1385 he built the Chapel of the College de Beauvais. He was employed, in 1387, on the royal palace on the Ile de la Cite (Paris). In 1401 he made a visit of inspection to the Cathedral of Troyes (France). Du Temple is undoubtedly the author of

the Chateau and Chapel of Vincennes, near Paris, which was built for Charles V about 1379. [ARCHITECT]

Remigius: d. 1092. Remigius was a monk of Fecamp in Normandy who was appointed Bishop of Dorchester, England, in 1067 by William the Conqueror. After 1075 the see was removed to Lincoln, where it could be under the protection of the castle then being constructed. He began at once to build his cathedral, which was completed in 1092. Of this original Norman building almost the entire western front remains and the lower stories of the western towers. [BISHOP]

Rennie, John, F.R.S., F.S.A.: 1761-1821. He was born in Scotland and educated in Edinburgh. In 1780 he removed to London. Rennie built in London the Waterloo Bridge, begun Oct. 11, 1811, and dedicated on the second anniversary of the battle of Waterloo, June 18, 1817, whence its name. He built the Southwark Bridge, London, begun 1814, and designed the new London Bridge, which was built after his death by his son Sir John Rennie. [ENGINEER]

Rennie, Sir John, F.R.S.: 1794-1874. Son of John Rennie. He was associated with his father in the construction of Waterloo and Southwark bridges, London, and built new London Bridge from his designs. He was knighted on the completion of London Bridge in 1831. Rennie was employed in many important works. [ENGINEER]

Renwick, James: 1818-1895. He graduated from Columbia College at the age of 17, and devoted himself to engineering and architecture. He was employed on the Erie Railroad and the Croton Aqueduct, and built the reservoir, Forty second Street and Fifth Avenue, New York City. He built Grace Church in New York and designed the Smithsonian Institute and Corcoran Gallery in Washington. His plans for a Catholic cathedral in New York City were accepted, and on Aug. 15, 1858, the corner stone of that building was laid. It was dedicated May 25, 1879. The spires were added in 1887. He planned and built numerous other buildings of importance in New York. [ARCHITECT]

Revett, Nicholas: ca. 1721-1804. He visited Rome in 1742 and met James Stuart, with whom he went to Athens in 1750. He was associated with Stuart in the preparation of the *Antiquities of Athens* (1762-1816). He also prepared the drawings Parts I and II of the *Antiquities of Ionia* (1769-1797) published by the Society of Dilettanti.

He designed and decorated various residences in England. [ARCHITECT]

Ricchini (Ricchinio) Francesco Maria: From 1605 to 1638 he was supervising architect of the Cathedral of Milan. He was also employed at the Ospedale Maggiore where he built the portal on the Via Ospedale. His greatest work is the Palazzo di Brera, the court of which is one of the finest in Italy. He built also the Palazzo della Canonica and many other buildings in Milan. [ARCHITECT]

Richardson, Henry Hobson: 1838-1886. Richardson was born in Louisiana. In 1860 he entered the *Ecole des Beaux Arts* under the direction of L. J. Andre. The outbreak of the Civil War having destroyed the resources of his family, he secured through Andre a position as drafter in a government office in Paris. Returning to America in October, 1865, his first commission was for a Unitarian church in Springfield, Massachusetts. This was followed by the construction of the offices of the Boston and Albany railroad in Springfield and a church in Medford, Massachusetts. On October 1, 1867, he formed a partnership with Charles Gambrill. In July 1870, Richardson's design for the Brattle Street Church in Commonwealth Avenue, Boston, was successful. This Romanesque church is noted for its fine tower, bearing a frieze sculptured with colossal figures. The best known of his works is Trinity Church in Boston, begun in 1872 and finished in 1877. In 1876 he was associated with Leopold Eidlitz and Frederick Law Olmstead in the completion of the State Capitol in Albany. Richardson built the Allegheny Courthouse Sever Hall in Harvard University, and numerous public and business buildings. In most of his works he followed a style of his own based on the Romanesque architecture of southern France. [ARCHITECT]

Richier, Ligier: b. ca.1506-1567, at Geneva Switzerland. His first work is the Nativity of Haton-Chatel (1523). In 1532 he executed for the Church of S. Etienne at Saint Mihiel the famous group of the Sepulchre, his most important work. In 1544 he made the monument of the Prince of Orange for the Cathedral of Bar-le-Duc (Meuse), France, and in 1545 that on Rene de Chalon for the Church of S. Pierre in that city. In 1547 he made the monument of the duchess of Philippe de Gueldre for the Cordeliers at Nancy. In 1549 he made a design for the Chapel of the Collegiate Church of S. Maxe at Bar-le-Duc and in 1555

decorated this chapel with sculpture. [ARCHITECT AND SCULPTOR]

Rietveld, Gerrit Thomas: 1888-1964. This Dutch architect studied drawing at the Municipal Evening School and was apprenticed to his father, who had a joiner shop. He opened his own cabinet shop in 1911. He got to know the founders of the De Stijl movement, including Robert van't Hoff. This association inspired his furniture designs. His most famous building is the Schroeder House, built in Utrecht in 1924 and done in collaboration with Truus Schroeder-Scrader, the interior designer. After World War II, Rietveld's buildings included the Netherlands Pavilion at the Venice Biennale (1954), the sculpture pavilion in the Sonsbeek park in Arnhem (1954), and the Rijksmuseum Vincent van Goh, built in Amsterdam between 1963 and 1972, this latter being designed in collaboration with J. van Dillen and J. van Tricht. [ARCHITECT]

Robbia, Luca della: 1399 or 1400-1482. The principal member of a family of sculptors in Florence in the fifteenth century. He was apprenticed to a goldsmith. The best known of his works and the earliest which can be dated with certainty is the marble cantoria which was formerly in the Cathedral of Florence and is now in the Museo Nazionale (Bargello). It was begun in 1430 and finished about 1440. The companion piece is by Donatello. Between 1437 and 1440 Luca made five bas-reliefs, completing the series begun by Giotto in the first story of the Campanile, Florence. The bronze doors of the sacristy of the Cathedral of Florence were begun by Luca with the assistance of Michelozzi in 1447, but not placed until 1474. In 1455 he began the marble monument of the Bishop Bonozzo Federighi in the Church of S. Francesco di Paolo near Florence (finished 1451). To Luca is due the application of the art of glazed terra cotta to figure sculpture and to elaborate architectural decoration. He was assisted and succeeded by various members of his family. Luca's earliest work in Robbia ware, of which the date is known, appears to be the bas-relief of the Resurrection over the door of the sacristy of the Cathedral of Florence (1443). The Ascension also in the Cathedral was made between 1446 and 1450. A series of medallions on the facades of Or S. Michele (Florence) are among his earlier works. The works of Luca are more severe in style and more simple in color than those of his successors. [SCULPTOR]

Robert de Coucy: d. 1311. The architect of Reims Cathedral, after the fire of 1211, was either Robert de Coucy or Hue Libergier, who began the Church of S. Nicaise at Reims in 1229. The Robert de Coucy known to the records became architect of S. Nicaise at the death of Libergier in 1263. He was also architect of the Cathedral of Reims at this later time. [ARCHITECT]

Roche, Keven: b. 1922. This Irish-born architect was educated at the National University of Ireland in Dublin. After short terms at the firms of Michael Scott in Dublin and Maxwell Fry and Jane Drew in London, Roche emigrated to the United States in 1948, where he joined Eero Saarinen's company. A few years later (1954) he became head partner in charge of design. When Saairnen died in 1961, Roche took over the firm with John Dinkeloo. Notable among this partnership's designs are the Oakland Museum in Oakland, California (1961-1968) and the Ford Foundation Building in New York City (1963-1968). The Ford Building catapulted Roche to internationally famous standing within the architectural community. Distinctly important other works include the Knights of Columbus Building in New Haven, Connecticut (1965-1969), the extension of the Metropolitan Museum of Art in New York City (1967-1978), the Cummins Engine Company in Columbus, Indiana (1972-9) and the Fiat company headquarters, located in Turin (1973). [ARCHITECT]

Rohault de Fleury, Charles: 1801-1875. A son of Hubert Rohault de Fleury. He was educated at the *Ecole Polytechnique* and the *Ecole des Beaux Arts* (Paris). In 1833 he was appointed architect of the hospitals of Paris and about 1837 built important works at the Jardin des Plantes. He was associated with Hittorff in designing the houses in the Place de l'Etoile (Paris). Charles Rohault de Fleury is best known by his important works on Christian archaeology: *L'Evangile, etudes iconographiques et archeologiques* (Tours, 1874); *La Messe, etudes Archeologiques sur les Monuments* (Paris, 1883-1889); *La Sainte Vierge, etudes archeologiques et iconographiques* (Paris, 1878). [ARCHITECT]

Rohault de Fleury, Hubert: 1777-1846. A pupil of Durand. He won the premier *grand prix de Rome* in 1802. In 1806 he was appointed inspector of the works at the Arc-de-Triomphe de l'Etoile. From 1817 to 1833 he was architect of the hospitals in Paris. [ARCHITECT]

Rondelet, Jean Baptiste: 1743-1829. In 1763 he came to Paris to study under J. F. Blondel and later assisted Soufflot as inspector of the works at the Church of S. Genevieve, afterward the Pantheon (Paris). In 1783 he obtained a royal pension and visited Italy. In 1785 he superintended the construction of the dome of the Pantheon under Brebion, who had succeeded Soufflot. In 1799 he was appointed professor at the *Ecole des Beaux Arts*. Rondelet published *Traite theorique et de l'art de batir* (Paris, 1802), *Memoires historiques sur le dome du Pantheon francais*(Paris, 1814), *Traduction des commentaires de Frontin sur les aqueducs de Rome*, etc. [ARCHITECT]

Root, John Wellborn: 1851-1891. He was born in Atlanta (Georgia) and in 1864 was smuggled through Federal lines and sent to England. Returning to America after the war, he graduated at the College of the City of New York and entered the office of James Renwick. He afterward became an assistant of John B. Snook, and under his direction superintended the construction of the Grand Central Station in New York City. In 1872 he entered the office of Drake & Wight in Chicago and later formed a partnership with Daniel H. Burnham. Root held the important office of consulting architect of the World's Fair Commission in Chicago. [ARCHITECT]

Roritzer, Konrad (Thomas and Wolfgang): Konrad Roritzer was architect of the Cathedral of Ratisbon (Regensburg) from 1459 to 1465 and built also the choir of the Lorenz Kirche at Nuremberg between 1459 and 1477. Thomas Roritzer was cathedral architect at Ratisbon (Regensburg) in 1482 and Wolfgang Roritzer held that office in 1514, when he was decapitated for sedition. [ARCHITECTS]

Royers de La Valfeniere, Francois des: 1575-1667. The chief member of a family of architects that was employed at Avignon and at Lyons in the seventeenth century. In 1636 he was appointed architect of the Chartreuse of Villeneuve-lez-Avignon, which he enlarged and decorated. In 1646 he finished the Palais de Justice at Carpentras and in 1647 made the plans of the abbey of the Dames de S. Pierre (now Palais des Arts) at Lyons. [ARCHITECT]

Ruggieri, Ferdinando: Ruggieri rebuilt (1736) the interior of the Church of S. Felicita, designed the facade of the Church of S. Firenze (1715), and assisted Carlo Fontana in the construction of the Palazzo Capponi, all in Florence. He is best known by his

Studio d' Architettura Civile. [ARCHITECT]

Ruskin, John: 1819-1900. While engaged in the study of painting, especially Italian and British landscape painting, he studied also the Medieval architecture of Europe and made many accurate drawings, engravings from some of which illustrate his published works. In 1849 was published *The Seven Lamps of Architecture,* a series of essays, and in 1851-1853, *The Stones of Venice,* one chapter of which, *The Nature of Gothic,* has been reprinted separately. He also published lectures and detached essays. John Ruskin is not widely known as an architect, rather, his contributions lay in the philosophies which he espoused and the styles which he encouraged architects to adapt. His book, *Seven Lamps of Architecture,* gives architects seven principles by which their designs should be governed: sacrifice, truth, beauty, obedience, power, life and memory. Major points include the design of buildings using natural materials (rather than machine-made), imitation and inspiration of nature, building for endless admiration, and styles which conform to universal acceptance. His second work, *The Stones of Venice,* proposed the new idea of using the Medieval beauty of architecture and the pleasure felt by the people who actually bring about the work involved in building. Ruskin deeply influenced Morris, whose contributions included workshops and socially reforming architectural designs and ideas. [WRITER AND ARCHITECT]

Saarinen, Eero: 1910-1951. Finnish-born Saarinen was the son of Eliel Saarinen, a renowned architect in his own right, and Loja Gesellius Saarinen, a talented artist. In his early years, he studied sculpture, a love which he never lost and which is evident in the sculpture contained in many of his designs. In 1923 Saarinen emigrated to the United States, then returned to Europe to study sculpture at the Academie de la Grande Chaumiere in Paris between 1929 and 1930. He returned to the United States. to begin his studies in architecture at Yale University between the years 1930 and 1934. He travelled back to Europe before settling down to start his career in his father's office in Ann Arbor, Michigan, in 1937. For the next 13 years, he worked first with his father and then in partnership with J. Robert Swanson, finally opening his own practice in 1950. Pelli, Roche, Dinkeloo started their careers under the direction of Saarinen. Eero designed the General Motors' Technical Center at Warren, Michigan (1948-1956), which consists of rectangular buildings of steel and glass arranged around an artificial lake. The Kresge Auditorium at Massachusetts Institute of Technology (1953-1955) features a warped roof. The chapel at M.I.T. has waving walls of brick and a sculptural dome. The Trans-World Airline's terminal at J.F.K. Airport in New York City (1956-1962) epitomizes flight, with the arches' outward pitch. The Dulles Airport in Washington, D.C. (1958-1963), which was completed after his death in 1961, is considered his greatest achievement. Saarinen's constant aspiring to new forms in architecture was his trademark; therefore, his work does not adhere to any particular school. [ARCHITECT]

Saarinen, Eliel: 1873-1950. Eliel studied painting and architecture at the University and Polytechnic College in Helsinki. His early works were influenced by the Gothic Revival, the Arts and Crafts movement and the Neo-romantic style reminiscent of H. H. Richardson. He married Loja Gesellius, who was related to Herman Gesellius, one of Eliel's partners and a gifted artisan herself. He won a competition in 1904 for the design of the railway station in Helsinki. It was completed in 1914 and is considered to be his most famous work. In 1922, Eliel won second place for his design of the Chicago Tribune building and decided to emigrate to the United States as a result of that prize. He opened his own practice in 1923 at Evanston, Illinois and moved it to Ann Arbor, Michigan, in 1924. In 1937, his son Eero joined his father in the company. Eames, Feiss, Weese, and Knoll all got their start in Saarinen's office or at the Cranbrook Academy of Art in Bloomfield, Michigan, which he designed and where he taught. His wife and others contributed to the interior design of the Academy; hence, it became a place where art and architecture are integrally combined and which shows a great harmony in design. Eliel's central belief was that the building should be in harmony with the city and include open spaces within its walls. [ARCHITECT]

Salvart, Jehan: On March 13, 1398, he replaced Jehan de Bayeux as architect of the Cathedral of Rouen (Seine Inerieure, France). In 1407 he restored the west portal of the Cathedral. From 1400 to 1411 he was employed on the Chateau of Tancarville (France). In 1430 he enlarged the windows of the choir of the Cathedral of Rouen. In 1432 Salvart appears as *maitre d' oeuvre* (city

architect) of the city of Rouen. [ARCHITECT]

Salvi, Niccolo: 1699-1751. Salvi was a pupil of Antonio Cannevari. His most important work is the fountain of Trevi in Rome (1735-1762). [ARCHITECT]

Salzmann, Max: ca. 1850-1897. Architect of the Cathedral of Bremen, Germany. At the time of his death he had finished the towers and the decoration of the northern side of the building. [ARCHITECT]

San Gallo, Battista (il Gobbo): b. ca. 1496. A brother of Antonio (II) da San Gallo, assisting in much of his work. [ARCHITECT]

San Gallo, Sangallo, Antonio (I) da (Giamberti): 1455-1534. Antonio Giamberti, brother of Giuliano da San Gallo, began life as a woodworker. He went to Rome about 1492 and was employed by Alexander VI (Pope 1492-1503) to remodel the Castel Sant' Angelo and build the gallery connecting it with the Vatican. He appears in the records as *curator*. About 1496 he was appointed *Capomaestro* of all the works of the Signoria of Florence, Italy, including the improvement of the Palazzo Vecchio and the fortresses of Firenzuola and Poggio Imperiale. He enjoyed a large practice as military engineer until about 1518, when he seems to have settled at Montepulciano, where he built the Cervini, Tarugi, and Bellarmini palaces and the important Church of the Madonna di S. Biagio. The Palace of the Cardinal, Del Monte (Palazzo Communale), and the Loggia del Mercato, at Monte San Savino, are attributed to Antonio. He built also the nave of the Church of the Annunziata at Arezzo. [ARCHITECT, ENGINEER, AND WOODCARVER]

San Gallo, Sangallo, Antonio (II) da (Antonio Picconi): 1485-1546. Antonio (II) was the son of a sister of Giuliano and Antonio (I) da San Gallo. His given name was Picconi. He was employed by Bramante as a drafter, assisted Giuliano da San Gallo at S. Peter's Church, and in 1517 was made Raphael's associate in the superintendence of that building. On May 1, 1518, he was appointed architect of the church and the Vatican Palace and retained that office until his death. The model which he made for S. Peter's is still in existence. Antonio was for many years the leading architect in Rome and controlled a large military and civil practice. He had in hand at one time the fortresses of Florence and Ancona, the completion of the buildings at Loreto, the enlargement of the Vatican, and the fountain and aqueduct at Orvieto. The villa Madama, Rome, is attributed to Raphael by Vasari, but existing drawings by Antonio and his brother, Battista, indicate that much of the work was done by them about 1530. About 1542 he built for Paul III (Farnese, Pope 1534-1549) the Pauline Chapel in the Vatican, which was decorated by Michelangelo. For the same Pope, also, he began the famous Farnese Palace in Rome. At About the beginning of the third story, the work was transferred to Michelangelo, whose design for the cornice was preferred. A long list of Antonio's palaces and churches is given by Vasari. He was assisted in much of his work by his brother, Battista San Gallo (il Gobbo). Many of his drawings are in the gallery of the Uffizi (Florence). [ARCHITECT]

San Gallo, Sangallo, Bastiano da (Aristotle): 1481-1551. Bastiano was a son of the younger sister of Giuliano and Antonio (I) da San Gallo and a cousin of Antonio (II) da San Gallo. He was apprenticed to the painter Perugino in Florence and studied the great cartoon of Michelangelo Buonarroti. He earned the name, Aristotle, by his intelligence and application. With his brother, Giovanni Francesco, he was employed to build the Pandolfini Palace, in Florence, from the designs of Raffaello Santi. The building was not finished until after 1530. He attached himself to the court of Cosmo I de' Medici. [PAINTER AND ARCHITECT]

San Gallo, Sangallo, Giuliano da (Giamberti): Giuliano was born in Florence the oldest son of Francesco Giamberti, a woodworker who trained his sons to his own trade. Francione was also his teacher and associate. The name San Gallo may derive from his residence near the Porta di San Gallo in Florence. In 1465 he was in Rome, and was employed by Paul II (Pope 1464-1471) on the Palace of S. Marco, the tribuna of S. Peter's, and the Vatican. In 1848 he fortified and defended, unsuccessfully, the city of Castellina against Ferdinand I of Naples. For Lorenzo de' Medici, Giuliano designed the octagonal sacristy of S. Spirito in Florence (begun 1489), and the famous villa of Poggio a Cajano (about 1485-1489). His *chef d'oeuvre*, the Church of the Madonna delle Carceri at Prato, was built between 1485 and 1491. On Dec. 9, 1507, Giuliano was chosen *capomaestro* (chief architect) of the Duomo, Florence. The cloister of S. Maddalena de' Passi, in which he copied an Ionic capital found at Fiesole, was begun in 1479. The Palazzo Gondi

(Florence) is ascribed to Giuliano by Vasari. For the Cardinal della Rovere, afterward Julius II, he restored the fortress of Ostia (1484) and built the Palace of Savona (1494). On one of the sketches of the Barberini collection is written an account of a journey to France in 1496. Giuliano built the dome of the church at Loreto, Italy (1497-1500), and was employed as civil and military architect in many Italian cities. During the reign of Leo X (Pope 1513-1521), he was associated with Raphael as architect of the Vatican and S. Peter's. On July, 1515, he returned to Florence. Several of the designs which he made in competition for the facade of S. Lorenzo in 1516 are still preserved at the Uffizi Gallery. The San Gallo had a *botega* (shop) in Florence for woodcarving and sculpture. The wooden crucifix at the Annunziata, a part of the high altar at the Duomo (Florence), and other works at Perugia and elsewhere are attributed to Giuliano. Between Sept. 19, 1489, and Feb. 16, 1490, Giuliano da San Gallo was paid 115 *lire*, 10 *soldi* for the model, still in existence, of the Strozzi Palace (Florence), of which he was undoubtedly the designer, instead of Benedetto da Maiano, as Vasari asserts. There is an album of his sketches in the Barberini Library

(Rome). Another collection is in the library at Siena. They contain drawings of monuments in Italy, France, and Greece, which have disappeared. [ARCHITECT, ENGINEER, AND WOODCARVER.]

Sanmicheli, Michele: 1487-1559. Sanmicheli was born at Verona (Italy). About 1500 he went to Rome, where he came under the influence of Bramante and Raphael. As early as Nov. 27, 1509, he is mentioned as cathedral architect at Orvieto, Italy, and appears in the records of that building until 1528. Michele built the altar to the three kings in this Cathedral. His earliest independent work is the Church of the Madonna delle Grazie at Montefiascone (1519). After the sack of Rome in 1527, Sanmicheli was employed by Clement VII (Pope 1523-1534) to assist Antonio (II) da San Gallo in the fortification of several Italian cities, notably Parma and Piacenza. This was a beginning of an immense practice as military engineer, which included the construction of the defences of Milan, Urbino, and Naples, and the superintendence of the entire system of fortifications for the territory under Venetian rule in Italy, Dalmatia, Crete, and Cyprus. He is said to have invented angular bastions. The most architecturally important of his military works are the fort of S. Andrea di Lido, Venice,

the bastions of Verona, and the superb series of semi-military portals in the walls of Verona, the Porta Nuova, the Porta Palio (or Stuppa), the Porta S. Zenone, and the Porta S. Giorgio. The most important of his palaces are the Bevilacqua, the Canosa, the Pompeii, Versi, and Gran-Guardia in Verona, and the Grimani (on the Grand Canal) and the Cornaro Mocenigo (in the Campo S. Paolo) at Venice. The architecture of these palaces is in the main a development of the type established by Bramante in the so-called Palace of Raphael (now destroyed) in Rome; heavy rustication below crowned by a single order above. Sanmicheli designed the domical Church of the Madonna di Campagna, the famous circular Chapel of S. Bernardino, the facade of the Church of S. Maria in Organo, and portions of the Church of S. Giorgio in Braida, all in Verona. He designed the monument of Alessandro Contarini in the Church of S. Antonio at Padua. [ARCHITECT AND MILITARY ENGINEER]

Sansovino (Sansavino), Andrea (Andrea Contucci): 1560-1529. Andrea was the son of a laborer of Monte San Savino in Tuscany, and his first teacher was Antonio Pollajuolo. His earliest known work is a terra-cotta altar with figures of S. Lorenzo, S.

Sebastiano, and S. Rocco, now in the monastery of S. Chiara at Monte San Savino, Italy. In 1480, on the recommendation of Lorenzo de' Medici (1448-1492), he was invited to Portugal by King John II A bas-relief and a statue of him are still in the church of the monastery of S. Marco, near Coimbra (Portugal). In 1490 he returned to Florence and was employed in the decoration of the Church of S. Spirito. In 1500 Andrea was commissioned to execute the marble statues of Christ and S. John Baptist over the door of the Baptistery (Florence). The statues of the Madonna and S. John Baptist in the Cathedral of Genoa were finished by him in 1503 (signed *Sansovinus Faciebat*). His earliest work in Rome appears to be the monument of Pietro da Vicenza (dated 1564) in the Church of Ara Coeli. His chief work, the monument of the Cardinal Ascanio Sforza, brother of Ludovico il Moro, Duke of Milan, at S. Maria del Popolo, was finished in 1506. The similar monument of the Bishop Hieronimus Bassus in the same church was begun in 1507. The monument of the Cardinal Johannes Michaelius and his secretary Antonio Orso in the Church of S. Marcello (Rome) is by Andrea. Among his works in his native city (San Savino)

is the cloister of S. Agostino, which is especially interesting on account of optical refinements introduced to correct the effect of its irregular plan. He built the great stairway between the Cathedral and the Bishop's Palace at Arezzo. [SCULPTOR AND ARCHITECT]

Sansovino (Sansavino), Jacopo or Giacomo (Jacopo Tatti): 1486-1570. Jacopo was born at Caprese, near Florence. He attached himself to the sculptor Andrea Sansovino, from whom he received his name and artistic training. About 1467 he went with Giuliano da San Gallo to Rome, where he met Bramante and entered the service of Julius II. Sansovino made a design for the facade of the Church of S. Lorenzo (Florence), which was not executed. He designed the Church of S. Giovanni dei Fiorentini in Rome which was continued by Antonio (II) da San Gallo. The facade is by Alessandro Galilei. After the sack of Rome (1527) Sansovino went to Venice, where he remained the rest of his life. He had charge of the church, campanile, and Piazza di S. Marco, and the adjacent public buildings except the Doge's Palace. The Palazzo Cornaro della Ca' Grande appears to be one of his earliest Venetian buildings. In 1535 the Council of Ten (Venice) commissioned him to build the Zecca, in which he used a fireproof iron construction. Sansovino's greatest work is the library of S. Mark. He began the Loggietta of the Campanile (Venice) about 1540. Sansovino built also in Venice the Church of S. Francesco della Vigna in 1534 (facade by Palladio), the church of S. Giorgio dei Greci about 1550, the church of S. Salvatore (restored), the church of S. Maria Mater Domini about 1540, and the facade of the Scuola di S. Giorgio dei Schiavoni about 1551. He made the monument of the Doge Francesco Venier (d. 1556), with the fine statues of Hope and Charity, in the church of S. Salvatore (Venice), and the monument of Livio Podocataro, Archbishop of Cypress, in the church of S. Sebastiano (Venice). He built also the Palazzo Delfini, now Banca Nationale, and began the Procuratie Nuove continued by V. Scamozzi. On Dec. 18, 1545, the great vault of the Libreria fell. Sansovino was held responsible for the loss, imprisoned, and fined. He was restored to his position Feb. 3, 1548. His most important works of sculpture at Venice are the statues of the loggietta, the colossal figures of Mars and Neptune which give its name to the Giant's Stairway at the Doge's Palace, the evangelists over the choir screen of S. Marco, and the famous bronze door of the sacris-

ty of S. Marco (begun 1546, finished 1569). He made also a bas-relief for the church of S. Antonio at Padua. He was much assisted by Alessandro Vittoria. [SCULPTOR AND ARCHITECT]

Sant'Elia, Antonio: 1888-1916. Sant'Elia was an Italian futurist architect who was educated in Milan. He never had a chance to build his visionary designs because he was killed in World War I. However, he left behind more than 300 drawings which paved the way for Rationalism and included terraced skyscrapers, magnificent roads at varying levels, and bridges made of steel or concrete. [ARCHITECT]

Santi (Sanctius, Sanzio), Raffaello; called Raphael: 1483-1520. Raphael was born at Urbino (Italy), the son of Giovanni Santi, a painter. About 1499 he entered the atelier of Perugino and probably assisted in the decoration of the Cambio at Perugia, which was done at this time. He assisted Pinturicchio in decorating the library at Siena, begun in 1502. He visited Florence in 1504 and spent much time in that city until 1509. Raphael was called to Rome by Julius II (Pope 1503-1513) in 1509, to assist in the decoration in fresco of a suite of apartments (*stanze*) in the Vatican already begun by Sodoma, Perugino, and others. The first *stanza* was finished in 1511. The second *stanza* was painted between 1511 and 1514; much of the execution was deputed to his assistants. The third *stanza*, still less the work of Raphael, was finished about 1517 by Giulio Romano. The decorations of the loggie of the Vatican were begun in 1517. In 1514 he painted at the Villa Farnesina (Rome) the fresco of "Galatea," and later made the designs for the "Marriage of Cupid and Psyche." The splendid sibyls in the Chigi Chapel at the church of S. Maria della Pace (Rome) were painted at about the same time as the "Galatea." When Bramante died (March 11, 1514), Raphael succeeded him as architect of S. Peter's; with him were associated Fra Giocondo and others. Raphael's principal innovation was to substitute a Latin for the Greek cross of Bramante. He may have designed those portions of the Villa Madama (Rome) which were built before 1520, although existing measured drawings for that building are by Antonio (II) and Battista da San Gallo. The Pandolfini Palace (Florence) is ascribed to Raphael, but was begun after his death. The Farnesina villa was undoubtedly the work of Baldassare Peruzzi. Raphael may have designed the Chigi Chapel at the church of S.

Maria del Popolo and the Palace of Giovanni Battista dell' Aquila (Rome), which has disappeared. By a brief dated Aug. 27, 1515, of Leo X (Pope 1513-1521), Raphael was authorized to inspect and purchase all marbles in the ruins within 10 miles of Rome. This enabled him to institute an extensive series of important excavations. He began a work on the topography of Rome, the text of which, by Andreas Fulvius, was published in 1527. The plates were never completed. [PAINTER AND ARCHITECT]

Scamozzi, Giovanni Domenico: ca. 1530-1582. From a simple carpenter he became an accomplished architect. He visited Budapest and Warsaw, where he reconstructed the royal palace. Giovanni made the index (*indice copiosissimo*) of the edition of Serlio's works, which was published in Venice in 1584 and 1619. In his introduction to this edition, Ludovico Roncone mentions some of Giovanni's buildings. [ARCHITECT]

Scamozzi, Vicenzo: 1552-1616. The name Scamozzi is derived from *camoccio* (*camoscio*), chamois leather, indicating some ancestral occupation. Vicenzo was a son of Giovanni Domenico Scamozzi and a pupil and rival of Andrea Palladio. He studied mathematics under the Padre Clavio, who was employed by Gregory XIII in reforming the calendar. Scamozzi made a thorough study of the Roman monuments. In 1582 he went to Venice to continue the Libreria di S. Marco, begun by Sansovino. Scamozzi added the Anti Sala. He also continued Procuratie Nuove, begun by Sansovino, adding a third story. In 1593 Scamozzi designed and began the fortress of Palmanuova in Friuli (Italy). In 1600 he accompanied a Venetian embassy to France, Germany, and Hungary. An autograph account of the visit, with drawings, is in the museum at Vicenza. He built a casino at Lonigo, another at Castelfranco near Treviso, the Palazzo Trenta at Vicenza, the Palazzo Trissino at Vicenza, the Palazzo Verlato at Villaverla (1574), the Palazzo Raveschiere at Genoa, and the second story of Buontalenti's Palazzo Roberto Strozzi in Florence. About 1604 he designed the Cathedral of Salzburg (Austria) and a part of the Schloss at Prague (Bohemia). Scamozzi published *Discorsi sopara l' Antichita di Roma* (Venice, 1582) and *Dell' Idea dell' Architettura universale* (Venice, 1615). There is a nineteenth century edition, *Pubblicata per cura di S. Ticozzi e l. Masieri* (1838). [ARCHITECT]

Scharoun, Hans: 1893-1972. Scharoun was born in Germany and took his education at the Polytechnic in Berlin. His early work included being director of the architectural advisory council for reconstruction of East Prussia (1915-1918). Later, he was a professor at the Academy for the Arts in Breslau (1925-1932). Scharoun's buildings can be grouped into pre- and post-World War II categories. Prior and during World War II, his designs were mostly residential. The houses which he built made the best possible use of the views and interior spaces (e.g., Schminke House, Lobau, Germany, 1933). Because of the Nazi regime, Scharoun was only able to build residential units; however, after the war ended, he began to come into his own as one of the early Expressionists. Post-war buildings include the Berlin Philharmonic Center (1956-63), his best-known work. Scharoun was not noted for his exteriors, rather for his interiors, and the Philharmonic is an excellent example of his talent for designing dramatic spaces within the walls. He also built the German Embassy in Brasilia (1970) and the National Library in Berlin (1978). [ARCHITECT]

Schaubert, Edward: b. 1800. He studied in Breslau and Berlin and in 1830 went to Greece, where he held several public offices. He was associated with Ludwig Ross and Christian Hansen in the restoration of the temple of Nike Apteros on the Acropolis and in the publication of *Die Acropolis von Athen...der Temple der Nike Apteros* (1839). [ARCHITECT]

Schindler, Rudolf, M.: 1887-1953. Schindler was born and educated in Vienna. At the age of 26, he emigrated to the United States, where he went to work with Frank Lloyd Wright. In 1921 he opened his own office. His style was greatly influenced by Wright and others of the International Modern School, and also by the Cubists. His specialty was designing homes for the wealthy and his most famous home is the Beach House (Lowell House) in Newport Beach, which was built in 1925. [ARCHITECT]

Schinkel, Karl Friedrich: 1781-1841. In 1797 he entered the Academy in Berlin and studied under David and Friedrich Gilly. In 1820 he was appointed professor in the Academy at Berlin and in 1839 *Oberlandbaudirector*. He visited Italy, including Istria and Sicily, France, and England. In 1834 he made a design for a royal palace on the Acropolis at Athens, which fortunately, was never executed. Among the most important of his buildings are the museum in

Berlin (1824-1828), the Royal Theater in Berlin (1819-1821), the fine Nicolai Kirche at Potsdam, the Konigs-Wache in Berlin, the Schloss-Wache in Dresden, the fine architectural school in Berlin, the *Charlottenhof* and Casino at Potsdam, etc. Schinkel was much interested in the construction of Protestant churches in the Gothic style, the most important of these being the Werder Kirche in Berlin. He made a design for the completion of the Cathedral of Cologne, which was never executed. [ARCHITECT]

Schluter, Andreas: 1664-1714. After the death of his father, Gerhard Schluter, a sculptor, Andreas became a pupil of the sculptor Sapovius in Danzig (West Prussia). Between the ages of 20 and 30 he visited Italy and in 1691 entered the service of Johann III Sobieski, King of Poland, at Warsaw. Here he attracted the notice of Prince Friedrich of Prussia (afterward Elector Friedrich III and in 1700, King Friedrich I), who in 1694 made him court sculptor at Berlin. After 1696 Schluter built the greater part of the Palace of Charlottenburg in Berlin. In 1697 he made the model of the equestrian statue of the Elector Friedrich III in Konigsberg. The famous equestrian statue in Berlin of the Great Elector Friedrich Wilhelm was begun by Schluter about 1698 and placed in position in 1705. Schluter superintended the sculptural decoration of the Zeughaus (Berlin) and made the series of 21 masks of dying warriors in the inner court of that building. About 1699 he was made architect of the Schloss in Berlin and held that office until 1796, when he was superseded by Eosander. In 1713 he was chief architect of the Russian court and died the next year in Saint Petersburg. [SCULPTOR AND ARCHITECT]

Scott, Sir George Gilbert: 1811-1878. In 1827 he was articled to James Edmeston and in 1832 entered the office of Henry Roberts. In 1844 he won first prize in the competition for the church of S. Nicholas at Hamburg, Germany, to replace the building burned in 1842. This he built in the German Gothic style of the fourteenth century, with a tower 475 feet high. In 1847 he was appointed architect of Ely Cathedral, and architect of Westminster Abbey in 1849, where he restored the chapter house, monuments and northern portal. His *Gleanings from Westminster Abbey* was published in 1862. After completion he was appointed in 1858 architect of the building of the War and Foreign Offices, London. His first designs were Gothic, but he was required by Lord Palmerston's government to

substitute a design in the style of the Italian Renaissance, according to which the building was erected (begun 1861). He afterward completed this block of buildings by erecting the Home and Colonial Offices. Between 1863 and 1868 Scott designed and built the Albert Memorial in Hyde Park, London. In 1866 he was one of the six competitors for the Royal Courts of Justice in London. He won the gold medal of the Royal Institute of British Architects in 1859, and was president of that body from 1873 to 1876. He was appointed professor of architecture at the Royal Academy in 1868. His lectures were published under the title *Mediaeval Architecture* (1879). [ARCHITECT]

Scott, Sir Giles Gilbert: 1880-1960. At the early age of 24, Scott achieved notoriety with the winning of a competition and design for the Liverpool Cathedral. This famous design has elements of Gothic and was evidently inspired by Bodley. Other famous churches of note designed by Scott include St. Joseph Church in Norfolk, England and the Chapel at Charterhouse School. They show less influence by others and more originality on Scott's part. Scott's prolific designs also included the Battersea Power Station in London (1932), establishing the beginning of using brick for power stations all over England. The Waterloo Bridge (1939-1945) was also built by Scott. His Cambridge University Library (1931-1934) and Guildhall Building in London (1954-1958) do not exhibit his early creativity. [ARCHITECT]

Semper, Gottfried: 1803-1879. He went to Paris to study architecture and was later associated with Gartner in Munich and Gau in Cologne. In 1830 he visited southern Italy, Sicily, and Greece, studying the use of color in architecture, which he published in *Bemerkungen uber bemalte Architektur und Plastik bei den Alten* (Altona, 1834). In 1834 he was appointed professor of architecture in the academy at Dresden. He built the synagogue in Dresden (1838-1840), and the Hoftheater (1838-1841). Other buildings in Dresden by Semper are the Gothic fountain in the Post-platz (1843-1844), and the Villa Rosa (1839). In 1847 he began the new museum at Dresden. Semper left Dresden during the political disturbances of 1848-1849 and settled in London, where he supported himself as a designer for metal work and decoration, and wrote some of his smaller essays on art and architecture. In 1855 he was appointed director of the architectural section of the *Polytechnische Schule* in Zurich, Switzerland. In Zurich he built the Polytechnicum (1858), the observatory (1861), the city hospital, and other buildings. He built also the Rathhaus in Winterthur. During this period he wrote his important work, *Der Stil* (2d ed. Munich, 1878-1879). In 1871 Semper was made architect of the new museums and the Hofburgtheater in Vienna. He made the plans for these buildings, which were, however, executed by Baron von Hasenauer, who changed them considerably. The exteriors of the two museums are, however, probably much as Semper designed them. [ARCHITECT]

Serlio, Sebastiano: 1475-ca. 1555 (at Fontainebleau, France). The date of Serlio's birth is established by records of the church of Tommaso della Braina in Bologna. About 1515 he went to Rome and was intimately associated with Baldassare Peruzzi, who, at his death in 1536, bequeathed to him his notes and drawings, which were afterward used by Serlio in the composition of his books. He seems to have gone to Venice about 1532. He measured the ancient monuments of Verona and was the first to draw the ruins at Pola in Istria. In 1541 he was established in France by Francis I as consulting architect at Fontainebleau. Neither in Italy nor in France is there any building of importance which can with certainty be ascribed to him. Serlio commenced the publication of his works with the fourth book, entitled, *Regole generali di Architettura di Sebastiano Serlio Bolognese, sobra le cingque maniere degli edifici ...Venizia, 1537*. The third book appeared next with the title, *Il terzo libro di Sebastiano Bolognese nel quale si figurano e si descrivono le antichita di Roma...Venizia, 1540*. The first book followed: *Le premier livre d'Architecture de Sebastien Serlio Bolognois, mis en langue francais par Jehan Martin* (Paris,1545). The second book was published with the first, *Le second livre de Perspective de Sebastien Serlio Bolognois, mis en langue francaise par Jehan Martin*. The fifth book was published next: *Quinto libro di Architettura di Sebastiano Serlion nel a Paris*, (1547). The sixth book was published at Lyons: *Extraordinario libro di Architettura di Sebastiano Serlio...trenta porte di opera Rustica mista con diversi ordini...Lione, 1551*. The seventh book was bought by Strada the Antiquary, and was published after Serlio's death: *Il settino libro d'Architettura di Sebastiano Serlio Bolognese, nel quale si tratta di molti accidenti, etc., ... Francofurti ad Moenum*, (1575). An eighth book, on military architecture, was also bought by Strada with Serlio's collection of drawings, but appears

not to have been published. The first complete edition of his works was printed at Venice in 1584. [ARCHITECT AND WRITER]

Sert, Jose Luis: 1902-1983. Born in Barcelona, Sert worked for Le Corbusier from 1929-1932. He emigrated to the United States in 1939 and became Gropius' successor at Harvard. Some of his designs include the Spanish Pavilion in Paris (1937), the U.S. Embassy in Baghdad, and the Fondation Maeght near Nice, France (1962-1964). [ARCHITECT]

Servandoni, Jean Nicolas: 1695-1766. Servandoni studied painting under Giovanni Rossi and later was established in Paris as director of decorations at the opera. In 1732 he won the first prize in the competition for the construction of the facade of the church of S. Sulpice in Paris. At S. Sulpice also he built the great altar of the Cathedral of Sens (Yonne, France) and in 1745 that of the Cathedral of Reims, and about the same time that of the Church of the Chartreux at Lyons. In 1752 he took part in the competition for the creation of the Place Louis XV, now Place de la Concorde, in Paris. In 1755 Servandoni was made court architect of King Augustus at Dresden, Saxony. He built the great staircase of the new palace at Madrid, Spain, and was employed at Brussels. Servandoni was especially successful in organizing fetes, processions, and the like. [ARCHITECT AND PAINTER]

Sheppard, Richard: b. 1910. An English architect, Sheppard studied at the Architectural Association School in London. His partnership with Geoffrey Robson and others was responsible for designing mainly educational buildings, including the Churchill College, which was won by competition in 1959, the Harrowfield Boys' School in Essex (1954), and the West Midland Training College in Walsall (1960-1963). [ARCHITECT]

Silis: Silis was probably from Aegina, Greece. He flourished in the sixth century B.C., and was associated with Theodorus and Rhoecuss in the construction of the labyrinth at Lemnos and the Temple of Hera at Samos. He made the statue of Hera in that temple and a group of the "Hours," which was preserved in Heraion at Olympia. [SCULPTOR AND ARCHITECT]

Silva, Joaquim Possendonio Narcisso da: 1806-1896. Da Silva spent his childhood in Brazil and returned to Lisbon in 1821. In 1827 he entered the *Academie des Beaux Arts in* Paris. In 1833 he was appointed court architect at Lisbon. He transformed the convent of La Pena into the residence of the King, Dom Ferdinand, and restored the Palace of the Duke of Palmella. [ARCHITECT]

Sinan, Abdullah, Pacha: The most important early Turkish architect. He is credited with a large number of mosques, minarets, schools, palaces, etc. His three principal works are the mosque of Sultan Selim I (built 1521-1527), the mosque of Sultan Suleiman I (built about 1550), and the mosque of the Sultana Valideh, built for the mother of Sultan Murad III, all at Constantinople (Istanbul). [ARCHITECT]

Skidmore, Owings, and Merrill: (estab. 1936) This partnership's founders were Louis Skidmore (1897-1962), Nathaniel Owings (1903-84) and John Merrill (1895-1975). The early years of the partnership were spent establishing branch offices and structure for the firm itself. The firm believed in teamwork and individual creativity and responsibility, as well as individual anonymity and economic working procedures. The Lever House in New York City (1952) firmly established the firm in the international community. This 21 story building set the style of combining different elements into one structure and features a curtain walled skyscraper on a pedestal of the first few stories and a garden court in the middle. Other important buildings are the Hilton Hotel in Istanbul, the United States Air Force Academy in Colorado Springs (1955), the Manufacturer's Trust Bank in New York (1952), the Connecticut General Life Insurance Building in Hartford, Connecticut (1953-1957), the National Commercial Bank in Jeddah, and the John Hancock Tower in Chicago, Illinois (1970). Mies van der Rohe, Le Corbusier, and others of the International Modern School influenced the firm's designs, and the firm itself has made an impact on American architecture. [ARCHITECT]

Smids, Michael Matthias: 1626-1692. He was court architect of the great Elector Friedrich Wilhelm and rebuilt the Marstallegebaude (Berlin) about 1666. [ARCHITECT]

Smirke, Sir Robert: 1781-1867. In 1796 he entered the office of Sir John Soane, then occupied with the building of the Bank of England, and in the same year became a student of the Royal Academy. In 1799 he won the gold medal for design. He visited Athens in 1803 while Lord Elgin was removing the sculpture from the Parthenon. He also visited Sicily and made drawings of the architectural

remains there. Smirke was employed on the mint, London, in 1809, and in 1845 was placed by Sir Robert Peel on the commission for London improvements. He built Lowther Castle and Eastnor Castle and in 1808 rebuilt Covent Garden Theater (burned in 1858). One of his most important works is the main facade of the British Museum (London). [ARCHITECT]

Smirke, Sydney: A brother of Sir Robert Smirke. In 1828 he was clerk of the works at S. James's Palace (London). At the British Museum, about 1855-1857, he designed and built the great circular reading room. [ARCHITECT]

Smithson, Peter and Alison: This English husband and wife team studied at the University of Durham. They opened their own practice in 1950 in London. Their contributions to New Brutalism were started with the Hunstanton School in Norfold (1949-1954). Mies van der Rohe was an influence on their designing style. The Economist Building (1964) was another important building designed by the Smithsons, as were the Robin Hood Gardens in London. [ARCHITECTS]

Soane, Sir John: 1753-1837. His name was originally Swan. He changed it to Soan and afterward to

Soane. He was the son of a bricklayer and in 1768 entered the service of the younger George Dance. He afterward studied with Henry Holland and at the schools of the Royal Academy. In 1776 he won the gold medal of the Academy and a travelling stipend which enabled him to spend three years in Italy. From 1788 to 1833 he held the office of architect and surveyor to the Bank of England. The facade of this building is one of the best of his works. Between 1791 and 1794 he was clerk of the works at S. James's Palace, the Houses of Parliament, and other public buildings in Westminster, and in 1807, clerk of the works at the Royal Hospital, Chelsea. In 1802, Soane was made Royal Academician, and in 1806, professor of architecture at the Royal Academy. In 1836 he built the Stat Paper Office, destroyed in 1862. His house in Lincoln's Inn Fields and his large collection of art treasures were left to the nation and constituted by act of parliament the Soane Museum. [ARCHITECT]

Solari, Cristoforo (il Gobbo): An architect of the school of Bramante in Milan. His most important building is the Church of S. Maria della Passione (Milan). He is supposed to have worked on the facade of the Certosa at Pavia and the tombs of the Visconti and Sforza in that monastery. In 1495 he entered the service of Lodovico Sforza (il Moro), Duke of Milan, and made the monument to his duchess, Beatrice d'Este, which was originally placed in the Church of S. Maria delle Grazie (Milan). He was employed upon the sculpture of the Cathedral of Milan until 1519, when he was appointed supervising architect of the Cathedral. Solari was probably related to Pietro Lombardo. [SCULPTOR AND ARCHITECT]

Solari, Guiniforte: d. ca. 1481. One of the Milanese family. He succeeded Filarete as architect of the Ospedale Maggiore in Milan, Italy, and was at one time architect of the Certosa of Pavia. [SCULPTOR AND ARCHITECT]

Sostratos: He built the Pharos (lighthouse) at Alexandria about 320 B.C. [ARCHITECT]

Soufflot, Jacques Germain: 1709-1780. After a journey to Asia Minor he returned to Lyons (France) about 1737, where he built the Church of the Chartreux and enlarged the Hotel Dieu. In 1752 he took part in the competition for the creation of the Place Louis XV, now Place de la Concorde, in Paris. In 1754 he was charged with the reconstruction of the Cathedral of Rennes and in the same year the theater of Lyons was begun from his plans. In 1755 he designed the Hotel de Ville at Bordeaux and in that year replaced Cailleteau as *controleur general* of the embellishments of the city of Lyons. Soufflot published *Suite de plans, coupes, etc., de trois temples antiques ... a Pestum* (Paris, 1764), and *Oeuvres ou Recueils de plusieurs parties d' architecture* (Paris, 1767). [ARCHITECT]

Soynere (Sunere), Heinrich: The first architect of the Cathedral of Cologne, Germany. The first stone of the choir was laid Aug. 15, 1248. [ARCHITECT]

Spavento, Giorgio di Pietro: d. 1509. Spavento succeeded Antonio Celega as *inzegnerius prothus dominorum procuratorum Sancti Marci*. He built the new sacristy of S. Marco in Venice (begun August, 1486) and at the same time the Church of S. Teodoro and that of SS. Filippo e Giacomo in Venice. About 1498 he restored the Sala del Gran Consiglio at the Doges' Palace. He assisted in the construction of the Palazzo della Ragione at Vicenza in 1500 and the Ponte delle Nave at Verona in 1502. At the same time he built the Capella di S. Niccolo at the Doges' Palace. In 1506 he made the model for, and began the construction of, the Church of

S. Salvatore in Venice, but was superseded the next year by Pietro and Tullio Lombardo. In 1507 he was again employed at the Doges' Palace. [ARCHITECT]

Specchi, Alessandro: In cooperation with Francesco de' Sancti he built in Rome between 1721 and 1725 the immense stairway leading from the Piazza di Spagna to the Church of S. Trinita de' Monti, the facade of which was built by Domenico Fontana. He built the stalls of the Palazzo Quirinale, Rome. [ARCHITECT]

Spence, Sir Basil: 1907-1976. Born in Bombay, Spence emigrated with his family to Edinburgh and received some of his education there. He designed the Sea and Ships Pavilion for the Festival of Britain in 1951. Spence's winning of the competition for the Coventry Cathedral (1954-1962) no doubt had a strong influence on his future work. This church building has been praised by critics as being one of the paramount churches of the twentieth century. Many artists and craftsmen were given opportunities to participate in the design of certain elements of the Cathedral. Spence's firm went on to design the British Embassy in Rome (1971), a building which fit into the design of others surrounding it, while at the same time exhibiting special character. [ARCHITECT]

Spintharos: He built the latest temple of Apollo at Delphi, in Greece. This building was not begun before 536 B.C. [ARCHITECT]

Stackelberg, Magnus, Freiherr von: 1787-1837. Educated in Dresden, he went to Rome, and in 1810 to Greece, where he assisted in the excavation of the temple of Athena at Aegina and the temple of Apollo at Bassae. He published *Der Apollo tempel zu Bassae in Arcadien* (Rome, 1826), and *La Grece, vues pittoresques et topographiques* (Paris, 1834). [ARCHITECT]

Staroff, Iwan Igorowich: A Russian architect who built about 1790 the Alexander Newski Church in Saint Petersburg, also called the Pantheon. He built, according to the designs of Guadagni, the Church of S. Sophia in Saint Petersburg. [ARCHITECT]

Statz, Vincenz: b. ca. 1819. 1841 he was associated with Zwirner on the works of the Cathedral at Cologne. He became diocesan architect in 1863 and in 20 years built about 60 churches in the Gothic style, most of them in the archbishopric of Cologne. He published *Gothische Einzelheiten* (1874), and with Ungewitter, *Go-*

thisches Musterbuch (Leipzig, 1856). [ARCHITECT]

Stirling and Gowan: (Estab. 1956.) This London partnership was formed by James Stirling (b. 1926) and James Gowan (b. 1924). Influenced by Le Corbusier, Stirling and Gowan designed such buildings as the houses at Ham Common (1955-1958), and the Leicester University Engineering Building (1959-1963), the latter being their most major work. Stirling left the partnership in 1963 and worked alone until 1971, at which point he went into partnership with Michael Wilford. Some of that partnership's major buildings were the Olivetti headquarters building (1971) and the Wallraf-Richartz Museum in Cologne (1975). Of his work, Stirling said, "I believe that the shapes of a building should indicate - perhaps display-the usage and way of the life of its occupants, and it is therefore likely to be rich and varied in appearance, and its expression is unlikely to be simple." This philosophy is reflected in his architectural designs. [ARCHITECT]

Stone, Nicholas: 1586-1644. Stone was a pupil of Isaac James, a mason, and assisted Hendrick van Keyser at Amsterdam. In 1614 he returned to England and executed many works from the designs of Inigo Jones, such as the banqueting house, Whitehall (1619-1622), the portico of old S. Paul's, the water-gate at York Stairs, and the fine portal of S. Mary's, Oxford. He was appointed master mason at Windsor by Charles I and was employed in the execution of a vast number of monuments. He was assisted and succeeded by his sons Henry, Nicholas, and John. [SCULPTOR, ARCHITECT, AND MASTER MASON]

Strack, Johann Heinrich: 1805-1880. He studied architecture with Schinkel and in 1834 went to Italy. After his return he was made professor in the Academy of Berlin. In 1862 Strack went to Athens and superintended the excavation of the theater of Dionysos. He published *Das altgriechische Theatergebaude* (1843); *Zeigel Bauwerke des Mittelalters und der Renaissance in Italien* (Berlin, 1889,); *Baudenkmaler Roms des XV-XVI Jahrhunderts; erganzung zu Letarouilly* (Berlin, 1891,) etc. [ARCHITECT]

Street, George Edmund R.A., F.S.A.: 1824-1881. In 1844 he entered the atelier of Sir George Gilbert Scott. In 1852 he was appointed diocesan architect at Oxford, England, and afterward held the same office for the dioceses of York, Ripon, and Winchester. In 1856 he established his office in London. He restored a large number of Medieval monuments, the cathedrals of York, Carlisle, Bristol, and Dublin, the Church of S. Peter Mancroft at Norwich, the church at Hythe, etc. He built a very large number of new churches in the Gothic style, being especially successful in the smaller designs. In 1867 he entered the memorable competition for the new Courts of Justice in London and in 1868 was appointed architect of that work. Street was made a member of the Royal Academy in 1871 and was afterward elected president of the Royal Institute of British Architects. He published *Brick and Marble Architecture in Northern Italy* (1855), *Gothic Architecture in Spain* (1865), and numerous contributions to periodicals, especially the *Ecclesiologist* and the *Transactions of the Royal Institute of British Architects*. His notes on the sepulchral monuments of Italy were published by the Arundel Society (1883). [ARCHITECT]

Stuart, James, F.R.S., F.S.A.: 1713-1788. He studied painting and in 1742 visited Italy. His *De Obelisco Caesaris Augusti* was published at the expense of Pope Benedict XIV (1750). On January, 1751, with Nicholas Revett and W. Pars, a painter, he visited Greece and made a careful examination and measurements of the ruins at Athens. He returned to England in 1752. The first volume of Stuart and Revett's monumental *Antiquities of Athens* was published in 1762, the second in 1788 (the year of his death), the third, edited by W. Reveley, appeared in 1794, and the fourth, edited by J. Woods, in 1816. A supplementary volume, *Antiquities of Athens and Other Places in Greece, Sicily, etc.*, was published by C. R. Cockerell, W. Kinnard, T. L. Donaldson, and W. Railton (1830). From 1758 until his death Stuart held the office of surveyor at Greenwich Hospital. [ARCHITECT AND PAINTER]

Suger (Sugger): Suger, Abbot of S. Denis, near Paris, rebuilt the church of his abbey about 1137-1140. This contains much of the earliest existing proto-Gothic work in France. Suger was also minister to Charles VI of France. [ABBOT AND BUILDER]

Sullivan, Louis Henry: 1856-1924. Although American-born Sullivan only had three years of formal architectural training, his influence on modern architecture was profound. Starting in 1879, Sullivan joined Dankmar Adler and remained in partnership with him until 1895. One of their first projects was the Auditorium in Chicago (1889), a complex project rich in technical details. Sullivan was a major influence on the shaping and refining of the skyscraper. The Wainwright Building in St. Louis (1890-1891), the Schiller Building and the Stock Exchange in Chicago (1892 and 1894) are examples of the firm's designs. The design of the Schlesinger and Mayer Department Store (1899-1904) reflected Sullivan's belief that art and the scientific method were inextricably bound. This building was designed after the partnership with Adler was dissolved and was Sullivan's last great contribution to the field. After Adler died in 1900, Sullivan found himself less and less in demand and in financial distress, having to accept less than noteworthy projects. He was alone in a hotel room when he died in 1924, a poignant ending for one of the greatest architects of modern times. [ARCHITECT]

Talenti, Francesco: d. ca. 1369. The Talenti came from Ponte-a-Lieve, near Florence. Francesco is mentioned among the sculptors working on the Duomo of Orvietio in 1329. His name next appears in an inventory of marble for the campanile of the Florentine Cathedral, dated 1351. This marble was for four windows. The three upper stories of the campanile are probably his work. He is last mentioned in the records of the campanile in 1357. On May 29, 1355, Talenti was commissioned to make a model for the Cathedral (S. Maria del Fiore), which should determine the position of the windows of the nave. At this time it was decided to make the four vaults of the nave square instead of oblong, as designed by Arnolfo di Cambio, thus increasing the length of the nave to its present dimensions. In 1358 Giovanni di Lapo Ghini was associated with him as *capomaestro*. On Dec. 20, 1364, Talenti was discharged, but on July 22, 1366, appears again in a position subordinate to Ghini. His salary was stopped in 1369, which is probably about the date of his death. The nave was nearly completed. [SCULPTOR AND ARCHITECT]

Talenti, Simone: The son of Francesco Talenti. He assisted his father at the Duomo (Florence) and in 1366 presented a model for that building. In 1375 he succeeded Francesco Salvetti as *capomaestro* of the Duomo. In 1376 Benci di Cione was associated with him, and they, with the assistance of Taddeo Ristoro, designed and began the building now called the Loggia dei Lanzi (Florence). In June 1377, the three architects were superseded both at the Duomo and the Loggia and executed all the carvings on the piers and brackets, fin-

ished Nov. 29, 1379. About 1378 Simone filled in the lower arches of Or S. Michele (Florence) and decorated them with tracery. [SCULPTOR AND ARCHITECT]

Talman, William: d. ca. 1700. His principal work was Chatsworth House in Derbyshire, England, built in 1681 for William Cavendish, Earl, and afterward Duke, of Devonshire. He built Thoresby House (1671), which burned before 1762. In 1694 he was appointed by King William III comptroller of the works in progress at Hampton Court. Sir Christopher Wren was surveyor at Hampton Court at the same time and was much disturbed by Talman's interference. [ARCHITECT]

Tange, Kenzo: b. 1913. This Japanese architect was born in Osaka and studied at Tokyo University. He joined the office of Kumo Mayekawa, who had formerly been associated with Le Corbusier. His design of the Peace Center in Hiroshima (1949) raised him to international recognition and reflects his sensitivity to traditional Japanese tradition, while at the same time incorporating all the techniques of modern technology. This prolific architect also designed the Tokyo Metropolitan Building (1952-1957), the Tokyo National

Gymnasium (1964), St. Mary's Cathedral in Tokyo (1965), and the Yamanashi Press and Broadcasting Center (1966). He believed that "only the beautiful can be functional," and this statement is indicative of all of his elegant buildings. His specialty was synthesizing form and function. In 1967 Tange was appointed master planner of the international exhibition at Osaka, a privilege which he shared with Uzo Nikiyama. Beginning in 1960, Tange's work had evolved to show less and less of the Japanese traditions which his designs up until that time had displayed. [ARCHITECT]

Tasso, Giovanni Battista del: 1500-1555. Battista belonged to a famous family of wood carvers which flourished during the fifteenth and sixteenth centuries in Italy. He was a *protege* of Pier-Francesco Riccio, majordomo of Duke Cosmo I dei' Medici, and was much employed in the improvement of the Palazzo Vecchio. There is a ceiling by him in the second story of the palazzo on the side toward the Uffizi. The curious door which he built for the Church of S. Romolo is preserved by Ruggieri. His most important work is the loggia of the Mercato Nuovo of Florence, which was begun by the order of Duke Cosmo I, Aug. 26, 1547. [WOODWORKER and ARCHITECT]

Tatlin, Vladimir: 1885-1953. This Russian artist studied art in Moscow and was influenced by Cubism and Futurism. He went on to become well-known for his work in theater design, abstract sculpture and painting. His works furnished the inspiration for Constructivism. In 1919 he designed a Monument to the Third International, a building which never came to fruition. His design was studied by many, however, for its marriage of steel and glass. [ARCHITECT]

Tecton: (Estab. 1932.) This group of English architects was established in 1932 by Berthold Lubetkin. Other members of the group were Anthony Chitty, Lindsey Drake, Michael Dugdalee, Valentine Harding, Godfrey Samuel, Frances Skinner and later, Sir Denys Lasdun. Among the projects designed by the firm were the London Zoo (1932-1937), The Highpoints I and II (1933-1938), and the Finsbury Health Center in London. [ARCHITECT]

Telford, Thomas: 1757-1834. He was apprenticed to a stone mason and in 1780 went to Edinburgh. After 1782 he was employed on Somerset House in London. Between 1795 and 1805 he constructed the Ellesmere canal, with its great aqueduct, and between 1773 and 1823 the Caledonian canal in Scotland. He made many roads in the highlands of Scotland, with about 1,200 bridges. His name is associated with a peculiar form of pavement for roads. [ENGINEER]

Tessin, Nicodemus (I): Little is known of his life. He studied in Italy and in 1645 succeeded Simon de Lavallee as architect of the Swedish Court. Among his principal works in Sweden are the Palace of Drottningsholm, finished by his son, the royal villa of Stroemsholm, and the mausoleum of Charles Gustav. [ARCHITECT]

Tessin, Nicodemus (II): 1654-1728. He was the son of Nicodemus Tessin (I) and was educated at the universities of Stockholm and Upsala, Sweden, and learned architecture from his father. He visited Italy and worked four years under Bernini and Carlo Fontana. In 1669 Tessin was appointed royal architect in Sweden. The royal palace in Stockholm, burned in 1667, was rebuilt by him. He finished the Palace of Drottningsholm, begun by his father, designed the parks of Drottningsholm and Ulriksdal, and made plans for the reconstruction of the palace in Copenhagen, Denmark. He took an

important part in public and political affairs. [ARCHITECT]

Texier, Jean le (Jean de Beauce): Le Texier was employed in the construction of the Church of La Trinite at Vendome (Loir et Cher). On Nov. 11, 1506, he contracted with the chapter of the Cathedral of Chartres to rebuild the northern spire of that edifice according to a design on parchment which he that day exhibited. This new spire, entirely of stone and one of the most splendid examples of the flamboyant Gothic style in France, was completed in 1513. In 1514 Le Texier commenced the beautiful sculptured screen that surrounds the choir of the Cathedral. This work, on which many sculptors were employed, was not finished at his death. Before 1410 he enlarged the Church of S. Aignan at Chartres by means of an arch with a span of 14 meters thrown across the river Eure, on which he built the new choir of the church. Le Texier and Martin Chambiges were the last great champions of the Gothic style in France. [SCULPTOR AND ARCHITECT]

Theodorus of Samos: Theodorus flourished during the early part of the sixth century B.C., and was one of the principal artists of the earliest Greek school. In much of his work he was associated with Rhoekos and Smilis. Theodorus, Rhoekos, and Smilis built the labyrinth at Lemnos. According to Herodotus, Rhoekos built the Temple of Hera at Samos, a description of which was written by Theodorus. Theodorus was consulted about the construction of the temple of Artemis at Ephesos, begun about 576 B.C., and advised laying the foundations in charcoal. Theodorus designed the building called the Skias, at Sparta. Numerous temple statues and works in the precious metals were attributed to him, among others the famous ring of the tyrant Polykrates of Samos and the silver wine cooler which was sent by Croesus to Delphi. [ARCHITECT AND ARTISAN]

Theodotos: According to an inscription, Theodotos was architect of the temple of Aesculapius at Epidauros, Greece, built between 380 and 375 B.C. [ARCHITECT]

Theotocopuli, Jorge Manuel: d. 1631. A son and pupil of Domenico Theotocopuli (El Greco). On March 10, 1625, he was made architect and sculptor of the Cathedral of Toledo in Spain. In 1626 he began the cupola of the Capilla Muzarafe in this Cathedral and finished it in 1631. [SCULPTOR AND ARCHITECT]

Theotocopuli (Teoscopoli) Domenico (el Greco): 1548-1625. A pupil of Titian in Venice, in 1577 he was in Spain painting altar pieces in the style of Titian. He designed the Church of the Caridad and the city hall at Toledo, Spain, the church of the college of Dona Maria de Arragon at Madrid, and the church of the Franciscan Monastery at Illescas with the marble tombs of its founders, which have been destroyed. [PAINTER, SCULPTOR AND ARCHITECT]

Thornton, Dr. William: (late 18th-early 19th century.) The first advertisements in the competition for the Capitol at Washington were published in 1792. In October of that year Dr. William Thornton of the island of Tortola in the West Indies wrote to the commissioners asking permission to compete. His plans were submitted early in 1793, were much admired by the commissioners, and on April 5th were approved by President Washington. The designs that were second in point of merit were those of Stephen Hallet, who was placed in charge of the construction of Thornton's design under the general direction of James Hoban, architect of the White House. Hallet was discharged Nov. 15, 1794. On Sept. 12, 1794, the President appointed Thornton to be one of the commissioners in charge of the District of Columbia, and he had general supervision of the Capitol until his office was abolished in 1802. At this time the north wing of the older part of the Capitol, now occupied by the Supreme Court, was complete, and the foundations and basement story of the south wing were partially laid. After retiring Thornton was placed in charge of the Pension office and remained there until his death. [ARCHITECT]

Tibaldi, Pellegrino: 1527-1598. Tibaldi began as a painter, the pupil of Danielo da Volterra. He was especially patronized by San Carlo Borromeo at Milan. Tibaldi applied the principles of Vignola to a large number of churches and palaces. In 1560 he began the reconstruction of the facade of the Cathedral of Milan. Of this work five doors and five windows remain. He built the fine Church of S. Fidele, Milan, begun 1569, the court of the Archbishop's Palace, Milan, 1570, the Palazzo della Sapienza, Pavia, 1562, the Church of S. Gaudenzio, Novara, 1577, the Church of S. Francesco da Paola, Turin, and the court of the University, Bologna, 1570. [ARCHITECT AND PAINTER]

Tino di Camaino: A pupil of Giovanni da Pisa who was employed on the Cathedral of Siena after 1300. He made several monuments in Florence, the most important of which is that of the Emperor Henry VII. In the will of Maria, widow of Charles II of Naples, Tino is chosen to construct her tomb. He is mentioned in other documents as architect of several buildings in the vicinity of Naples. [SCULPTOR AND ARCHITECT]

Tolsa, Manuel: ca. 1750-ca. 1810 (in Mexico). In 1781 he went to Mexico as government architect. He directed the erection of the towers of the Cathedral of Mexico City, 1787-1791, designed the College of Mines in Mexico, 1797, and other buildings. In 1798 he was appointed director of the Academy of S. Carlos, Mexico City. His chief work is the fine equestrian statue of Carlos IV, now in the Pasco de Bucareli, Mexico City. [ARCHITECT, ENGINEER, AND SCULPTOR]

Torelli, Giacomo: 1608-1678. Torelli was especially associated with the rapid development of the construction and decoration of theaters and scene painting in the seventeenth century. He made improvements in his native city, Fano, in Italy, which were engraved and attracted much attention. He was called to Venice and at the theater of SS. Giovanni e Paolo in that city invented a method of changing scenes which was universally adopted. Torelli was called to Paris by Louis XIV, and remained there until 1662. He arranged the theater of the Petit Bourbon. The *Andromeda* of Corneille was first placed upon the stage by him. Returning to Fano, he built the Teatro della Fortuna. [ARCHITECT AND PAINTER]

Tresguerras, Franciso Eduardo: 1745-1833. "The Michelangelo of Mexico," Tresguerras was a pupil of the painter of Miguel Cabrera for a short time at the Academy of S. Carlos in Mexico City. He did not have the advantage of European travel and study. His activity was confined to a group of cities in the vicinity of Celaya. He began as a painter and afterward took up wood carving, acquiring extraordinary skill in that art. He probably learned the elements of architecture from the Jesuits, who supplied him with a Vignola and other architectural works. Tresguerras's work as an architect is characterized by great originality and beauty of proportion, especially in domes and towers. His interiors are extremely rich. His best building is the Church of Nuestra Senora del Carmen, at Celaya. Other important works are the convent churches of S. Rosa and S. Clara in Queretaro, the Alarson Theater in San Luis Potosi, the bridge of La Laja, the beautiful Church of La Concepcion in San Miguel de Allenda, and other works. His most important picture is the altarpiece of the Church of S. Rosa in Queretaro. At the age of 70 he became an enthusiastic supporter of the Mexican Revolution. [ARCHITECT, SCULPTOR, PAINTER, MUSICIAN, AND POET]

Ulrich von Ensingen: d. 1429. Ulrich (from Ensingen, a village in Switzerland near Fribourg), was chief architect of the Cathedral of Ulm, (begun 1377) from 1390, when the most important part of the construction was actually undertaken, until his death in 1429. From 1410 to 1429 he was also employed in some capacity at the Cathedral of Strasbourg. In 1387 he was called to Milan to advise concerning the construction of the Cathedral. He was succeeded by his sons, Gaspard and Mathias. [ARCHITECT]

Upjohn, Richard: 1802-1878. He was apprenticed to a builder and cabinetmaker in 1829, came to the United States, and settled in New Bedford, Massachusetts. He went to Boston in 1833 and assisted in the construction of the City Court House.

In 1839 he went to New York to take charge of proposed alterations in the old Trinity Church. This scheme was abandoned, and Upjohn designed and constructed the present Trinity Church, which was finished in 1846. He built also S. Thomas's Church, Trinity Building, the Corn Exchange Bank, and other buildings in New York, several churches in Brooklyn, and other buildings. He was president of the *American Institute of Architects* from 1857 to 1876. [ARCHITECT]

Valdelvira, Pedro de: A contemporary and rival of Berruguete, Valdelvira studied Michelangelo's works in Italy. In the town of Ubeda, Spain, he built the castle of Francisco de los Cobos, secretary of Charles V, and the Church of S. Salvador. [SCULPTOR AND ARCHITECT]

Valence, Pierre de: The chief member of a large family of French architects. In 1500 he was employed on the Church of S. Gatien at Tours (Indre-et-Loire). Jan. 11, 1503, Valence was called by the Cardinal Georges I d'Amboise to inspect the works at the Chateau of Gaillon, near Rouen, and in 1506 undertook the construction of the water works and fountains of that Chateau. In 1507 he directed the construction of the fountain of Beaune in Tours. On Jan. 22,

1511, he made a contract for the fountains at Blois. His sons, Germain and Michel, succeeded him. [ARCHITECT, ENGINEER, AND SCULPTOR]

Vallee, Simon de la: He was called to Sweden by Queen Christina. At Stockholm he built the Palace of the Nobility (begun 1648), the Churches of S. Marie, S. Catherine, etc. [ARCHITECT]

Vanbrugh, Sir John: Vanbrugh devoted the early part of his life to literature and distinguished himself as a dramatist. In 1702 he succeeded Talman as comptroller of the royal works. His first completed building was a theater (1703-1705) in London, afterward destroyed. In 1701 he began for the Earl of Carlisle the palace called Castle Howard in Yorkshire, England. As a reward for the distinguished services to John Churchill, Duke of Marlborough, the royal manor of Woodstock (England) was granted to him and to his heirs by Act of Parliament of March 14, 1705, with half a million pounds to build the great palace called Blenheim, which is Vanbrugh's most important and characteristic work. In 1716 he succeeded Sir Christopher Wren as surveyor of Greenwich Hospital (London). Among the residences built by Vanbrugh are Eastbury in

Dorsetshire (1716-1718), Seaton Delaval (1720), portions of Audley End (1721), Grimsthorpe (1722-1724), etc. [DRAMATIST AND ARCHITECT]

Vasari, Giorgio: 1511-1574. Giorgio Vasari was born at Arezzo (Italy), a kinsman of Luca Signorelli. His first teacher in painting appears to have been Guillaume de Marcillat. His literary training was superintended by Aretine poet Giovanni Pollastra. About 1523 he went to Florence, and entered the service of Ottaviano de' Medici and the Duke Alessandro de' Medici. He went to Rome afterwards with the Cardinal Ippolito de' Medici. From 1555 to the end of his life he was court painter to Cosimo I de' Medici, Duke of Florence. The most important of his undertakings are the frescoes of the Cancelleria in Rome and those of the Palazzo Vecchio in Florence. As architect he prepared in 1536 the decorations of the triumphal entry of the Emperor Charles V into Florence. He made the original plans of the Vigna di Papa Giulio (Julius III, Pope 1550-1555) in Rome. He remodelled the Palazzo Vecchio and built the Palazzo degli Uffizi in Florence. At Pistoia he built the cupola of the Church of the Madonna dell' Umilta and at Pisa the Palazzo dei Cavalieri da S. Stefano. He built the Badia and the Loggie Vasari at Arez-

zo. Vasari's most important work is his series of biographies of artists *Le Vite de' piu eccellenti Architetti, Pittori e Scultori*. The first edition appeared in 1550. The second, in 1568, was more complete. The standard edition of Vasari is that of Gaetano Milanese, which was published in Florence between 1878 and 1885. The *Vite* were translated into English by Mrs. Foster in 1888. A selection of 70 of the *Lives* from Mrs. Foster's translation, with introduction, annotation, and bibliography by E. H. and E. W. Blashfield and A. A. Hopkins was published in New York in 1896. [ARCHITECT AND PAINTER]

Vassallectus (Vasaleto): The name Vassallectus, variously spelled, appears in inscriptions on several monuments of the thirteenth century in the vicinity of Rome. The most important of these, the cloister of S. Giovanni in Laterano, which was probably built about 1230, bears this inscription, discovered by Count Vespignani in 1887: NOBILIS ET DOCTUS HAC VASSALLETTUS IN ARTE, CUM PATRE COEPIT OPUS QUOD SOLUS PERFECIT IPSE. The inscription indicates that the sculptor belonged to a family of *marmorarii* (marble workers). A throne with lions, which was made about 1263 for the Abbot Lando, and is now in the museum of the Cathedral of

Anagni, Italy, is signed *Vasaleto de Rome me fecit*. The name appears also on an oedicula for holy oil in the Church of S. Francesco at Viterbo. It is supposed by some authorities that the fine monument of the Pope Adrian V in this church was made by the same person. Less important works are a lion before the Church of SS. Apostoli (Rome), and a candelabrum in the Church of S. Paolo fuori le Mura (Rome). There is also an inscription which belonged to a monument that stood in the old basilica of S. Peter's (Rome). These works may be by one person or several. A screen in the Cathedral of Segni, dated 1185, and a canopy in the Church of SS. Cosmo e Damiano (Rome) appear to be by an earlier member to the family. [ARCHITECT, SCULPTOR, AND MOSAICIST.]

Vaux, Calvert: 1824-1895. He studied architecture under Lewis N. Cottingham. He became the assistant of A. J. Downing and later formed a partnership with him. The firm of Downing and Vaux laid out the grounds of the Capitol and of the Smithsonian Institution in Washington. In association with Fredrick Law Olmsted, Vaux made the plans according to which Central Park in New York was laid out and retained his position as consulting landscape architect of the department of parks in New York until his death. Olmsted and Vaux designed Prospect Park, Brooklyn, the parks of Chicago and Buffalo, the State Reservation at Niagara Falls, and the Riverside and Morningside parks in New York. [LANDSCAPE ARCHITECT]

Verdeman de Vries, Hans (Jan): 1527-1588. A pupil of Reijer Gerritszen, glass painter, of Amsterdam. In 1569 he assisted in the erection of the triumphal arch in honor of the entry of Charles V into Antwerp. De Vries painted many perspective decorations in Mechlin, Frankfurt, Braunschweig, Prague, Hamburg, Danzig, and elsewhere, and made many designs for buildings, furniture, monuments, etc. He published works on perspective and architecture. [ARCHITECT AND PAINTER]

Viollet-le-Duc: 1814-1879. He was educated at the College Bourbon (Paris) and in the atelier of Achille Leclere. At the suggestion of his father, who was employed in the conservation of public buildings, he made a journey through France, studying and sketching the monuments. He travelled through Italy in the same way. Returning to France in 1840, he undertook the restoration of the abbey Church of Vezelay (Yonne,

France) and the Church of S. Pere Sous-Vezelay. About this time he restored the Hotel de Ville at Narbonne (Aude, France) and was appointed auditor of the *conseil des batiments civils*. He was associated with Lassus in the restoration of the Sainte-Chapelle in Paris. In 1842 Lassus and Viollet-le-Duc were commissioned to superintend the restoration of the Cathedral of Notre Dame (Paris). At the death of Lassus in 1857, Viollet-le-Duc retained sole charge of that work and designed the central spire and great altar, as well as the new sacristy and treasury adjoining the south flank. In 1846 he began the restoration of the abbey Church of S. Denis, near Paris, and had charge of that building until his death. From 1849 to 1874 he was architect of the diocesan buildings of Reims and Amiens. In 1852 he took charge of the restoration of the *cite* of Carcassone (France), with the ancient fortifications, and in 1853 was appointed *inspecteur general des edifices diocesains*. In 1858 he began the reconstruction of the Chateau of Pierrefonds (Oise, France). In 1862 he restored the Church of S. Sernin at Toulouse and in 1863 the Chateau of Coucy. In 1863 he was appointed professor of aesthetics at the *Ecole des Beaux Arts* (Paris). As his lectures were not in

agreement with the traditions of the school, the students refused to listen to him. He resigned his position the following year and published the material which he had prepared as the *Entretiens sur l' Architecture*. In 1873 he began the restoration of the Cathedral of Lausanne (Switzerland) and built the fine spire of that church. Viollet-le-Duc restored many less important monuments and erected many new buildings throughout France. Among his many publications, the most important are *L'Art Russe; Les Origines, etc.* (Paris, 1877); *Comment on Constuit une maison* (4th ed., Paris, 1883); *Description et histoire du chateau de Pierrefonds* (8th ed., Paris, 1876) *Dictionnaire raisonne du Mobilier francais* (Paris, 1858-1875); *Entretiens sur l'Architecture* (Paris, 1863-1872); *Essai sur l'Architecture Militaire au Moyen Age* (Paris, 1854); *Habitations modernes* (Paris, 1875-1877); *Histoire d'un Hotel de Ville et d'une Cathedrale* (Paris, 1878); *Histoire d'une forteresse* (Paris, 1874), and with Lassus, *Monographie de Notre Dame* (Paris, no date). [ARCHITECT AND ARCHAEOLOGIST]

Visconti, Louis Tullius Joachim: 1791-1853. A son of Ennius Quirinus Visconti, the archaeologist, who came to Paris in 1798. Between 1818 and 1817 Louis studied architecture at the

Ecole des Beaux Arts and with Charles Percier. In 1814 he won second *Grand Prix* and the *Prix Departemental*. In 1822 he was employed as under inspector under Destailleur. He replaced Delannoy in 1825 as architect of the Bibliotheque Royal. His projects for this building were not carried out. Visconti was appointed in 1832 *conservateur* of the eighth section of the Monuments of the City of Paris. In 1835-1839 he built the Fontaine Louvois (Paris). He arranged the ceremony of the reception of the remains of the Emperor Napoleon I, Dec. 15, 1840 and in 1842 was commissioned to construct the monument of the emperor in the Church of the Invalides. In 1842 he completed the Fontaine Moliere (Paris) and in 1846 commenced the Fontaine of the Place Saint-Sulpice (Paris). In 1850 he was appointed architect of Napoleon III, and in 1851 made the plans for the completion of the Louvre and the gallery uniting the Louvre and Tuileries on the north. This work was begun July 25, 1852. After the death of Visconti, in 1853, it was continued by Lefuel according to his designs. He built numerous residences in Paris and the monuments of the Marshals Lauriston, Saint Cyr, Soult, and Souchet. [ARCHITECT]

Vitoni, Ventura: 1442-ca. 1522. He was brought up as a carpenter and, according to Vasari, was a pupil of Bramante. All the buildings attributed to him are in Pistoia (Italy). The earliest is the Church of S. Maria delle Grazie (begun 1484). That of S. Giovanni Battista was begun 1495 and completed in 1513. Parts of the Church of S. Chiara may also be by him. Vitoni's great work is the Church of S. Maria dell' Umilta, a combination in plan of the Pazzi Chapel and the sacristy of S. Spirito at Florence. The large closed atrium and the choir were begun in 1494 and the central octagonal portion in 1509. That date is inscribed on the building. At his death he had carried the church to the windows of the third story. The dome is much later. His will is dated March 11, 1522. [ARCHITECT]

Vitruvius (Pollio), M. C. L.: b. ca. 83-73 B.C. The author of a Latin work of 10 books on architecture, the earliest existing manual on that subject, dating from about 30 B.C. Considerable portions of his book are quoted by Pliny in his *Historia Naturalis* without acknowledgment, and he is mentioned by Frontinus in his work on aqueducts. The little basilica at Fano described in his book is the only building that can be attributed to him. Among the many sources from which he derived information are the writings of Anaxagoras, Ctesiphon, Ictinus, Theodorus etc. In a letter of the Councillor C. F. L. Schultz to the poet Goethe, the theory was first brought forward that Vitruvius' work was really a compilation made in the reign of the Emperor Theodosius, and afterward ascribed to Vitruvius, a well-known architect of the time of Augustus. The work was highly esteemed during the Middle Ages and frequently transcribed. The manuscript of S. John's College, Oxford, was made as late as 1316 and belonged to the Abbey of Canterbury. There was a manuscript of Vitruvius in the Palace of the popes at Avignon, which was carried to Spain in the fifteenth century. The *editio princeps* was published by Johannes Sulpitius Verulanus about 1486. During the reign of Julius II (Pope 1503-1513), Fra Giocondo published his critical edition, which he dedicated to that Pope. The most important editions of the text are that of Poleni (1825-1830), and the standard edition of Marini (Rome, 1836). There are English translations by Newton (1791), Wilkins (London, 1872), and Gwilt (1826). [ARCHITECT]

Wailly, Charles de: 1629-1798. De Wailly entered the school of Jacques

Francois Blondel and was associated also with Legeay and Servandoni. In 1752 he won the *Grand Prix d'Architecture* and visited Rome. In 1767 he entered the *premiere classe* of the *Academie d'Architecture* in Paris and in 1771 the *Academie de Peinture*. In 1779-1782, in collaboration with Marie Joseph Peyre, he built the theater of the Odeon (Paris). He enlarged the choir of the Church of S. Leu (Paris) and built a Chapel in the Rue Hoche at Versailles. The plans which he made for the embellishment of the city of Kassel (Germany) are in the library at Kassel. He had an atelier in the Palace of the Louvre and died there. [ARCHITECT AND PAINTER]

Walter, Thomas Ustick: 1804-1887. In 1819 he entered the office of William Strickland as a student in architecture. In 1831 he designed the Philadelphia County Prison and in 1833 the fine building of Girard College (Philadelphia), which was built entirely under his direction. In 1851 he was appointed architect of the Capitol in Washington, superseding Robert Mills. The old Capitol was completed according to the designs of Charles Bulfinch when he left it in 1829 and remained practically unchanged until 1850, when Walter presented his scheme for the addition of two wings containing accommodations for the Senate and House of Representatives. The cornerstone of the new work was laid by Daniel Webster, July 4, 1851. Walter rebuilt the western front, which had been destroyed by fire, and added the library. At the close of 1854 the walls of the wings had reached the height of the ceiling. In 1855 the old dome was removed and the new dome begun. Both wings were covered in 1856. The House of Representatives first met in its new quarters Dec. 16, 1857, and the Senate Jan. 4, 1859. The government ordered the suspension of the work in 1861, but through the patriotism of the contractors, operations were continued during the entire Civil War. The exterior of the dome was completed in 1863 and the entire work in 1865, when Walter retired from office. [ARCHITECT]

Wast (Vast), Jean (II): d. 1581. At the death of his father Jean (I), he succeeded him as *maitre en second* in the construction of the Cathedral of Beauvais, serving under Martin Chambiges until his death in 1532, and after that under Michel Lalye. In 1557 he had succeeded Lalye as chief architect. Wast made the plans of the famous central tower of the Cathedral of Beauvais and built the lower stories, which were of stone. The wooden spire was added by Florent

Dailly. This tower fell in 1573. [ARCHITECT]

Wilars de Honecort: Wilars, thought to have belonged to Honnecourt, a village near Cambrai (Nord, France), is known by an album of sketches preserved in the collection of manuscripts taken from the Abbey of S. Germain des Pres, which are now in the Bibliotheque Nationale, Paris. In the fifteenth century the volume contained 41 leaves of vellum. The drawings are made with lead or silver point, sometimes inked in. The book contains numerous figures probably taken from sculpture or glass, sketches of architectural details, such as the plan of the towers of Laon, the rose window at Chartres, the rose window at Lausanne, and many mechanical devices. From internal evidence contained in his book, it is supposed that he was one of the leaders in the development of Gothic architecture in the thirteenth century and that he built, between 1227 and 1251, the choir of the Cathedral of Cambrai, which was destroyed during the French Revolution. About 1244 he visited Hungary. The apse of the church at Meaux, the church at Vaucelles, and also some buildings in Hungary which show French influence, have been attributed to him by different writers. [ARCHITECT]

William of Sens: d. 1180. In 1175 the chapter of the Cathedral of Canterbury (England) undertook the reconstruction of that building, which had been destroyed by fire in 1174. William of Sens (Yonne, France) was employed as architect and built the walls, pillars, triforium, and clearstory of the choir, when (about Sept. 13, 1178) he was thrown from a scaffold, receiving injuries from which he died two years later. It is supposed by Viollet-le-Duc and others that he built a considerable part of the Cathedral of Sens before he went to England. [ARCHITECT]

William of Wykeham: 1324-1404. He was born at the village of Wickham near Winchester (England) and was educated at the priory school at Winchester. He early became known to Bishop Edingdon of Winchester, who employed him on the Cathedral and recommended him to the King. In 1349 he was appointed King's Chaplain. On October 30, 1356, he was appointed surveyor of the works at Windsor Castle. On July 10 he was made chief warden and surveyor of the royal castles of Windsor, Leeds, Dover, and Hadleigh. Wykeham made important additions to Wind-

sor Castle. In 1361-1367 he built Queensborough Castle. He was made keeper of the Privy Seal and King's secretary in 1364. On October 17, 1367, he was made chancellor of the kingdom and on October 10 of the same year was consecrated Bishop of Winchester. On March 5, 1380, he laid the foundation of New College, Oxford, and on March 26, 1387, commenced S. Mary's College at Winchester. In 1394 he commenced alterations at Winchester Cathedral. He began the reconstruction of the nave and aisles, which was not completed until after his death. In rebuilding the church Wykeham used the exciting Norman masonry, transforming it into the perpendicular style of the time. [ARCHITECT]

William The Englishman: (12th century.) He succeeded William of Sens as architect of Canterbury Cathedral, ca. 1178, and in much of his work simply carried out the designs of his predecessor. The new Trinity Chapel or Chapel of Becket was built entirely under his direction. [ARCHITECT]

Woronichin, Andrei Nikiforowitsch: 1760-1814 (in Saint Petersburg). He studied at the Academy of Saint Petersburg and was sent by Catherine II to Germany and Italy. In 1791 he was appointed architect to the court of Saint Petersburg. His most important work is the Church of Notre Dame in Kasan, Saint Petersburg. He built numerous palaces. [ARCHITECT]

Wren, Sir Christopher: 1632-1723. He was a student at Oxford (B. A., 1650; M.A., 1653) and afterward a fellow, and in 1660 was appointed Savilian Professor of Astronomy in that university. His scientific work was known throughout Europe. He was an original member of the Royal Society at its foundation in 1662 and was elected president of that body in 1681. Having gained a great reputation as a mathematician, he was consulted in architectural matters during the confused times of the Restoration. In 1661 he was made a member of the commission in charge of the restoration of old S. Paul's Cathedral in London. The first building which Wren actually designed and superintended was the Chapel of Pembroke Hall, Cambridge. He began the fine library of Trinity College, Cambridge, in 1676. His Sheldonian Theater at Oxford was opened July 9, 1669. He visited Paris in 1665 and met Bernini, then occupied with his design for the facade of the Louvre. Wren never visited Italy. The Great Fire of London occurred Sept. 2, 1666. Immediately afterward Wren made a plan

for the reconstruction of the burned district, which was not followed. He also began to made designs for the reconstruction of S. Paul's Cathedral, which had been burned, and in 1673 was commissioned to prepare the fine model which is now in the South Kensington Museum. This model, being in the form of a Greek cross, did not satisfy the ritualistic tendencies of the court, which required a long nave for processions. A design in the form of a Latin cross was finally accepted May 14, 1675. The Cathedral was begun on the site of the old Cathedral and finished in 1710. It was paid for by a tax on the coal brought to London by sea. The Monument in Commemoration of the Great Fire was begun by Wren in 1671. In 1675, with the assistance of the astronomer Flamsteed, he built the observatory at Greenwich, London. About 1695 he took charge of the reconstruction of the old Greenwich Palace and was instrumental in having it transformed into a seaman's hospital. The double colonnade of coupled columns at Greenwich is one of his finest works. Wren repaired the spire of Salisbury Cathedral. He began the construction of Chelsea Hospital in 1682. He made a fine design for a mausoleum for Charles I which was not executed. On the Accession of William and Mary in 1689 he began the enlargement of Hampton Court Palace, one of his most characteristic works. In 1708 the erection of 50 new churches in London was ordered by act of Parliament. Wren actually designed 53. Among the most important of those are S. Mary-le-Bow, S. Stephen, Walbrook, S. Bride, Fleet Street, S. Lawrence, Jewry, S. Michael, Cornhill, etc. He sat in Parliament for many years. There is a collection of his drawings in the library of All Souls' College, Oxford. [ARCHITECT

Wright, Frank Lloyd: 1867-1959. Wright, considered by many to be the greatest architect who ever lived, spent the first 50 years of his career in virtual obscurity. During his childhood years, there were two influences which would later define his designs. The first was his training in the Froebel kindergarten, wherein he learned order, proportions, and the relationship between geometric figures. Later on, he would translate this early training into his "unit" theory of design. Additionally, Wright spent his summers at his grandfather's farm. There he learned an appreciation of nature and land and the relationship between the two. The influence of these summers shows in Wright's use of natural un-

stained wood and the blending of construction with the environment. Trained briefly at the University of Wisconsin (yet never received an official degree), Wright spent the first few months of his career at the office of J. L. Silsbee, an architect who specialized in the design of homes. Next, Wright applied for work at Adler and Sullivan's office, was accepted, and spent the next several years with these two architectural giants, prior to establishing his own practice with partner Cecil Corwen in 1893. The writings of Henry David Thoreau and Thomas Jefferson, the Arts and Crafts Movement, and the work of architects H. H. Richardson, Bruce Price and McKim, Mead & White were formative in Wright's early years as an architect. In 1896, Wright established his own practice. An early design, the Winslow House in River Forest, Ill. (1894) shows Sullivan's influence. However, Wright's own style of overhanging roofs, rooms converging on each other, gardens coming together with terraces is more evident than anything else and launched Wright into his unique "prairie house" designs. The Unity Temple in Oak Park, Ill. (1905-1906) and the Larkin Building in Buffalo, New York (1904) were his first commercial commissions and soon led to larger projects. These include: the Park Inn Hotel in Mason City, Iowa (1909-1910); Midway Gardens in Chicago (19130); The Barnsdale House in Los Angeles (1917-1920); and the Taliesin Community (Wisconsin, 1925-1927) and Taliesin West Camp in Arizona (1937) are monuments to this architect's masterful blending of building and environment. Taliesin West firmly established Wright's position as an extraordinary designer within the national and international communities. Finally receiving the recognition he deserved, the commissioned project list reads like a small volume. Included would be the following designs: The Fairmont Hotel remodeling and Tower in San Francisco, California (1944); The Price Tower in Bartlesville, Oklahoma (1953-1956); The Marin County Civic Center in San Rafael, California (1957-1966); the Beth Sholom Synagogue in Elkins Park, Pennsylvania (1958-1959); the First Christian Church in Thousand Oaks, California (1965-1972); and the Westfair Shopping Center in Huntington Beach, California (1968-1969). But the bulk of his designs remained in the residential arena, and this truly great architect designed an amazing number, nearly 80 homes and housing projects between 1937-1957.

Wright's designs influenced such renowned architects as Gropius, Breuer, and Saarinen, not to mention thousands of students and architects who have studied and imitated his work and will continue to do so for many years to come. [ARCHITECT]

Wyatt, James: 1748-1813. A brother of Samuel Wyatt. Wyatt was taken to Rome at the age of fourteen by Lord Bagot, ambassador to Italy. He studied also for two years in Venice with Visentini. In 1770 he made considerable reputation by adapting the old Pantheon in Oxford Street, London, for dramatic performances (burned 1792). Working originally in the Classic style, he afterward imitated Gothic architecture, and built in that style Fonthill Abbey, Wiltshire, for W. Beckford, and other important works. March 16, 1796, he was appointed surveyor general and comptroller of his Majesty's office of works, succeeding Sir William Chambers, and held that office until it was dropped in 1815. He was made a member of the Royal Academy in 1785, and temporary president in 1805. He built the royal military academy of Woolwich, and restored Salisbury and Lincoln cathedrals. [ARCHITECT]

Wyatville (Wyatt) Sir Jeffrey:
1766-1840. His name was originally
Wyatt, a son of Samuel Wyatt. He
exhibited at the Royal Academy after
1786, was created associate in 1823,
and royal academician in 1826. From
1784 to 1799 he worked with his father and his uncle, James Wyatt. In
1799 he went into partnership with a
builder and engaged in extensive
government contracts. He enlarged
Wollaton Hall, Nottinghamshire
(1804), Woburn Abbey, Bedfordshire
(1818-1820), Chatsworth in Derbyshire, and other residences. From
1824 until his death he was architect
in charge of Windsor Castle. He
completed the quadrangle and staircase of George III, rebuilt the Bruns-
wick Tower, etc. On August 12, 1824,
his name was changed to Wyatville
by royal license. On December 9,
1828, he was knighted. His *Illustrations of Windsor Castle*, edited by
Henry Ashton, was published in
1841. A list of his works is given in
the *Architectural Publication Society's
Dictionary*. [ARCHITECT]

Xamete: An important master working in Spain in the early sixteenth
century. In 1537 he made the candelabra of the Capilla de la Torre in the
Cathedral of Toledo. He also executed the fine portal of the cloister
of the Cathedral of Cuenca. [SCULPTOR
AND ARCHITECT]

Xenaios: The walls of Antiochia in
Asia Minor were built under his
direction when that city was founded
by Seleukos in 296 B.C. [ARCHITECT]

Ybl, Nikolaus von: d. 1891. A distinguished architect of Hungary, he
was a pupil of Pollak in Pesth and
afterward of Gartner in Munich. He
was constantly engaged on important
works, was raised to noble rank, and
made a member of the upper house
of the Hungarian Parliament. [ARCHI-
TECT]

**Zampieri, Domenico (Domenichi-
no):** 1581-1641 (at Naples). The celebrated painter, Domenichino, was
much employed in the construction
of villas. He assisted at the Villa Negroni, Rome, and designed the Villa
Belvidere at Frascati and the Villa
Ludovisi in Rome. His most important architectural undertaking was
the design of the Church of S. Ignazio
in Rome (begun 1626). [ARCHITECT AND
PAINTER]

Zwirner, Ernst Friedrich: 1802-1861.
He studied architecture in Breslau in
1821 and with Schinkel in Berlin in
1824. He devoted himself especially
to the revival of Gothic architecture
in Germany. In 1833 he was ap-

pointed inspector of the construction
of the Cathedral of Cologne and in
1853 architect of that building. The
completion of this work was largely
due to his efforts in interesting the
people of Germany, and especially
Freidrich Wilhelm IV, King of Prussia, in it. Many leading German architects were educated by him and
assisted him in his work. Zwirner
built also the castle of Herdringen
(1844-1852) for the Count of Fursten-
berg, the Church of S. Apollinaris at
Ramagen, near Bonn, etc. [ARCHITECT]